MUIRHEAD LIBRARY OF PHILOSOPHY

An admirable statement of the aims of the Library of Philosophy was provided by the first editor, the late Professor J. H. Muirhead, in his description of the original programme printed in Erdmann's *History of Philosophy* under the date 1890. This was slightly modified in subsequent volumes to take the form of the following statement:

'The Muirhead Library of Philosophy was designed as a contribution to the History of Modern Philosophy under the heads: first of Different Schools of Thought—Sensationalist, Realist, Idealist, Intuitivist; secondly of different Subjects—Psychology, Ethics, Aesthetics, Political Philosophy, Theology. While much had been done in England in tracing the course of evolution in nature, history, economics, morals and religion, little had been done in tracing the development of thought on these subjects. Yet "the evolution of opinion is part of the whole evolution".

'By the co-operation of different writers in carrying out this plan it was hoped that a thoroughness and completeness of treatment, otherwise unattainable, might be secured. It was believed also that from writers mainly British and American fuller consideration of English Philosophy than it had hitherto received might be looked for. In the earlier series of books containing, among others, Bosanquet's *History of Aesthetic*, Pfleiderer's *Rational Theology since Kant*, Albee's *History of English Utilitarianism*, Bonar's *Philosophy and Political Economy*, Brett's *History of Psychology*, Ritchie's *Natural Rights*, these objects were to a large extent effected.

'In the meantime original work of a high order was being produced both in England and America by such writers as Bradley, Stout, Bertrand Russell, Baldwin, Urban, Montague, and others, and a new interest in foreign works, German, French and Italian, which had either become classical or were attracting public attention, had developed. The scope of the Library thus became extended into something more international, and it is entering on the fifth decade of its existence in the hope that it may contribute to that mutual understanding between countries which is so pressing a need of the present time.'

The need which Professor Muirhead stressed is no less pressing today, and few will deny that philosophy has much to do with enabling us to meet it, although no one, least of all Muirhead himself, would regard that as the sole, or even the main, object of philosophy. As Professor Muirhead continues to lend the distinction of his name to the

Library of Philosophy it seemed not inappropriate to allow him to recall us to these aims in his own words. The emphasis on the history of thought also seemed to me very timely: and the number of important works promised for the Library in the very near future augur well for the continued fulfilment, in this and other ways, of the expectations of the original editor.

H. D. LEWIS

MUIRHEAD LIBRARY OF PHILOSOPHY

General Editor: H. D. Lewis
Professor of History and Philosophy of Religion in the University of London

Action by SIR MALCOLM KNOX

The Analysis of Mind by BERTRAND RUSSELL

Belief by H. H. PRICE

Brett's History of Psychology edited by R. S. PETERS

Clarity is Not Enough by H. D. LEWIS

Coleridge as Philosopher by J. H. MUIRHEAD

The Commonplace Book of G. E. Moore edited by C. LEWY

Contemporary American Philosophy edited by G. P. ADAMS and W. P. MONTAGUE

Contemporary British Philosophy first and second Series edited by J. H. MUIRHEAD

Contemporary British Philosophy third Series edited by H. D. LEWIS

Contemporary Indian Philosophy edited by RADHAKRISHNAN and J. H. MUIRHEAD 2nd edition

The Discipline of the Cave by J. N. FINDLAY

Doctrine and Argument in Indian Philosophy by NINIAN SMART

Essays in Analysis by ALICE AMBROSE

Ethics by NICOLAI HARTMANN translated by STANTON COIT 3 vols

The Foundations of Metaphysics in Science by ERROL E. HARRIS

Freedom and History by H. D. LEWIS

The Good Will: A Study in the Coherence Theory of Goodness by H. J. PATON

Hegel: A Re-examination by J. N. FINDLAY

Hegel's Science of Logic translated by W. H. JOHNSTON and L. G. STRUTHERS 2 vols

History of Aesthetic by B. BOSANQUET 2nd edition

History of English Utilitarianism by E. ALBEE

History of Psychology by G. S. BRETT edited by R. S. PETERS abridged one volume edition 2nd edition

Human Knowledge by BERTRAND RUSSELL

A Hundred Years of British Philosophy by RUDOLF METZ translated by J. H. HARVEY, T. E. JESSOP, HENRY STURT

Ideas: A General Introduction to Pure Phenomenology by EDMUND HUSSERL translated by W. R. BOYCE GIBSON

Identity and Reality by EMILE MEYERSON

Imagination by E. J. FURLONG

Contemporary Philosophy in Australia edited by ROBERT BROWN and C. D. ROLLINS

𝕸𝖚𝖎𝖗𝖍𝖊𝖆𝖉 𝕷𝖎𝖇𝖗𝖆𝖗𝖞 𝖔𝖋 𝕻𝖍𝖎𝖑𝖔𝖘𝖔𝖕𝖍𝖞

EDITED BY H. D. LEWIS

Gifford Lectures

THE ELUSIVE MIND

THE ELUSIVE MIND

*Based on the First Series of the
Gifford Lectures
delivered in the University of Edinburgh
1966 - 1968*

BY

H. D. LEWIS

LONDON. GEORGE ALLEN & UNWIN LTD
NEW YORK. HUMANITIES PRESS, INC

FIRST PUBLISHED IN 1969

SBN 04 130013 0

PRINTED IN GREAT BRITAIN
in 11 *on* 12*pt Imprint type*
AT THE SHENVAL PRESS
LONDON, HERTFORD AND HARLOW

PREFACE

This book contains the substance of the first series of Gifford
Lectures which I was privileged to give in the University of
Edinburgh in the period 1966–68. I have combined with this the
Hobhouse Memorial Lecture, 'Dreaming and Experience', given
in London in 1967 and my Presidential Address to the Aristotelian
Society in 1962, 'Mind and Body'. Although offered to a more
limited public already these papers, with appropriate changes of
detail, seemed sufficiently relevant to the main purpose of the
present work to warrant their inclusion as separate chapters at the
point where I have placed them.

I am grateful to the Athlone Press Board and the Aristotelian
Society for permission to reproduce the papers which they have
already published.

I am also very glad to have this opportunity of publicly thanking
the Principal and the Senatus of Edinburgh University for the
honour they did me in asking me to give the Gifford Lectures. Of
the kindness of the audiences which attended the lectures, and of
the warmth of the personal hospitality extended to my wife and
myself during our several visits to Edinburgh, it is hardly possible
to write adequately in so impersonal a context as the preface to a
book. Our hosts will know already how much we treasured their
kindness. Nor can anyone who has been fortunate enough to spend
several months in the city of Edinburgh break away easily from the
sense of enchantment, the spell, which is cast on those who spend
their time as agreeably as we did in this delightful and historic
place.

Much of this book is concerned with the problem of mind and
body. I pass in review some well-known and much admired
examples of ways of dealing with this problem today, beginning
with those which seem to me least attractive and proceeding to
positions which concede more to the points I myself consider
essential to a satisfactory treatment of the problem. On the basis
of my discussion of the work of Professor Sydney Shoemaker,
with whose views I am in many ways in close agreement, I set
forth in outline, in chapter XI, the main features of the position I
wish to take up myself; and I bring out the bearing of this, in the
remaining chapters, on some of the issues in philosophy and reli-

gious thought to which they have most relevance and which have most affinity with the matters discussed in earlier chapters. In the sequel to this book, I set out more exhaustively the themes of chapter XI of the present work and relate them to further issues in religious thought and ethics along the lines indicated very briefly in the closing chapter of this book.

I am much indebted to two of my friends, Professor C. A. Campbell and Dr A. C. Ewing, for reading the whole of my typescript and making very helpful suggestions. The proofs were read for me by Dom Illtyd Trethowan and by my gifted former pupil Mr Anthony Ellis. Mr Ellis also made the Index. I am grateful to all these gentlemen for their help and encouragement.

H. D. LEWIS

CONTENTS

CHAPTER I

RYLE AND DESCARTES

Anyone who proposes, as I do, to defend the view of the soul as some reality altogether other than the body must take the closest account of the extensive and vigorous criticisms of dualist accounts of mind and body advanced by some of the most influential and gifted thinkers of our time. So powerful has the onslaught on the dualist position been of late that many now consider it to have been finally and utterly demolished. Forlorn indeed must appear to them any attempt to re-establish a position subjected to such caustic and apparently devastating comment by a number of talented and confident writers. That is nonetheless the course which I believe should be taken. I shall not attempt an exhaustive survey of recent controversies about the mind-body problem. My plan will be to select some typical and influential discussions of the question and subject those to fairly detailed examination.

The first position on which I wish to comment is that of Professor Gilbert Ryle in his well-known work *The Concept of Mind* and other writings. This work has already been very widely discussed in recent times and it might well be thought that not much would be gained by traversing some of this ground again. There are, however, weighty reasons for doing so, and I hope this part of our task can be accomplished without undue weariness to those who have already heard a great deal in one way or another about *The Concept of Mind* and the aftermath of its publication in philosophical controversy.

The reasons to which I allude are these.

(1) Critical discussions of Professor Ryle's work have stayed, in the main, at the level of general critical comment without coming very closely to terms with details in the presentation of his views. In the light of what I say as point 4 below I shall have reason to consider Professor Ryle's procedures fairly closely.

(2) Although much in Professor Ryle's position has been formally repudiated by those who share his general approach to philosophical questions, the views which prevail among many influential and fashionable philosophers of today, in English-speaking countries, deviate little in substance from those of Ryle

on questions like the nature of our minds and their relations to our bodies. The style of argument remains largely the same and, where the conclusions appear to differ, the difference is more in method of presentation and language than in the essentials of the positions defended. Issues are joined, sometimes with heat and vigour, but within the framework of a general agreement about aims and method. The pattern which Ryle laid down in *The Concept of Mind*, and some of the basic assumptions he makes, remain legislative for a large and influential body of philosophical writers and teachers. These expend a considerable amount of ingenuity and literary skill in presenting variations on themes which remain, in vital respects, the ones we encounter in *The Concept of Mind*. To consider the latter in some detail is thus to investigate, at a point where it is seen to the best advantage, a vein of philosophical thought which is still very confidently worked. I hope to make this plain in due course.

(3) Many writers on religious topics have thought that Ryle has rendered their cause a quite signal service, whether or not he had that intention, by his strictures on dualistic views of mind and body to which many, not excluding Ryle himself at one time, are very prone. This is also a matter which will be made clearer later.

(4) I pass now to a point of the utmost importance for the main theme of these lectures. It concerns a peculiarly elusive character of mind or of mental processes. There are various ways in which, for ordinary purposes, we think of ourselves. I sometimes picture myself mainly in terms of my body, although it would certainly be going too far to say that I identify myself in that way with my body. My bodily movements or postures may be uppermost in my thought of myself, as when I think of myself singing in the bath or sitting up at the table, and I may likewise think mainly of my friend as the person whose hands are engaged in the movements of lighting his pipe just now. 'Which of you is Brown?' someone asks. 'That one just lighting his pipe', we reply, and here it is the physical movement which matters mainly. But we are also apt to think that there is more than the physical movement, the motions of the hands are intended and there is much else that goes on in Brown's life at this moment. He may have a far-away look and although he seems to get his pipe to draw we may also say that he is not 'with us', he is thinking of the fish he will catch in the lake this afternoon. At these times we are apt to draw a sharp distinction between mind and body, Brown is physically here but his mind is

'far away', and while we no longer take 'far away' in a literal sense we come vividly to think that there is a good deal more involved in being Brown than the movements and location of his body. There is also something 'going on in his mind' as well. This may not be the right way to view the matter, Ryle certainly thinks it is not, but it is a way of talking and thinking to which we are all very prone, and Ryle admits that he has had to school himself not to lapse into it. All this has come about, according to Ryle, through the influence, mainly in recent centuries, of certain misguided philosophical theories, but this is a point where most of Ryle's followers think that he has overplayed his hand. The dichotomy of mind and body comes easily to us in many contexts, whether or not it is ultimately warranted. There is also much support for it in our more sophisticated thinking. In our thought of immortality, for instance, it is natural to suppose that the soul is some entity that survives the dissolution of the body. When Socrates told his friends half mockingly that when he died it would not be easy to catch him, they would not find it hard to know what he meant. In some primitive cultures it is thought that the soul may leave the body and return to it, and we read today of some paranormal experiences in which a person seems to be observing his own body from a point of view outside it. The true significance of these matters does not concern us now. All that I wish to note is that, in some contexts at least, it is natural to think of ourselves as composite entities, as being (or having) a mind and a body. A person can have a deformed body and an excellent mind, and this seems to imply that our minds are quite distinct from our bodies. There appear at least to be reasons for regarding this as a very natural view to take. When clearly presented it is not hard to win assent to it. In what other way, it might be argued, could we think of ourselves except as some kind of composite beings having a mind as well as a body?

Natural indeed it may be to think in this way but by no means easy if we think hard. For what, it may be asked, can we say about this mind or soul which is distinct from the body? How do we characterize it? How is it observed, of what is it made? There are no doubt ways in which we can distinguish different mental states or activities, feeling angry or being afraid or setting out to amuse oneself or to solve a problem. But what is it for these to be mental and not physical? What am I at this moment over and above my body? Where are these thoughts that guide my movements?

They are not in my head or elsewhere in my body. No one can see them, and the more I try to think of the sort of reality they can have the more they seem to evaporate and be nothing at all. It is not that they are screened or hard to detect. In one sense it is quite easy to describe them. I can tell you what I am thinking and you may discover at least some of it in other ways. But how can there be anything which is so intangible and without location as mental processes altogether distinct from what I am as a body? We seem to be concerned here with something so elusive that it seems like being nothing at all.

This is not unlike the quandary in which Hume found himself in his search for some kind of substantival self. As he put it in his famous affirmation—'I never catch myself at any time without a perception, and never can observe anything but the perception'. Hume was helped to come to this conclusion by the firmness of his adherence in general to a strict empiricism. But he seems in any case to be saying something very plausible to us in certain moods. And, in like manner, when we try to be down to earth and explicit we find ourselves wondering, not only whether there is some abiding soul or self, but also how there can be anything so evanescent and unsubstantial as thinking appears to be; and this induces a doubt about the reality of thinking in any way which makes it altogether supplementary to the movements of my body. The most we are disposed to allow, in this mood, are physical sensations and we remain very uncertain about their status.

There is not, however, real justification for scepticism of this kind. We lapse into it, or are manoeuvred into it when we allow our thought to be imposed upon in a certain way, when we get ourselves conditioned to looking for something tangible and manageable, as body is, in all our search for reality. After all I do know quite well what I am thinking now, and that is why I am so confident that I can tell you what I am thinking; and my thinking is certainly not the movement of my hands holding the pencil, or anything else of that sort. It seems absurd to deny that there is thinking about philosophy 'going on', as we say, as part of my experience now. It only seems unreal when I set myself to look for the wrong sort of thing or attempt descriptions in terms that are not at all appropriate. That was the trouble with Hume; and it is much more the trouble with his progeny today who have got themselves into a frame of mind in which the only reality they can recognize has to have something of the character of the objects we find in the world around us. Nothing seems real to them unless it is in some way tangible or substantial in the manner, whatever that ultimately proves to be, of external things. It is easy to get into this way of thinking. There is a certain imperviousness about external things, they cannot be gainsaid, and it is natural to assume, in the moods in which external things impose most upon us, that everything there is must at least have something resembling the seemingly solid tangible character of the world of nature. We look for something of that sort in the alleged world of distinct mental processes, and when we fail to find it we lapse into a general scepticism, and doubt the reality of things which are otherwise obvious to us, like our normal mental processes.

There is the additional difficulty of finding any terms in which we can properly characterize mental activity. We can compare such activities with one another, but even for this purpose we have to borrow the terms we use in designation of external things. No metaphor will help us to say what mental activity is as such. There is nothing to regret in that. If there are radically distinct sorts of things in the world—and why should there not be?—they have to be recognized in their distinctness without seeking to find terms common to both or reduce one to the other. By material standards mental activities are odd, for although they take time, they are not in space or extended at all. This is what makes them so elusive when, accustomed as we are normally to be outward looking and coping with the world around us, we try to comprehend them; and when we find that, to handle mental reality at all, we have to borrow terms from the world around us, there is the aggravated temptation to suppose that mental realities, like external ones, must have some kind of quasi-tangible or solid character.

Two things, closely related, result from this. On the one hand, many of us fall into the way of thinking of mental activities in material or quasi-material terms, and if we become seriously inclined to do this we are at once open to grievous objections and indeed ridicule. Some of the ways in which we talk of memory as a storehouse, if we go beyond obvious metaphor, or of the unconscious as a subterranean place, or of there being some all-pervasive mind-stuff, at once invite the severe censure of our critics. We are invited to produce those quasi-material activities, and of course we are unable to do so. Good sense in the philosophy of mind and in psychology turns much on our care in heeding this point. But if we lapse further and allow ourselves to be misled, not only when particular concepts are confused by misuse of metaphor, but by thinking generally of mental activity in quasi-material terms, we expose ourselves to the challenge of those who require us to produce these mythical realities on pain of surrendering all claims to distinct mental existence. On the other hand, the critic, assuming, in what is substantially the same terms, that if there are distinct mental processes they must partake in some way of the reality of observable things, finds himself unable to detect any entities or processes of that sort, or to elicit any plausible account of them from us, and he thus concludes that there cannot be any mental reality wholly distinct from what we encounter in the world of observable bodies.

Both these matters are very closely illustrated in Professor Ryle's work. He has undoubtedly helped to disabuse philosophers and others of our proneness, understandable in the light of what has just been said, to manufacture mythical entities and distort what is true about our minds through misuse of metaphor. He is not of course an innovator here. Other positivist and linguistic philosophers have anticipated him, and they have been anticipated by a long line of others, reaching back at least as far as Socrates and Plato, who have warned us of the deceptiveness of metaphor and of words in general. Many have cut through misleading hypostatizations of metaphors used in psychology or philosophy of mind without recourse to anything partaking more of a philosophical technique than common-sense. But I do not wish to withhold from Professor Ryle the credit for helping to straighten out our thought in this particular way.

The extent of his achievement here, and of our debt to him, is, however, uncertain. For his main examples and illustrations do not come from the more obvious misuses of metaphor. They are of a much more questionable nature and concern ways in which, it is alleged, all references to quite distinctive mental realities, or at any rate the presentation of these as altogether other than observable processes, come about through the postulation of quasi-material processes for which no evidence can in fact be found. This is what is most distinctive in his philosophy of mind, at least on the negative side; and it is this that I wish first to consider.

By doing so I hope that two things will be achieved. We shall, in the first place, be turning the edge of much confident fashionable criticisms of dualism, as a theory of mind and body, and dispelling many general doubts and misgivings which many besides pro-

fessional philosophers may feel about it. In the second place, by
showing how mistaken it is to take material representations of
the life of the mind too seriously, we shall throw into prominence
and sharp relief the peculiar and elusive inwardness of mental
activity, and indeed of all experience, to which I wish to draw
special attention and which will be central to much that I shall
want to maintain later.

Let us begin where Ryle himself begins, namely with his own
reference to 'Descartes' myth' and what he himself also calls 'the
Official Doctrine'. I do not believe that Ryle is altogether justified
in claiming that this doctrine 'hails chiefly from Descartes'.[1]
Positions very similar to it are common in Oriental thought, and
in Western philosophy the teaching of leading thinkers like Plato
and Augustine about the soul have a great deal in common with
that of Descartes and his followers in modern times. There are
also thinkers, in recent centuries, notably Berkeley and Kant, and
in some respects Leibniz, who have defended views which have
much in common with those of Descartes without being too
obviously indebted to him and with innovations of considerable
importance. My own firm impression is that the Official Doctrine
has held its place, in modern times as also earlier, because it
reflects what we are much inclined, whether rightly or not, to
think in certain moods.

This point need not however detain us here, and we must resist
the temptation to deviate into an historical excursus. There can
be little doubt about the persistent influence of Descartes in
modern philosophy, and his view is as firm and precise an example
as any of the position Ryle is so anxious to rebut. It does not follow
that we have to defend Descartes on all counts, although I shall in
fact take my stance closer to that of Descartes himself than that
of some of his defenders.

Ryle presents Descartes' doctrine in these terms:

'With the doubtful exceptions of idiots and infants in arms every
human being has both a body and a mind. Some would prefer
to say that every human being is both a body and a mind. His
body and his mind are ordinarily harnessed together, but after
the death of the body his mind may continue to exist and function.'[2]

---

[1] *The Concept of Mind*, p. 11.
[2] *Op. cit.*, p. 11.

Let me quote further:

'Human bodies are in space and are subject to the mechanical laws which govern all other bodies in space. Bodily processes and states can be inspected by external observers. So a man's bodily life is as much a public affair as are the lives of animals and reptiles and even as the careers of trees, crystals and planets.

But minds are not in space, nor are their operations subject to mechanical laws. The workings of one mind are not witnessable by other observers, its career is private. Only I can take direct cognisance of the states and processes of my own mind. A person therefore lives through two collateral histories, one consisting of what happens in and to his body, the other consisting of what happens in and to his mind. The first is public, the second private.'

A person 'may have great or small uncertainties about concurrent and adjacent episodes in the physical world, but he can have none about at least part of what is momentarily occupying his mind'.[1]

This seems to me to put the position well on the whole. I have no quarrel of substance with it as a statement of the position to which I myself subscribe. But there are some points even in these fairly straightforward statements which are worth noting carefully as indication at the outset of some of the ways in which Ryle fails to do justice to the views he attacks.

Note, for example, the phrase, 'with the doubtful exceptions of idiots and infants in arms'. I am not aware that Descartes himself made any such exception, and if he, or anyone else defending a dualist view, were to do so he would be doing his position a grave injustice. The truth seems to be that Ryle has very much the impression that anyone defending a dualist view must think of mental processes, mainly if not exclusively, in rarefied intellectual terms. This will become plainer later. But in fact the limited intelligence of the idiot or the infant is found in processes as distinct from the movements of their bodies as are those of the most sophisticated or reflective person. We do indeed speak of one person being intelligent, the other not. But this is a distinction which has no relevance except where there is at least some modicum of intelligence or mental activity. The idiot is not very bright, but there would be no point in saying this of a being who could not exercise his wits at all. His dim attempt to understand, or whatever

[1] *Op. cit.*, p. 12.

his mental processes are thought to be, are activities as distinct from physical processes as the most abstract operations of a genius. The distinction of intelligent and stupid or unintelligent activity (or beings) cuts right across and presupposes the more basic distinction of mental and physical processes.

A further slight modification of the first statement quoted is possible. We do certainly speak of people 'having' a mind—so and so 'has a very good mind'. This is a harmless way of saying that someone is intelligent, but when we get beyond a rough and ready idiom I doubt whether we would want in seriousness to say that someone *has* a mind—a person *is* his mind in a way in which he is not his body. I can say in seriousness that I *have* a body, but in serious thought it would be odd to think of my mind as just belonging to me, I am my mind in a quite fundamental sense. So, in strictness, the dualist would not say that 'every human being is both a body and a mind'.

Consider next the word 'harnessed', as it is used in the first quotation. There is no very serious objection to this term in its context. We have to rely on a metaphor of some kind here. Our minds and bodies are united or joined in some very special way, and we cannot easily refer to this without some figure of speech derived from the relations of physical objects to one another. All the same the relationship is a unique one, and if we are not careful we are apt to lose sight of its quite peculiar character. For this reason we have to be very careful about our metaphors here, and it seems to me that Ryle is using a metaphor so strongly suggestive of the relations of physical entities to one another as to give away at the start his inability to appreciate how very special and distinctive the alleged relation of mind and body is taken to be. He is thinking already, and no doubt has led many of his readers to think, of alleged distinct mental processes as some kind of duplicate of physical ones.

In the second quotation we read of human bodies being subject to 'mechanical laws'. As a statement of Descartes' position this is strictly correct. He took over the view which the science of his day appeared to require, namely that the entire physical universe, or the whole 'world of nature', was like one elaborate machine, a vast system of parts interacting in accordance with strictly mechanical laws. How far Descartes himself contributed to this view, how far he was the victim of it, may not be very easy to settle. It was certainly the view which many others, some by no means holding his strictly dualist position about mind and body, also shared, eminent scientists as well as philosophers. Who was most at fault, scientist or philosopher, may also be hard to say. But to the extent that Descartes was at fault it is well to remember that he was subscribing to, if also to some extent shaping, the view that was fashionable, and in some quarters beyond question, in his day. We can certainly not lay the whole blame for it at Descartes' door; I much doubt in fact whether he was the worst offender; and in any case it is easy to understand how this theory came to be widely held in the circumstances of the time.

Moreover, Descartes, unlike other eminent thinkers of his day, made a firm exception of human activity. Man, he held, had a 'liberty of indifference', that is he could choose what he would do independently of the operation of mechanical laws. These laws did not apply to human volition, and if our choices were to be effective in the world there was required an interaction of mind and body. The state of our bodies affected the state of our minds, and mental operations in turn had an effect on our bodies. It did not seem possible, therefore, for everything that happened in the world of nature to be wholly determined by mechanical laws; for there could be a variation of this due to the interference of the different determination of our acts of will. The point will come up again shortly. For the moment it must suffice to note that Descartes would not consider the system of nature to be a completely closed mechanical one, and movements of bodies are not therefore exclusively subject to mechanical laws.

This is one of the sharp points of difference between Descartes and Hobbes or Spinoza, for both of these thought of the world of nature, as such, as subject throughout to rigid mechanical determination. The ways in which they supplemented this differ. It was possible for Spinoza to speak of freedom in terms of another aspect which all processes have, and we are not here concerned with the adequacy of this conception. Nor is it necessary here to consider how far Descartes' understanding of the laws of nature, in the form in which he accepted them, allowed him to make an exception of the interventions of human actions in the world of nature. The point is that he did make this exception and was, to that extent, much less the slave of the prevailing mechanistic ideas than some of his contemporaries.

Moreover, even if Descartes' position was made difficult, or even impossible, by his adoption of certain views about the operation of mechanical laws in the world of nature, this would not apply to those who sought subsequently to defend his kind of dualism on the basis of a better understanding of how events occur in the external world. What is sound at the centre of Descartes' contentions is not impaired by error, if error there is, in a subordinate and relatively incidental feature of it arising from the state of thought in his day about something which is not vital to his main thesis.

Let me refer next to the allusion to 'the lives of animals and reptiles'. This is also most revealing. It shows how little Professor Ryle is aware of the inwardness of mental activity as something which characterizes experience at all levels. Just as he wonders whether the dualism of the Official Doctrine could be made to apply to infants and idiots, so he assumes quite firmly that it could never be extended to sub-human creatures. But, as I shall stress again, there is an inner, non-material character to all experience, even the lowest forms of sentient life. 'Crystals and planets' (and trees presumably) are not in the same class here as 'animals and reptiles'. And if Ryle had grasped firmly what was at stake he would have realized that the claim to be rebutted did not concern superior levels of mental activity, or turn on the quality which made these superior. It concerns something alleged to belong to all experience as such.

A concession on a historical point may, however, be made here. For it seems that Descartes himself was so much under the dominance of the mechanistic view of the world of nature that he thought that the activities of all sub-human creatures could be accounted for entirely in the same terms as the movements of inanimate bodies. It is hard to understand how anyone could believe this, but for anyone who did so—and Descartes seems to have made no exception apart from human action—it would be a moot point whether anything of a properly mental character, even very low-grade mentality, could be ascribed to brutes. But here again what we have is a peculiarity, a very odd one admittedly, of a particular period and fashion in matters of thought. It should not determine what we are to think today about mental and material existence.

I pass now to a point in Ryle's presentation of the Official Doctrine which is already incipient criticism and which anticipates much that he says later in more explicit criticisms. Ryle complains that nothing is said about the way our minds and bodies are alleged to influence one another. 'The actual transactions between the episodes of the private history and those of the public history remain mysterious, since by definition they can belong to neither series.'[1] The expectation here seems to be that, if there is inter-action of mind and body, it should be possible to describe the form which this takes, the means of communication should be open to inspection. How does the mind send its message to the body, and how does the body instruct the mind? These are, of course, questions to which no answer is ever given, the alleged 'transactions' 'remain mysterious', as Ryle puts it. And it might seem that there is something very disconcerting here. That is certainly the suggestion. If there are these 'transactions' between mind and body, it should be possible to say something about them and indicate how we came to know them. The conclusion we are expected then to draw is that the influence of distinct mental processes on physical ones, and vice versa, is a wholly fictitious one.

It should be noted further that, if the criticism held, it would have a double sting—as Ryle himself is fully aware. For if we could point out certain exchanges or transactions by which the two processes in question affected one another, the question would then arise of how these transactions in turn made their impact on the mind, on the one hand, and, on the other, on the body—and, if answer were forthcoming to this, a still further question would arise about the transactions which made the impact possible; link after link would need to be forged, different modes of influ-ence or exchange would have to be invented *ad infinitum*. We shall see how this anticipates similar moves made by Ryle later in the course of his attempted *reductio ad absurdum* of the Cartesian position.

There is, however, little in these arguments or their implications to cause us serious anxiety. We only find ourselves in difficulty if we let ourselves be manoeuvred into the position of seeking desperately to supply the necessary 'transactions'—as some may have done. The 'transactions' remain mysterious because they are non-existent, we say nothing about them, and are baffled if we try, because there are none. And why should there be? Even when we think of causal relations in the external world, we do not look for links (or 'transactions') between cause and effect to explain how the one leads to the other. No one after Hume should make that

[1] *Op. cit.*, p. 12.

mistake, and if he did he would soon find himself committed to a hopeless infinite regress. We find that things behave in a certain way, that given certain conditions something else happens. In terms of what we learn in these ways we can explain a great deal that occurs, and we can bring out in ever more detail the way things affect one another, but we do not postulate some mysterious medium by which influence is transmitted from cause to effect or speculate about modes of exchange or mysterious messages.

The position is, of course, more complicated if we assume, as Descartes himself seems to have done, that there must be some *a priori* connection between cause and effect or that 'like is caused by like'. Even this, however, would not lead to the postulation of mysterious transactions, and Descartes himself could get out of the difficulties presented by his special views about causation by insisting that God could cause anything he liked to be related. There is not, in any case, any need for us to follow Descartes at all points in order to accept the substance of his interactionist theory. If Ryle were just finding fault with an incidental feature of Descartes' general position, that would be one thing. But the impression he conveys, and seems plainly to want to convey, is that the dualist Cartesian position as such is open to fatal objection because it essentially requires the postulation of the alleged mysterious transactions. We can cope quite well with the point by just noting that there need be no such transactions.

It does not follow that there is no problem about cause and effect. There certainly is. For how is it that we are so confident that things will continue to behave as they have done and that, allowing for concomitant variations, we can predict the future on the basis of past experience? Am I, as Hume supposed, simply conditioned to expect the kettle to boil when placed on the fire? Or have I justification for this hope? Is the fact that, in endless variations in the past, there seems to have been no break in the systematic continuity of events, itself part of the justification for assuming that this must continue? Many have sought to solve the famous problem of induction in those terms. Others find this circular or in some other way inadequate and they are either content to leave it that we have found things behaving according to rule or system hitherto and hope that our luck will last, or they seek for some foundation for a *necessary* causal continuity in some way—in religion perhaps—outside the course of events themselves. The problem need not worry us here. For what matters is this, that however we deal with the philosophical problems presented by cause and effect, the last thing we should try to do is to look for some link or transaction between one event and whatever it necessitates. We do not in the last resort explain causal relations, except in the sense of unfolding in greater detail the way things do in fact behave or of providing, in some of the ways suggested, some general justification for causality itself or for our confidence in it. We do not see why causal relations must be such as they are, we just accept what we find subject to the underlying assumption of consistency or continuity. We can, on the basis of what we know already, insist that certain things must be—and that others cannot be—but there is nothing beyond this, in the nature of the processes themselves, to show us why they are followed by certain others. To seek for an explanation of causal relations by peering ever more closely at events to discover some occult influences or transactions which account for their interconnections, to try to pass to some level beyond that of the way in which we find in fact that things do behave, is to follow the wildest will o' the wisp; and no philosopher should be so led astray today.

But if this holds of cause and effect in the external world, why should it be different in respect to the influence of minds and bodies on one another? There could conceivably be some 'go between', there could, for all we know, be some mysterious medium—some ethereal substance—through which the influence of mind on body occurs. But even if there were we would need at some point just to accept it that certain sorts of things influence other things in certain ways. In the meantime there is no evidence to show that any such medium exists or is needed. All we can say is that the state of our minds influences our bodies in certain ways, and that the state of my body affects my mind. Why this should happen we do not know, it may well be that we shall never know, or that there is nothing to know, that these determinations are ultimate in the nature of things—at least for finite understanding. We must be content to accept what we find, and in that case the search for mysterious transactions or exchanges is an entirely unnecessary requirement. We do not have to postulate or seek for anything of the sort, any more than we have to provide some extra-scientific account of the laws of nature. We must go by the facts.

This does not mean that the influence of mind and body on one another is not more remarkable or astounding in certain ways than the influence of one physical thing on another or the inherent determination of our thoughts in accordance with their meaning and logic. The latter determination does in fact to a large extent explain itself, it is less brute fact than physical relations. But in the case of mind and body we have determinations in very different media, and some find this bewildering. Whether there is a serious problem here will be considered again, but it may be well to say now that, in my own view, there is nothing in the last resort more perplexing or astonishing about my mental processes affecting the movements of my body than about a flame consuming the paper to which it is applied. In the last resort, in both cases, we simply find that certain sorts of things happen.

I must add that there is nothing out of place in seeking in another way to determine just how the impact of mind on body takes place. This means trying to locate the part of the body which is most directly affected—and the relation between this and the rest. We are all well aware now that the brain is vital in all such operations, although nothing in our normal experience suggests this. I decide to write, and my fingers move as I wish. But as an educated person I know a good deal more about the way this happens, I know that certain changes take place in my brain and that these are 'relayed', as we put it, along the nerves to the appropriate muscles. A vast amount of detailed information about the physiological process involved here is available now, and there are highly complicated studies of the brain. We shall no doubt learn a great deal more in these ways and correct past errors. But all this is a process of filling out, in most illuminating ways indeed, the details on one side of the interaction; it may give us specific points of contact, for example when some parts of the human brain seem more important than others for different mental states or operations, like perceiving or remembering. But this tells us nothing about the mode of determination of the strictly mental process on the physical one, or the other way round. That is still something we just accept. Nor does new knowledge about the molecular structure of brain cells and the functioning of electrical charges in them, affect the substance of this point at all. It still leaves us on one side of the interaction.

In the light of this consideration, the attempt of Descartes, naive though it seems to us, to locate the precise part of the brain where interaction occurred is not in itself as absurd as some have supposed. It will be recalled that Descartes located the point of contact in the pineal gland, situated between the two main parts of

the brain. Much scorn has been poured on this supposition from
time to time, and not least of late. But it was not an inherently
absurd suggestion, there is some point after all, namely the brain,
where the contact is normally, and perhaps invariably, made; and
we can now make this knowledge more specific. To that extent
Descartes was not in error on a philosophical matter or seriously
confused philosophically in what he had to say about the pineal
gland. He was simply ill-informed about physiological matters,
and that was not surprising when systematic study of the body
was still in its infancy, Descartes himself helping much to stimulate it. The same may be said about Descartes' notion of 'animal
spirits' which conveyed messages to and from the brain. This
could also be mainly a shot at explaining physiological processes
in the absence of the physiological knowledge which subsequently
became available.

I do not, however, wish to deny that Descartes himself had
further expectations here. He seems to have thought that what he
had to say about the unity of the pineal gland and the subtlety of
'animal spirits' made these seem more like minds than other
material things. This would help him out of difficulties caused by
his particular views about causation. To that extent he was also
philosophically in error. But there was nothing improper in itself in
trying to find out, with very limited physiological knowledge, just
where the impact of mind on body occurred and how it worked
in detail.

The reason why all these matters should have been overlooked
by Ryle is not far to seek. It is found in a general presupposition
of so much of his thought, namely that, if we are to think at all of
some paraphysical reality, we must suppose that it somehow
resembles the reality of the observable external world. If, that is,
there are two very different worlds operating on one another, there
must be some medium through which this occurs or some transactions between them to be detected. The modes of the alleged
interaction must be witnessable in some way. But the more we
realize the quite radically different nature of mental processes
and physical processes, the less disposed we shall be to look for
any explanation of the relations between them on the basis of what
either of them are taken to be in themselves.

Professor Ryle also refers to the notion of 'two different kinds
of existence or status'.[1] There is physical existence and mental

[1] *Op. cit.*, p. 13.

existence. These are somewhat unusual terms, but no one could object to them seriously as they stand. They might mean no more than that there are mental realities and physical ones, or two sorts of things, mental and physical, to put it a little more crudely. But Professor Ryle appears to be saying more, namely that the existence itself is somehow different, there are two ways as it were of existing. This may seem a very slight, almost trivial, point. But in the light of what we find Ryle saying later about the occurrence of mental events, it is not without significance; and we have thus to protest that it is not the existence that is different, but the nature of the things that exist. There may be some context in which we find it proper to speak of different ways of existing, for example when we contrast the necessary being of God with contingent being. But even here existence as such means the same. To say that something exists is simply to say that it *is* or is real; and at the finite level at least there is no difference in the existence of entities as such but only in the nature of the entities. They may differ radically, but this does not preclude us from meaning the same thing when we say that they both *are*.

Two points of greater substance, as it seems to me at least, remain to be noted in Ryle's first approach to his subject. They both concern the claim that we have direct cognizance of our own minds. If this holds, it is urged in the first place, we cannot be mistaken about ourselves. 'Mental states and processes are (or are normally) conscious states and processes, and the consciousness which irradiates them can engender no illusions and leaves the door open for no doubts.'[1] This is how Ryle understands the Official Doctrine, and he is not slow to point out that in fact we are often mistaken about ourselves. Men are sometimes 'thoroughly gulled by some of their own hypocrisies and they successfully ignore facts about their mental lives which on the official theory ought to be patent to them'.[2] The teaching of Freud has made this particularly plain.

This is not the place at which to consider closely how much Freud has accomplished or what must be conceded to him. It may well be that he and others who share his views have exaggerated or distorted the ways in which we may be deluded about ourselves. But we can certainly allow that there are some ways in which we may be mistaken about ourselves and that our friends

[1] *Op. cit.*, p. 13.
[2] *Op. cit.*, p. 14.

and others may understand us better than we do ourselves. Nor do we need the help of Freud to teach us as much as this. It is common knowledge. But what follows? Is there anything here to embarrass those who maintain that in some way we have immediate awareness of what goes on in our own minds?

I do not think there is. The dualist can readily accept what we commonly believe about self-deception. For there are many ways in which this may happen. We may be in error, for example, about what we were like on some past occasion, perhaps in the very recent past. The liability to error here diminishes, other things being equal, with the nearness of the event to be recalled, but logically at least it is always present. One may likewise fail to anticipate what he shall feel or do on some future occasion, since a person may prove to be bolder or more afraid, as the case may be, than he expects when in danger. Here it is a case of understanding, or failing to understand, what our own natures are like. We have more or less permanent tendencies to react or behave in certain ways, and these tendencies or dispositions guarantee the continuity of our conduct. Ryle himself, as we shall see, makes a great deal of our dispositions in the more positive features of his own teaching. But obviously a disposition is not something to be inspected or known about directly. We cannot peer beyond our actual states of mind or conduct at the structure of our character as we might examine some mechanisms like the engine of a car to determine what it can do or where it is likely to fail us. We learn about character from what we or others know of our actual states of mind. To allow that we may be mistaken about our own dispositions is not, therefore, disconcerting for those who affirm that we have immediate and privileged access to our own states of mind while we have them. The claim need not be extended to what lies behind these states or determines them in the way of permanent tendencies—and it would be most unwise to do so.

It is worth adding that most of what Freud and others have to say about the way we may not always understand ourselves concerns mainly at least our dispositional tendencies. Freud himself may not always have thought very clearly about this; he sometimes writes as if unconscious tendencies were some sort of existent realities. But this is usually ascribed to his anxiety to maintain the genuineness of the forces in our nature which he claimed to have revealed. The confusion, so far as there is one, has been largely, but not perhaps entirely, dispelled by his followers. The serious claim made is that we have certain tendencies of which we are not aware and that these are often due to events in our past which we have forgotten. But there is no reason why teaching of this kind, and further ramifications of it, should not be fully accepted by those who claim immediate awareness of our own mental states. The dualist need have no serious quarrel with Freud.

A further point to be stressed here is that it is very misleading to think of mental states as quite distinct isolable episodes. The life of the mind, as I shall stress again, is more like a stream with many currents and eddies in it. There is a great deal which is happening to us at a particular time, and it is not odd if some of this fails to arrest attention and that our over-all picture of ourselves at any time should sometimes become easily dimmed. Mental events merge into one another and their outlines may thus become easily blurred. It is only if we take, or are manoeuvred into taking, a crude and over-simplified episodic view of mental occurrences that the complexities of our mental life and the confusion, not, however, as extensive as some suppose, to which we are liable about ourselves becomes hard to understand or acknowledge.

The second main point which Ryle makes at this stage is that, if the Cartesian view is right, it must be impossible for anyone to know any mind other than his own. 'The workings of one mind are', on the view in question, 'inevitably occult to everyone else.'[1] 'Absolute solitude is on this showing the ineluctable destiny of the soul. Only our bodies can meet.'[2] The Cartesian is bound to be a solipsist.

This is obviously a very serious accusation. No theory which failed to rebut it could stand at all. For it is certain that we do communicate and have fellowship with one another. If we had no knowledge of other people's thoughts and feelings, life would become impossible. A highly sophisticated person might manage to cope in some fashion with a solipsist position. But most persons would find it intolerable, and some, we are told, have been driven mad by trying to hold it. It is certainly not a position of which a philosophical defence can be offered with any consistency. For to whom would the defence be addressed? At best we would be trying to account to ourselves for the illusion of communication

---

[1] *Op. cit.*, p. 14.
[2] *Op. cit.*, p. 15.

B

with others which had made life possible hitherto. I do not know if anyone would care to undertake so forlorn and quixotic a task. We all of us normally assume that we know a great deal about one another, and this assurance is not seriously upset by any difficulties we meet in trying to account for knowledge of other minds. We conclude that there must be something radically wrong with a theory which rules out the possibility of such knowledge, and, if Professor Ryle's accusation at this point held, most philosophers would at once concede to him a total victory.

But has the point any substance? Is there any reason to suppose that a Cartesian must be a solipsist? None, to my mind. There are two aspects of a Cartesian view, firstly that mental processes are distinct from physical ones and, secondly, that we have some direct access to our own mental processes. Neither of these closely related assertions preclude at all the possibility of knowing the minds of other persons in some wholly reliable indirect way. This is surely how we normally think of the matter. I know that I have pain the moment I feel it, I learn that you are hurt from your behaviour or what you tell me, involving in the latter case hearing the sounds you utter and interpreting them or some equivalent. There may be difficulties in accounting for this indirect awareness we have of one another, and there may be certain ways in which it seems odd; philosophers have been much concerned about such questions for a long time. But it is quite another matter to hold up the dualist to scorn on the grounds that his view involves the repudiation of all communication. That is not how the dualist himself understands the matter, and the fatal consequence which his view is alleged to have is by no means evident; it is not something immediately involved in claiming direct or private access to one's own states of consciousness. For the claim would always carry with it the insistence that *in another way* we do have the sort of knowledge we normally think we have of one another. There is, thus, no way of putting the dualist out of court from the start by accusing him of the absurdity of solipsism. The absurdity is clearly not so evident that it can be boldly proclaimed from the start. It must at least be shown that, contrary to what we normally suppose and what the dualist himself maintains, the private access theory involves the absurdity in question.

What attempt does Ryle himself make to substantiate his criticism? Very little. His procedure—as we shall see—is in the main to just let it be assumed that a dualist view is tantamount to the repudiation of all communication and thus to make such a view seem immediately ridiculous. He does, however, offer, with the utmost brevity, one argument in support of his procedure at this stage. It is the following:

Ryle declares that 'the supposed arguments' which people may use 'from bodily movements similar to their own to mental workings similar to their own would lack any possibility of observational corroboration'.[1] I do not think a dualist would admit that this contains a satisfactory statement of his position. But in any case, the substance of Ryle's complaint seems to be defective. He assumes that we have no warrant for any affirmation of fact without 'observational corroboration'. If pressed, this assumption would make it very difficult—to my mind impossible—to account for our knowledge of the past. I believe that Napoleon lost the battle of Waterloo but we cannot have the scene itself re-enacted, as we may put on a film at will. We draw our conclusion, and we do so with every confidence, on the basis of the evidence available to us now. It is likewise claimed that we have good reason for supposing that the bodily movements of other persons are of such a nature as to afford us perfectly reliable evidence as a rule of thoughts and intentions which we cannot know as they are known by the persons having them. If there is error in this assumption this must be clearly shown and arguments must be carefully advanced to counter those of thinkers who defend the alleged indirect knowledge of one another. Simply to state that the claim lacks 'observational corroboration' is to restate what the theory essentially maintains; it is no rebuttal of it.

This brings us to the close of Ryle's general presentation of the position, the official doctrine in his terms, which he hopes to demolish; and it is evident already, I hope, that Ryle has brought little openness of mind or care to his examination of the themes to which he is opposed. The opening presentation already contains much misrepresentation and anticipation of the distortions on which subsequent criticisms are made to depend. We are well prepared, in this way, in the opening pages of the book, for the declaration made, in proceeding to more explicit criticisms and exposure of 'The Absurdity of the Official Doctrine',[2] that the author intends to speak of the theory 'with deliberate abusiveness'.[3] In the latter respect I do not think it can be doubted that

[1] *Op. cit.*, p. 14.
[2, 3] *Op. cit.*, p. 15.

Professor Ryle succeeds. Whether this contributes to better philosophical understanding or is consistent with the attitude we expect from a philosopher is another matter. We can judge better when we see how Ryle proceeds, and I believe it can be shown, when we look more closely at Ryle's procedures, that he is especially liable to error through his proneness, almost deliberately cultivated, to look for nothing which is not in some fashion like the impression we have of the natural world which we come to know from observation of it. Let us then pass to Ryle's criticisms of the Official Doctrine which he associates especially with Descartes.

At the start of his criticism of the 'Official Doctrine', also described as 'the dogma of the Ghost in the Machine', Professor Ryle introduces us to a notion which has since become very familiar, namely the notion of a category-mistake. This is the mistake of presenting something as if it belonged to one logical type or category when in fact it belongs to another. There is no doubt that philosophers and others do fall into error in this way at times. One familiar example is that known as hypostatizing an abstraction. This happens when we speak of an abstraction as if it were a particular entity. Many instances of this may be found in the history of thought and controversy. During the nineteenth century it was often the tendency of political thinkers, especially post-Hegelian idealists, to write of the State as if it were some entity or super-structure over and above its individual members organized in a certain way. Much of the work of writers like L. T. Hobhouse, in his *Metaphysical Theory of the State*, turned on the exhibition of that fallacy in the political theories of idealist writers. Traditionalist theologians have likewise been led to write on occasion as if our lives, or the lot we have in this world, belonged to some all-inclusive 'man' who had a Fall and a subsequent history throughout the ages. Many traditionalist errors, in respect of sin and responsibility, have been ascribed in fact to that misconception. Others have been induced, in a similar way, to think of values as if they were some peculiar sort of entity with a 'realm' of their own. These are familiar errors, and although the thought of recent times, preoccupied with clarity and much afraid of being misled by abuse of metaphor, has been much concerned with the exposure of such errors, the commission and the exposure of them is by no means the monopoly of our day, and they are persistent features of intellectual controversy. We need not then question the idea of the category-mistake in itself, but we must not suppose that there is anything very novel in the discovery of it today. There is nothing new in it beyond the name, and we have also to be on our guard against looking for it and thinking we have found it where there is no genuine evidence of it. We must not become obsessed with the category-mistake.

It will be well to note here the examples of the category-mistake with which Ryle himself introduces us to this idea. He refers to the visitor to Oxford who, after being shown the colleges and so on asks to be shown the university, oblivious of the fact that the university is just 'the way in which all that he has already seen is organized'.[1] Again, someone who has seen battalions, batteries, etc., march past might request to see the division, unaware that these make up the division. Another, when watching a cricket match might request to be shown the team spirit or those whose role it was to display it, as the bowler does the bowling and so on. In the same way, someone might suppose the British Constitution to be of the same logical type as the Home Office or the Church of England, or we may suppose that the Average Taxpayer is like an individual we may encounter somewhere.

These are reasonable instances of a category-mistake. But there is one thing we should note about them. The likelihood of anyone making them, except in make-believe or jest of the Lewis Caroll type, is remote; and I think it is only by stretches of his own imagination that Ryle can make out that the mistake has been seriously made in the alleged instances of it he detects in philosophical arguments.

The commission of a category-mistake by Descartes is thought to have started with his adoption of the mechanistic explanation of events in the external world. It was deemed improper to regard mental events as 'just a variety of the mechanical',[2] for that would put religious and moral concerns in jeopardy. Recourse was thus had to 'non-mechanical causes', to the notion of 'minds as extra centres of causal processes rather like machines but also considerably different from them'.[3] This gives us the 'paramechanical hypothesis'.

I see, however, little evidence in fact for the supposition that Descartes' thought moved in this way. True he accepted the

[1] *Op. cit.*, p. 16.
[2], [3] *Op. cit.*, p. 19.

mechanistic views of physical processes, as we have seen; and it is plain that he also wished to exempt human beings from the operation of such laws. That was the point of insisting on 'liberty of indifference'. But this gives us no reason for supposing that Descartes would not in any case have wished to regard mental processes as quite distinct from physical ones. He could well have done this as his direct impression of what in fact he found to be the case, and this seems to me the natural and plausible account to give of the matter. He would also in the interest of liberty and human dignity have wished to show that mental processes were not subject to the mechanistic determinism which he thought prevailed in the external world. But this would be a subsequent consideration which itself presupposed initial detection of the radical difference between extended or spatial physical entities and 'the non-spatial workings of minds'. It can only be on the assumption that the Cartesian position is inherently implausible that it becomes sensible to look for an explanation of it on the basis of some alleged postulation of quasi-mechanical processes for which there is little evidence and which seems so much out of accord with Descartes' concern to stress the radical difference between mind and body.

Ryle adds, as a reflection which he believes much strengthens his case, that 'there was from the beginning felt to be a major theoretical difficulty in explaining how minds can influence and be influenced by bodies'.[1] I am not sure how far this was 'the notorious crux' it is alleged to be. True, it is strange that processes as different from one another as mental and physical ones should affect each other. But this is not very much stranger than other forms of causation, and, in any case, to be amazed that there should be some variety of causal determination tells us nothing in particular about our recognition of it and does nothing to call it in question. Even if it can be shown that some thinkers, including Descartes, have wished to have a further explanation of how the interaction of mind and body took place, this would be a separate error which casts no doubt on the soundness of the belief in interaction as such.

Ryle further contends that Descartes, having some general adherence to mechanistic notions, was driven to 'avert disaster', in respect to human understandings and worth, by adopting an 'obverse vocabulary' still to that extent determined by 'the gram-

[1] *Op. cit.*, p. 19.

mar of mechanics'.[1] In this way 'the workings of minds had to be described by the mere negatives of the specific descriptions given to bodies; they are not in space, they are not motions, they are not modifications of matter, they are not accessible to public observation'.[2] But just how did Professor Ryle expect Descartes to describe his theory except in these terms? If one holds a dualist view, what can one say, in presenting it, except that mind is radically different from body in the ways indicated—and that we know positively what mind is like in having mental experience? That is what the theory means and what Descartes thought was the case. If there are two ultimate sorts of things in the world as we find it, what can we say of the one in relation to the other except by pointing the contrast? Descartes took the only course open to him and this affords us no warrant for supposing that, in adopting the alleged 'obverse vocabulary', he was somehow proceeding under the spell of the mechanistic theories and having his views shaped by this. True, he would have thought that minds 'are not bits of clockwork' but just what is the justification—or the point of suggesting—that he thought of them as 'just bits of not-clockwork'?[3] I suspect that it is Ryle who is really obsessed with the mechanistic notions in question and finding some baleful influence of them in matters susceptible of a much simpler explanation.

Further reference is also made here to the Freedom of the Will. It is suggested that a problem arises about this solely because our thought is shaped for us throughout by mechanistic models. We assume that 'minds belong to the same category as bodies and since bodies are rigidly governed by mechanical laws, it seemed to many theorists to follow that minds must be similarly governed by rigid non-mechanical laws. The physical world is a deterministic system, so the mental world must be a deterministic system'.[4] A solution is found by supposing that laws governing mental processes are 'only rather rigid'. 'The problem of the Freedom of the Will was the problem how to reconcile the hypothesis that minds are to be described in terms drawn from the categories of mechanics with the knowledge that higher-grade human conduct is not of a piece with the behaviour of machines.'[5]

Now it is undoubtedly the case that anyone who supposes that certain processes are determined in mechanistic ways is liable to

[1,2] *Op. cit.*, p. 20.
[3,4,5] *Op. cit.*, p. 20

look for some means of exempting mental processes in the interest of their worth and of freedom. But it does not follow that this is the only way in which a problem of freedom arises. Even when it has been shown that our activities are not subject to any mechanical determination there remains the question, and this is the serious problem of the Freedom of the Will, whether in other ways we are not bound to act according to the sorts of persons we are. This is an additional problem, it has force on its own account and not as any kind of legacy from the adoption of mechanistic ideas in respect to other processes; and it is thus a sad mistake to suppose that the postulation of mental processes of a paraphysical nature only comes about as an attempt to extricate ourselves from a bogus difficulty created by supposing that all activities must at least be quasi-mechanical. The existence of a problem of freedom is by no means the grist to Professor Ryle's mill that he takes it to be. It arises in quite other ways than the one he supposes.

Ryle also observes that the alleged attempt to 'avert disaster' in the way indicated is in a further way 'broken-backed'. The postulation of 'spectral machines' which are in some way like, but not quite like, material ones, fails of its purpose, because we 'could never get access to the postulated immaterial causes'[1] of our observable behaviour. 'Save for the doubtful exception of himself' no one 'could ever tell the difference between a man and a Robot'.[2] Those who seem intelligent may really be idiots and vice versa. But all this of course turns on the assumption that, if we have no direct access to other minds such as we claim for ourselves, there is no way *at all* in which other minds are known. This, we have already urged, is quite gratuitous. We do have good reason for supposing that other minds are known indirectly, although by no means always without error—the apparent idiot may be a clever actor and so on. Professor Ryle's point would only hold if he had already and independently shown that the account of our knowledge of one another in indirect or analogical ways could not be sustained, and this he has not really begun to do, he has just dismissed the supposition with scorn, although it is the essential feature of the view he opposes.

The truth is that Descartes and others were not seeking at all to avert the particular disaster which Ryle has in mind. They thought on quite other grounds that mental processes were other

[1], [2] *Op. cit.*, p. 21.

than physical ones. But Ryle supposes that they were misled by asking the wrong questions. We already know, he declares, 'how to apply mental-conduct concepts', and although it is not clear what that means at this stage, it becomes evident later that Ryle is thinking of what we normally intend when we speak of someone being intelligent, someone else not so bright or stupid, and so on. We decide this in terms of what people do; some people solve puzzles more quickly than others or see the point of a joke more readily and so on. That, and a host of kindred things, is why they are said to be intelligent, or to 'have intelligence'. Ryle assumes that this answers all the problems we could have about what is involved in being intelligent, and then he contends that Descartes, instead of giving this sort of straightforward answer in terms of what we would normally say and do, mistook 'the logic of his problem' and, on finding that the principle of mechanical causation affords us no criteria for distinguishing intelligent from non-intelligent behaviour, asked what other causal principle could do this. 'He realized that the problem was not one of mechanics and assumed that it must therefore be one of some counterpart to mechanics.'[1] This is where the category-mistake is most lurid.

Now it seems to me that if anyone is a victim of a category-mistake here it must be Professor Ryle himself. He starts with the question of how we normally apply the word 'intelligence' and determine what is intelligent and what is not, and he assumes that this is the only question to ask and that it was in some way the question which philosophers like Descartes were trying, in a very confused way, to answer. They were in fact concerned with a quite different question, and it is Ryle who has here got the logic of the *philosophical* problem mistaken. Descartes was trying to say something, not about why one person is thought clever and another not so, but about what it means to be exercising intelligence of any kind at all. This is not a question we ask from day to day, and it is not, for that reason, reflected in what we normally say, in our standard or paradigm use of terms as it is sometimes put. It is the philosopher's question and it applies as much to the low grade intelligence of the stupid or slow-witted person as to the high grade intelligence of the person of whom we go out of our way, in ordinary parlance, to say that he is intelligent. A person would not be unintelligent unless he had intelligence in the general sense in

[1] *Op. cit.*, p. 22.

some measure. Stones are not stupid, they just do not have understanding at all; and what philosophers have been concerned about is what is involved in having mental powers of any kind. It was about this that Descartes was seeking to say something, and what is sound or mistaken in his views is not affected at all by whatever is relevant to a very different sort of question and one which is normally of less interest to philosophers. In failing to recognise this and have a grasp of properly philosophical procedures, Ryle himself seems to be mistaking considerations of one logical type for those of another.

This becomes especially evident when he complains of the futility of Descartes' procedure in asking questions about minds and machines when 'everyone already knew how to apply mental-conduct concepts'.[1] The questions were superfluous and the answers in consequence bound to be distorted. But the upshot of this is not to ask philosophical questions at all, and instead to be content with finding what is most appropriate to say for ordinary non-philosophical purposes; in short Professor Ryle is giving up the ghost at the start of his book in more senses than one.

It is not surprising, therefore, that he should proceed to flourish very boldly before us still further instances of the alleged category-mistake. It would be absurd to say of someone that he had bought a left-hand glove, a right-hand glove, *and* a pair of gloves; and if we say of someone that she came home in a sedan-chair and a flood of tears, we do not mean that these are disjunctive terms to be used and conjoined in the same sense. To come in a flood of tears is not the same thing as coming in a chair or a box. In the same way, Ryle argues, it is absurd to 'maintain that there exist both bodies and minds; that there occur both physical processes and mental processes'.[2] It is not altogether clear how this is to be understood. For Ryle insists also that he is 'not, for example, denying that there occur mental processes'.[3] We do long divisions and we make jokes. This seems to take the sting out of his earlier statement; he is not, it would seem, after all denying anything we are seriously concerned about, and his position is quite innocuous. Much of his case, throughout the book, owes much to his skilfully conveying the impression that he is not calling in question the sort of things he seems at first to be doubting. But under cover of seeming to grant us all that we are properly concerned to defend

[1] *Op. cit.*, p. 21.
[2], [3] *Op. cit.*, p. 22.

Ryle does in fact put forward views of a highly controversial kind which are quite out of accord with what many others think and consider important. That certainly happens in the present context.

For while he is prepared to say that in one sense there are, or there occur, mental processes, he is equally insistent that these do not exist or occur in the same sense as physical processes. 'I am saying that the phrase "there occur mental processes" does not mean the same sort of thing as "there occur physical processes", and, therefore, that it makes no sense to conjoin or disjoin the two'.[1] 'It is perfectly proper to say in one logical tone of voice, that there exist minds and to say, in another logical tone of voice, that there exist bodies. But the expressions do not indicate two different species of existence, for "existence" is not a generic word like "coloured" or "sexed". They indicate two different senses of "exist", somewhat as "rising" has different senses in "the tide is rising", "hopes are rising", and "the average age of death is rising".'[2]

This is an issue we have already met. I can only add here that the use of the words 'are', 'occur', 'exist', just do not seem to me to belong to different logical types when applied to bodies and to minds. Mental processes are real, they 'are' or they go on just as physical ones do. My mind is very different from my body, and to that extent they exist differently, but I mean substantially the same thing when I say that they both exist. My thoughts at the moment are as real (they go on) as the movements of my hands. My thoughts are not abstractions, they do not exist in some sense similar to that in which there is an average taxpayer. They occur as particular occurrences distinct from the physical occurrences which go on at the same time and which affect, and are affected by them. To question this is to question something substantial, and we cannot redeem that situation by allowing that in some other ambiguous or esoteric sense it may be said that there *are* minds and bodies. Professor Ryle must stand by what he seriously maintains without being allowed to make it appear more innocent than it is.

Where he does stand might seem plain in the declaration that 'the hallowed contrast between Mind and Matter will be dissipated', but how are we to understand the reservation that follows—

[1] *Op. cit.*, p. 22.
[2] *Op. cit.*, p. 23.

'but dissipated not by either of the equally hallowed absorptions of Mind by Matter or of Matter by Mind, but in quite a different way'?[1] It is perhaps plain already that the different way is not so very different after all, except in the curious procedures by which the denial of the reality of mental processes is sustained. We can now look more closely at some of these procedures.

[1] *Op. cit.*, p. 22.

CHAPTER II

'KNOWING HOW' AND VOLUNTARY ACTION

A prominent place, at all stages in his work, is accorded by Ryle to a distinction he draws between 'knowing how and knowing that'. This is, in some ways, a distinction we can all easily recognise and allow; and that lends much plausibility to Ryle's contentions until we look more closely at the way he understands it and the use he makes of it. Examples of the distinction in general are easy to provide. We all know that many things are the case (or true), that Edinburgh is north of London, that New York is in America, that the battle of Waterloo was fought in 1815, that the sum of the angles of a triangle is 180 degrees, that two and two make four, and so on indefinitely. I may at any time call something of this sort to mind, or discover it for the first time, as when I first learn that Labour has won the election; and I may state or affirm that something is the case in this way for the benefit of others. But this is very different, or appears to be so, from knowing how to do certain things, like knowing how to swim, how to ride a bicycle, how to type, how to spell, how to play chess and so forth. In some fashion we can all recognize such a distinction. The question then is what does it involve.

The important point, according to Ryle is that, in the case of 'knowing how' we are not having knowledge of 'this or that truth' but simply displaying the ability to do certain sorts of things; and this, at a certain level seems evident also. I do not seem to call to mind that anything is the case when I exercise my skill in playing cricket, I just play the stroke, and my skill lies in knowing just how to play it, I swing deftly round and cut the ball low down between the slips so that it races to the boundary. I might be very poor at saying just how this is done. At some stage a coach may have given me instructions, he will have urged me to keep my eye on the ball, not to move too far out of my crease, not to swing too soon and so on. But I certainly do not call all this body of instruction consciously to mind, at least this is not what normally happens. I may on occasion remind myself of some rule or advice, or something I have discovered myself that helps me to play. But

I would not be likely to play well if I were all the time theorising in this way. The teaching has soaked in and disappeared and it only shows itself in my skill when I have to play the stroke. Perhaps I never had, and never gave myself, any formal instruction. I may never have been told (or have told myself) to keep a straight bat or to watch my timing. I have just watched and played cricket and acquired the knack.

Indeed, it is a well-known fact that people who are thinking too much about the rules do not show up very well in practical skills. No one likes to sit next to a driver who is always telling himself or thinking what to do; we are much more confident with those who drive 'without thinking' or automatically. These are in no way careless drivers, they may well be experts, but they do not distract themselves by calling to mind the rules. Hardly anyone could afford, after the first experiments in driving (and not much then) to be thinking how far to swing the wheel round, we just turn with the bend, we know how to do this without having to think, and, if we had always to pull ourselves up first to think, we could never act with the promptness and smoothness which good driving requires. Even if it is a good thing to go over the technical rules now and then, like refreshing our minds about the highway code, good driving is not a matter of self-consciously applying a code.

Perhaps I can venture on one further illustration, in one way a very effective one. It might seem to make Ryle's case for him very conclusively. This concerns the way we type. When we first learn to type we have to study the keyboard, to note where the letters A, B etc. are placed. But once the skill is acquired we have no need to be telling ourselves where the letters are, we just get on with the typing, 'automatically' or 'instinctively' as it is sometimes rather loosely put. It is moreover true that an expert typist might find it very difficult to describe the keyboard—she might have to take her time and think hard. I certainly could not tell at once how the letters go, but I am a tolerable typist. If asked to list the letters on the board I would have at least to simulate the action of typing and record the position of the letters as my fingers found them for me. But my fingers find the letters without difficulty; if they did not, if I had to try to visualize the keyboard each time or in some other way remember where each letter was, I would never be able to type. The process would be much too laborious to be worthwhile. Here then we seem to have a clear instance of expertly knowing how without knowing what is the case.

But what does Ryle tell us further about this? To what use does he put the idea of 'Knowing how'? It is here that I would begin to part company with him. For he seems to think that between abstract and deliberate theorising, on the one hand, and the observable performance, on the other, there can be nothing further in the way of distinctive intellectual activity. Whatever is thought to go beyond an outward performance of a certain sort must, as he understands it, be some kind of theorising. If I do not call to mind the keyboard, or something of that sort, then there is nothing besides what my fingers do.

This might appear to be out and out materialism. But Ryle would certainly not admit that. There is a vital difference between our behaviour and a merely physical process. When we say that someone is witty or tactful 'we are not considering only the muscular movements which we witness'.[1] A parrot might make the same remark without being credited with a sense of humour, a lout may chance to do the same thing as the tactful man. In what then does the difference consist? It consists in the fact that the humorist (or the tactful man) did what he did 'on purpose'. The clown 'trips and tumbles on purpose and after much rehearsal and at the golden moment'.[2] But here all turns on what is meant by 'on purpose'. And what this involves, according to Ryle, is not that the performance is the 'effect of any hidden internal cause', but that it is 'the exercise of a skill'.[3] That is what distinguishes intelligent behaviour.

But what then is involved in being an exercise of skill? The answer to this question is central, not only to what Ryle has to say about 'knowing how' and 'knowing that', but to his philosophy of mind at all points. We must look closely at what he says.

A skill is 'neither a witnessable nor an unwitnessable act'.[4] 'It is a disposition, or complex of dispositions.'[5] The idea of a disposition is a fairly straightfoward and familiar one. We use it, for example, when we describe glass as brittle. 'The brittleness of the glass does not consist in the fact that it is at a given moment actually being shivered. It may be brittle without ever being shivered. To say that it is brittle is to say that if it ever is, or ever had been, struck or strained, it would fly, or have flown, into

[1] *Op. cit.*, p. 32.
[2, 3, 4, 5] *Op. cit.*, p. 33.

fragments.'[1] This has much, though not everything, in common with being subsumed under a law. 'To possess a dispositional property is not to be in a particular state, or to undergo a particular change; it is to be bound or liable to be in a particular state, or to undergo a particular change, when a particular condition is realized.'[2]

The dispositions of human beings include habits as well as skills. 'We build up habits by drill', by the 'imposition of repetitions', 'but we build up intelligent capacities by training'.[3] The point of importance here is that 'many disposition-concepts are determinable concepts',[4] that is they can be realized in a vast, almost unlimited variety of ways. The 'higher-grade dispositions of people' are 'dispositions the exercises of which are indefinitely heterogeneous'.[5] And the claim which Ryle is making here is that intelligence and doing things on purpose consist in our exercising determinable dispositions in a great variety of ways. It is not a case of repeating hackneyed moves or following a single track but of being able to vary our moves according to need. In judging a performance to be intelligent we are thus considering the 'abilities and propensities of which this performance was an actualization'.[6] A person may hit a bull's eye by chance, but, if he hit it through good marksmanship, then this must be borne out in 'his subsequent shots, his past record, his explanations or excuses, the advice he gave to his neighbour and a host of other clues of various sorts'.[7] He must be able 'to get on or near the bull's eye again, even if the wind strengthens, the range alters and the target moves'.[8]

'Knowing how' then consists in our having and exercising determinable dispositions in a variety of ways as occasion requires; and we seem, therefore, in respect to this sort of knowledge or intelligence at least, to be dispensing with any occurrence beyond the observable performance considered as an exercise of a skill or capacity. Nothing seems to be involved beyond our 'capacities, skills, habits, liabilities and bents'.[9] There is therefore no need to postulate causes of our performances, least of all 'occult causes'. The story is complete as it stands, once we have invoked the dispositions or skills of which the actual performance is a manifestation.

It might be thought necessary at this stage for Professor Ryle

[1, 2] *Op. cit.*, p. 43.
[3] *Op. cit.*, p. 42.
[4, 5] *Op. cit.*, p. 44.
[6, 7, 8, 9] *Op. cit.*, p. 45.

to tell us more about dispositions and skills. Questions have at
any rate been raised about them by others. What are general
properties and how do they belong to a particular entity? What are
dispositions and how do they belong to a person? To the first
question the answer may be given that there is nothing that can be
said beyond the fact that objects of a certain sort do behave, or
are bound to behave, in certain ways. The brittleness of the glass
is just its liability to be shivered. Nothing more can be said, and
in the main this seems to be sound. Few would wish today to
postulate some Lockean substance in which physical properties
inhere, and we can go seriously astray if we think of general
properties as if they were in turn some peculiar sorts of entities,
that is if we hypostatize them. But it might be thought that something further requires to be said about the element of dependability or necessity which seems to be involved in a general property.
I shall not consider further here what this might be, as the answer
I would be disposed to give would lead out to questions of a
religious nature about the ultimate dependence of all things on
God. Beyond this I doubt whether anything can be said about
general properties beyond noting them, and I do not think therefore there is any serious complaint to be made against Ryle at this
point. He has no need for his purpose to go beyond anything we
might say in a finite context about the qualities of things.

It is more of a moot point, however, how far this is also true of the
dispositions of persons. We have again to avoid the errors of hypo-
statization. But when we have done so, is there nothing remaining
to be said about the way our interests and tendencies belong to us
as persons? Do not self-conscious beings, at least, display a special
sort of unity? But these are questions best left over till we come to
consider later what Ryle has to say more explicitly about the self
or subject in experience. It must suffice here to note, without too
serious a complaint, that Ryle does not tell us anything further
about dispositions and capacities, and that he probably does not
think there is anything to be said beyond noting them.

The really important question at the moment is whether the
account of intelligent behaviour in terms of performances and the
skills displayed in these is adequate. Is there something which
Ryle has not covered? It seems that there is and that his arguments, at this crucial point in his theories, involve a very serious
false disjunction. We can allow the importance of what he says
about skills and dispositions and be grateful to him for bringing

them into prominence in the philosophy of mind, provided we do not suppose, as some seem to do, that he was the first to discover them. We can also admit that practical activities do not depend normally on giving ourselves general instructions, or telling ourselves what to do, and then doing something. That is what he considers to be the alternative to his account of our activities in terms of the witnessable performance considered as the exercise of skills. He complains, therefore, that champions of 'the intellectualist legend', as he puts it, are apt to try to reassimilate knowing *how* to knowing *that* by arguing that intelligent performance involves the observance of rules, or 'the application of criteria' and that a person must in this way 'preach to himself before he can practice'.[1] He 'must do a bit of theory and then do a bit of practice'.[2] As it is also put, the 'act is preceded and steered by another internal act of considering a regulative proposition', 'there must be some anterior internal operation of planning what to do'.[3] There must be 'two processes, one of doing and another of theorising'.[4] But this is obviously not a proper account of the way we behave. If anyone seriously held it, the question would at once arise, as Ryle himself is not slow to point out, of how we come to do the initial theorising. Would not this require an anterior act of planning how to plan, would not an agent have to 'first reflect how best to reflect how to act',[5] and so on in an endless regress?

All this seems patently true. We do not have to plan every action before we perform it. In this sense, it is certainly true that, when I do something, 'I am doing one thing and not two'.[6] In writing these words I do not have first to tell myself how to write them, I do not have to rehearse the performance in that sense, and if I had I could hardly get on with anything. We do have to plan unusual or difficult activities, but if everything had to be planned with deliberation, we could hardly achieve anything. This is what was shown in the instances of 'knowing how' given above.

But can we then conclude that, because an act cannot be divided into two in the way Ryle has in mind, that because there is not invariably or normally any prior 'theorising' about it, there is nothing to be said beyond noting the performance and the skills it is found to display? Admittedly, reference to the skills, as disclosed

[1, 2] *Op. cit.*, p. 29.
[3, 5] *Op. cit.*, p. 31.
[4, 6] *Op. cit.*, p. 32.

in a variety of kindred performances, is how we come in practice to pronounce the act an intelligent one—or at least that is involved in doing so—but does this tell us everything of substance about the act?

I do not think so. When I write these words now on the page there seems to be clearly more going on at the time than the movement of my fingers and the pencil. This holds even if we leave out of account the meaning the words have for me as part of my argument. In my actual writing more is involved than the physical movement, and this more is not of a merely dispositional kind. It is part, and to my mind the essential part, of what goes on, as I have put it. What is this more? Clearly it is my sustained understanding of what I am doing and my continuous purposing to do it. This cannot be dissolved into dispositional attitudes. They are indeed required in a variety of ways, but they are also actualized at the time in an on-going or continuous mental process which determines my physical movements. In the absence of such a process it is hard to see what could be meant by regarding the performance as a conscious or a willed or a deliberate one. It would not be mental activity at all. If we reduce the actual activity entirely to the physical movement, the position cannot be redeemed by reference to skills, adaptations and so on. These bring out part of what is involved in doing something 'on purpose', 'with heed', on 'the *qui vive*', and so on. But it would all be Hamlet without the prince if we tried to tell the story entirely in these terms. There must be some conscious happenings as well.

This is what is very badly misrepresented when it is thought that, when I am doing one thing, I am doing something else as well, that I am doing not one thing but two, purposing to write and writing on the page. There are indeed two processes involved, but they are not the two processes that Ryle has in mind. He says, of a clown's tumblings, that there are 'not two processes, such as one process of purposing to trip and, as an effect, another process of tripping'.[1] That is certainly true, and it is what has made Ryle's position seem so convincing to many. But the dual process involved is not that of one act preceding another—my doing two things instead of one etc.—but of the one act having a mental component and a physical one. More strictly, I would prefer to say that the act proper, that is my on-going purposing, induces or is accompanied by the physical movement. The real question, when we think of the clown's tripping, is what is involved in the

[1] *Op. cit.*, p. 33.

tripping. If we have given a proper account of the tripping, there is no further need to refer to the purposing to trip. Tripping, in the clown's performance, is tripping on purpose, and this is what makes it seem absurd to suppose that we have to refer, in addition, to the purposing to trip. The act of tripping, in this case, would not be an act without purposing, it would be a mere physical movement or an accident. What makes it not an accident is that the clown is aware all the time that he is doing it and has all along the intention to do it. Sustaining the intention, even though in this case for a very short interval, is what makes the act a genuine or purposed one; and however much the purposing in this sense may depend on dispositional skills and attitudes, as it certainly does, there could be no purpose or genuine action unless the dispositions were actualized in the sustaining of a purpose consciously over a period, however slight. The dispositions are not just actualized in the physical tumbling. There is another item, the essential one in fact, which Ryle altogether overlooks and which is so grievously travestied in the supposition that the two processes involved consist of one process of acting and another of purposing to act.

We can agree with Ryle that 'a skill is not an act'[1] and that it cannot be 'recorded by a camera'. 'It is a disposition, or complex of dispositions, and a disposition is a factor of the wrong logical type to be seen or unseen, recorded or unrecorded.'[2] But we have also to insist that there is something involved in an act beyond the skill and the overt performance, and that this something more cannot be captured by the camera just because it has not the physical quality which anything must have in order to be photographed. It is a mental, non-extended, occurrence. We cannot, therefore, agree that 'the traditional theory of the mind has misconstrued the type-distinction between disposition and exercise into its mythical bifurcation of unwitnessable mental causes and their witnessable physical effects'.[3] It is Ryle himself who has fallen into a considerable fallacy of false disjunction.

In doing so, and in seeking in desperation to account for our activity solely in terms of outward performance and skills, Ryle is much influenced, here as elsewhere, by his assumption that if any process is postulated beyond a physical one it must at least be like the latter. 'We are still tempted,' he declares, 'to argue that . . . there must be occurring in the clown's head a counterpart performance to that which is taking place on the sawdust.'[4] But

[1, 2, 3, 4] *Op. cit.*, p. 33.

of course no one who understands his business holds that the mental process, the purposing proper, takes place in the clown's head, and it is a moot point whether we would say that even in metaphor; we certainly do *not* think of the extra-physical process as 'a counterpart performance', an 'occult or ghostly' tumbling about in private rehearsal in one's head or anywhere else. It is indeed not a performance, in the sense in which the physical tumbling, or the whole activity as involving that, is so. It is a quite different mental process not at all in space or in quasi-space.

There are further revealing observations made in these contexts. Ryle declares, for example, that 'On the assumption of the antithesis between "physical" and "mental", it follows that muscular doing cannot itself be a mental operation'.[1] But would we ever want to say that muscular doing is a mental operation? Muscular doing is surely physical, indeed strictly speaking it is not proper to use an expression like 'muscular doing', since 'doing' involves something more than muscular. The latent materialism of Professor Ryle comes close to the surface in expressions like these. Note again the statement: 'Nor does the surgeon's skill function in his tongue uttering medical truths but only in his hands making the correct movements.'[2] This seems to me a glaringly confused and misleading statement. No one would wish to hold that the surgeon's skill consisted in his tongue uttering medical truths, nothing of the sort has ever been held by anyone. Nor do we imagine that the surgeon calls to mind in any other way anything we would normally understand by 'medical truths'. He does not have his text books or any other before him, and he is not thinking of them or of any equivalent. He is much too busy and absorbed in what he is doing, and only on some very rare occasion, when faced with some unusual emergency perhaps, would he have to think of anything as general as the terms 'medical truths' imply. Those truths have become, as we say, a part of him, and they remain largely dispositional. But what he knows in this dispositional way is subtly actualized, as the situation requires, from moment to moment in conscious processes in his understanding. In other words, although he is not uttering medical truths, he is going through an intense mental activity of concentrating with acute understanding on what he is doing. This is how his skill comes to be exercised, and if his mind wandered, through his being worried

---

[1] *Op. cit.*, p. 32.
[2] *Op. cit.*, p. 49.

perhaps about something else, we would certainly not be happy to leave it to his 'skilled hands' to make the correct movements. The skill, in short, does not lie solely, or at all strictly, in the hands, although we do for rough and ready purposes speak of the skilled hands of the surgeon. The skill involves a sustained and subtle mental activity in the closest co-ordination, without our knowing how, with responsive muscles, nerve endings, brain cells and so on. The surgeon, like the athlete, must no doubt train his hands and keep them steady and responsive, but he does not do this as he might keep a machine in good trim for some job it might be left to do. The hands can only function when the appropriate mental process continues as well; and this is so obvious that one would feel apologetic about labouring the point were it not so widely assumed that pronouncements like those of Professor Ryle here, in speaking of 'the hands making the correct movements', are the last word in good sense and the originality which will really advance the subject in the philosophy of mind. That it should gain credence at all must be largely due to the wholly misleading disjunction which makes it the only alternative that the tongue should be uttering medical truths. The latter travesty lends its cover to a form of materialism which is here very thinly disguised.

There is a further point much overlooked by Ryle, and unhappily it is one which much hinders the importance he has rightly ascribed to skills and dispositions from taking its proper place in an adequate philosophy of mind. Mental activity does not take the form of easily isolable episodes. It is a subtly changing flow of variegated events. At any particular time I am conscious of many things. At the moment I am thinking about philosophy. That, as it is put, is in the forefront of my mind. But I am also aware of my hand holding a pencil, I glimpse the pencil and note the marks as they appear on the paper, I am aware of the table beyond that, and I have the sensations of my arms resting on the table and my body against the chair, I am aware of the cool wind blowing in through open windows, of the trees and fields beyond these, of the sounds of children at play, of the occasional motor-car in the road, and o on. Some of these things may quite slip out of my consciousness, and there is a problem, which need not delay us here, of what could be meant if it were held that I still note some of them subconsciously or unconsciously. Does whatever falls below the threshold of consciousness become merely dispositional, or are there in addition subconscious mental occurrences—as the well-known illustration of the clock which we seem not to note till it stops tends to suggest? We need not try to answer now. It is enough to draw attention to the richly varied state of one's consciousness at any particular time.

Much of this richly varied content of a conscious state is moreover constantly changing, some shifting more to the centre of attention and drifting away again. In the main the centre continues to be occupied by my thoughts about what I propose to write, but my mind may also wander a good deal, I may not be certain how to proceed and, until I do so, the scene out of the window may arrest my attention more. It is probably quite a good thing to allow one's mind, within limits, to wander in this way; and there are no doubt subtle variations on the more obvious forms of these fluctuations. The interchange between disposition and actualization is also very subtle here. At one moment a thought may be actually entertained by me, and at the next it may only be something I am capable of actualizing at need. What in fact shapes itself in the way of thoughts I actually entertain, out of the vast reservoir of what I only know or believe dispositionally, is therefore subtly varied from moment to moment, and not, for that reason, easy to describe or always to detect. This is an additional reason why mental activity is apt to seem elusive and difficult to note by contrast with external events. It has been well compared to a stream or flow in which there are many currents, whirls and eddies. But if instead of thinking of mental processes in this way as a constantly changing stream we envisage it as a series of distinct isolable episodes each with its easily noted link with the external world, then we are again making it peculiarly difficult for ourselves to appreciate properly how we do have mental processes distinct from external processes and subtly interacting with them—and this is just what Professor Ryle does. He thinks of our purported mental activity almost as a series of jerks or spasms.

Intimations of this are found in the frequency of references, in the passages I have just been discussing, to 'mental happenings', 'internal operations', 'occult causes'. Such language might be innocuous if it were balanced by turns of speech which are more indicative of the continuous nature of mental processes. But, far from our finding such a corrective, it becomes clear, as soon as Ryle proceeds to more specific explications of his views, that it is the severely episodic notion of mental activity that he ascribes to his opponents. This becomes particularly plain when he passes from his general account of 'knowing how' to discussion of 'the Will' and of further problems about the freedom of will.

Ryle's concern here, as we might expect, is to show that our 'overt actions' are not the 'results of counterpart hidden operations of willing'.[1] 'The language of volitions is' the misleading 'language of the para-mechanical theory of the mind'.[2] Two observations are at once made in support of this. They are made together and not very clearly distinguished. I shall note them separately.

The first point is that no one ever speaks 'in the recommended idioms', 'save to endorse the theory'.[3] No one ever says 'that at 10 a.m. he was occupied in willing this or that'.[4] 'An accused person may admit or deny that he did something, or that he did it on purpose, but he never admits or denies having willed. Nor do the judge and jury require to be satisfied by evidence, which in the nature of the case could never be adduced, that a volition preceded the pulling of the trigger.'[5] Novelists describe the actions of their characters: 'but they never mention their volitions'.[6] All this seems to me, however, beside the point. It is the well-known appeal to what we normally say as a way of settling philosophical questions, and for this procedure there seems to be no warrant. It is peculiarly irrelevant here, for it is evident why we do not normally speak of our volitions or say that we were engaged in willing. This is because willing is involved in, is in fact the essential ingredient in, all our actions. Professor Ryle himself is prepared to speak of our actions, but it would be equally absurd to say that I was acting (except in the special and irrelevant theatrical sense) at 10 a.m. It is not relevant to any ordinary purpose or query to say that I was occupied in willing at a certain time. What normally matters is what I was willing to do. We are willing all the time that we are conscious. An act of will is not the rival of walking, eating, writing, and so on. I do not suspend these activities to perform an act of will. My willing is the continuous maintaining of my intentions, and for that reason we do not normally have occasion to mention it. Only theorists do so, and Ryle admits that they have done so freely.

One might almost use an argument like that of Ryle here to show that we are never alive. No one would say that he was occupied with being alive at 10 a.m., unless he were seriously ill and trying hard not to be overcome. I would not say that one of

[1, 2, 3, 4, 5, 6] *Op. cit.*, p. 64.

the things I had been doing during the last hour was living. It would be very uninformative if I did. It is plain, that whatever I was doing I was alive, and my friends, or a judge or anyone else, would be concerned, on the contrary, to know whether I was awake or sleeping, at work or at play,—or what game I was playing. But the fact that we never have occasion to say that we were alive or living does not even begin to prove that we were not. We could not do what we do without being alive, and it is therefore pointless to mention the fact as a description of what we were doing.

It will be noted that Professor Ryle denies that the judge and jury are interested in whether a volition preceded the pulling of the trigger. This is ambiguous as it stands. For 'pulling the trigger' would normally be taken to mean the full action, including the volition. No one wants to know whether this was preceded by a volition to do it—and so on *ad infinitum*. But if 'pulling the trigger' means the physical movement, then the question how this came about, whether it was willed or not, is obviously of the utmost importance in a court of law. If the gun has gone off by accident, then this radically alters the case. The issue really turns on whether the movement was a willed one, and in addition of course on whether the agent rightly understood the situation—that the gun was loaded and so on. Ryle might say that it was enough to say that the trigger was pulled 'on purpose'. I have no quarrel with that in itself, but then we have to decide what 'on purpose' means. That is where I part company with Ryle, for it seems to me evident that we cannot give a proper account of what is meant by doing things on purpose without recourse to the notion of some non-physical activity of willing.

The present argument of Ryle against this is not unlike the well-known argument of Socrates in Book 1 of Plato's *Republic* where he tries to show that justice is useless and the just man a thief. The only difference is that Socrates knew that he was talking nonsense and only argued as he did to show a rather raw young man how little he had thought about the subject. The argument is that there does not seem to be any sphere or activity especially reserved for justice. We may sometimes be engaged in navigating a ship or in building a house or cooking a meal, but when are we engaged in being just—we always seem to be doing something else? The defect in this argument is of course the supposition that in building houses or cooking meals we are excluded from being just, as if being just meant the same sort of thing as building a house; it is on the contrary something involved in the way we engage in such activities. It does not compete with them, and to suppose that it does is a good example, it seems to me, of what Ryle himself understands by a category-mistake. But it is just such a mistake which he himself makes in supposing that acts of will, if they occurred, would have to be detached from other activities and rival them in such a way that it could properly be said that we were engaged in performing acts of will and not eating or talking and so on.

The point of this complaint becomes even more apparent when we turn to the second point made by Ryle in this context. It is closely related to the one I have just been noting, but also distinct from it and should have been noted as such.

Ryle observes that no one would say that he had, on some occasion, 'performed five quick and easy volitions and two slow and difficult volitions'.[1] He also asks how volitions could be described: 'Can they be sudden or gradual, strong or weak, difficult or easy, enjoyable or disagreeable? Can they be accelerated, decelerated, interrupted or suspended? Can people be efficient or inefficient at them?'[2] These rhetorical questions all imply that 'performing a volition' is a distinct operation in the same class as the activities to which these questions would be pertinent. To perform an act of will as such is neither hard nor easy, it does not take a long time or a little; the question would depend on what in fact we are doing. An act of will is not like a jolt we give to our bodies to set them in motion, like starting up a machine or spinning a wheel. We do not take time off our other activities to wind up our bodies like winding a clock, we are continually willing to sustain and modify our intentions throughout the entire enactment. I do not will to eat my supper as a preliminary to sitting at the table. I am continuously willing each movement as I make it. I do not will to reach for a piece of bread, and then leave it to my arm. I sustain throughout the intention to make the appropriate movement; I could stop at any time. Willing is not something we do in detachment. There is no instance of just willing, we will to do this or that, and the questions 'how long', 'how difficult' etc. have no point except in relation to what we are willing to do, and we have to bear in mind that we are all the time willing to do something or other.

There are also different senses in which we might speak of an

[1, 2] *Op. cit.*, p. 64.

activity being difficult or agreeable, as the case might be. It may be physically difficult, like lifting a weight or climbing a rock. This will affect the difficulty of sustaining the intention to do these things, but the one is not strictly relative to the other. I may be so fond of lifting weights, or so anxious to lift this particular weight that is pinning someone down, that I can put my whole heart easily into what I am doing. I may find other things that are physically easy very distasteful. Other things are mentally difficult, like solving a mathematical puzzle, but I very much enjoy doing them. They are difficult in one sense, they involve intellectual strain, and I may feel washed out at the end. But in another sense I might have been thoroughly enjoying myself and for that reason not finding it hard to keep at it. Questions of difficulty, in respect of volitions, have thus to be made precise and we have to ask them in respect to the content of whatever is being willed. But the content, in this case, is not the physical movement that ensues, even when engaged in physical activity. It is what I envisage as what I set myself to bring about, and it is only in relation to that, in the first instance and directly, that questions of ease and enjoyment etc. apply.

The questions 'how long' or 'at what time' depend also on what exactly, in our activities, we are hoping to measure. Professor Ryle asks, 'At which moment was the boy going through the volition to take the high dive?'.[1] This is one of those seemingly simple questions which are not simple at all. The boy is sustaining his intention to do this or that throughout the whole activity in which he is engaged. His particular physical movements will happen almost immediately at the point at which he is willing them to happen. This holds not only of the spring he takes from the board, but of his setting his foot on the ladder, mounting up and so on. He is mentally active all this time initiating the appropriate movements leading to what he ultimately wishes to accomplish. Just when he willed the movement which actually precipitated him off the board is of course difficult to say with precision, since the physical movement follows with only a gap that is not perceptible to us on the willing of it. The boy would have had the end in view in all the preliminary movements, and at some point he would will the consummation of it; we could not time that as we might the instant of his foot leaving the board, but it would have been at some time.

[1] *Op. cit.*, p. 65.

Ryle asks what answers the boy himself might give to these questions about his dive. When would he say that he performed the act of will? The intention here is to make the question seem ridiculous. The boy would know just when he put his foot on the ladder, and when he took his dive. He would be rather flabbergasted to be asked when was he willing to do this. Ryle supposes his opponent would fall back, in the face of this onslaught, on the untrained person's lack of familiarity with the dictions appropriate to inner behaviour. But the first and most important thing to say is that the questions themselves are misleading, since they wholly overlook the close integration of sustained mental activities with the physical processes that they condition. There is no noticeable break, no gap while something else goes on, between the mental processes and the physical ones they initiate, but only integration so smooth as not to be noticed. The whole has the feel of being one process, and for most ordinary purposes can be treated as such. We cannot ask about the one process in dissociation from the other. This, as well as not being trained in the sort of question being asked and the appropriate terms, is why a boy might be taken aback if asked when he was willing to take the dive. The strict answer again would have been, 'when I dived'; for the important thing about the dive was the willing. If the boy had been asked whether he meant to dive, he would have answered, 'Yes', and if asked when he was meaning this, he would either have referred to the time he formed the intention (again not always easy to specify precisely) or he might have said very properly that he meant it all the time he was doing it.

It is for similar reasons that it is absurd to ask a man, in another of Ryle's examples, 'how long ago he executed his last volition, or, how many acts of will he executes in, say, reciting "Little Miss Muffet" backwards.'[1] The sensible answer is that he was willing what he did all the time he was doing it. It is not a question of 'ghostly thrusts', or of thrusts at all.

There are further difficulties about timing, or as it is sometimes put, dating a mental activity, and these can also be invoked, indirectly at least, to discredit the notion of mental activity itself. These difficulties apply, to some extent, to the dating of overt activity also but they have more force in the measuring of mental events. The basic difficulty is that we have no obvious standard of measurement. What, in other words, is to count as *an* activity?

[1] *Op. cit.*, p. 65.

Suppose I go for a walk. We can ask, from time to time, how many minutes have elapsed, and we could count how many steps I have taken. Beyond this there is no obvious unit. We would not ask, 'how many bits of walking have I done?' Convention usually defines *a* walk in terms of when I leave the house and return, but we could not apply even this very strictly—if I return to fetch a coat, have I had two walks or one? More generally, how do we answer if asked how many things we have been doing within the last hour? Suppose I have been sitting at my table; it could still be said that I have been doing many things. Perhaps I had a cup of tea in the middle of my writing. Is this a distinct event? And what about stirring my tea, the various movements of drinking it, putting the tray outside? Even in the physical sense, it is not easy to say how many things have happened to me within an hour. It is much harder if we think of our experiences in their fullness.

For there are so many levels and varieties of experience. I experience and purpose many things at a particular time. I have many perceptual experiences at the moment, seeing books, table, trees out of the window, etc., hearing and touching many things. I am thinking about philosophy, but this in itself involves many changes of thoughts and interests as the subject develops; in any case I do not, even when concentrating hard and work goes well, keep my mind wholly on what I am writing. There are fluctuations of interest, strange associations take one's thoughts off their course, one is sometimes more and sometimes less aware of one's surroundings, one's mind has developed its own techniques of subtle diversionary activities which actually help the main movement of one's thought. It is a somewhat arbitrary matter where within all this we have distinct units of experience or activity.

The most we can say is that there are continuities at various levels, and that, according to our interest in making the divisions, these afford a basis for fairly rough demarcation. Some of these demarcations can be much more precise than others. This is because some slices of experience have a more uniform character than others and more clearly defined edges. I can say that I worked till lunch-time, that I spent three hours at a theatre, that I have just been hearing a shrill noise which lasted a few minutes, and so on. But within and around these demarcations there is a variegated flow of experience and activity within which it is by no means easy to find sharp delimitations. There are, as I have put it earlier, various currents, swirls and eddies within a continuous flow. This makes it difficult, in some regards, to specify certain mental activities distinctly and date them, and, because there are no obvious or easy ways of deciding how certain activities are to be measured, some have been apt to conclude that they are not activities at all. But this only happens to those who are led, by a misconstruction of the use to which terms like 'acts of volition' can be put, to expect mental activity, if it is real at all, to consist entirely of easily isolable episodes.

The discussion of alleged internal volitional activity culminates, for Ryle, in considerations of freedom and praise or blame. He argues, in the first place, that we can do no better, on the official doctrine, 'than guess that the action was willed'.[1] Much turns here on the word 'guess'. If the statement means that we have no good reason for concluding that certain bodily movements— and what results from these—are willed by various people, then it is certainly false. I can have ample grounds for believing that someone who pulled a trigger intended to do so in the expectation that it would lead to someone else's hurt or death. The conclusion I draw here is quite reliable, we take drastic action on the basis of it. But, on the other hand, if it is meant that there is no conceivable possibility of error, that is also mistaken. What we have, is a degree of probability so high that we can discount the possibility of error. Professor Ryle, however, writes as if we had no justification at all for ascribing the untoward event to the prior willing of it, and the only reason he adduces for this is that the volition would have to be inferred from 'an observed overt action'.[2] As nothing has been done, and very little attempted, to discredit such an inference, the main point has very little force.

Two supplementary arguments repeat the points made earlier about the mysterious nature of the alleged transactions between mind and body and the supposed vicious regress whereby each volition requires a prior volition to make it, and so *ad infinitum*. Replies have already been made to these points, and so we come to what seems to be the crux of the present arguments for Ryle. He urges that we decide whether an act was voluntary or involuntary, or whether it could have 'been helped' without any reference to the 'hypothesis of the occult inner thrusts of actions'.[3] If this means that we make practical appraisals of actions without raising

[1] *Op. cit.*, p. 66.
[2] *Op. cit.*, p. 65.
[3] *Op. cit.*, p. 67.

general questions about the nature of mental activity, then it is
certainly true. But this is because we take certain things to be true
about our actions in a way that does not require to be restated on
each occasion of making an appraisal. The position here is like
the one we met before when Ryle complained that no one declares
that he has been engaged in making volitions. No one would make
such a declaration because, unlike the assertion that he had been
doing this or that, it would not be helpful or informative—a man
'makes volitions' continuously whenever he is doing anything at
all. For the same reason we do not remind ourselves of the distinct
mental character of acts of will in deciding whether an action was
a genuine one for which the agent could be called to account. We
might apply the same tests as Ryle to decide whether an act was
done 'on purpose', but we understand a good deal more by its
being done 'on purpose' than he does.

In his determination not to invoke, at this point, any processes
other than the external observable ones Ryle is compelled to complete his account of all we think about the voluntary character
of actions in terms of the capacities we can be known to have,
thus placing the burden of explanation again squarely on dispositions of one sort or another. He begins his task here with a somewhat odd insistence that we only think of actions as voluntary or
involuntary when it is a case of blaming or finding fault. To apply
such terms to meritorious actions that are to someone's credit is
'an unwitting extension' of their ordinary sense. This goes also
for the word 'responsible'. But here it seems to me plain that
Ryle is mistaken. We surely think that our good actions are free
and as much exercises of our responsibility as our evil ones. It
would make nonsense of all appraisal if accountability did not
mean the same in good as in evil conduct. We admire and praise
as well as blame; the two attitudes are correlative and imply the
same basic conditions. I do not see how anyone could deny this
except in the desperation of maintaining a theory subjected to
particular strain. It is true that we may have more occasion, in
ordinary activities, to think of responsibility and use the term
when it is a question of assigning blame. But this does not alter
in the least the fact that we are responsible in other activities in
the same way.

The next step taken by Ryle is to maintain that the question
whether fault is to be found depends on whether we could help
what we did in the sense of having a practical competence or skill

of a certain kind, this being thus the only important and legitimate meaning of 'voluntary'. When we blame someone 'we mean that he knew how to do the right thing'.[1] We learn that a boy 'was competent to tie a reef-knot, though what he unintentionally produced was a granny-knot. His failure or lapse was his fault'.[2] This is a bewildering example and it shows how little at home Professor Ryle is in the matters with which he is dealing here. In what sense, for example, is the word 'fault' used? If used in the moral sense, it is plainly not appropriate; we do not blame people morally for what they produce unintentionally. The most we could say was that the boy had made a mistake, and once attention is centred on what is involved in making mistakes it is at least a little more plausible to maintain that the condition that matters, in making such a claim sensible, is whether one has or has not a certain capacity.

Even with the present restriction, however, the position is not as straightforward as might appear. It is true that in practice we are usually content with knowing whether the boy, in Ryle's example, had the requisite skill. Questions of error or mistake would not arise if the boy had never been taught anything about knots. Even so we take it that the actual performance was not a mere movement of his fingers. He would be continuously conscious of what he was doing or aiming to do, there would be the on-going mental process as well as the physical one. Otherwise we would not think of the action as an action at all, it would be in the class of a reflex or kindred physical movement. This is not something of which we would normally take note, we take it for granted; for it applies to all actions and would thus have no particular relevance to specific questions like what is involved in making a mistake. It is a basic condition of making mistakes that we should be mentally active, but for ordinary purposes there is no need to affirm this. That is no justification for overlooking, much less denying, it in philosophical reflection or analysis.

But in any case it is not in respect of mistakes that we mainly think of responsibilities and finding fault. We do indeed use the terms in such a context, but that would generally be thought to be a rather loose use of the words. We have in any case, in careful thinking, to go beyond the day-to-day use of words and not to be dominated by it; and it is evident that there is a basic use of 'fault' and 'responsibility' which could not be extended at all to

[1, 2] *Op. cit.*, p. 70

mistakes. When we find fault in the more serious sense we are thinking of a person purposing or choosing to do what he did. We would not seriously blame a man for genuine error, we blame him for what he intends. It is for this reason, and not because certain activities are meritorious, that we refuse to extend the notion of responsibility to meritorious activities listed in this context by Ryle. He notes how absurd it would be to ask, 'Could you have helped seeing the point of that joke?' or 'Could you have helped solving the riddle?' Provided we hear it, we do or we do not see the point of the joke, and if we are trying to solve the riddle we succeed or we do not; the most we can do is try; beyond that it is a matter of good or bad luck. It is for this reason, and not for anything to do with being meritorious, that it is absurd to ask someone who has 'done a sum correctly', 'could you have got it wrong?'. It is indeed absurd to ask whether someone is 'sufficiently intelligent and well-trained' 'to make a miscalculation'. Training and intelligence are related to success. But Professor Ryle's pleasantry does not bring out, but on the contrary obscures, what is radically wrong with asking 'Could you have helped getting it right?'. It is that getting things right or wrong in the present sense is not something we can control or choose, we can only try. And the important point is that it is in respect of choosing, purposing, or setting ourselves to do something, that we can be properly blamed—or praised, in the correlative sense, as the case may be.

When questions arise about the sort of praise or blame involved here and the conditions of ascribing responsibility, well-known difficulties appear. Granted that I meant to do something, could I have helped this? Being the sort of person I was in a certain situation, having had my sort of upbringing and history and so on, could I have done anything else at the time? The delinquent knew that he was wrecking the railway compartment, that the glass would be shivered when he struck the mirror, but was it inevitable in some way that he should be doing this? Should we treat him, and other wrong-doers, as we might treat a sick person—or at least assume that, whatever practical needs may require, there is no radical difference? Various answers can be given to these questions. Perhaps the questions themselves are the result of some basic confusion. But they certainly do not come to be asked in the way Professor Ryle suggests, namely by our stretching the use of 'voluntary' to meritorious activity in a way which involves the

C

absurdity of implying that we had a capacity to fail in some task in which in fact we succeeded. The questions concern what we purpose, and I am, like many philosophers today as in the past, far from convinced that they are 'a tangle of largely spurious problems'. Ryle believes that he has got rid of such problems by what he says about finding fault and knowing 'how to do the right thing'. But in fact he has only shown us how little he understands the genuine problem of the Freedom of the Will.

Some of those who have considered the latter problem have urged that responsibility, in its strict moral sense, involves a special sort of freedom which is not displayed in all our conduct. This is the freedom to do, or not to do something, whatever one's nature as a whole is like at the time. If they are right—and the question whether they are right is largely the question of moral freedom—this seems to highlight the fact that our mental activities are distinct from our physical movements, but it is only one sharp indication of what is true of mental activity in all regards. There could be no freedom of will without distinct mental processes, but there could well be such processes without any of them consisting in the sort of choice which many consider to be the essential condition of moral responsibility. In other words, the problem of freedom, in its ethical form at least, is a special problem which is not to be identified with the more general question of the non-physical character of all mental activity. Without the latter there can be no freedom, but with it freedom is not guaranteed, it must be shown to be genuine on its own account. For this reason it is most regrettable that the two questions should be merged, as they tend to be in Ryle's treatment of them. That can only lead to confusions in the handling of both, as is very evident in Professor Ryle's work.

One further point must be made here. In practice, in seeking to assign responsibility, what we are concerned to establish is whether a person had the appropriate physical or mental capacities. We want to be sure, as Ryle puts it, that he was 'not acting under duress or in panic or high fever or with numb fingers',[1] and so on. This is what the judge and jury have to settle. But it is a further question what is involved in their attitudes and procedures, and whether these call for some modification. It could be argued, and many (as we have seen) do so, that in addition to these capacities there is required a special freedom of choice. Our views

[1] *Op. cit.*, p. 71.

on such a question could affect our attitude in general to legal proceedings and others like them, but it is, all the same, a general philosophical question which is not a subject for proper controversy in the courts of law as such. We must not allow what is proper to say and consider, in settling the immediate practical problem in the court of law and elsewhere, to determine for us what is sound to think on either the special question of freedom of the will or the more general question of the nature of mental activity. Much that seems true about these questions has to be taken for granted, as a general truth about our activities, when considering this or that specific problem of practice and dealing with it. That, it seems to me, is what Professor Ryle, like many others today, is apt to overlook.

This is one major reason why Ryle is able to persuade himself that there are no mental occurrences beyond our overt behaviour. The distinctness and inwardness of mental activity does not need special reference made to it all the time, and for this reason it is very misleading to go by what we would normally be saying and thinking. But closely related to this is the other major mistake which Professor Ryle makes, namely that of supposing that, if there is the alleged inner activity, it must resemble or be a strict counterpart of the overt behaviour. This is also a point that has been much stressed already earlier. But it is worth making special note here of how prone Ryle is to this in the passages dealing with voluntary action and freedom of the will. In line with his earlier pronouncements he declares that 'to frown intentionally is not to do one thing on one's forehead and another thing in a second metaphorical place'.[1] We do not, however, have to think seriously of the mental occurrence as being in any sort of place. It is not a rehearsal of the physical frowning and no one supposes that it involves the activity of some 'non-bodily organ' or the 'frown-causing exertion of some occult non-muscle'.[2] It is in the use of misleading terms of this sort that Ryle achieves best the deliberate abusiveness which he has made his unfortunate, and not very responsible, policy. He is himself the worst victim of it.

[1], [2] *Op. cit.*, p. 74.

CHAPTER III

SOME FURTHER THEMES OF
THE CONCEPT OF MIND

Professor Ryle brings his main thesis to bear on a number of other important issues in the philosophy of mind. His procedures follow the same general pattern, and I shall not, for that reason, weary the reader with more detail than I can help in following Professor Ryle further. Let us note first what he says about emotions.

Here again there seems to be something of an internal or private character involved. An emotion is essentially, we would be disposed to say, something the person himself feels or is aware of. He is swayed, we might say, by his feeling of anger or fear, and he himself, in the first instance, is peculiarly conscious of this, though others may soon learn about it. This is, however, according to Ryle a very muddled view. We are led to think in such terms by not understanding the extent to which our emotions can be described in terms of what we are liable to do. 'Motive words' are 'elliptical expressions of general hypothetical propositions'[1] and have not to do with 'narratives of episodes'.

There is of course much truth in this. If a person is frightened he is liable to run away, to cry out, and so on. But the question is whether there may not be something else which cannot be described in this way. Professor Ryle thinks there may be. But he conceives it in terms of 'flutters', 'qualms', 'throbs', 'itches', and so forth whose status is somewhat obscure. There is a strong suggestion that the 'flutter' is a physical occurrence. We are reminded that 'these names for specific feelings, such as "itch", "qualm" and "pang" are also used as names of specific bodily sensations'.[2] 'Moreover, we are in some cases ready to locate, say, the sinking feeling of despair in the pit of the stomach or the tense feeling of anger in the muscles of the jaw and fist. Other feelings . . . like glows of pride, seem to pervade the whole body in much the same way as do glows of warmth.'[3] James, it is added, 'boldly identified feelings with bodily sensations', but Ryle himself

---

[1] *Op. cit.*, p. 85.
[2, 3] *Op. cit.*, p. 84.

thinks it is possible that there is 'a tinge of metaphor'[1] in the talk which suggests this. That is indeed a faint admission. But, even so, it seems a serious one. For how could this 'tinge' be understood without implying the occurrence of at least something of a non-bodily kind? There is only one way to avoid this, and that is to take the 'tinge' entirely in terms of allusions to dispositional traits. It is not made as clear as it should be that this is what is done. But it is hard to find anything else of which Ryle can be thinking.

The feeling to which he gives most attention is that of vanity. This choice, whether of set purpose or not, rather favours his case. For we do tend to think of vanity mainly in dispositional terms. The vain person is, as Ryle describes him, disposed 'to talk a lot about himself, to cleave to the society of the eminent, to reject criticisms, to seek the footlights and to disengage himself from conversations about the merits of others'.[2] We are also told that there can be 'feelings of pique and buoyancy' but these are not thought to be particularly indicative of vanity, and there is again a hint that they are either physical (feeling 'light of toe' etc.) or vaguely metaphorical. The impression conveyed is that the distinctive thing about vanity is what can be put, as above, in dispositional ways. This invites two comments.

In the first place, the dispositional tendencies in question here can only be themselves actualized and conceived in terms of activities which raise again the question whether something occurs here beyond physical activity related in certain ways to dispositions. What does it mean 'to talk a lot', 'to reject criticisms' etc.? Must there not here be on-going mental processes, must we not be understanding what goes into our talk, and will not a lot of this, in the case of the vain man, be accompanied by emotions of varying intensity and length? But, secondly, will there not also be occasions when the vain person finds his thought peculiarly centred on himself, on his prospect of success or his appearance and so forth? This will also stir up accompanying emotions. These cannot be described except in terms of the situation and thoughts which occasion them. They have no other recognizably independent hallmark, and why should they be thought to need any—except by the mistake, a category one it seems, of assimilating them to things with which they should not be classed? But what Professor Ryle

---

[1] *Op. cit.*, p. 84.
[2] *Op. cit.*, p. 86.

straightway proceeds to do is to suppose that if there are feelings of vanity which affect our conduct they must be understood in terms of peculiar prickings or impulses thought of in detachment from everything else, as if we had a feeling of vanity, coming unannounced like a hiccough, impelling us out of the blue and making us boast. We all know that mental life is not of this kind. Our thoughts and emotions are more sustained and more interwoven. We do not have to hold that every time the vain man behaves vaingloriously he experiences a 'palpitation or pricking of vanity'. In this sense perhaps 'the vain man never feels vain'.[1] But we are obviously looking for the wrong thing. The vain man could hardly be vain without some explicit thought about himself accompanied by emotions, sometimes more and sometimes less arresting in themselves. The emotion and the thought do not vie with one another, nor do either of these have to be suspended for us to act appropriately. It is again a sorry travesty, and a total misapprehension of the subtle interchanges of modes of experience, which suggest that our feelings are peculiar twinges which disrupt everything else until they prompt, most mysteriously, some physical response.

The distortion and over-simplification in Ryle's account of feelings is seen very clearly in what he also says about 'feelings of interest'. He asks, for example, 'whether these feelings are sudden, like twinges, or lasting, like aches; whether they succeed one another several times a minute or only a few times an hour; and whether (a man) feels them in the small of his back or in his forehead?'[2] The answer is of course that a person who is deeply engaged in a train of thought does not have to interrupt his thought and charge himself up, as it were, by undergoing these peculiar twinges from time to time; he remains absorbed in what he is doing, he does not stop to attend to his emotions, he is lost in what he is doing. But this in no way rules out there being the sustained desire to do what he continues to do and the appropriate emotional accompaniments of this. These do not obtrude themselves or hinder the actual performance, whether mental or physical, they are well geared into it. But they are no less indispensable on that account. It is not at all true that we are 'free from feelings' while doing the work. We are subject to them in a sustained integrated way all the time. What we are not subject to are peculiar 'twinges' 'cropping up, maybe, about every two or twenty minutes'.[3] Ryle

[1, 2, 3] *Op. cit.*, p. 87.

correctly points out that even if there were such occasional twinges they would hardly explain our interest in our work in the meantime. But who has ever supposed that they did?

It is further maintained by Ryle, in support of his general account of emotion, that even if we did have the twinges or spasms he mentions, we have no good reason for supposing that they are the causes of our action. They could be 'one of a thousand other synchronous happenings'.[1] Perhaps this is true, but it does not by any means follow that we cannot regard the thoughts we entertain, in sustaining a purpose, and the emotions connected with them, as the main and immediate determinants of the physical events which occur so consistently in accordance with them. Motive as thought, with the glow or stir of emotion within it, is a very different matter, at any rate, from motive as an unspecifiable itch with no inherent connection with the events that follow.

There remain of course many problems about the way our thoughts are involved in sustaining a purpose, whether to follow out a train of thought or bring about a physical change. How distinctive is the sustaining of a purpose or the setting ourselves to accomplish some end and what, if anything, can be said further about the relation of this to the ensuing events?—these are hard problems in the philosophy of mind, and there are problems of analysis and definition also about the use of the word 'motive'. Shall we, for example, understand by this word the state of mind immediately preceding the change we bring about, and so virtually identify it with action, or shall we reserve it for some other feature of the many-sided mental process, itself involving purposing of some kind all the time, by which some particular action or purposing comes about—and are there actions not motivated in that way? These, as I have said, are hard problems, but they are not problems for Professor Ryle.

This is because he is content to think of motives entirely in terms of dispositions. We do of course use the word 'motive' in that way. We may say that an action was done from kindness, or from spite, jealousy, greed or ambition, and so on; and what we mainly mean here is that the action is due to certain traits of character or relatively permanent interests, it can be brought under some 'law-like proposition'. Explanations by motives are, to this extent, explanations by 'the character of the agent'. It is in line with saying that the glass was shattered because it was brittle. We could

[1] *Op. cit.*, p. 90.

also say that a stone hit the glass, and this would be the properly causal explanation. We do not provide a causal explanation when we say that an action was due to greed or ambition understood as traits of character. My general tendency to be angry or kind or ambitious is not an event, and it cannot therefore be the cause of anything.

It is, moreover, possible to subsume one trait of character under a wider one, to bring my interest in watering a particular rose under a more general interest in having a nice garden, and so on. We can thus provide explanations of actions, in terms of interests and traits of character, at various levels of comprehensiveness or detail as the case may be. This is one important way in which our conduct admits of being explained. It can also be accounted for in causal terms, and this for Ryle consists solely in indicating some external situation which called it forth. We might ask, 'Why did someone pass the salt?' and the answer could be, in the first place, 'because he is a polite or considerate person', but we could just as well say, 'because his neighbour asked for it'. These are two very different, and quite proper and normal, ways of accounting for what we do. But are they complete, do they, as Ryle supposes, tell the whole story?

It does not seem so. For the occasion of the action could not bring about a specific exemplification of a man's politeness except in the form of a sustained intention, however short, to accommodate the neighbour, that is as a live experience or mental process of which the agent himself, and no other, is immediately conscious in having it. This takes its place in sustained conscious activity, and while it is the other levels of explanation that matter most for ordinary purposes, we must not forget that they themselves derive their significance from the continuous conscious process which does not require to be mentioned, in ordinary discourse, except where some feature of it, as could well happen, is the one most relevant to a specific enquiry. Reasons for actions are of various kinds, and Professor Ryle believes he has told the whole story when he has only mentioned parts of it.

Here again the main mistake is due to a wrong and much simplified conception of what to look for. We could not act from the motives of love or hate, in the dispositional senses, unless we had also experiences of loving and hating, and these cannot be reduced solely to behaving in certain ways towards others. If I hate someone there will be occasions when I entertain disagreeable thoughts about him and have emotions coloured by these thoughts. We know from first-hand experience what it is to have such emotions, and there may not be much that we can say about them beyond indicating the thoughts which extend into them and determine which they are, but that does not prevent us from knowing what they are like, as we all do. But Ryle is looking for itches or 'agitations' which have their power and reality solely in themselves and not as part of an integrated process.

Even so, he feels he must give some account of the way we sometimes seem to be subject to distinctive and strong emotions. He treats these, significantly enough, under the head of 'agitations', as if all powerful feeling took the form of 'gusts or storms'. These agitations are, moreover, thought to be themselves just 'liability conditions' of a certain kind, and they fall thus into the class of traits of character. What distinguishes them is, in the first place, that they are 'moods', and moods are taken to be inclinations, again in the dispositional sense, which dominate other motives. To be sulky is to be liable to act in a vague but recognizable way on each turn which the situation takes while the mood lasts. But it is also possible for a mood to be frustrated in certain ways, the inclination in which it consists cannot find a proper outlet. This is what it is to be distracted or agitated. The agitation is not itself a motive, it is not itself an inclination to do anything; nor is it an experienced state or process of any kind. It is the state of having certain inclinations, strong or dominant at a particular time, which are inhibited due to factors in the external situation or to some contrary inclination.

This is very ingenious and it certainly tells us much that we recognize to be sound and relevant about certain ways in which we may be agitated. But it seems also to leave out the main matter, namely the conscious experience in which there is involved a recognizable factor of distressful felt emotion deriving from the state of our thoughts. Nor is it the case that all powerful felt emotions take the disagreeable form described by Ryle. We may also have very pleasant feelings of excitement. Ryle mentions these also, but in a quite casual way to bring them within his general account in the form of tensions or fatigue, and so on, which we can in some way enjoy in spite of their being also unpleasant. But there are positive feelings of enjoyment, consequent upon some pleasing experience or glad tidings. We can say of all, or of most, of these of course that they involve the removal of obstacles in some sense, and that some element of being thwarted is thus present at some level, but this in no way deprives the feeling of gladness of its distinctive positive character.

No one wants to multiply unnecessary entities or states. But, in our anxiety to prune away all but the indispensable minimum, we must be careful not to throw over undisputed features of our common experience which we all recognize however hard it may be to describe them or allude to them apart from their accompaniments in other modes of experience. Traditional distinctions are not sacrosanct, but neither is it true that major distinctions to which importance has been ascribed in the past are inevitably confused and misleading. It is as absurd to be iconoclastic in principle as it is to be immovably conservative. There may have been misleading ways in which the distinction of feeling and thought has been handled on occasion in the past, and some of the things said in what is sometimes denounced as faculty psychology may fall into that class. We may have allowed our figures of speech to harden and mislead us in describing emotions or acts of will, but the remedy for that is a more cautious appreciation of the sort of reality which belongs to emotions or acts of will and of the subtle intertwining of different modes of conscious experience in the total event of a mental process. If our references to these have, not altogether surprisingly, borrowed too much from modes of speech pertinent only or mainly to external reality, and if analysis has tended to over-simplify or to partition what is very closely interlinked, this should have been itself a guide and a warning to critics also not to direct their batteries against travesties of what a subtle rounded conscious experience is like.

The elimination of feeling, as a distinct mode of experience, by reducing alleged states of feeling to the thwarting of certain behavioural tendencies, has close affinity with much that is said in disposing of sensations also as modes of private experience. In a paper entitled 'Feelings', published in the *Philosophical Quarterly*,[1] Ryle considers what is involved when a person feels a tickle. If I have a tickle I have an impulse to scratch. But the latter is not the effect of the former. There is no cause-effect connection here at all. Nor are there two things, the tickling sensation and the impulse to scratch. The tickle is just having the impulse to scratch in conditions which impede that impulse. This is analogous to the derivative use of 'tickle' when we use it of being amused and where

[1] April 1951, p. 199.

it means, apparently, 'wanting to laugh, in the sense of "want" in which a dog wants to scratch when prevented from doing so'. This is again ingenious but about as implausible as anything can be. The tickle, like a sensation of pain, seems obviously something I feel or experience in a way that cannot be reduced at all to any mode of my dispositional states. I shall mention briefly again what Ryle has to say about pain, but here, if anywhere, it seems to me, is a point where only a thinker desperately, one might almost say recklessly, determined to hold on to a theory, would keep his account to conditions pertaining to what we are disposed to do.

Consider the following case in relation to Ryle's example of a tickle. Suppose someone were to give a lecture, and just as the meeting was about to start it was pointed out to him that he had left some soap on his face; then he would have an impulse at once to rub this out and go through motions identical with those we make in scratching. But he could also tell himself that it was too late for that now and just hope that no one would notice it much. As the meeting went on, however, the impulse to rub out the soap would recur and have to be resisted. We would have here all the ingredients of Professor Ryle's tickle, but we would not have a genuine tickle at all, though of course we might induce one.

A further point at which Professor Ryle's view is subject to considerable strain is that of perception and mental images, particularly dreaming. For here again it seems peculiarly hard not to find something, in the experience of the individual, to which he alone has immediate access. But these are topics to which I shall be returning in another context, and so I shall not consider here what Professor Ryle has to say about them. I proceed instead to the topics which are central in the philosophy of mind, namely those of the nature of belief and knowledge, consciousness of oneself and the operations we consider to be more distinctively intellectual.

Here Ryle begins by insisting that 'belief' and 'knowledge' are dispositional words. There is, as we have seen, much truth in this. Little that we know or believe is in our thoughts at any time. But Ryle has to go further than this and deny that there is any episodic or occurrent sense of knowing and believing. They can both be accounted for entirely in terms of our dispositions.

To some extent grammar and language support this claim, or seem to do so. For we would not say of anyone at any time that he was now knowing or believing, as we might say that he was swimming or thinking hard about some problem. But it is very questionable indeed whether anything of substance turns on this. It would be quite unilluminating to say of anyone that he was knowing or believing, for the simple reason that he must be doing one or other of these all the time. We do of course say that someone is thinking, although we usually qualify this by indicating what sort of thinking it is, thinking hard or thinking about this or that. But 'thinking' in this context stands for a fairly precise activity of reflection and concentration that is more sustained or systematic or intense than normal. We would not otherwise describe anyone as thinking, for all conscious activity, and dreaming too, involves that. It is only helpful to refer to a certain kind of thinking.

This is itself reflected in a very strange contention to which Ryle next proceeds. He first observes that disposition words like 'know' or 'believe' are 'highly generic or determinable'. There is a great variety of ways in which we may do either of these things. Ryle then ascribes to his opponents this procedure, namely that they suppose that, over and above believing or knowing this or that in some specific way, there must, for each case, be further operations of knowing or believing as such. In the same way, it might be thought, a solicitor, in addition to drafting wills, defending clients and so on, must also be engaged, in a way no one observes or 'behind locked doors', in solicitoring. Thus it comes about that dualists locate states of believing or knowing 'inside the agent's secret grotto'.[1]

No evidence is adduced for anyone having blundered in this particular way. It is all highly speculative and hypothetical, and it is far removed from any position or procedure adopted by any sensible dualist. No one holds that there are private states of just knowing or believing. It is always a case of knowing or believing something. But the fact that there must always be something known or believed in no way precludes these total states from being states of someone's personal experience. In being aware of entertaining some belief I must be aware of myself as believing something in particular. No dualist, to my knowledge, suggests the contrary. In holding that dispositional beliefs may be actualized in mental states of believing, no one would think of this except as a case of believing what the disposition expressly requires.

The suggestion, however, that there must, in addition to dispositions of knowing and believing, be episodes or occurrences

[1] *Op. cit.*, p. 119.

in which the dispositions are actualized is countered by Ryle in terms of the concept of heeding. The expression 'mental acts' belongs to the much derided 'two-worlds story'. It implies that 'some things exist or occur "in the physical world", while other things exist and occur not in that world but in another, metaphorical place'.[1] We know by now what Ryle thinks of this belief, and it is hardly necessary to point out yet again how misleading it is to suppose that mental events occur in some kind of 'place'. But how then does it seem plausible to refer to distinct mental acts, and what in fact happens on the occasions we are actually prone to describe as mental occurrences? Ryle replies that these are cases of doing various things 'heedfully', that is in an 'alert' or 'ready' frame of mind. In such cases I am 'noticing' what I am doing, I am 'applying my mind' to it. This means in turn, not that I am internally watching my performance, but that I can take appropriate action in the various contingencies with which I may be presented or give proper answers to questions about what I am doing or arising from it. If I drive my car heedfully I shall not pass over the white line, I shall notice a car parked round the bend the moment it comes in sight, I shall stop the moment the bus ahead of me looks like stopping, and so on. I can also give a good account of what I have been doing, of people I passed on the road etc. I have been alert and aware of what I am doing, on the *qui vive* and ready for surprises, and this it seems is what happens when we wrongly suppose that there are mental occurrences distinct from the overt performance.

To this we must again reply that we are being offered a part of the story for the whole. It is true that driving heedfully involves all that Ryle indicates here, and that is one thing we would have in mind in saying that someone knew what he was doing or was alert. But we would not say this unless it were also assumed that the driver was continuously purposing to do all he was doing as part of an on-going mental process which would be equally genuine and distinct from the bodily movements if he were driving badly, or in an absent-minded frame of mind. The absent-minded driver is continuously thinking about some things, and he must also be giving some of his attention to the road, the wheel and so on. There is, of course, a problem here, about what is not in the focus of our attention, as in the case of someone driving home deep in thought about something else and hardly aware, as we put it, of what he was

[1] *Op. cit.*, p. 135.

doing—he remembers little of the journey and so on. But whatever we say about this (and it is hard to see how we could begin to tackle it and kindred questions on Ryle's assumptions), we cannot suppose that there was no consciousness at all of what was going on. If we did suppose that, we could not even regard it as driving in one's sleep, it would be a quite incredible physiological performance of which no reference to dispositions could begin to take account.

Ryle, in short, is taking some things that may be said, in such terms as heedfully or alert, about a certain kind of behaviour to cover and exhaust the sort of thing we want to say, not about some kind of behaviour, but about all. The dispositional story tells us something relevant and sound enough in itself. But it must not be allowed to do duty for the quite different affirmations which the dualist in his turn is also fully entitled to make.

I need hardly add now that the insistence on distinct mental processes of which each is aware in the first instance himself does not imply that we are 'watching', 'inspecting' or 'monitoring' what we do. We might be doing that, for some psychological purpose perhaps. But we do not normally monitor what we do. Nor do we normally engage in retrospection either. But this in no way precludes our being aware of what we are doing (or thinking) in the very process of doing it. This is not an additional 'piece of theorizing', to suppose that it is is the wildest travesty, it is not theorizing but being aware of what we are about in the very process of being engaged in it. Whatever problems may be involved in describing this, they cannot be burked or explained away by directing attention to something quite different.

I should like to add here that there can be no case in which we may be said to know or believe anything unless we have at some stage actually had it in mind. Some readers will recall here Plato's famous simile of the cage in the *Theaetetus*.[1] There can be no birds flying about to be caught unless they have been caught and put in the cage in the first instance. This will be widely denied at the present day. Many philosophers take it for granted that, as we can all be relied on to behave or respond in certain ways on the basis of the knowledge we do have, these activities reflect (or are identical with) abiding knowledge of things that only come to light in those activities themselves. But we do not, in fact, have the knowledge or belief in question until we achieve it at the time. All we had previously was the means of speedily learning something new.

[1] 197 B.

This has, however, been so much disputed of late that further comment is called for.

Consider the sort of case which has been given much prominence. Suppose I were asked, 'Do you know that Oxford is south of the river Humber?', I would answer at once, 'Of course I do'. But, if I were asked whether I had ever thought of Oxford and the river Humber at the same time before, the answer would have to be 'No'. It would seem then that I know something to which I have never given a thought, and this is taken by many to be quite conclusive, an unanswerable argument that only needs to be stated to carry conviction. But the position as presented is, in fact, much over-simplified. It is true that I have never before explicitly thought of Oxford and the river Humber together, but in learning the location of the river Humber I would learn that this place is north of all towns, whether named or not, in the South of England. The thought of where the Humber is, in short, is not just a matter of considering that locality by itself. It involves also the general exclusion of other localities. This is part of what we mean when we locate the river in the North of England. It is part of our thought that it is north of all places we find to be south of it, and in learning, or knowing already, where Oxford is, I *ipso facto* place it south of where I also know the Humber to be. In this case we have not to draw any further inference, but only to take a sensible view of what is involved in locating something.

There is a further reason for the initial plausibility of the argument here rejected. This turns on the way we are apt to confuse meaning and mental image. When being told where the river Humber flows and gets to the sea I may have a map before me, and failing a map I am very likely to have a mental image of a certain sort of countryside or a mental picture not unlike an enlarged map. It becomes easy in this way to suppose that the thought itself, or the meaning of locating the river, is delimited in a similar way, and my belief about the Humber becomes in this way a very circumscribed belief in which thoughts of Oxford or Reading and so on have no more place than the corresponding localities have on a map of the North of England. But this of course overlooks the general or universal elements in meaning, it is a lapse into the 'rigid pieces' theory of thought against which Bradley and Bosanquet directed constant criticism in their rebuttal of 'atomic' theories of the mind in the nineteenth century.

But take now the case where there is a genuine new item of

knowledge concerned. Where the means of obtaining this is fully and immediately available to me the impression may again be given that we have had the actual information all along. Suppose I were given a list of the trains from Oxford to London every day. It could then be said that I have the times of the trains in my possession, and this might be taken as tantamount to my actually knowing them. In the same way we might find it proper, for a rough and ready purpose, to say that they know the times of the trains at the station or at the Enquiry Office. But this would not be strictly accurate. In the first example, I do not properly know (or believe) that the train leaves for London at a certain time until I have actually consulted my list, and if I look at the list hastily I may conclude that the next train leaves at 6.03 when I would decide that it left at 6.08 if I had taken more care. The man in the Enquiry Office may also make a mistake. The truth then seems to be that, however obviously a conclusion may seem to follow from materials already available, it does not become a matter of belief until the inspection is made or the deduction drawn. It is not enough to be on the way, we must arrive. In a detective story the clues are there for all to see, but alas only the clever detective sees their significance. The others who remain obtuse and puzzled can hardly be said to know (they may not suspect at all) that X is the culprit until it is all explained to them.

The position is the same when someone is said to know how to find his way about in parts of the country which he has not visited and has an impression of particular places which would prevent him from being at a loss in seeking closer acquaintance with them on his own. Such a person could not properly be said to know the places he has not visited or to have the detailed information about them which he is equipped to discover with ease. What he knows are certain directions, outlines, patterns, together with some points of detail or filling, and from this he is able to set about other discoveries and make various deductions. But until the latter have in fact been made we have not the beliefs or knowledge they yield; we have only very complete conditions for attaining it.

It is also worth noting here that we rarely, if ever, recover some item of information without setting it in a new context or combination of other facts, determined by our aim at the moment, and in this way immediately extending its significance. Thought is always alive and developing, it is not the manipulation of static material but the extension of meanings which are continuously given new forms (as idealist philosophers have again much helped us to realize). The old is thus intimately fused with the new, the one seeming to participate so much in the nature of the other as to induce, in some cases, the impression that what we learn for the first time had in fact been mysteriously in our possession earlier.

This seems to have taken us away from Ryle's arguments, but the digression, if such it is, is not irrelevant. For what I wish to bring out is how easy, and also how mistaken, it is in some cases to conflate a live awareness with the conditions which make it possible. This is closely bound up with the general mistake of accounting for belief or knowledge entirely in dispositional terms and reducing our actual mental processes to the conditions and the implications of our having them.

A further move made by Professor Ryle here is to describe 'knowledge' as an 'achievement' word. He obviously attaches much importance to this, and so do his followers. But it is not altogether clear what difference it makes to his main position. For he allows that achievement words are 'genuine episodic words'.[1] Someone scores a goal or finds a thimble at a particular moment. The main point, however, is that achievement words involve some state of affairs beyond one's own performance. I cannot win a race if my opponents run faster, I cannot score a goal if the ball does not go where I intend it. In the same way I cannot know anything unless the facts are in accordance with what I think. This certainly means that knowledge, unlike belief, is not entirely a personal state or process, but that does not in any way preclude it from being a process; and while there are, as I fully admit, dispositional states of belief and knowledge, there must also be occurrent states of mind where we think what is true or entertain ideas which comply with any further conditions of knowledge. The latter will be thought by some to exclude the possibility of error. But we have no need to go into that question to establish the reality and privacy of knowledge as an occurrent state of mind.

The application of these arguments by Ryle to questions of the more explicit consciousness we have of ourselves follows the course we now expect. First there is the usual travesty. The dualist is thought to claim knowledge of a world other than the physical world in the form of 'counterparts to our ways of discovering the contents of the physical world'.[2] It will be evident now, I hope,

---

[1] *Op. cit.*, p. 149.
[2] *Op. cit.*, p. 154.

how much this fails to reckon with the peculiarity of mental processes and the way they are known. We do not observe or inspect
our thoughts as we watch events in the world around us.

Beyond these distortions of the position he attacks, Ryle's main
further contention is that, when we know what we are doing or
thinking, we are doing it in the heedful or prepared frame of mind
described already. A person is in this way 'alive to what he is
doing'.[1] A yachtsman knows what he is about in this sense when he
lowers his sails at the sign of an impending storm. He can indicate
why he is doing what he does, and if he does something unexpected, if he crowds on more sail when we should expect him
to reduce it, someone who knows how experienced a sailor he is
might observe, 'Oh, he knows quite well what he is doing'. This
means that the yachtsman has the situation in hand, that he knows
what the results of his actions will be and is suiting his moves to the
true requirements of the situation.

This is a perfectly proper use of the words 'knowing what one is
doing'. The driver of a car knows what he is doing when he speeds
up to overtake another car. His action can be explained in terms
of the sense it makes, one move leads appropriately to another. In
this sense we can say just as well of another person as of oneself
that 'he knows what he is doing', and this is a point which Ryle
makes very firmly himself. These questions of 'facility', as he puts
it, 'do not derive from, or lead to, a difference in kind between a
person's knowledge about himself and his knowledge about other
people'.[2] This is of course quite true as far as the limited use of the
terms 'knowing what he is doing' is concerned in the sort of context in question. I am 'alive to' or know what another person is
about in this sense in just the same way as I know what I myself
am doing, that is I understand the action in terms of the various
moves it involves and what is being achieved, or guarded against,
in this way.

The difficulty arises when we ask what this kind of argument
proves. To what sort of philosophical issue is it relevant? We have
noted one use of the words 'knowing what he is about', but the
words, in that context, are not meant to refer at all to the question
how do we come to know our own actions, and those of others, in
the general sense with which the philosopher is concerned. I am
not talking philosophy when I say of a driver who risks an odd

[1] *Op. cit.*, p. 179.
[2] *Op. cit.*, p. 181.

move that 'he knows what he is doing'. Such expressions, in that context, are quite neutral as far as philosophical questions are concerned. The appeal to ordinary language settles as little here as anywhere else. The question still means how, not in this or that sort of situation, but at all times do we know initially what are our own thoughts and purposes, and do we know the thoughts of others in the same or in a different way? We have not begun to make any attack on this question when we have considered how the words 'knowing what I am doing' are understood in the sort of context Ryle has in mind. This is why it is particularly hard to come to grips with his argument. It does not come properly into the discussion.

The desperation with which Ryle has to plead his case is also evidenced in his extension of the preceding argument to cases of 'our own silent monologues'.[1] He does not indicate what such a monologue could be except to treat it as something 'muttered or said in our heads'.[2] It certainly is not literally said in our heads. It must surely be said in a way which can only be known in the first instance to ourselves, even in the rare cases where our expressions might give it away to someone who knows us well. But all that Ryle says about a very crucial issue (for him) is that we 'notice' these silent monologues solely in the sense of 'preparing ourselves to do something new,[3] namely to describe the frames of mind which these utterances disclose'.[4] Surely we notice them in the first instance in the much more radical sense, and the one which matters for the philosophy of mind, of knowing what they are like in the very process of conducting them. This is not 'eavesdropping' on ourselves. It is much more immediate and has no parallel in any way we monitor or eavesdrop on the utterances of other persons.

At one point Ryle is tempted to ask, in the guise of a critical reader, why he does not use the verb 'to think' in contexts like the ones in question. He replies, in the first place, that we need to take account of utterances not in the indicative mood, such as questions, commands, and so on. 'Secondly, we tend to reserve the verb "to think" for the uses of those studied and severely drilled utterances which constitute theories and policies.'[5] There is truth in this, as we have already seen. But the point of it seems to be missed, namely that we limit the use of 'think' in this way because it would otherwise be uninformative in ordinary contexts. It does

---

[1, 2, 4] *Op. cit.*, p. 184.   [5] *Op. cit.*, p. 185.

[3] Professor Ryle offers some further and more subtle variations on this theme in a lecture, 'Thinking and Reflecting', published in *The Human Agent* (Royal Institute of Philosophy Lectures, Vol. I, Macmillan, 1968). But he does not take up the objections to his general treatment of the subject which have been

not follow that we are not in another, more basic, sense thinking when we ask questions or issue commands; much less can we turn aside the question what is involved in processes of thought in general by hinting that there is no special question to be asked about the nature of thought beyond consideration of the difference between thinking in the specialized use of the word and its use as involved in all mental activity.

It is not surprising, in the light of Ryle's general procedure, that he finds little difficulty in accounting for what seems to be perplexing in the way we think of ourselves as persons. It was noted earlier how elusive is the nature of mind, and, if persons are essentially minds, they share in this radical elusiveness. This accounts for Hume's failure to look into himself and find something tangible which he could note and describe. Under such analyses the self seems to melt away. We seem not to know what we are, and when conditioned to look for something quasi-physical, something which has form and image like outward things, we seem to be nothing at all. And yet what could be more real or more evident to us? We know quite well, in a way, what it is to be and to be ourselves. The difficulty is to tell what sort of existence this peculiarly personal existence is, to lay hold upon it in any way other than in the recognition of it by each one in his own case. But for any perplexity we may feel here (and who, child or philosopher, has not felt it?) Ryle has a simple, if curious, explanation.

He observes that we can perform certain mental operations upon other operations, or with the latter as their object. I can criticize or mimic your rendering of a song, I can blackmail a deserter. This is called 'higher order' activity, though not of course in a valuational sense of higher. There is no causal transaction here, but only one process involving the thought of another, or taking some account of it. A person may, moreover, perform such higher order activities upon another activity of his own. I may deplore my own solecism, or tell others of my apt remark, or feel remorse about my treachery. But no such performance or comment can be its own object, no higher order activity is ever performed upon itself. No 'act of ridiculing can be its own butt'.[1] It could 'be the target only of another commentary. Self-commentary, self-ridicule

[1] *Op. cit.*, p. 195.

voiced by many in the twenty years since the publication of *The Concept of Mind*. He thinks that Rodin's *le Penseur* presents a special case for him, and deals with it in terms of greater 'disengagement' and 'independence of adjuncts' etc.; but there would be no acute problem here were there not a problem already presented by the tennis-player.

and self-admonition are logically condemned to eternal penulti-
macy'.[1] There is, therefore, something we cannot catch in our self-
directed activity, any more than a man can jump on the shadow of
his own head. Thus it comes about that, while I can exhaustively
describe my past self, 'my today's self perpetually steps out of any
hold of it that I try to take'.[2]

This argument gives us one way in which we may consider the
self to be elusive and hard to lay hold upon. But it is hard to see
what relevance, except by a curious and unilluminating parody, it
has to any serious problem which besets the philosopher when he
thinks about his own self. There is no problem of our not being
quite aware of what the initial activity and the 'higher' activity
performed upon it are like. All we have is the logical impossibility
of a commentary being about itself, and this appears to have
nothing to do with the genuine perplexity we have about the way a
self is to be indicated or described. Nor does it bear on the problems involved in saying that some experience is one of my own and
not that of another. We say nothing in further description of an
experience when we claim it as our own, but in what then does this
claim consist, what are we affirming? The problem of finding the
answer to this sort of question does not seem to be affected by the
peculiarities found in the alleged higher order statements. If there
is an elusiveness about the self it is certainly not the sort of
elusiveness that Ryle has in mind.

There is, of course a well-known problem of how the self as
subject or knower can become an object of knowledge to itself,
and I have more than hinted already at the way this problem may
be solved in terms of the way we 'enjoy' or 'live through' our
experiences. But there is only a formal and remote resemblance
between this genuine philosophical problem and the 'systematic
elusiveness' of which Ryle treats in his account of 'higher order'
performances.

Ryle reminds us also that pronouns like 'I' or 'You' are index
words. That is, they are not names of particular persons. But
some, it is alleged, have taken them to function like proper names,
and this is a further way in which it has come to be assumed that
in addition to the persons who 'are known abroad by their ordinary
surnames and Christian names',[3] there are extra queer individuals
hidden behind the former and denoted by pronouns like 'I' or

---

[1] *Op. cit.*, p. 195.
[2] *Op. cit.*, p. 196.
[3] *Op. cit.*, p. 187.

'You'. But until some indication is given of who are the persons
who have erred in this peculiarly foolish way, it is hard to take this
argument seriously. Neither in *The Concept of Mind*, nor in other
writings of Ryle and his followers, is there any indication of where
the evidence relevant to the alleged confusion is to be found. We
are left with the vaguest of insinuations which, in the circumstances, we cannot properly confirm or refute.

In the same context Ryle takes up again, very briefly, the problems of the Freedom of the Will. The idea of 'higher order' performance provides a final simple solution to this problem also. My
future is 'systematically elusive to me', not because it is not determined, but because a prediction cannot take account of itself. The
prediction may itself make a difference to what I do or think, and
my prognosis cannot take account of that. But the extent to which
anyone's conduct is varied in this way is extremely limited and
does not seem to have anything to do with the limitations we would
normally impose on our exercise of freedom. Ryle himself, moreover, admits that even the variation in question is in principle, and
usually in practice, predictable. My career is thus in no way
'unpredictable to prophets other than myself', nor is it 'inexplicable
to myself after the heat of the action. I can point to any other
thing with my index-finger, and other people can point at this
finger. But it cannot be the object at which it itself is pointing'.[1]
The problems about the Freedom of the Will fall into the same class.

These considerations seem to me as remote from serious understanding of the problem of the Freedom of the Will, and the concern that has been felt about it, as anything can be. The 'feeling of
spontaneity' seems to have little to do with any way in which a
prediction of our own may affect our immediate conduct; whatever the final account to be given of it, this feeling is much more
inherent in the actual performance than Ryle's account implies,
and it is much too widespread to be due to the sort of sophistication he has in mind. The problem has, moreover, much to do with
questions of praise and blame, and if it is felt that blame, in a
proper moral sense, and remorse are out of the question if our
conduct is predictable, this can hardly be affected by any way in
which we may not be able to predict the effect of our own prediction on our own actions. What has worried people about Free Will
is the thought of their future, whether known to themselves or
not, being preappointed. It is hard to see how we can be blamed

[1] *Op. cit.*, p. 197.

or praised morally if all is mapped out already, however this comes about. There may be a way out of this difficulty, although I myself do not think there is one short of the acknowledgment of some genuinely open choices. But the point for us now is that the issue is surely not affected by who is able to make the prediction. It is the predictability as such that is troublesome, and in any case we do not just consider *ourselves* to be subject to moral praise or blame. We take the lives of others to be subject to moral distinctions in precisely the same way, and the solution proposed by Ryle has plainly no relevance there. He tells us that we find no 'absurdity in the supposition that the futures of other people are so pre-appointed'.[1] There may or may not be absurdity in this, but that there is something, on the face of it at least, hard to reconcile with responsibility seems evident; and the easy assumption by Ryle that he has happily got rid of the main difficulties, in a moral or any other context, seems to betoken nothing more than extraordinary ineptitude in grasping what certain philosophical problems are like and how they arise.

We have the same impression, together with a sense of the author's mounting desperation, when we turn to Ryle's account of the remaining major topic to which he applies his main themes and techniques, namely the nature of our more strictly intellectual activities, such as handling theories and arguments. It is significant that Ryle draws a very sharp distinction between these operations and other intellectual activities like those of the engineer and chess-player. The latter have a practical aim and are not thus, it is alleged, concerned with the discovery of truth, they do not add to knowledge. The engineer builds bridges, just as the labours of the legislator, although he thinks in abstract terms, 'issue not in theorems but in Bills'.[2] This seems to me again a misleading dichotomy. The chess-player only gains the victory because he is able to discover what the position will be, or what is likely to happen, if he moves his piece in a certain way. The engineer builds a sound bridge because he finds out what stresses can be borne by various columns and arches and so on. In substance the pursuit of truth is the same here as anywhere, and it is upon it that achievement mainly depends. But let us set this aside. What can be said of these more obviously and severely intellectual activities of forming

[1] *Op. cit.*, p. 196.
[2] *Op. cit.*, p. 281.

or presenting theories where again it would seem, on the face of it, that private mental processes must be involved?

Here Ryle draws a further sharp distinction between the theory or argument as finally formed and presented, on the one hand, and, on the other, the process of building or shaping a theory. There is 'travelling' and there is 'being at one's destination', there is the making of a path and there is sauntering along it. This is again a distinction we can all recognize in a rough and ready way, but it is doubtful whether it is as sharp as Ryle supposes. He claims that failure to heed this distinction is responsible for grievous errors. 'Epistemologists', it seems, 'very frequently describe the labours of building theories in terms appropriate only to the business of going over or teaching a theory that one already has.'[1] This is how they come to think of processes of judging, deducing, abstracting and so on. These words and distinctions belong only to the classification of the final product. There are premisses and conclusions in arguments and we foolishly read these and kindred distinctions back into the process through which we come by our argument or theory, the initial 'pondering'. We postulate 'counterpart' elements corresponding to 'the classified elements of achieved and expounded theories', and in this way we manufacture bogus mental episodes or cognitive acts of judging and so on.

At this point it would have been particularly helpful to have had firm instances of the culprits Ryle has in mind and of where precisely in their works they fall into the mistake in question. As Professor C. A. Campbell has pointed out,[2] he might find it very difficult to produce any; Ryle seems, for the most part, to have invented an error into which people might fall, though how is far from clear, and then boldly assumed or announced that many have in fact been the victims of it.

To consider the matter further let us first think of the finished product or expounded theory. We can refer to such a theory without thinking of any particular person advancing or holding it, and we might discuss the theory of evolution in such terms, indicating what we take to be right or wrong in it. But the theory of evolution as such is nonetheless an abstraction, it has no reality or significance apart from certain ideas entertained at some time or another by various people and communicated to others through wellknown conventions in speech or print. There is no reason to

[1] *Op. cit.*, p. 289.
[2] 'Ryle on the intellect', *Philosophical Quarterly*, 1953

suppose that Ryle would quarrel expressly with this point, and if he did he might find himself falling foul of the bogy he has raised himself, the much advertised category-mistake. But what then of the process of going over or expounding the finished product? At this point we are first reminded that having a theory is to be 'prepared to state it or otherwise apply it'.[1] This is true, but how can we state or apply the theory without also thinking or entertaining it at the time? The theory is not just words or mere talk.

Apparently, however, Ryle seems to think that the theory just is a certain kind of talk and material behaviour. We may teach a theory or we may use it. If we teach it or go over it, we engage in 'further didactic talkings',[2] and those who listen attentively learn in due course 'how to say just those same things, or things to the same effect, or at least how to talk in that manner'.[3] But this is tantalizing indeed. Just what does 'talk' and 'say' mean here? It must surely mean more than uttering the appropriate sounds or making marks on paper. To this vital question no answer is given, nor are we told how we can use or apply the theory, making a variety of moves and so on without understanding what we are doing and entertaining thoughts of what we expect to follow. We are left with the ambiguities of words like 'say', 'talk', 'cite' etc. But what Ryle would say can well be guessed when we pass on to the other, preliminary, stage of *building* a theory.

Such work does not 'consist only in operating with pens, but also in operating with microscopes and telescopes, balances and galvanometers, log-lines and litmus-papers'.[4] This, we must add, is not mere material movement. Presumably Ryle would say here, as elsewhere, that the movement is an intelligent one, that is that we understand what we do when we note the colour of the litmus paper, merely in the sense that we are dispositionally ready to make certain other movements—the 'appropriate' ones, but how are they deemed appropriate? And on this no more need be added here. But in addition to the operations instanced there will also be 'a lot of soliloquy and colloquy', of 'debating and experimental asseverating'.[5] This activity, I think we should add, is peculiarly closely intertwined with the first. But what matters most is how the alleged asseverating etc. is to be understood. We are told it consists of 'self-addressed interim reports of sub-theories'[6] which

[1] *Op. cit.*, p. 286.
[2], [3], [4] *Op. cit.*, p. 288.
[5], [6] *Op. cit.*, p. 291.

help us to get the full theory with which we are at last content. So here, in the process of building theories, there is a place for other theories as we proceed. What of these? They are also, it appears, a matter of what we say, of what one says tentatively—'I roll them on my tongue'.[1] But here again it is not a matter of mere saying, indeed I would have thought a scientist deeply absorbed in his experiment would not be concerned at all to roll words on his tongue, as the poet or the actor might be. It is not rolling the words on one's tongue that matters, but saying things to oneself, perhaps without words in the conventional sense at all, in the sense of thinking certain thoughts, thinking something out or thinking along certain lines, and this is not initially or primarily being prepared to make certain moves, but understanding, or seeming to understand, certain things.

Ryle, in short, is offering us, along with the exposition of established theories, a process of travelling which consists in certain ambiguously conceived practical operations together with the enunciation of sub-theories which, in principle, fall into the same class as the finished theory in consisting essentially in talk and being prepared to talk in a certain way. What is obviously, indeed glaringly, missing in this is the one ingredient that gives point to it all, namely the process of understanding or grasping meaning. This is continuous whereas much that Ryle specifies is intermittent and dispensable.

Ryle anticipates that this objection will be raised against him, and he senses the importance of it. He thus directs a barrage of typical critical comment against the idea that terms have a meaning except in the use of them on the *qui vive* in his special understanding of that notion. If they had, he implies, we would have to ask 'When and where do these meanings occur?'.[2] To the first part of the question an answer is possible; I was thinking of certain events in Vietnam while reading about them in the paper this morning. To the second part no answer is possible, or necessary, except in a thoroughly metaphorical sense. We might say that thoughts or meanings are in my mind, but *in* does not properly signify any kind of place. We are saying no more than that we have these thoughts or that they occur. They do not need to occur in a place, and by their very nature they could not do so; it is only by the gravest philosophical misunderstanding that anyone could think otherwise.

[1] *Op. cit.*, p. 291.   [2] *Op. cit.*, p. 295.

Contempt is poured also on the idea that an 'expression is on a lead held by a ghostly leader called a "meaning" or thought'.[1] 'Ghostly leader' is the usual travesty, but the use of an expression is surely determined by the thought I wish to convey. My thought may find immediate expression in suitable terms, but I would not use these particular terms did I not have a definite thought to communicate. So subtle is the intertwining of thought and words that we often acquire or shape our thoughts in the very process of finding the right words. But the words are nonetheless not the thoughts. The thought could be expressed in other words, or in other languages.

It is added that the fact that 'an expression is made to be understood by anyone shows that the meaning of an expression is not to be described as being, or belonging to, an event that at most one person could know anything about'.[2] This turns of course on the assumption, already shown to be entirely unwarranted, that belief in 'private' access is tantamount to solipsism. The simple fact is that we have conventional ways of conveying our meaning, and that one person's thoughts can, therefore, be understood by many others. My own thoughts become in this way a common possession, but it can only be so in the form of thoughts which I and other persons have; my meaning is understood when it is known by others what I am thinking. My meaning has no other existence—in either a public or private place. It is not made public in the sense of being part of the events we observe in the world around us.

We are told also that the meaning of an expression is not an event, 'and *a fortiori* not an occult thing or happening'.[3] In one sense this is true. Meaning, as an abstraction, stands for the factors common to our thoughts likely to be stirred by accepted or conventional expressions. But as such it could not have any significance apart from the actual thinking of various persons. Meaning can have no reality apart from persons thinking—and thinking is an event.

Scorn is poured also on the idea that each word has a meaning strictly monopolized by it. In this also there is a half-truth. I can indeed indicate *the* meaning of a term like 'table' in the sense of giving a dictionary definition of the term by describing the main features of the objects it denotes. But no one could actually just think 'table'. We can only think things like, 'here is the table', 'mind the table', 'what a fine table', 'put it down on the table' and

[1, 2, 3] *Op. cit.*, p. 295.

so on, all of which could well be conveyed in a certain context or situation by the one word 'table'. The unit of thought never falls below the level of judgment, and this has been admirably brought out by idealist logicians like Bosanquet whose work is also much neglected by fashionable philosophers of today. But the fact that words have no meaning in a fixed and static way, but only as involving some modification of thought through the units appropriate to it, does nothing to undermine the notion of thought as an event or process.

I need hardly add that meanings are not 'ghostly doubles of the words, phrases or sentences themselves'.[1] There is no 'shadowy naming, asserting, or arguing'.[2] The meaning is the arguing, but the arguing is not the saying or writing of the words. Here Ryle takes an almost exactly opposite view. To say something significant is not, for him, 'to do two things'. It is to do one thing 'in a certain frame of mind'. 'Saying something in this specific frame of mind, whether aloud or in one's head, *is* thinking the thought.'[3] The frame of mind, of course, is the dispositional one of being on the *qui vive* etc. But that takes away not one whit of the absurdity of identifying thinking with saying. There just are two things that we do, two very different things whose difference Ryle does not begin to appreciate, namely thinking and saying.

A further butt of much ridicule for Ryle is the idea ascribed to wrong-headed but unnamed epistemologists of a passage from premiss to conclusion in an argument. The distinction of premiss and argument belongs to 'the anatomy of the limbs, joints, nerves of the statements of built theories'.[4] It does not reflect any movement of thought as such. There is truth in this also. In seeing the point of an argument there is no event of passing from the premiss to the conclusion, it is one insight in which we see the conclusion as following from the premiss. But we can (indeed we must) be aware of the premiss first and we may know the purported conclusion. And when, in due course, we see how the one follows from the other, this must occupy *some* time, however infinitesimal. That it is practically instantaneous does not make it strictly timeless.

Ryle ironically asks how long the alleged trip from premiss to conclusion took for someone, and whether he enjoyed his trip. I think most persons would be disconcerted if they were asked how

[1] *Op. cit.*, p. 295.
[2], [3] *Op. cit.*, p. 296.
[4] *Op. cit.*, p. 293.

long it took them to blink, although this could be measured by suitable equipment. We could invent nothing that would measure, even with signals from ourselves, just when we see the point in an argument. It is, as I said, practically instantaneous. But it could not happen without taking *some* time. As for enjoyment, this must surely qualify longer stretches of thinking in which much is perceived, pondered and thought over again, and so on. It must be added, again, that thought, as event, is not made up of easily isolable momentary episodes. Our thought is sustained by continuously seeing connections of various sorts. To itemize this in detail would require considerable skill, and in many cases would not be possible at all.

This is where the intended appeal by Ryle to common sense, in the person of John Doe, is so singularly inappropriate. For not only is John Doe little familiar with the terms and idioms of philosophers or with philosophical thinking, but he is being asked questions, about enjoying his trip from premiss to conclusion etc., which are bound to dumbfound him because they are questions which it would be absurd for anyone to try to answer, just as it would be absurd to ask a person how much he enjoyed the various steps he takes, or the change-over from lifting his foot up to bringing it down, in the course of a walk pronounced as a whole to be extremely enjoyable. One might as well ask a bather, just back from an enjoyable swim, just how exhilarating he found it to move his arms in this or that way in the course of making his breast stroke—and how much precisely this contributed to his enjoyment of the swim as a whole.

At one point in this context Ryle seems to be giving up his case by referring, in his account of a detective solving a problem, to 'the one occasion when the light burst upon him'.[1] Does not this imply an occurrence of some kind? Ryle does not expressly tell us, and presumably, if he were to take up this crucial issue, he would have to insist that nothing is involved beyond reaching a point at which we acquire new capacities to say certain things and make certain moves. We are not, in fact, told this, or anything else, about the occasion when the light bursts because Ryle's serious concern, in making the allusion, is to reduce its significance almost to vanishing point. It is, indeed, uncertain whether he really believes that the light does ever burst. For his main contention is that normally at least it does not. The light 'dawns'. The loopholes in

[1] *Op. cit.*, p. 299.

the detective's theory 'became gradually smaller and smaller until, at no specifiable moment, they dwindled away altogether'.[1]

There is here also something we can recognize. But it also cries out for analysis. What does the 'dawning' in this case involve? It must surely involve coming to certain conclusions as we proceed, the loopholes are closed when we judge certain things to be the case, all of which must happen and take some time; the dawn consists in the breaking of light this way or that. There need be no blinding flashes, but only perhaps imperceptible gradations of fitting things together. But any perception of any connection, whether intermittent or continuous with others, must be a process which takes some time. This may be a merging of insights in which none is very marked or obtrusive by itself, but there must be movements of thought which draw themselves together in some way to yield the essential result. There is no difference in principle, and certainly none that affects the present issue, between the dawning of truth and the bursting of light on our minds, and in many, if not most, of the matters that are highly problematic, the solution will present itself with startling suddenness—Professor Ryle can hardly have forgotten Archimedes.

As a desperate defence against this sort of criticism Professor Ryle boldly reaffirms his view that what I have described as a movement of thought is simply someone saying this or that (or, in argument, 'this, so that') but with the additional proviso of 'knowing that he is licensed to do so'.[2] This seems innocent and plausible enough. But, in fact, it just takes us back to the beginning of our problems. For we have to ask at once 'what is involved in this knowing?' and can any answer to this question be given in behavioural terms from which mental processes are entirely excluded? I hope by now that I have said enough to show that that is not the case.

A curious defence of Ryle's procedures as a whole has been advanced, again it seems to me in some desperation, by some of his followers. They contend that Ryle did not seriously intend to attack positions actually held by outstanding philosophers, or indeed by any known thinkers at all. Nor did he, on this view, seriously intend to defend the position he seems to hold. His aim, on the contrary, has been to show what regrettable consequences

[1] *Op. cit.*, p. 299.
[2] *Op. cit.*, p. 301.

follow from making certain mistakes, notably category ones; he is setting up various signs and signals to warn us off certain danger areas, and if parodies of well-known theories serve this purpose best, together with deliberate abuse of famous thinkers, what of that? The end is so splendid that it justifies the means and the extensive travesty of truth in other ways; to appreciate the importance of Ryle's work we have to realize how extremely oblique it all is.

I do not know whether Professor Ryle welcomes this sort of defence. On the face of it, it is not a very flattering one. Something might be said for the procedure in question, as a desperate form of intellectual bludgeoning or a means of awakening us out of deep dogmatic slumbers, if it could be shown that we were in fact prone to stray into the perilous areas envisaged. We may shriek very loudly and take desperate courses to keep someone away from a cliff edge which he does not see, and we may tell the wildest stories to such a person if we think he is not of very sound mind. But when the dangers seem entirely mythical, or at best very remote, and when there is no evidence of the sort of insanity envisaged, it can only be ridiculous and gravely misleading to treat sound and sensible people as if they were in imminent and deadly peril. We do not, to change our metaphor, need remedies for non-existent maladies, and only hypochondriacs heed them.

It is indeed always perilous to tamper with the truth, however high the intention. One may of course state the case carefully for a position one does not actually hold, and a somewhat Socratic teacher may disguise his own position for a while to force a sluggish pupil to think. But disguises should not be worn for long in the pursuit of truth, most of all when the masks tend to leave their imprint on our features. Nor should anyone play *advocatus diaboli* without in due course declaring his real sympathies and interests. Otherwise the utmost confusion follows, and those who should be our shepherds to keep us away from disasters are the ones most likely to bring us to catastrophic ruin. If Professor Ryle did not seriously believe that Descartes and others have held the positions ascribed to them, and if there are no epistemologists who can be shown to have committed the errors ascribed to such thinkers, and most of all if Ryle does not seriously hold to the sort of behaviourism he seems to be defending, then we must certainly allow that he has had his fun, that he has produced a witty and entertaining work; but we have also to remember, in a much sadder and more sombre mood, that the better part of a generation of gifted younger scholars have met their academic destinies largely by ringing the changes on his various moves and disjunctions. This can hardly be thought to be in the interest of truth at a time when culture and indeed the very life of society stand in as grave a need as at any time of the steady guidance of the philosopher, prepared to follow 'the wind of the argument' wherever it takes him, prepared as well to appreciate, and make it clear to others, that the world is in many ways a stranger place than we first take it to be; but concerned above all, like the great thinker who first spoke of the wind of the argument, that our objective should always be, and be known to be, not ingenuity for its own sake, but the attainment of truth and the deepening of sound understanding.

In my criticisms of Professor Ryle, I have tried to make it plain, above all, that the mistakes which he seems to me to be making come about mainly through his being under the impression that any reality of a non-material kind, or anything which cannot be sensibly observed, must somehow resemble the latter, that alleged mental processes must be some kind of ghostly double of the witnessable performances of persons. This is an understandable error, although it by no means justifies the excesses in which Professor Ryle seems to indulge. It is natural to try to visualize, in some fashion, all of which we can think, and it may indeed be difficult to think at all without some imaging or visualizing in that way. But I hope I have shown by now how perilous it is to neglect the representative or metaphorical character of all such imaging in dealing with various modes of mental activity. The lesson above all which we learn from study of Ryle's work is how radically different the mind is from the body and how elusive are the activities of minds, not in the sense that we do not properly know what they are in themselves, but in the sense that we cannot lay hold upon them in the same way as events or entities in the world around us or describe them in essentials except in terms of what each person finds his experience to be in having such experience or living through it. The failure to appreciate this and to grasp properly the sense in which the in-wardness and elusiveness of mental processes must be understood is an outstanding feature also of much further work on the philo-sophy of mind by several writers who have taken up the subject after Professor Ryle; and my next aim will be to trace the course of the same basic error in some representative and highly regarded studies of the same questions in recent years.

CHAPTER IV

THE NEW MATERIALISM

The fashion set by Professor Ryle has been followed by many others. It would take long to trace the ramifications of it in recent thought. The best way for me to advance the subject further at this stage will be to give an account of some positions which have much in common with that of Professor Ryle but are also sufficiently different to be of interest in themselves. I begin with the views of Professor Stuart Hampshire as he presents them in a work which has also been much praised and admired, namely *Thought and Action*.

This book is a difficult and obscure one. It is quite different in style from *The Concept of Mind*. One has no difficulty in knowing what Professor Ryle is maintaining and by what sort of arguments he hopes to advance his case. This is why his work is in some ways an easy target for those who oppose it. He is bold and ruthless, and if we think his position breaks down it is fairly easy to indicate how this occurs; he has, as in the case of notorious fallacies in John Stuart Mill's work, been explicit enough to be found out. But many who follow Ryle in their main contentions have been much more cautious and covered their tracks in a way that makes pursuit and capture less easy. This is certainly true of Hampshire, his arguments proceed at a highly rarefied and abstract level, there is very little instantiation of what he claims, and one has sometimes to work out his position for him and choose between various ways in which his views may be taken. I hope I shall do him no grave injustice.

Of Hampshire's general alignment with Ryle there can, however, be not much doubt. Both are firm in their rejection of anything approaching a Cartesian position, and, if at all, Hampshire is bolder in the affirmation of the materialistic strain in his thought. Not that he, any more than Ryle, could be said to be in all respects an out-and-out materialist. But that is the position in which he seems more unmistakably to come to rest at times. For him also the awkwardness that is created by the repudiation of distinct inner processes is covered by the role he ascribes to behavioural tendencies and action.

D

The drift of Hampshire's main contentions may be found in observations like the following: 'Every observer is aware of himself as one item in the furniture of the world, and, when he identifies the objects around him, he also thereby fixes in his own mind his own situation in the world'.[1] 'The line that we draw between "inner sensations" and features of the external world depends upon this distinction between the active subject, who is a body among bodies, and who from time to time changes his own point of view, and the common object observed from many points of view.'[2] 'The observer is always a self-moving body among other bodies which he observes and intentionally manipulates.'[3] 'We are in the world, as bodies among bodies, not only as observers but as active experimenters.'[4] 'We have therefore no reason to look for some criterion of personal identity that is distinct from the identity of our bodies as persisting physical objects.'[5] 'These philosophers fall into absurdity who suppose that the public actions of making meaningful statements and of asking questions must be said to be *accompanied* by a corresponding shadow process.'[6]

The affinity with Ryle is very evident in the last quotation and that affords us a very convenient link with what has gone before in this book. That may be all the more necessary because of the great disparity of style and sustained procedures between the two authors. But the point of noting these passages here is to afford the reader a glimpse of the main jumps before he is set to negotiate the course. The test must come in considering how such passages are to be understood more strictly and by what sort of arguments they are supported. We must look at them in their context, and to that task I now turn.

We approach the main themes of Professor Hampshire in his repeated insistence that there can be no completely detached items of experience to be identified on their own account. This is certainly not a novel view in itself. It has a long history and was very vigorously asserted by idealist thinkers in the last century. Their way of putting it was, in the words of Bernard Bosanquet, that 'we can get at no data unqualified by judgment'.[7] There is

---

[1] *Thought and Action*, p. 45.
[2] *Thought and Action*, p. 46.
[3] *Op. cit.*, p. 50.
[4] *Op. cit.*, p. 53.
[5] *Op. cit.*, p. 75.
[6] *Op. cit.*, p. 165.
[7] *The Essentials of Logic*, p. 28.

indeed a peculiarly close affinity between the way Bradley and Bosanquet presented their case for 'the impossibility of getting at an original datum'[1] and a great deal of the early part of *Thought and Action*, so much so that it is surprising to find no explicit reference to such writers. In view of the vigour of the reaction against idealism which gave much of its impetus to contemporary philosophy one must regard the present coincidence of emphasis as a peculiarly interesting unconscious meeting of extremes.[2] But one does not have to be either an out-and-out idealist or a fashionable contemporary philosopher to agree readily with the substance of the claim that there are no wholly isolable elements in our experience of the world.

The novelty comes in with the prominence given by Hampshire to the role of language and convention in making it impossible for us to reduce our experience to merely 'transitory impressions'. We can single out nothing in our own lives or the world around us that has not already been identified and characterized in some way. There is a great variety of ways, indeed according to Hampshire 'an indefinite number of alternative ways',[3] in which something may be classified, and the way we go about the task on any particular occasion is in large measure determined for us by the ways in which things have already been classified. 'Whatever I may be referring to and identifying as a thing of a certain kind, I am always and necessarily amplifying the description that might originally be given of it: "that heap of stones is a tomb". Having established these two identifications, I can go on to a third identification of the same form and so on indefinitely. There is no necessary end to the series. Nor is there a necessary starting-point, as so many philosophers have assumed, in a type of classification which most nearly corresponds to the true divisions in experience or reality. It must depend on our permanent and common interests, and the forms of our social life, whether we tend to single out one or another type of object in our language as constant objects of reference.'[4] It is thus a grave mistake to assume 'that there must be natural, pre-social units already discriminated as the ultimate subjects of reference in our experience: that social convention and artificiality enter only at the second tier of language, resting on a

[1] *Op. cit.*, p. 30.
[2] *Cf.* also Chapter XIV below.
[3] *Thought and Action*, p. 19.
[4] *Op. cit.*, p. 20.

first tier of basic and natural discrimination which is independent of any institutions of social life'.[1]

I do not wish to quarrel with the substance of this claim. It certainly appears to be true that 'description of reality is essentially inexhaustible'.[2] Nor does anyone start from scratch with neat unqualified items of experience. We begin where others left off and with interests shaped for us by those who have gone before us. But it would be wrong to understand this in a way that made classification wholly a matter of convention and language. The way we discriminate within our experience, and the way others over the ages have predisposed us to do so, are determined in the last resort by what the world is like. We do not manufacture the world in which we find ourselves, even if we bring various conspectuses to bear on it. The suggestion that the main matter is convention and language is a further curious parallel to the idealist notion of an earlier period whereby the mind was thought to make its own world of objects. In both cases we have a major error, namely that of overlooking the fact that we can only classify objects in a certain way in the last analysis because of what they are like. No classification can be wholly arbitrary.

Idealist thinkers were, in fact, nearer the truth in this matter than many of our conventionalists at the present day. For they at least recognized and emphasized certain *a priori* conditions or characteristics of experience which thus held for all times and places. No individual or group manufactures these. But there must also be some 'given' particularity in all things, and we describe things as we do because that is what in fact we find them to be like. It is true that we never get at wholly raw or neat items of experience, and this is due in part to the reason given by Hampshire, namely that we come in where others have largely set the course for us. But that is not the only reason. There is a more basic reason in the nature of things, namely that we could not ascribe any significance to an item of experience that was not characterized in any way at all. We could not think of anything without taking it to be one sort of thing, however vague, as being different in some way from other things or being in one place or time rather than another. This seems very clear, and this is what Stuart Hampshire appears to be saying most of the time. But it is equally plain that it is not a mere matter of convention or language and that we have to

[1] *Op. cit.*, p. 26.
[2] *Op. cit.*, p. 21.

bear in mind the character and divisions of reality itself which ultimately govern our thought about it.

Subject to these qualifications we can readily agree that objects do not single themselves out in some quite spontaneous way in our experience altogether divorced from our purposes and habits of thought. There is, as Hampshire puts it, 'no limit that can be placed on the variety of objects of reference that may be singled out in reality',[1] and we have thus to participate ourselves in making the world meaningful for us. We take part in a process by which things are identified.

I pass now to a more questionable and very revealing move made by Hampshire, namely to suggest that the method of identification of items within the course of our own experience as such is in no radical way different from the way we specify and single things out in the external world. In neither case can we merely 'record the impressions of the moment'.[2] But here the implication seems to be, in the context, that there is nothing involved in the way we identify and describe our own states of mind beyond the procedures we follow in coming to recognize objects in the world around us, 'the identification of the state of mind' is no different from 'the identification of the object'.[3] I identify my state of mind as anger in the same way as I conclude that I am looking at a horse. 'We pick out resemblances in certain respects as the basis of our classification and neglect other resemblances which, in pursuance of some new need or interest, may be marked later.'[4] But this is at least much too simplified for internal processes. When I learn that I am angry or frightened there is nothing in the way of sensations or feelings that plays the same role as 'the look of things, of sounds, colours, tastes, smells',[5] in the way I identify a horse or a tree. Physical sensations may, of course, be involved, although physical is not quite the right word. I may have a sinking feeling or feel faint or flushed or feel my pulses beating or catch my breath or choke. But I do not know that I am angry or frightened at such times by placing these sensations in some wider system or 'situation', in Hampshire's term, such as those in which the looks of external things enable us to identify them. The fear or anger is identified in the complex or unity of the meaningfulness

---

[1] *Op. cit.*, p. 25.
[2, 5] *Op. cit.*, p. 29.
[3] *Op. cit.*, p. 27.
[4] *Op. cit.*, p. 31.

of which it is a part. I recognize it in the thought in which it consists. The physical sensations are incidental, and I could be angry or frightened without them. Hampshire is quite right in holding that I could not recognize my anger for what it is by some clear disjunctive mark of a momentary mental state, but this is because no mental state can be what it is apart from the apprehension of meanings reaching well beyond it which I discover in the very process of having it. I know that I am afraid, not because of the choking sensation or any external concomitants of it, but in just being afraid, which of course involves thoughts of various kinds involving in turn my hopes and expectations of many sorts.

The truth seems to be that Hampshire has not emancipated himself as much as he should from the atomism of isolable data against which he is mounting his attack. He seems to think that we identify a state of anger or fear initially through some sensation we have at the time and the placing of this in some 'situation' in relation to others. But this is to overlook the radical difference between mental processes and events in the world around us. The problems of identity are by no means the same in the two cases. Stuart Hampshire seems to think they are.

Proceeding on this assumption, his next main contention is that nothing can be referred to or identified except from a certain 'standpoint', and in terms of his basic assumption the standpoint will depend expressly on a physical location. We identify nothing raw, but as objects already determined in some way. But this itself presupposes something else. 'Below the level of communication in language and the making of statements, there is the act of intentional pointing, away from oneself and towards an object. The act of pointing is performed from a point of view and standpoint, which is the present situation of myself, as a persisting object placed among other objects. . . . No sense can be given to the notion of a situation and a point of view, if the perceiver is not thought of as a self-moving object among other objects. It becomes impossible to understand how any identifiable object could be indicated, and therefore how any statement with external reference could be made, if the perceiver is thought of as an extensionless point, an unsituated consciousness, unable to make the distinction between "here" and "there". As soon as the possibility of external reference is conceded, and therefore the possibility of marking the situation of the thing indicated in relation to the situation of the observer, the perceiver must be thought of as a persisting body among others.'[1]

There are jumps in this argument which I am quite unable to follow. Admittedly, we cannot identify anything in space except in relation to some physical location, but it does not follow, from this consideration at least, that I must be myself a spatial entity of some kind to make the initial entry, as it were, into space. It would seem to be enough to have a point of view, and the question whether this is possible without my having a body could then be asked. In practice I function in this way, as in others, by having a body, but it is not inconceivable that I should accomplish a great deal at least of what I do now merely by having a distinct point of view, and Professor H. H. Price has worked out very ingeniously what it would be like to be disembodied to that extent.[2] There may be other considerations which make it unlikely, or impossible, for there to be disembodied existence. But physical existence is not directly required to give one a point of view or perspective from which objects could be perceived. Certain kinds of correlation within experience would do the trick.

But even if it were held that one could not have perception and identify objects in space without having a body, it does not follow at all that I must myself be the body which makes that possible. My distinctive perceptual experiences are in fact made possible for me by the body I have, I see these trees now because this is where my body is and so on; my brain and nervous system must be in a certain state. But the perceiving itself is not a physical process, my eyes and my brain have a physical location, but the seeing itself is not physical; and thus, even if it is the case that I could not have perceptual experience and identify objects in space without having the body I have, this would not in any way make me, as the person having these experiences, myself a physical entity in relation to which other things are placed. As far as the present considerations go, I could just as well be a composite entity having a mind as well as a body.

Nor is perception everything. What about further thoughts, resolutions and emotions? Here Hampshire takes a very bold course. Consider again the well-worn example of pain. I seem to know what sort of pain I have, and when, in having it. Hampshire seems at first to admit this, although in a curious way. We cannot,

---

[1] *Op. cit.*, p. 41.
[2] *Brain and Mind* (Ed. J. R. Smythies) p. 1–24.

he notes, say of a pain that *it is* of a certain kind until it is brought 'within my range of perception now. The pain itself has no identity to be established by tracing the history of its appearances. Therefore "I feel a pain" comes to the same as "I am in some pain". Feeling is not here a species of perception'.[1] But instead of admitting, on the basis of this contention, that I have some experience or awareness that is not a matter of external observation, the obvious conclusion to draw, Hampshire questions 'the independent existence' of the feeling apart from its place as it comes within the range of perceptual experience. 'It is only constituted as a separate subject of reference by the separate description offered on this particular occasion.'[2] This means, I take it, that I could not have a pain without having it at a certain time and place, and that I have to note such things to identify the pain. But that does not make the pain itself a part of the world I perceive; the pain is not deprived of its genuine non-physical quality as the feeling I feel.

Hampshire continues: 'Alongside the solid furniture of the world, concrete persisting objects, I may certainly perceive objects—flashes of lightning, rainbows, effects of light, and many others—to which the contrast of real and momentarily apparent properties does not apply; they can be referred to and identified through their spatial relations to concrete things and therefore to the observer.' This is again very like the procedure of some idealist thinkers who have been derided for making incomplete contrasts the bases of bold speculations. There is one sense in which the contrast of real and apparent holds only with respect to 'concrete persisting objects'. But this certainly does not mean, as should have been evident long ago from the *Sophist* and other works of Plato, that the flashes of lightning and so on are wholly unreal.

The truth seems to be that Hampshire has taken it for granted from the start that there is no question of real or unreal except within perceptual experience and that the paradigm case of identification is the identification of objects in the external world. His case is made to seem plausible because everything in our present experience is closely related to perceptual experience. We live in a material world and must always be finding our way around in it. But this does not of itself make everything material. Even if a

---

[1] *Op. cit.*, p. 43.
[2] *Op. cit.*, p. 44.

person could not, in fact, ever be aware of himself except in identifying objects in an external world, this would certainly not prove that 'Every observer is aware of himself as one item in the furniture of the world'.[1]

To the extent that Hampshire is forced to recognize that we have some non-material side to our nature, he seems happy to dissolve it into some activity we perform, as bodies, on other bodies. 'The line that we draw,' he declares, 'between "inner sensations" and features of the external world depends upon this distinction between the active subject, who is a body among bodies, and who from time to time changes his own point of view, and the common object observed from many points of view.'[2] Much importance is ascribed to the part played by our own physical movements in the process of identifying other bodies, and the neglect of this is said to be 'the deepest mistake in empiricist theories of perception'. The latter complaint, levelled in particular against Berkeley and Hume, seems to me only partially true, the corrective lies already within much that Berkeley said. But we can certainly agree that the way we manipulate things is an important feature of the way we identify them and learn what they are like. 'A perceived surface is a perceived point of potential resistance and abstraction. . . . The expanse of blue, the so-called visual datum, may be the mark of recognition of the object; but the nature of the object itself is determined by the range of its possible manipulations, its possible actions and reactions in the context of standard social interests and customary intentions.'[3] No one need quarrel with this as it stands, and it may well be that there is something here which theories of perception have insufficiently heeded. But what is questionable is the subtle identification of the physical manipulations in question with the total activity involved and the consequent reduction of the agent in perception and elsewhere to 'a self-moving body among other bodies which he observes and intentionally manipulates'.[4]

The word 'intentionally' may be thought to redeem this kind of declaration. But whatever the force of it, and that is by no means clear, it is not intended as any acknowledgment of any process or constituent in our activities that is not itself a bodily operation.

[1] *Op. cit.*, p. 45.
[2] *Op. cit.*, p. 46.
[3] *Op. cit.*, p. 48.
[4] *Op. cit.*, p. 50.

On the contrary the insistence on the prominent place of activity in perceptual experience paves the way for further dissolutions of alleged interior and non-bodily reality into activities of our bodies or, as in the case of Ryle, behavioural tendencies. The case is considered, for example, of sensations we may have in awakening from sleep before we have become aware of our situation in the world. Hampshire seems plainly embarrassed by this case and he first hastens to remind us that we could not in fact raise any questions about such sensations until we had begun to be aware of our situation. But this will hardly suffice, and he has, therefore, recourse to insisting that if I am reduced to making statements like 'I feel cold', 'I am in pain', 'I feel giddy', 'these statements so far imply only a disposition or tendency to behave in a certain way'.[1] This desperate manoeuvre is coupled with the curious insistence that 'organic sensations are not in any sense perceived; they simply occur'.[2] Perceived they may not be, but when they do occur they have their own reality distinct from their physical causes and any feature of the perceptual situation in which they happen.

Hampshire tries to turn the edge of this kind of comment by dwelling on the importance of pain as a reason for action. It is no doubt an important fact about pain and pleasure that they are reasons for action, but they could not be this independently of what they are in themselves, whatever further problems that presents. There may be no better way in practice to indicate what a pain is like than to present it as 'the sensation that one has when so and so is happening' and which sets up a 'disposition of the person to avoid whatever it is that he is feeling'.[3] But devices of this sort do not deprive the pain of its distinctive 'interior' character as something in the first instance which a person feels.

So also in the case of dreams and associated mental phenomena like our having mental images, after-images and hallucinations. These also appear to have a peculiar inwardness and privacy of which it seems exceptionally hard for Hampshire to give an adequate account. I do not wish in the least to imply that such phenomena as dreams and hallucinations are the crucial considerations for a philosophy of mind; they are peripheral, and the main attention must be given to normal waking consciousness. A theory about mind and body should prove itself first in respect to what experi-

[1, 2] *Op. cit.*, p. 60.
[3] *Op. cit.*, p. 63.

ence of any sort, or experience as such, is like. All the same certain sides of the problem can be highlighted by reflection on our less common modes of experience, and matters may be revealed in that way which might otherwise be neglected. A sound theory must also be able to accommodate all manner of mental phenomena. And it is here that Hampshire's view seems to be subject to particular strain. This is most evident in the case of the quite familiar phenomenon of dreams. For it is hard to see how Hampshire's theory could extend to these.

'In a dream,' as Hampshire himself observes, 'all things are possible, because both the dreamer, and the objects and persons about which he dreams, may change their nature and their position without any continuity being preserved.'[1] The normal pressures and resistances do not hold in dreams, and I cannot, therefore, be said to manipulate objects from my standpoint as one body among others in the usual way. Indeed, as when I am awake, there is a sense in which my proper body does not come into it, it operates in a causal way only. My physical body is stretched out in bed while I, in my dream, wander through the fields and talk to my friends. If a body is involved in the way I identify myself here it must be a dream body (I am quite unaware of my real body being in my bed) and that certainly does not conform to all that Hampshire has in mind about the way a body functions in making me aware of things and of my own identity. Nor is it altogether clear that a body of any kind is needed. Might not a point of view or perspective suffice, especially if I myself do not figure much in the events of which I dream?

One might have thought that Hampshire would seek a way out of this quandary by making the difference between dreaming and waking a partial one and thus contending that the conditions of self-identity he has in mind are at least partially realized in dreams. I do not in fact think that this concession could be made without serious disruption of some of the things Hampshire is most emphatic about. But it would seem on the whole the more attractive course. It is not at all, however, the course he follows.

His procedure, on the contrary, is boldly to deny the reality of dreams though without, if I understand aright, taking the extreme course followed by Professor Malcolm[2] of denying that there is any process or experience of dreaming. Hallucinations and illusions,

[1] *Op. cit.*, p. 64.
[2] See below chap. VI.

even madness, have some place, so Hampshire admits, in relation
to the stable realities of normal experience, and one's sense of
identity may thus be preserved in spite of them. But dreams are
'the model of unreality'.[1] 'Dream is a total hallucination', and for
this reason I lose the sense of my own identity within it. 'In
dreaming I may lose the sense of my own identity as a thing
occupying a particular position in space at a particular time',[2]
and with that, on Hampshire's view, goes all awareness of identity.

Now admittedly dreams are obviously unreal in one sense. What
happened in a dream, we would say, never happened at all. I am
relieved, when I awake from dreaming that my house is on fire,
to find that all is as it was and that there was no fire at all. I just
dreamt it. It never happened really. All the same something
happened, my relief springs directly from what the dream was
like and I can perhaps describe the dream in detail. Nothing
happened in the external world, but I lived through a certain kind
of experience which was in many salient respects just like witnessing my house on fire. The dream was not wholly unreal, I was
aware of flamelike shapes and shapes like the bodies of men
handling hose-pipes etc. Even if the dream had been much wilder
and hard to describe in ordinary terms, it would still have some
reality and what went on would be of one sort or another. We
cannot, in short, brush aside the problems created by dreams by
the rather high-handed discounting of all their reality. They
are certainly not unreal in the sense that we never have them.

Nor is it in the least evident that I lose my identity in a dream.
What seemed to go on in my nightmare was that *I* was witnessing
my own house on fire. I 'recognized' the place and the friends who
hurried to help me. I knew quite well who I was myself, I was
perhaps particularly alarmed to see the flames get near the study
where my notes and manuscripts are kept. My heart may have
warmed to the neighbour who consoled me. I may even have given
particulars of myself to the police or an insurance agent. I am not,
in other words, at all oblivious of who I am in my dreams. I could
make little of them were there no sort of continuity with waking
life. I think of myself in my dream very much as I do when awake.
I have not forgotten who I am.

Even if the dream were of an extremely disruptive kind akin,
in that respect, to states of schizophrenia or loss of memory,
I do not think there would be a loss of identity or of the sense of it,

[1, 2] *Op. cit.*, p. 64.

in the most ultimate sense. Self-identity does not wholly, or even mainly in the last analysis, depend on my being able to say who I am in the sense of giving my name, saying where I live and work, what my past history has been and so on. There is a basic sense in which I know myself to be myself apart from all this. But that is not a point I can press now. It must be expounded and defended properly in due course. But even with that point set aside there should be enough in the common undisputed substance of dreams to disconcert Stuart Hampshire. Even if my dream is a very very odd one, and my surroundings in my dreams most unfamiliar, it is still of myself being in this peculiar state that I think—even if I am not struck or puzzled by the oddity of it. On the whole it would not be different from finding myself literally mutilated or in strange surroundings.

The changes have often been rung on the familiar joke about a person falling into a drunken stupor and waking up to find his beard cut, his clothes changed, and so on, and exclaiming dazedly, 'Who am I?' But the point of this joke is of course that no one would in fact react in that way. The genuine reaction would be—'What has happened to me?'. Even if a different form of words is used, the real puzzlement comes about just because I remember that I am a person whose appearance is normally very different.

In the same way there is no reason to suppose that when we find ourselves, in dreams, in an odd world where much of the normal continuity and stability of things is lacking, our normal consciousness of who we are is jeopardized at all. We think of ourselves as just the same persons as when we are awake. If it is argued that this would not hold in the more disruptive sort of dream, the reply is threefold. First I should repeat that there remains a basic sense of identity even in such cases, but secondly, and more to the point here, a similar problem would arise in some states of waking consciousness too. Would we say in these cases that self-identity was partial, that self-hood is a matter of more or less? Many philosophers, including most idealists and Stuart Hampshire, would say 'Yes'. But that would, I believe, be a much more questionable view, and fraught with much graver consequences, in ethics and other spheres, than many seem to realize. I shall note the point again. Finally, and still more pertinent to the points at issue now, the admission that in most dreams (or even in a few if that were the case) we are fully aware of who we are in all normal senses would be fatal to a view which makes our awareness of our own identity turn, in the way suggested, on our having a particular body occupying a particular position in space.

In the case of dreams we find Hampshire, in fact, taking a course very similar to that of Ryle, namely that of bluntly denying the distinct reality of the sort of phenomena which cause them most embarrassment.

This is indeed a desperate policy. It is only matched by the contentions of those who have tried to save the same situation, and at the same time avoid an apparent confession of weakness, by making out that, although we must say that we dream, there is nothing, in the case of a dream, which strictly happens—in other words, that a dream is no sort of experience. I shall consider a well-known example of this view in a moment.

In the meantime note should be taken of a further way in which Hampshire stands very firmly in the fashion typified especially by Ryle, namely in his failure to pay much heed to differences in ways we become aware of our own identity and those in which we become aware of other persons and their identity. The assumption seems to be that there are no differences of principle in the two cases. Thus we read: 'However successful one may be in suggesting to others how one feels by some analogy, there is still no sure way of identifying recurring states of consciousness except by some reference to the recurring situations in which they are enjoyed, and to the behaviour which is their natural expression.'[1] This may be true of the way we indicate to others what our experiences are like and identify ourselves for them. But we ourselves surely know our own states of mind more directly. Hampshire admits that 'I may self-consciously watch my own anger or disappointment growing, or attend with care to my own bodily sensations, noting and describing their changes'. But he adds: 'Yet when I try to describe the felt quality of my experiences, putting my intimate feelings into words, I must always have the sense that the words fall short, that any description can only be indefinite and untestable and liable to mislead. This is because feelings cannot be thought of as objects which can be surveyed by different observers from different points of view and which, when surveyed from one point of view, may seem to be other than they are. I cannot therefore pick them out as separate entities and label them and give an inventory of my feelings at any particular time. The kind of determinateness and precision that I can attain in describing

[1] *Op. cit.*, p. 65.

myself or another person as an object among other objects, or as an agent acting upon other objects, cannot be attained when I try to separate my inner experiences from my environment. I am then no longer referring to socially recognized behaviour, and I am trying in my descriptions to go beyond any conventional classifications.'[1]

In this passage, as elsewhere, we have an admission, disconcerting in a way, that there are 'inner experiences'. But they seem to be thought of wholly on analogy with organic sensations and to have no meaning or intentionality except in their linkage with external processes, they are no system of meanings in themselves. And the way this comes to be assumed so firmly is that the same criteria seem to be applied to the description of another person and to oneself. The warrant for what we say is thought to be the same in both cases, and this, as has already been urged, is a fatal flaw in much that is advanced today in the philosophy of mind.

Hampshire also shows himself a close, though not always very explicit, follower of Ryle in a further way in which he opposes the notion of distinguishable mental events, namely in an ambiguous use of the word 'doing' in the refusal to acknowledge an act of will separable from the external doing. 'An ordinary human action', we are told, 'is a combination of intention and physical movement. But the combination of the two is not a simple additive one. The movement is guided by the intention, which may not be, and often is not, distinguishable as a separate event from the movement guided.'[2] This is a tantalizing statement. No one wants to hold that the combination in question is 'a simple additive one'. The movement is 'guided' by the intention. But how can this be if the two are not distinct? How does the guiding function? The point of this question is, however, obscured by a subtle transition whereby the 'movement' is itself treated as the action proper, as seen especially in the statement with which Hampshire continues: 'I often cannot in reflection or introspection, distinguish as separable episodes the thought of what is to be done from the actual doing of it.'[3] This is sensible enough as it stands. We do not have to suppose that when I rise from the table I must first clearly envisage this, I simply get up. Otherwise we would have the infinite regress with which Ryle threatens us. But 'rise' and 'get up' do not refer merely to physical movements. They have them-

[1] Op. cit., p. 66.
[2, 3] Op. cit., p. 74.

selves mental and physical components. The doing, in other words, does not have to have a thought of doing preceding it every time, as a prior act of will. It itself involves willing, it has within it 'the thought of what is to be done'. More strictly the doing is itself a mental process on which normally the anticipated physical movement promptly ensues. But if 'doing' stands for the physical movement then it must plainly be preceded by 'the thought'. Hampshire gains his point and concludes that 'a philosophical dualism . . . does not give a possible account of the concept of action'[1] under cover of the ambiguity of the word 'doing'; and it will be evident, I hope, how reminiscent this is of much in Ryle's procedure in discussing the notion of an act of will distinct from the overt behaviour.

There are, however, some points where Stuart Hampshire seems to be forced by his own arguments to admit that in some sense we have an inner world of thought which cannot be reduced to organic sensations or feelings which are analogous to these. To prevent this, however, from being a damaging admission he straightway characterizes such inner life as a 'shadow' of outward reality in the form of inhibited action. Corresponding to 'identifiable action, there may be an arrested or inhibited form of it, when the publicly identifiable change is not actually made'.[2] The 'truncated or arrested action, the momentary intention or belief' can be 'represented' 'as a *disposition* to act, or publicly to affirm, in a certain way'.[3] 'If I had never had the power of saying "No", and if I did not have the power of inhibiting my actions, it would never be right to attribute unexpressed beliefs to me. A man to whom we attribute a rich inner life of belief and disbelief, of unexpressed doubt and self-questioning, must be a man of great powers of self-restraint, to whom the inhibition of action is natural. He has cut away the substance of human routines and chosen to live with their shadow. . . . The mental and inner life of men is the obverse of social restraint and convention.'[4] This is why it is thought absurd, in terms of the words quoted at the outset, to suppose that public actions are '*accompanied* by a corresponding shadow process. The shadow is that which remains when the public aspect of the action is inhibited; therefore it does not need to be added to the whole of which it is a detachable part'.[5] The most

[1] *Op. cit.*, p. 74.
[2] *Op. cit.*, p. 163.
[3], [4] *Op. cit.*, p. 164.
[5] *Op. cit.*, p. 165.

that has to be admitted, therefore, is that when I 'pause for reflection' an 'intelligent and thoughtful disposition is, while it lasts, separated from the action that will later incorporate it'.[1]

But is this all that a pause for reflection involves? Has it not its own reality as a mental occurrence and must not the richness of it be given more substance on its own account than could be wholly ascribed to the arresting and thwarting of outward action, however much the latter may on occasion contribute to it or stimulate it? I shall not, however, venture further on critical comment here, as I could hardly do so without much repetition of what I have tried to make clear in my more extended examination of Professor Ryle's arguments.

In advancing the views to which I have just referred Professor Hampshire has, like Ryle, a special concern about freedom. He declares that 'to show the connection between knowledge of various degrees and freedom of various degrees is the principal purpose of this book'.[2] His book *Freedom of the Individual* has the same theme, and he expects, like Ryle, that much in the age-long controversies about freedom will be dissolved when heed is paid to his main conclusions. On the face of it this is again a bold assumption. For a view which identifies a person with his body does not seem to hold much promise of dealing adequately with the spontaneity and power of initiative we claim for our conduct, most of all in responsible action. The idea of degrees of knowledge and degrees of freedom is also an ominous harking back to those central notions of idealist philosophers which have been shown to be peculiarly hard to maintain and most inadequate to questions of moral freedom. I shall not, however, launch out into this further subject now. It must be considered closely on its merits later.[3]

---

[1] *Op. cit.*, p. 166.
[2] *Op. cit.*, p. 133.
[3] Mainly in the sequel to this book. Cf. chap. XVI.

CHAPTER V

'THE HUMPTY DUMPTY ARGUMENT'

Another firm opponent of dualism is Professor John Passmore, and he also owes much to Professor Ryle and follows him closely. Passmore's attack on dualism is on a very broad front and again somewhat imprecise except where he follows Ryle closely. In chapter III of his book *Philosophical Reasoning*, he sets out his objections to all forms of dualism. His procedure, in spite of being adopted in support of the down to earth philosophy of today, is more boldly metaphysical than we would expect, and I think it shows well the rashness of those who return to metaphysics from a school where the subject has been held in poor regard and its principles not much heeded; for that is where we are today most likely to find repeated the faults of bad metaphysics which brought the subject understandably into ill repute not so long ago.

I have in mind especially Passmore's assumption that the many applications of the word 'dualism' have enough in common to enable them all to be exposed to some very general objections to the standpoint they all are taken to represent. This seems to me a very big assumption and an approach to the subject which may do much to obscure the real issues and the arguments most germane to them. We find for example that the word dualism figures much in controversies as to whether the universe is one or many. Of the views advanced in that context there is a great variety, and some of them appear to be much more plausible than others. No side appears to have a monopoly of the more interesting arguments, and it could well be that those who favour a dualist, as against a monistic, view of the universe should also consider that there is more to be said for some forms of monism than for certain kinds of dualism and that the arguments which make one or the other of these attractive vary a great deal with the precise position being maintained. A thinker who feels drawn to some kind of Hegelian idealism might find himself more repelled by a Spinozistic monism or a Parmenidian type of mysticism than by some of the pluralistic alternatives to idealism. In other words, it seems fairer to consider particular positions on their merits and in the light of the specific situations and reflections which suggest them than to try to settle the question in some once for all fashion, in terms of some very abstract considerations to which it is hard to attach clear and precise significance. Is not the best philosophy that which arises out of reflection on what we find the world and our experience to be like, rather than that in which issues about particular aspects of reality are prejudged in *a priori* ways or forced into some predetermined mould which may prove very ill-fitted to receive them? And if this is how the matter strikes us when we think of various forms of dualism or monism as views about the universe as a whole, how much more when we think of these in relation to specific issues of a more restricted character like the mind-body problem? How much have the arguments which bear on the latter question to do with the sort of considerations which lead people to maintain that the universe is one or many in any of the many ways in which such notions have been understood and defended? Very little directly, it seems to me. A person could hold a dualist view about mind and body, for example in agreement with Descartes and using the arguments by which Cartesian views are normally defended, and yet claim that in some more ultimate sense the universe to which these belong is one and not many. We seem, therefore, apt to confuse ourselves if we neglect the particular arguments by which specific positions are defended, or subordinate them from the start to considerations about the nature of the universe or some kindred wide-ranging considerations arrived at without due heed to what we find specific aspects of the world or experience to be like.

This relates closely to a claim with which Passmore launches his own discussion of the subject, namely that 'the rejection of dualism is indeed one of the few points on which almost all the creative philosophers of modern times have agreed'.[1] What can we say of this sort of claim, except that it is so general that it is hard to see of what sort of appraisal it admits? Do major philosophical positions allow of the neat pigeon-holing which this kind of generalization presupposes? Are they not a great deal more mixed?

How, for example, should one classify Leibniz, dualist or monist? Strictly speaking some would say neither, they would prefer to say that Leibniz was a pluralist. This is certainly how the monadology is usually taken; it is often regarded as the pattern of a pluralistic view and one to which most subsequent defenders of a pluralistic metaphysics would wish to acknowledge some indebted-

[1] *Philosophical Reasoning*, p. 38.

ness. On the other hand, there is a case for saying that Leibniz was a monist, in as much as all the monads reflect the reality of a supreme monad and have their natures and history determined by their relation to the one reality which is variously mirrored in them all. Monism, then, we might say, but we almost immediately recall how spontaneous and independent, even 'windowless', the finite monads are taken to be in relation to one another, and this provides much of the starting-point for those who wish to defend a pluralistic view of finite beings in relation to one another. Where, then, could Passmore place Leibniz, and should he claim him as an ally or yet another of the exceptions to be deplored?

And what should we say of Spinoza? Plainly, in some regards, the model par excellence of monism. And yet those who wish to advance a pluralist view may find very valuable grist to their mill in the notion of the infinite attributes and the modes of them in which finite being consists. Spinoza gives us an invaluable glimpse of the infinite variety and richness of reality and we may well take our cue from this in presenting an ultimate view of the nature of things very different from the monism of Spinoza.

Where does Berkeley stand? I should have thought much more obviously with the pluralists than with the monists. Admittedly he can be regarded as holding the view that all reality is mental or mind dependent. This is what the alleged immaterialism of Berkeley generally means. But again the position is not as straightforward or simple as a facile *a priori* classification would require. In the first place, to be mental is not the same as being mind dependent. Colours and sounds are certainly not, for Berkeley, modes or states of our own minds; and the way in which the order of nature depends for its being, in the last resort, on being in the mind of God leaves it very open indeed just how it exists for God and what such a relationship means. Above all, we find in Berkeley's general account of perception the lead into some of the main considerations which induce us to regard each individual as being, in the first instance and *qua* finite being, a world of his own, although of course without being a prisoner in it cut off from all communication. I shall find occasion to stress this again and return with considerable interest to these features of Berkeley's philosophy which so much favour the notion of the distinctness of persons. Consider also the importance Berkeley ascribes to the different ways in which minds and external objects are known. The latter are known in being perceived, the former through 'notions'; and this involves also for Berkeley a peculiar and very ultimate indivisibility of individual minds. How then does the philosopher travel if he takes his start from Berkeley? Is he to find himself with G. F. Stout who, relying much on Berkeley, arrived at the view that finite minds are limitations of one universal mind, or is he to stress the distinctness and indivisibility of finite minds as his ruling conception? Here again we find a situation too rich and complex for neat generalization and admitting of further development in a variety of ways.

Where, finally, in our rigid classifications should Kant be placed? In some respects perhaps with mentalists and monists, although such appellations fit very ill indeed in his case. But we also recall the importance ascribed to the autonomy and freedom of our wills, the doctrine of the pure ego and the somewhat notorious bifurcation into phenomena and noumena from which some of the major difficulties in the Kantian system derive. Here again we need to be peculiarly wary of sharp classification, and I think we would find ourselves little better placed if we moved forward from these and kindred thinkers to more recent philosophers or traced our way back into earlier periods and the various cultures the world has seen. Even the predominant monism of Eastern systems of thought is by no means unrelieved or of a simple and uniform pattern.

But let us return to Passmore. What sort of monism does he defend, and how does this bear on the mind-body problem? Passmore begins by rejecting what he calls 'entity-monism', namely the view that 'there is only one entity' and that all that we regard as distinct things are appearances of this one entity. With this he contrasts 'existence-monism', making here a somewhat less familiar use of the term. This second type of monism is said to be 'difficult to define',[1] but the main point about it seems to be the assertion that 'there are not sorts, or levels, or orders of existence'.[2] There are many variations of this view, ranging, it is alleged, from Thales to Space-Time doctrines of today. It is by no means clear to me that all the theories envisaged have the aim mainly of showing that to exist is to be something or other, a quantity of water or to have a place in Space-Time. They might be merely holding that all that there is in fact, or all that there can be, is of a certain sort. This is not a view about existence as such, but about what there

[1,2] *Op. cit.*, p. 39.

happens, or has, to be, but we get a clearer view of what Passmore has in mind in his examples, namely phenomenalism, idealism, physicalism, naturalism or the merely 'implicit assumption, certainly widespread, that the traditional dichotomies of Mind and Body, God and Nature, are obviously untenable'.[1]

One had not thought the vogue of 'isms' to be very strong today. Have we not been at pains to rid our prospectuses of them? Was not that one of the good results of the hostility to metaphysics? Are there not features of all the famous 'isms' which are apt to be overlooked or distorted by the use of these blanket labels, and if one rejects some particular dichotomy is one bound *ipso facto* to line up in some general opposition to dichotomies as such? And how far is it true that there is a widespread assumption that the dichotomies instanced are untenable? The dichotomy of Mind and Body may be out for most influential philosophers in English-speaking countries, but it is not so obviously so elsewhere and it is making its way back among ourselves. The dichotomy of God and Nature is as firm as ever; indeed, whether one thinks of Biblical scholarship or theological doctrine or philosophy, few things have been more emphasized than the transcendence of God which requires the order of nature and all finite being to be very different from Him. Is not this one of the main features of the new Protestant theology and the renewal of Catholic theology as well? Is it not a prominent feature of the study of religions? Such emphasis may be misplaced, and the fashion may change again, but the present position shows very clearly how dangerous it is to generalize and to link the fortunes of answers to very different sorts of questions together as closely as Passmore does and without greater heed to what they are specially concerned to do. Is not that also a reversal to the bad metaphysics which tries to fit everything into a preconceived framework?

It is, however, to dichotomies of the sort instanced that Passmore seems to take exception. His main concern seems to be to rule these out. How does he hope to achieve this? By the use of a further, very general and, it seems to me, very tenuous argument. The dichotomies are all, irrespective of any specific considerations that suggest them, doomed from the outset because they are bound to fall foul of 'the Humpty Dumpty argument' which 'philosophers', we are told, 'have come to accept as unanswerable'. This argument is 'that once we break up any system in a certain

[1] *Op. cit.*, p. 40.

kind of way, it becomes quite impossible to put the pieces together again in a single situation: and yet, unless they can be so put together, the whole point of the breaking-up is lost'.[1] I have little notion of what philosophers could be listed as subscribing to this argument. But let us consider how, according to Passmore, the argument operates.

This is not an easy undertaking. For when we have reached this point we find that most of the remainder of the chapter is taken up with familiar difficulties in Plato's views about forms and particulars. If forms and particulars stand in some relation, participation or whatever it may be, how could this ever be known? It could not be known from the side of the forms themselves, for here all we deal with is absolute perfection and strict knowledge. On the side of particulars we seem limited to the particulars and to mere belief about them; and no way of bridging the gulf seems possible. If there is a mind—'let us call it God'—in the world of eternal objects it can know nothing of particulars. A mind which is part of the world of change can never get beyond particulars. On neither side can anything be known of participation. 'So the theory of forms leads to consequences which are incompatible with its *raison d'etre* as a theory.'[2]

This may be a fair account of a problem which lies at the centre of Plato's philosophy. No doubt there remains room for much dispute as to what precisely Plato meant by participation or imitation, and scholars will continue the debate on this and related topics. I should think that good note should be taken also of Plato's own consciousness of the quandary in which he was placed, of the protest into which he sometimes bursts against the remoteness and aridity of his own account of true reality as the world of forms, as in the warm insistence of the *Sophist* that there must be place in that which is perfectly real for 'change, life, soul',[3] and of the part played in the inter-relationships of being and becoming by *dunamis*, a Platonic conception whose lack of permanent place in the dialogues should not deprive it of its importance both as a key to Plato's thought and as a notion of the utmost importance for thought and culture at the present day. But these are not matters to be pursued closely here, they would take us far afield and keep us from our main topic. Let it be allowed then that

[1] *Op. cit.*, p. 40.
[2] *Op. cit.*, p. 42.
[3] *Sophist*, 248E.

the way Plato generally thinks of forms and of the contrasted world of becoming and particulars leaves us with no way in which there can be knowledge of the relation alleged to hold between them, grant to Professor Passmore, albeit somewhat reluctantly, all he claims on this score; what follows?

What follows is much less dramatic and inhibiting than Passmore supposes. For, in the first place, even if Plato provided no hint of a remedy himself, it would not seem particularly hard to see the lines along which it may be provided. For it has often been pointed out that Plato does grave injustice to what he himself tells us about reason when he supposes that the whole world of particulars, including our own appetites, is altogether a world apart from the reason by which they should be governed. The exercise of reason is involved in all knowledge of events, in our own lives and in the world around us, and we do ill to neglect the way reason permeates and transforms our own appetites, even the meanest. How much Plato's thought suffers from neglect of this point is well-known. But it might be replied that, with this correction, Professor Passmore's point is conceded. For we have no longer the bifurcation into two worlds or orders of being. That is not, however, quite the case, for there are radical distinctions still to be drawn, between universals, however conceived, and particulars, and between minds and the world of nature. We do not, in short, in rejecting or correcting a particular dichotomy dispose of all radical dichotomies, like those between God and Nature, Mind and Body—these must be considered on their merits.

At this point Professor Passmore interposes a brief comment on Berkeley. He has also apparently lapsed in the same way as Plato in his distinction between the way we know minds by means of notions and objects by perceptions. For this leaves open the question how this principle itself is known. It is not perception and it is not a knowledge of minds. This seems to me again to be a most unreal difficulty. We all know how Berkeley goes to work and what sort of considerations induced him to think, rightly or wrongly, that objects depend on being perceived. The fact that we know objects by perception and minds by notions does not in the least imply that minds must be empty of all except thought about themselves. Our thoughts have a content and there is nothing to preclude this from including reflections about what we find the world of nature to be like such as might lead to Berkeley's theory.

Passmore continues by insisting that not only is it impossible to know the relation between forms and particulars, but that there cannot be such a relation. For if the forms are required in any way to make the particulars what they are, they must somehow become particular themselves and their role in any other way is rendered useless. This again depends on how the alleged 'eternity' of forms is understood, it does not rid us of a genuine problem of universals and particulars; it simply makes more than is warranted of a peculiar Platonic problem. The same is true when the soul is found to be, for Plato, not among other things in the world of becoming and yet not itself a form. This is a problem for Plato but not for other ways of distinguishing sharply between the soul and its physical environment.

Passmore seems to me to press his case with peculiar desperation when he next cites the example of Butler's principle of self-love taken to be a means of mediating between reason and passion. Are we to suppose that Butler himself thought of the matter in this way? It would not be easy to prove that. But if the problem is the general one of how reason can affect practice or desire, is it not enough to note that what we want alters with better understanding of the situation? There is nothing odd about this, but it certainly does not follow that there is no sharp division between reason and desire or will. There may have been faults in the faculty-psychology which tended to hypostatize our powers, but that we function in very different ways seems beyond dispute. We do not dispose of an activity of willing by our refusal to think of the will as some detachable instrument by which the willing is done.

We come next to a very short way for the disposal of the problem of the natural and the supernatural, namely the repudiation of any possible transaction between them. The supernatural cannot affect the natural order, even in the way of creation, without itself being involved in the natural order. Creation is itself an act involving some kind of temporal particularity. This difficulty is pressed as if it had been little thought of before. Yet Professor Passmore must know that religious thinkers have at most times been acutely conscious of it. They have often met it, today as in the past, by stressing the mysterious nature of the relation of transcendent being to finite being. We know, it is argued, that God must be, but involved in this very knowledge is the awareness that we cannot know what it is to be God or how the world depends on God, the relation being in all respects different from what we understand a relation of one limited being to be to another. Creation does not, therefore, stand comparison with any finite enactment. Nor does any further knowledge of God, whether it be thought to come by analogy or by discernment of some other way in which God makes Himself known within the world, require any surmounting of our finite nature. There are well-known difficulties in such views, not least that of retaining the meaningfulness of notions which have always to be taken beyond their ordinary context or, in the term made familiar of late, 'habitat'. Passmore notes such difficulties, but he says nothing of the ways various thinkers have claimed, some very shrewdly of late, that they can be surmounted. The only thinkers he notes, and that very slightly, are those who afford most grist to his mill.

One of these is Caird who, as a typical idealist, would wish to bring all under the aegis of a reason not essentially dissimilar to our own and who could thus have no room for the sort of trans-cendence which most religious thinkers of today would posit and in terms of which they would hope to deal with the sort of problem Passmore has in mind. Another is Tillich who rightly objects to the sort of supernaturalism which is too closely modelled on natural process but leaves it extremely obscure what he would substitute for it, as Professor Paul Edwards has made particularly plain.[1] The notion of some intermediary, of creatures of a 'plastic nature', 'half-supernatural, half-natural' is also held, very properly, to be quite inadequate, for they 'either break down the gap they are supposed to bridge, or else they remain on one side or the other of it and so fail to bridge it'.[2]

My own complaint is that Passmore remains obdurately unwilling to turn his attention to the powerful thought, of today as of the past, which claims to have a way out of the dilemma in which he would hold us. Nor does it seem reasonable to speak with such boldness in a very brief compass about matters which have so much exercised the minds of some very able thinkers and to dis-miss, as one item among many others, the idea of supernatural being which is surely a major problem in itself and one least likely to be amenable to the application of a general technique taken to be a solvent of many problems at once. In the absence of patient discussion which takes proper heed of the most cautious and highly regarded discussion of the question, one can only conclude

[1] 'Professor Tillich's Confusions' *Mind* April 1965.
[2] *Op. cit.*, p. 52.

that one is being offered a preconceived dogma as a substitute for careful philosophical reasoning.

This is the impression which is confirmed for us when the discussion comes to its climax with an application of the main theme to our present problem of mind and body. The only consideration of substance adduced is a reiteration of one of the main points made by Professor Ryle, namely that if mind and body are thought to be altogether different, no account can be given of any transactions between them. Passmore takes the case a little further than Ryle, at least to the extent of presenting it as an example of a general principle which rules out the possibility of interaction from the start in common with all similar dichotomies. Ryle seemed mainly concerned to challenge us to say something about the alleged transactions and to complain of our reluctance to do so. But he does have also the infinite regress argument, and what Passmore seems to do is to push this a little further and present it in more general terms.

He tells us, in the first place, that the argument against interaction is a 'classical case of the two-world argument'.[1] But he insists that the difficulty, for the interactionist, arises, not just from the fact that mental acts and physical processes are different, but from their being given a different ontological status. This seems to take care of the objection that cause and effect are in any case often different—a lighted match, for example, and the subsequent explosion. But how then does the difference of ontological status affect the issue? It does so in two ways, as in the other examples. In the first place, it leaves us no way of knowing that any transactions between the two series of events had occurred— 'if we suppose that the mental life is known in one way and the physical in another, it will be impossible to give any account of our knowledge of the transactions between the two lives'.[2] But this of course presupposes that there are such transactions. If I am right in what I have maintained earlier, all that we need affirm is that physical changes supervene upon mental ones and vice versa. How this comes about we do not know, and we may never be able to, we find that it happens and we cannot rule out the obvious facts of experience on the basis of an *a priori* dogma—we must rather question the dogma. But even if there were, or if, for some strange reason, there had to be, some transactions or kindred

[1] *Op. cit.*, p. 52.
[2] *Op. cit.*, p. 54.

mediation between mental and physical events, there is no reason why these could not be known, unless we make the strange assumption that all knowledge must be knowledge of minds by minds.

But it is his second point that Passmore seems most concerned to press, the 'ontological' question as he puts it. But this I find it very hard to lay hold upon properly. We are told, most disarmingly, that 'if interactionism is simply the view that the mental can affect the non-mental—that, for example, if I am worried about something, this can affect my digestion—then it is obviously true'.[1] But this is what interactionism does mean, except that immediate effects, like my arm moving when I will it to do so, would be a better example. Passmore, however, adds that what goes wrong is the positing of 'an ontological gap between the mental and the non-mental'. He is apparently prepared to distinguish between the mental and the non-mental, but he will not have them accorded what he calls very vaguely a different ontological status.

As far as I can glean, what he means is this. Minds, on the view he opposes, can only obey mental laws and bring about mental effects. Bodies obey physical laws and only affect bodies. How, then, can they ever affect one another? In the writer's own words: 'Then the difficulty can be put thus: it has to be granted that in some sense the mind influences the body and vice versa. But the only force the mind has at its disposal is spiritual force, the power of rational persuasion; and the only thing that can move it is a purpose. On the other side, a body has no force at its disposal except material force and nothing can influence it except mechanical pressure. This means that bodies cannot appeal to minds to act; they can only push; and minds cannot influence bodies by putting purposes before them, because bodies are not susceptible to this sort of influence.'[2] I do not know who is being criticized in this passage, but clearly not any normal interactionist position, for the whole point of the interactionist thesis is that minds, in addition to conducting their own mental processes in certain ways, have the further power of affecting physical things as well; and physical things affect bodies. It is no reasonable criticism of the interactionist to foist upon him an assumption so opposed to what he maintains that he is bound to be put out of court at the start.

The interactionist certainly stresses the difference between mind and body, he declares, for example, that mental processes occupy no part of space. But there is no reason why this should commit

[1, 2] *Op. cit.*, p. 55.

him to so isolate mind and body that they can never meet. His main claim is that in fact they do meet, although he may not know further how this comes about. If the interactionist thesis cannot be stated without some assumption which undermines it, then this must be shown. And I fear that Professor Passmore has done nothing to show it. He has just clothed his antipathy to interaction in a dogma which he does little to justify.

The failure of Passmore to grasp just what the interactionist view involves comes out especially in the importance which he thinks the advocate of such a view must ascribe to the postulating of some further mediating entity, like, so it is suggested, the 'animal spirits' of Descartes. I am not at all convinced that Descartes in fact did invoke 'animal spirits' as a way of coping with any difficulties with which he thought his theory of interaction was fraught. He was curious, quite properly and understandably, about the way changes of a certain kind were relayed through our bodies, and, in the absence of the sounder and completer physiological knowledge of a later day, he put forward a guess which, for his time, is not particularly absurd. No evidence supports it and we reject it outright. But nothing in the dualism of Descartes calls for it, nor is it evident that Descartes thought so. The importance of this curious notion is, on the contrary, misplaced by Passmore and others who so construe the interactionist thesis as to imply that it needs some desperate rescue work by the invocation of some mediating entity.

If 'animal spirits' had the function Passmore supposes, it is plain that they could not fulfil it; for we could not think of them as anything other than either physical, presumably this, or mental; and whichever we said it was, the original difficulty, if genuine, would reappear. But the futility of the alleged rescue work ought in that case to make us more cautious in supposing that it was ever thought necessary. My impression is that Descartes found the interactionist thesis so obviously true as an account of common experience that it never occurred to him that it would require the salvage work in question—or any other.

It does not seem to me, therefore, that Professor Passmore has justified his claim that philosophy can 'show, by its own peculiar arguments', 'that dualism is untenable'.[1] On the contrary, what he seems to do is to take a questionable argument of Professor Ryle, committing the dualist to certain mysterious transactions,

[1] *Op. cit.*, p. 57.

and expand it, via a peculiar problem in Platonic philosophy, to the dimensions of a general situation in which all manner of philosophical views, including dualism of mind and body, are caught. But there is little of substance in this procedure beyond the dogmatic acceptance of the initial difficulty which can itself be shown to depend on a serious misunderstanding.

CHAPTER VI

DREAMING AND EXPERIENCE

Mention has already been made of certain types of experience which make it exceptionally hard to deny that there is some internal or private character of mental life. Such are hallucinations, having mental images and dreams. These are not, as was also stressed, the matters we should have mostly in mind in examining the basic issues in the philosophy of mind, and excessive attention to them might give us a distorted impression of the main issues. They do, however, have particular relevance to questions of interiority, and it is thus not surprising that those who are most eager to rebut any kind of dualism of mind and body should sometimes take the very bold course of denying that the phenomena instanced should be thought to constitute any kind of experience. Intimations of this in the cases of Ryle and Hampshire have already been given, and I shall not comment further now on what they have to say on the subject. But the outstanding recent example of the procedure in question is that of Professor Norman Malcolm in his ingenious and arresting account of dreams, in his book *Dreaming*. He takes his start more directly from Ludwig Wittgenstein whom he knew well and about whom he wrote a most illuminating book. But we could hardly find a better example of the desperation and strained ingenuity to which philosophers are driven, in dealing with topics like dreams, once they embark on the repudiation of all inner experience of which Ryle's work is the standard and most comprehensive example. Let us then pause to consider how Malcolm deals with the subject of dreams.

It should first be made clear that Malcolm has no intention of denying that we do dream. He is himself most explicit on this point; we must certainly say that we do dream. Indeed, that is for him the starting point of all sound philosophical thinking about dreams. We should begin with the fact that we 'tell' dreams, and we ought never to wander very far from this in any reflection on the subject. The direction and limit of our thought about dreams is set by the fact that we tell them.

But having a dream is not the same as telling it. What then is it to have the dream which in due course we tell? Not, it seems, having 'an inward state or process of the soul'.[1] There is no time during which we are dreaming, there is no sort of occurrence or process through which we pass while we are asleep and in which the dream consists, nothing happens which could be described as a dream. In one sense of course this is true and beyond all dispute. If I dream that I am swimming in the lake I know when I awake that none of this happened, my body is not wet and has not, in fact, been anywhere near the lake. I have not had my bathing suit on, none of this happened. Admittedly, but we usually suppose that during the dream I did have an experience similar to bathing in the lake and that I passed through a period, while still asleep, when I was myself convinced that I was bathing. This is how most philosophers and ordinary people have thought about the matter, and Malcolm lists a number of philosophers of today and of the past who have thought of dreams in just these terms. He is very frank about this at the outset. But this is also the point which he most wishes to challenge, and this is what makes his theory at least a very original one.

We must be careful, however, not to identify Malcolm's position with that of writers who identify the dream with certain impressions we have on awakening. These are certainly important for Malcolm's thesis, though not quite as basic as the fact that we tell our dreams. But the dream itself is not some impressions I have the moment I awake and which I soon discover to be quite contrary to the facts. 'The dream and the waking conviction', Malcolm firmly declares, 'are not one and the same thing',[2] a dream is not some curious and quite unfounded 'remembering' that we dream. It is something other than the waking conviction, but it is not, on the other hand, anything that happens to us or takes place in any sense while we are asleep.

This is a very perplexing position. Perhaps our best course will be to indicate first what reasons Malcolm has which so strongly induce him to deny that dreaming is in any sense a process and which thus lead him to what seems at least to be a very paradoxical position strangely at odds with what we all commonly assume.

The main objection to the view that when we dream we are having some kind of experience is that if this were the case there could be no means by which it could be known. No outside observation will confirm what is purported to be happening in a dream.

[1] *Op. cit.*, p. 54.
[2] *Op. cit.*, p. 59.

For no one could know the dream except from within it, and no one could report the dream at the time it is happening; for if he could that would prove that he was awake. The report of the dreamer himself will not help, for there can be 'no possible verification of his claim'.[1] Once he is awake, the dreamer is in no better case, so it is alleged, respecting his dream than anyone else; he shares the general predicament, as there is no way of linking the dream reliably with waking experience, the two never intersect.

In pressing these claims Malcolm makes much of the fact that no one can significantly say that he is asleep. It would be contradictory to affirm that one is asleep, for in making such an affirmation one betrays an awareness of other people which is not consistent with what we mean by being asleep. If I tell someone that I am asleep this will at once be taken to be a statement made in jest and not in earnest. This does not imply that the words 'I am asleep' could not come from the lips of a sleeping person, but if that happened the words could not be taken as an attempt of the sleeping person to inform someone in his neighbourhood that he was asleep. For anyone who set out to communicate in that way would plainly be awake.

A comparison is made here with the words 'I am dead'. For if anyone were to tell me that he is dead, that would be as good evidence as one could want of his being alive. I am not sure, however, that the comparison holds throughout. For the assertion 'I am dead' does not appear to be inherently absurd in quite the same way as the assertion 'I am asleep'. This is because we can conceive of situations in which it would not be contradictory to say 'I am dead'. If someone had survived his death he could, in principle and presumably in fact, communicate this to another departed spirit. He could also in principle communicate this to the living, whether or not there are in fact insuperable barriers to this in practice. 'I am dead' is only absurd when the assertion is made in circumstances which make it very plain that I am still alive, as when I appear and speak with my present body. But if we are able to communicate in any sort of way in a dream with other genuine persons this would appear to contradict altogether what we understand by being asleep and dreaming.

It seems then that no one can significantly say to another person that he is himself dreaming. But might he not believe this or say it to himself? Malcolm thinks this also is impossible. But he thinks so on grounds that seem to me very inadequate. The first of these is that 'there is something dubious in the assumption that there can be a true judgment that cannot be communicated to others'.[1] This would, of course, be true if we were thinking of some alleged judgment which in principle could not be communicated. But there are many judgments which in fact we are unable to communicate at the time we make them. If I am bound and gagged I cannot inform anyone that the house is being burgled. I know what is happening but I cannot tell anyone. The same would be true if I were struck with paralysis, I might know of something that needed to be done urgently—about my will perhaps—and yet die without being able to tell anyone about it; I might be in pain and not be able to say where it hurts. The same would hold even if I were in full possession of my faculties but among people whose language I did not know—there is a limit to what one can communicate without words.[2] And what about infants? They must surely make many judgments of some sort before they can speak (or understand speech), and some of these they might well be unable to communicate in any way. In most cases, when I am unable to communicate at a particular time, I can easily do so later—when the gag is removed or my health is restored, and so on. A dream seems plainly to be in the latter class. I cannot tell it at the time, but there is nothing to preclude my telling it later; indeed it is, as I have noted, to the telling of dreams that Malcolm himself attaches most importance.

One could, moreover, be addressing oneself to someone in the dream itself. In fact we very often do so. The recipient of my confidence is not in such a case a real person. I am not strictly speaking telling anyone anything. But does this make a difference? In my dream I am convinced that there are other people about, and I am doing all that I would normally do in communicating with them. This seems to be all that is needed, even on Malcolm's own assumptions, to make the judging a fully meaningful process for me.

There seems, therefore, to be very little substance in this first

---

[1] *Op. cit.*, p. 9.

[2] The late Professor Alexander Macbeath had a horrifying story of such an experience as a prisoner in a Turkish hospital. He knew, from a previous illness, that his dangerously high temperature was not due to the wounded leg which the doctors felt, in the circumstances, they must amputate. After much torment of mind he managed, with typical resourcefulness and determination, to struggle out of bed to get at a drug that brought down his temperature and saved his leg. But I gather that it was a near thing. (I hope I remember the story correctly from his telling it.)

argument of Malcolm's, and it is not strange that he tells us that he 'will not pursue this problem'.[1] He turns instead to what he presumably takes to be a weightier consideration, namely 'whether it can be verified that someone *understands* how to use the sentence "I am asleep" to describe his own state'.[2] The normal test would be, it is urged, that a person sometimes utters a sentence describing a state of affairs when that state of affairs does exist, and the negation of it at other times. But we can never do this for dreams, as we can never know that the person is making the judgment while he is asleep. If he himself told us he would obviously be awake; we cannot know what a person is dreaming at the time he is dreaming, he alone is aware of that. But can he not tell us when he awakes? Apparently not, but why this should be is not altogether clear. The main consideration seems to be that if anyone were to tell us after he awakes that something occurred to him while he was asleep he must have known that he was asleep while it was occurring; 'his claim that he said certain words *while asleep*, implies that he was *aware* of being asleep',[3] and this holds apparently even when the words are said to oneself. But on this two comments may be made.

In the first place, there appears to be no reason why we should not undergo a certain experience and only realize that it is happening to us in a dream after we awake. This is how we normally think of the matter. I dream that I am swimming in the pond. At the time I am certainly convinced that this is the case. I am quite convinced that I am swimming, and give that matter no further thought. This is partly what we mean when we say that certain dreams were very vivid, they hold us in their grip, and we would not be so terror-stricken during a nightmare did we not take all that seems to happen with the utmost seriousness; it is not, as a rule at least, like watching a horror-film which we know full well is nothing but a film. We do not normally doubt that what seems to happen in a dream is actually taking place. But this does not preclude us from realizing, the moment we awake, that it was only a dream. We awake and find ourselves in our familiar surroundings where we expect to be in the light of what we recall about the past. The realization would not, presumably, be so immediate had we not already had many similar experiences, and we recognize the mark of the familiar experience of dreaming the moment we are sufficiently awake to put it in its context against the world of waking consciousness. How more precisely this comes about, and what are all the processes involved in it, does not matter for us now—it is a subject in itself. All we need note is that it seems to be a fact of common experience that, when we dream, we do not normally believe that we are dreaming and that when we awake we realize that what went on only went on in a dream.

The only point made against this by Malcolm, as far as I can see, is that if a person says certain words to himself while asleep we have no means of testing whether he understood these words, for the test depends on his using them in the proper context. But we can know from a man's ordinary behaviour that he knows how certain words are used, and if he assures us that he said certain things to himself, or just thought them, on some past occasion we can quite properly take his word for it, if we have reason to think him an honest person and so on. Even if, in principle, we cannot test his claim at the time, there is nothing absurd in taking the claim seriously if we have good reason to suppose, from other occasions, that the person himself understands it.

It does not seem, therefore, that any case has been made, or can be made, for the general insistence that, to be able to give an account, on awaking, of certain things that went on in our private experience while asleep, we would have to be aware at the time that we were asleep.

But, secondly, there appear to be some cases when people are aware that they are dreaming. This is obviously unusual, as already stressed. But it seems to happen.[1] Perhaps we should note first the cases when we are awake but begin to wonder, from the strange turn of events, whether we may not in fact be dreaming. Malcolm anticipates this and he observes,[2] quite properly, that, when we use such words as 'I thought I must be dreaming', we are not implying that we are seriously wondering whether we were asleep. We are expressing surprise or bewilderment or exclaiming at the oddity of our situation. This is, no doubt, generally true, but is it true in all cases? May not the strange or unexpected character of some events induce us to wonder seriously whether we may not be dreaming? It is certainly said that this does sometimes happen, and would not this situation be like, in the relevant respects, the

---

[1] *Cf.* the account of 'lucid dreams' in C. D. Broad's *Lectures on Psychical Research*, chap. IV.

[2] *Op. cit.*, p. 21.

one in which a dreamer might consider whether or not he is dreaming? But, in addition, the claim is made, on occasion, that some person did in fact believe or realize in the course of a dream that he was dreaming, and even if we said that, in such case, he only dreamt that he was dreaming, this still leaves it possible for someone who is asleep to entertain at the time the thought that he is asleep. There are, in particular, the quite familiar experiences of slowly emerging from a dream. The dream, in such cases, seems to persist in our waking state, it has us in its grip; and, if we enjoy it we may try to perpetuate it or even to work our way back into it as some people claim they are able to do. Now it could be argued that we are in such cases strictly awake and merely under the influence of the dream, we have unusually vivid waking impressions. But is there all that difference? Can we hold, as presumably Malcolm would have to hold, that there is a precise point at which we no longer speak of dreaming but of being awake? That seems highly implausible, and if we cannot take such a course, and take it, *mutatis mutandis*, of the case of passing from a reverie into a dream, then there seem to be cases when we are dreaming and also aware that we are dreaming.

The last points are noted here as part of the rebuttal of Malcolm's specific argument that to claim we have had some experience while asleep we would have to be aware, *per impossibile* it is alleged, that we were asleep at the time. But they can also be made the basis of a more positive frontal attack. For it seems evident that Malcolm's position requires us to draw a peculiarly sharp distinction between waking and dreaming such that one is a process or experience and the other not at all so. Do not the processes of gradually falling asleep and of slowly pulling ourselves awake again make such a radical bifurcation extremely implausible? Can we, in the light of such experiences, deny the continuity, in many respects, of a dream state proper and the beginning of a state of being awake? We can, if we like, pedantically insist, in the interest of a theory, that dreaming is one thing, waking another, and that there must be some precise point where experience or process begins after sleep in which there is no mental occurrence at all. But we can only do so by going so sharply against what seem to be familiar incontrovertible facts that only the most overwhelming arguments could justify us. But if I am right there is very little substance in the strained arguments by which Malcolm seeks to buttress an otherwise impossible position.

It might be contended at this point, in defence of Malcolm, that what he wants seriously to argue is, not that it is impossible to claim that we had some experience while asleep without being aware at the time that we were asleep, but merely that we could not say, even to ourselves, that we were asleep. But in fact Malcolm does rely on the sort of tortuous argument I have noted, he seems to feel that it is not enough for him to claim that it is self-evidently contradictory for someone to say to himself 'I am asleep'. He puts his trust in the more general arguments which I have noted and tried to counter.

The truth, in fact, seems to be that it is odd to the point of self-contradiction in normal contexts for anyone to say that he is asleep and Malcolm draws upon this, in the course of a very terse statement of his view, to invest the more elaborate arguments by which he tries to buttress his position with an obviousness which they do not properly have, but only borrow from the absurdity of claiming in any normal situation that one is asleep.

This becomes plainer when we consider what the link might be between the insistence, as a main basis for further contentions, that it is absurd to claim to be asleep and the general conclusion that there can be no process or experience of dreaming. For what we find is, not that the latter conclusion is deduced from the absurdity of saying that one is asleep, but rather that the alleged absurdity here is set before us as one striking exhibition of an absurdity which is thought to characterize directly the possibility of making any kind of judgment, or having any other experience, while asleep. The difficulty in the case of saying that one is asleep is that it could not be verified without reference to behaviour which shows that a person is not asleep. But this, it is urged, 'would be so *whatever* the judgment was. . . . To verify that he was both asleep and making a judgment we would have to verify that he was both aware and not aware of saying certain words'.[1] 'It would be self-contradictory to verify that he had made *any* judgment while asleep. It is not that there is something unique about the fact of being asleep that keeps one from taking note of *that* fact while asleep.'[2] The absurdity is the same in all cases, and it turns on the fact that we could not obtain evidence of what is purported to be someone's experience while asleep without implying that he was awake, that is on the basis of utterances and behaviour of a person not asleep.

[1, 2] *Op. cit.*, p. 36.

Indeed, the argument holds, if at all, and is firmly alleged to hold, of all mental activities, perceiving, imagining, questioning and so on and 'for "passivities" like fear, anxiety, joy; illusions and hallucinations; and imagery'.[1] We cannot say that any of this happens in a dream, for we could not know that it happened without the response which implies that a person is awake.

The argument is, moreover, clearly firm if we are thinking of providing evidence that is adequate by itself to the outside observer. That kind of verification is ruled out. But what does this prove? As Malcolm himself puts it, 'it could be objected that my argument has shown merely that the *verification* that someone is both asleep and judging is self-contradictory, not that his *being* both asleep and judging is self-contradictory'. What, then, can we say of the latter, which is surely the crucial point? Only apparently that 'it is senseless in the sense that nothing can count in favour of either its truth or its falsity'.[2]

We are here at the crux of the matter. Is verification, in the sense that Malcolm has in mind the sole criterion? I am prepared to concede that if we had to rely on the sort of correlation by which we learn about events in the external world, that is, if no appeal is allowed to private experience and one's own recollections, we could never discover from external evidence alone that people had experiences of dreaming or that anyone was dreaming in the course of a particular sleep. For there is nothing, in the having of the dream itself, which could be linked at the time with any observable event. To that extent there is force in Malcolm's rejection of several cases that might be cited against him. Suppose, for example, someone said that he had some dream experience when it thundered. This would clearly not be right, for if he heard the thunder he was not fully asleep.[3] Suppose, again, someone says he had the sort of experience he only has when asleep; but how, on the present assumptions, could it ever be known that we have this or any other experience when asleep? Nor could we look for help to physiological phenomena. For we could only correlate these with the dream experiences if we had some other way of knowing in the first instance that the experience was occurring. On the whole, then, I grant Malcolm's main contentions here if the terms in which he frames the problem are sound.

[1] *Op. cit.*, p. 45.
[2] *Op. cit.*, p. 37.
[3] *Cf.* note p. 146.

The only point at which I would have a misgiving is this. Take the case of the person who looks frightened in his sleep or who, alternatively, has a beatific smile. We would be inclined to say that he is having a frightful or a very agreeable dream, as the case may be. We normally do this on the basis of what we know dreams generally to be like. But even if we never had dreams, or never remembered them, but came across a rare phenomenon of someone smiling sweetly in his sleep, would there not be a strong presumption, on the basis of what people look like and do when awake, for supposing that he was having a pleasant experience of some kind? Admittedly the inference would be weaker in this case, and we would have to allow for various physiological factors which might suffice to account for the smile. If it was an encounter with a creature from outer-space we might wonder whether smiles might not reflect something other than happiness in beings whose constitution and background might be very different from our own. In doing so we would have to ignore some inherent appropriateness and affinity which there seems to be between smiles and kindred expressions and what they convey to us. But for normal human beings there seems to be a fair presumption that, if people wear an expression during sleep which is akin to those which register certain experiences we have when awake, then they are having similar experiences. The agreeable dream experience sets in motion of its own accord, without our being aware of it or purposing it, the mechanism which produces the happy facial expression.

It is in the same way that we ascribe dream experiences, on occasion, to sub-human creatures. They do not tell their dreams, but when we observe the dog whining and twitching his feet in sleep we conclude very naturally that he is dreaming—and we even have a good guess what the dream is like, 'he is chasing rabbits again' we say. This might not be such an obvious conclusion to draw if we never had the experience of dreaming ourselves, although even then the solution might be suggested to us in the absence of any other sensible explanation of the dog's behaviour. But given our own experience of dreaming there seems to be nothing to hinder us from straightway ascribing a dream experience to the dog when he behaves in a certain way. This is undoubtedly the normal reaction, it is what most people think and say; and if they are right we seem to have here a substantial retraction of any concessions we may be disposed to make to Malcolm—the dream experience is known in this case from behaviour alone. The only reply which Malcolm himself makes is to say that when we say that the dog is dreaming 'This use of language is not quite serious',[1] we draw 'no practical consequences' from it. I do not know whether we do draw practical consequences in such a case. We might conclude of a rather over-sensitive pet that it was being over-indulged or given food or exercise that made it dream more than was good for it. But even if there were no practical consequences the statement would be quite serious in the sense that we meant what we said; and the failure of Malcolm to say more than he does on this point seems to me a serious indication of the weakness of his view.

There are cases, then, like nightmares, the happy smile, the motions of sleeping animals, when we do conclude, with obvious justification it seems to me, that dream experiences, and those the kind we may in some sort determine, are happening without having any report from the dreamer himself. I leave it open whether this would be possible if dreaming were not an experience familiar to all of us. I also allow that, in most cases, we have no adequate evidence of dreams apart from the subsequent testimony of the dreamer. The more sound and normal the sleep the less is there to indicate what, if anything, is occurring in the experience of the sleeper. We certainly cannot report our overt behaviour while asleep, for if we could we would be awake. Nor can we be aware of the world around us. This is the strength of Malcolm's position in the cases, like that of the clap of thunder while someone is asleep, which he himself discusses. In such cases, as Malcolm rightly insists, we have only the subsequent recollection of the dreamer. But will this not do?

This is a very vital question for the assessment of Malcolm's position, even if the reply to him does not turn solely on it. Malcolm rejects the appeal to one's own recollection, not in the sense that it is uncertain and not too reliable, but in principle. For all we have, he maintains, is the impression of the dreamer when he awakes, and how can we correlate this with what is alleged to have happened in a way of which no other record is available? However vivid the recollection it 'cannot be confirmed', it is 'theoretically undecidable'.[2] But just how strong is this point on which so much is made to rest? Can we put no credence in sheer recollection in

---

[1] *Op. cit.*, p. 62.
[2] *Op. cit.*, p. 40.

this matter? We certainly do so normally, we claim to remember what we dreamt and this is understood by most people to mean remembering some kind of experience they had, an experience in which certain things were happening which we now know did not happen in fact. Are we all hopelessly wrong in this and making a claim which is impossible in principle? If we are, then it seems to me that much weightier arguments need to be adduced to establish the point than the mere insistence that there can be no independent confirmation, which is all that Malcolm supplies.

There are, admittedly, very considerable problems about memory. Is it, in the last resort, inferential, or is it more direct? But such problems need not be considered now. They concern the general nature of memory, and, unless we are driven to the somewhat desperate view that our memories are wholly unreliable, there does not seem to be anything improper in claiming to remember what went on in a dream. After all, even if there is much in our ordinary memories that is confirmed and sustained by independent evidence, we do put the utmost reliance on memories of a very private character which do not differ very markedly from the memories we have of dreams. Suppose I sit in my chair thinking hard about some problem, or just lapse into a reverie (idly *dreaming* as we significantly say) about this or that, what evidence is there of what my thoughts have been like other than my own recollection? If I have been moving around or smoking my pipe, or have gone out to mow the lawn, there is the more tangible evidence of the changes so brought about, the empty pipe and the mown grass and so on. But even here there is little to show just what I was thinking about all the time. This is a matter of my own very clear memory, and if I am generally thought to be a sensible and honest person, no one would doubt that what I say does describe what the course of my thoughts were like at the time. Is there any difference of principle in the case of dreams? Admittedly they fade and we have only dim memories of them as a rule. But this is a practical, not a theoretical, difficulty. Is there anything in principle which precludes their being remembered? I can find no such difficulty that would not be part of the general problem of memory and the reliance we place upon it. Malcolm has certainly not adduced anything to support his case here, and he takes his stand on a dogmatic insistence on the sort of confirmation required by a highly questionable theory of truth and meaning which he does nothing to substantiate.

There is indeed one reference to the alleged 'remembering' of dreams, but only to assure us that this is 'a misuse of language'.[1] For 'when we think philosophically about memory' the paradigm case is that in which I do or say something and subsequently give an account of it which can be checked against the reports of other witnesses. But even if this is the normal situation we cannot make it legislative for all forms of memory or even take it to be straightway the essential guide to what memory as such is like and how it is warranted. One would have thought that the appeal to the paradigm case, most of all in the present very restricted and dogmatic form, had already been blown upon so much by the time Malcolm (in 1959) published his book as not to be invoked so naïvely without further argument.

At this point my criticism of Malcolm may be given a more positive turn. We have seen that he does not wish to equate a dream with the waking impressions of the dreamer. I tell the dream on the basis of these impressions, and in some way, one gathers, the telling is more fundamental, for understanding what it is to dream, than the impression. But what then is the dream itself? It is not the waking impression or the 'telling', although 'not logically independent' of these. This means, it appears, that there could not be dreams without the waking impressions, a view that is much opposed to what layman and expert generally believe in supposing that we may dream a good deal without having any remembrance of it afterwards. On the other hand, dreams and waking impressions are 'two different things';[2] we are very firmly told this, and Malcolm seems to be taking some pride in conforming here to what we normally think and say. The dream is not the telling, but something that we do tell, and it seems quite in order to say that we had a dream and so on—'people really do have dreams—which is undeniable'.[3] 'The dream and the waking conviction are not one and the same thing.'[4] But neither is the dream anything that happens while we are asleep or some experience we have. It has no duration. This is the main theme of the book, and when we recall this the question becomes very insistent indeed— just then what is a dream, what status do we accord it?

To this question there is no serious reply, but only a very tantalizing evasion. In a most disconcerting way Malcolm declares:

[1] *Op. cit.*, p. 56.
[2] *Op. cit.*, p. 60.
[3] *Op. cit.*, p. 58.
[4] *Op. cit.*, p. 59.

'Indeed I am not trying to say what dreaming *is:* I do not understand what it would mean to do that.'[1] In support of this line of
retreat there is invoked the celebrated wisdom of Wittgenstein
when he remarked in a lecture 'that it is an important thing in
philosophy to know when to *stop*'.[2] There is undoubtedly wisdom
in this observation, although why it should be specifically credited
to Wittgenstein when so many have said it as effectively before
him is hard to understand. There is, as Malcolm notes in words
made very familiar in philosophical writings somewhat alien to the
taste of Wittgenstein's followers, 'something given'. There are
points beyond which further philosophical arguments are not
possible, as in the claim, for example, that we know some things by
intuition. We certainly must stop somewhere, and it is part of the
wisdom of a good philosopher that he knows where argument is
possible and where it is not, and knows thus when to stop. But it
does not seem to me that Malcolm has reached such a point in the
present context. If a dream is neither the telling (and related
impressions) nor any kind of previous experience, the situation
cries out for some answer to the question—just what is a dream?
It must have some status, and one cannot, alas, avoid the conclusion that Malcolm has decided to stop, not where the logic of the
situation requires him but where it best suits his own argument.

There are many further ways in this very short study where the
strains to which the position as a whole is subjected, and the
lengths to which the author in desperation has to go, become very
apparent. We have already found it queried whether we should
ever say that dogs are dreaming or that people who struggle or cry
out in a nightmare are really asleep. In the same context it is
urged that, when we say of someone who smiles in his sleep that
he is dreaming about his sweetheart, we are either 'using his
behaviour as our *criterion* that he is dreaming or else as *evidence*
that he will be able to relate a dream',[3] some kind of prediction.
But what is involved in the former case? We are not told, for 'our
words', it is added, 'do not fall definitely into either alternative, and
indeed have no clear sense'.[4] In the same vein it is urged that it is
improper to say of someone that he is walking in his sleep,[5] for
this is very far removed from the paradigm case of sleeping where
the body is quite inert. Nor is a person in a hypnotic trance asleep,

[1] *Op. cit.* p. 59.
[2] *Op. cit.*, p. 87.
[3], [4] *Op. cit.*, p. 62.
[5] *Op. cit.*, p. 27.

for he responds to commands and suggestions.[1] This is indeed a short way with dissenters. A man in such a trance is lost to the world in all ordinary senses, he knows nothing of his environment by perception or in any kindred way; and while the phenomenon is indeed peculiar and baffling in many respects, it does mean that a person is cut off from ordinary contacts and awareness and also subject to certain physical conditions in the way we have mainly in mind when we say that someone is asleep. It is a very desperate course indeed to refuse to place this phenomenon more in the class of being asleep than of being awake. If it is sleep it presents Malcolm with a very hard case, as he is of course well aware in casting doubt upon it.

What Malcolm says about being 'sound asleep' should also be noted. He points out quite correctly that when we speak of 'a sound sleep' we are, mainly at least, thinking of how refreshed we are after and so on. We also, it is urged, use the words 'sound asleep' to indicate how certain we are that a person is sleeping, he is quite inert and so on. We also use the word 'asleep' in a dispositional way—he is asleep in his study in the afternoon; such a person may be dozing or even quite awake at times during such periods, as a man 'sawing wood' may be just mopping his brow. But it does not follow that we may not speak of a light or restless and a deep or sound sleep. What Malcolm says about this is that a person may be in one respect asleep, in another not, as one might say that one's leg is still sensitive but one's toe numb. But sleep is a more pervasive state than this. One could not be wide awake in one regard, fast asleep in another, and this shows again how we may be doing or thinking certain things *in* our sleep. A light sleep is not merely one from which a person is easily awakened but also one in which we presume there is much mental activity, not altogether precluded of course in sound sleep.

It is significant also that the meaning which Malcolm is prepared to give to the word 'asleep' is taken solely from physical conditions, it is 'not guided', he tells us, 'by any consideration of what is going on in someone's cranium, spinal column or other inward parts, but rather by how his body is disposed and by his behaviour or lack of it'.[2] The contrast is of course misleading. For the question is not whether something goes on in one's cranium over and above the visible disposition of one's body but whether something

[1] *Op. cit.*, p. 28.
[2] *Op. cit.*, p. 22.

goes on in a wholly non-physical way. And it seems to me that when we use the word 'asleep' what we have mainly in mind is the diminution or the total suspension of the state of consciousness we are in when awake. The physical inertness is our obvious clue to this as a rule, and when we see someone in that state we are quite happy to say at once that he is fast asleep—we are rarely mistaken. But what we mean is not just that his body is inert in a recumbent position and so on; we take this to be a reason for supposing that ordinary processes of thought are suspended; we think of being asleep by contrast with the sort of consciousness we have when awake. But in that case, that is if the state of being asleep is not described exhaustively in physical terms, we are not precluded from supposing that it can involve consciousness or experience of *some* sort.

It is commonly assumed by psychologists today that they can learn a good deal about the times and occasions when we are in fact dreaming. This is not, in the first place, due to the probings of the psycho-analyst, startling and significant though some of his disclosures may be. For these depend on what we say or do in moments of waking consciousness. Malcolm need not be all that perturbed by them and should not find it hard to fit them into the pattern of his general thesis. They would not lose their significance if no reference were made beyond waking impressions, they could still tell us a great deal about dispositional tendencies and some remote or forgotten occurrence which may have shaped these. But the position is not so simple in other ways. We have already seen that it is not unreasonable to suppose that certain expressions and other dispositions of our bodies could be taken to give some indication at the time of the course of our dreams, not perhaps to warrant seriously so precise an affirmation as that someone is dreaming of his sweetheart, but at least enough for us to say that it is a happy dream. But some experimental psychologists go much further than this today. They claim to know much more precisely when we are dreaming and when our dreams are more lively. They do this on the basis of certain physical conditions. I am not concerned here with the details of what is thought to be established in this way or the full interpretation of the available data. Different interpretations are in fact offered by different investigators, especially about the nature and extent of mental activity in the deepest states of sleep. It is the question of principle that concerns us.

How then, it may be asked, is the correlation with physical conditions established in the first place? How do we know that there is dreaming when certain states of the body are noted? No testimony can come from within the dream itself, and mere behaviour in restless sleep can hardly take us very far along the road of scientific precision here. The technique apparently is to awake the sleeper and record his immediate report of whether he was dreaming. States of the body are noted at the same time, and in this way correlations, involving especially certain movements of the eyes, are established in an initial way which prepares for further more elaborate experiments. This seems beyond objection provided the first links are sound. Further developments are possible in principle in various ways once the first obstacles are overcome, whatever the difficulties and limitations may be in practice. But what of the initial moves?

Malcolm would clearly have to repudiate these, and he expressly does so. This sets him at odds, not only with common sense or lay opinion, but also with a substantial body of scientific opinion and highly regarded scientific procedures. Psychologists do undoubtedly claim to discover much about the duration of dreams and about their physiological correlates in the ways indicated, as Malcolm is well aware. We cannot of course straightway summon the scientist to witness against the philosopher. The scientist may be confused or misguided in conducting his experiments or he may, through some error which the philosopher can correct, be taking a wrong view of the significance of what he discovers. That, it appears, is what Malcolm does say here. He insists that we do dream and that rapid eye movements and so on do 'stand in interesting empirical correlations with dreaming',[1] but they do not afford a criterion of dreaming or any indication of duration. This is because the idea of duration just 'does not belong to the common concept of dreaming at all',[2] there is no 'provision' for it, and there can, therefore, be no correlations with it. The only relations there can be are those 'between *reports* of dreams and physical occurrences',[3] and if the reports give no clue to a temporal occurrence then no other feature of the experiment can. If we can never get beyond the reports we can never make a start.

In all this Malcolm is of course quite consistent. Granted his

[1] *Op. cit.*, p. 81.
[2] *Op. cit.*, p. 79.
[3] *Op. cit.*, p. 77.

assumptions the answer is obvious. But the assumptions depend on its not being possible to put any credence in our impression when we awake that something has been going on in our experience just before we were awake; that is, memory must be shown to be inherently unreliable here. But nothing has been done to prove that, as has been already noted. It is simply ruled out on the ground that it does not admit of one, rather restricted, type of confirmation. If memory is allowed, and that of course is what the psychologists assume here, then there is no hindrance to the experiments proceeding and being illuminating in the way supposed by those who conduct them. If Malcolm is to impugn the validity of the experiments and what it is alleged they prove, he must surely do so on less slender grounds. The onus of proof seems to be upon him, and to that extent the weight of the scientific evidence and the strength of the presumption on which it rests must count heavily against him.

Moreover, as in other respects, we are entitled to expect from Malcolm some indication of his own of how precisely the experiments can be thought to have relevance. What sort of thing do they prove if they do not prove what the experimenters take to be plainly the result of them? In view of the vagueness of Malcolm's own concept of dreaming and his refusal to be explicit when it seems obviously necessary, one cannot easily anticipate what he might say. The onus is in any case again on him in the first place, and we can only complain that he fails to be explicit where we are most entitled to expect him to be.

Malcolm refers also to the notion of coherence, or being able to connect something with the whole course of one's life,[1] as a well-known test of being awake made familiar to us in writings ranging from those of Descartes to Russell and Ayer today. Against this notion there is, according to Malcolm, a simple knock-down argument, namely that we might dream that things were coherent in the way required. This is not, however, as deadly a blow as it seems. For if we could continue to link things in a sustained way with our present environment and our memories we would be awake in some fashion, even if paralysed or cut off in some other way from our usual contacts. Malcolm seems to think also that the suggested procedure implies that we could as easily assure ourselves that we were dreaming when dreaming as that we are awake at other times. But this does not follow. I have indeed mentioned earlier that it

[1] *Op. cit.*, p. 110.

might be possible for people sometimes to be aware that they dream, but normally the question does not arise as the dream experience is too confused and too arresting in the hold of some limited impressions upon us for us ever to raise a question about it. But that does not preclude us from applying the test successfully when we are awake and finding good reasons for ruling out the possibility that we are dreaming.

The most that Malcolm adds further here is the earlier insistence that judgment in sleep is unintelligible, as nothing could count for or against the truth of a claim that we are so judging. And with this I hope I have coped effectively already. But the desperation with which Malcolm holds to his course is well evidenced in his denial that we can ever affirm significantly that we are awake, as we seem quite plainly to do very often in one way or another. 'The sentence "I am not awake" is strictly senseless', it is urged and there cannot, therefore, be 'another possible statement which is its proper negation'.[1] 'You cannot know by observation that you are awake because if you could it would make sense to speak of knowing by observation that you are not awake.'[2] But if this holds, and I think I have shown that it does not, how does it seem to us to make such good sense to say that we are awake? The answer is that we never do affirm or judge that we are awake but only *show* that we are awake by uttering these words, and the words 'I am not awake' would do just as well. It is, however, very hard to believe that a person does not strictly understand and mean what he says in declaring himself to be awake; we understand the question and even if we are also showing that we are awake we make the move with the express intention of confirming thereby what we assert about our state at the time. There seems, therefore, to be no substance in Malcolm's suggestion, or indeed any plausibility, unless it can be shown initially that there is inherent absurdity in 'thinking that one *must* be able to know, to *see*, that one is awake';[3] and this, I have urged, is far from being the case.

I shall not attempt to follow Professor Malcolm further in the subtle and, as it seems to me, very desperate arguments by which he supports his view. I hope I have said enough to show to what remarkable lengths some contemporary thinkers are prepared to go in seeking to repudiate all appeals to any experience which is ini-

[1] *Op. cit.*, p. 118.
[2] *Op. cit.*, p. 119.
[3] *Op. cit.*, p. 120.

tially private to the subject of it and known in ways other than by the evidence directly available in principle to the outside observer. The samples of such procedures which I have given are not exhaustive, but they are typical, well-known and much admired. If I am right in what I have maintained about them I hope the reader will be convinced of the futility of the enterprise as a whole.

This does not mean, however, that we have done with monistic systems in accounts of experience and persons—far from it. There remains a very solid body of opinion which is firmly opposed in other ways to any dualistic view of mind and body. The thinkers in question do not deny that we must draw a clear distinction between what goes on in the mind and what goes on in the body. They are not out to deny all private experience, but they maintain in other ways that the distinction is not as ultimate or final as it seems, mental and physical processes belong to the same entity and there is no genuine wedge to be driven between them, they could not be thought to exist or function apart from one another, in the last analysis they are the same.

It is now time, therefore, for us to look at examples of this modified and seemingly less daunting form of monism; and I shall begin with a position that lies nearest to the ones I have already examined, a position which is not very easy to characterize as it seems initially to grant us more than is in fact intended. It is intermediate, being in some ways reminiscent of Ryle and in others opening out towards the views of those who admit very frankly that there is a radical difference between mental and physical processes although in the last analysis we must affirm that they belong in an inseparable way to the same entity. The view to which I refer is that of Professor Peter Strawson and I shall consider especially what he says about it in the chapter entitled 'Persons' in his book *Individuals*.

NOTE

One important point to raise about dreams, in any exhaustive study, is how we are to distinguish between various stages of being asleep and being awake. We say sometimes that a person is fast asleep, and sometimes we speak of being half-asleep and half-awake. There is an interesting borderland, and this gives us one way in which the sound of thunder could affect the course of a dream. If, however, we deny this and insist on saying firmly at all times that a man is asleep or awake, we close one very important avenue for the investigation of dreams and their significance.

CHAPTER VII

PERSONS AND THE STRUCTURE OF LANGUAGE

In the chapter entitled 'Persons' in his book *Individuals*, Professor P. F. Strawson opens his discussion of this subject with the observation that the group of questions he proposes to discuss might be denoted 'the issue of solipsism'. He realizes that this is not the customary use of those terms, but he contends that there can be no objection to his present procedure since solipsism, as normally understood, 'is not a genuine issue at all'.[1]

There can be no serious objection to the adoption of a term for a new purpose, least of all when the author is quite explicit about it at the outset. Even so the practice is not to be much commended, for it could be a source of misunderstanding. But in the present case that has less importance, for Strawson hardly uses the term in the subsequent discussion, and I mention his initial move in indication of the confidence with which it is maintained throughout that solipsism is not a genuine issue. That confidence is, in my view, quite misplaced.

It is, of course, true that no one wishes to make a case for solipsism as a final philosophical view. No one sets out to argue that only he himself exists, or that there are no very strong reasons for believing that we can know other persons. But philosophers have to ask questions about matters which we normally do not doubt at all in order, by this 'methodological doubt', to understand better what it is that we believe and to see what modifications in the way we normally believe it may be needed. They have thus been much concerned to discover in what way it is that we have knowledge of one another. This is the traditional problem of 'other minds', and it is the obverse of the problem of solipsism. The philosophers who have examined it, and very few philosophers have managed to avoid it in some form, have rarely, if ever, been seriously worried by the thought that there may be no one in the world but themselves. But they have usually thought it a difficult and fascinating question to determine how this assurance is obtained and warranted. Strawson, however, thinks this enthu-

[1] *Individuals*, p. 87.

siasm to have been entirely misplaced and disposes as boldly of the
problem of 'other minds' in a later context as he does of its counterpart, the problem of solipsism, at the outset. In both respects he
seems to me unable to justify his view by satisfactory arguments
and to be relying heavily on extremely dogmatic assumptions
about philosophy and language.

Professor Strawson settles down to his task with a reference to
some of the things we ascribe to ourselves. These include, on the
one hand, states of consciousness, thoughts and sensations, and,
on the other, physical characteristics like height, colouring and
weight. There is no particular problem about ascribing the latter
set of characteristics to 'something or other', for they can be
ascribed to one's body, a 'material thing' which 'can be picked
out from others, identified by ordinary physical criteria and
described in ordinary physical terms'.[1] But it is thought to be very
perplexing that we can ascribe states of consciousness and physical
characteristics *to the very same thing*'.[2]

Now here, in the very statement of the problem, there seem
to me to be unwarranted assumptions which careful analysis
ought to dispel. Is it strictly the case that we ascribe these different
characteristics to the same thing? We certainly do so in a rough
and ready way for ordinary purposes. We say, for example: 'I am
sitting at the table', 'I am running', 'I am writing'. There are
clearly two sets of characteristics involved here, as may be seen
most obviously perhaps in the last example. Writing involves
physical movement and it involves mental activity. We do not for
normal purposes distinguish the two. It is enough to say—'I am
writing'. This is because the two activities are peculiarly closely
linked and because it would be cumbersome and pointless to be
always noting the distinction between them. It would be much
too troublesome to say, for example—'I was intending to open the
door and my body moved towards it'. It is neater and apter, for
ordinary purposes, to say simply 'I went to the door' or 'I went to
open the door'. But while this is the best thing to say, as a rule, we
cannot allow that to be decisive in philosophy, and I fear that that
is ultimately just what Strawson does.

The truth seems to be that we do not strictly ascribe corporeal
characteristics and mental characteristics to the same thing.
When, for example, I say 'I am tall', I am not saying anything
about my mind but only about my body, which of course affects

1, 2 *Op. cit.*, p. 89.

my mind in a great many ways. My mind has neither height nor length nor breadth. It would be absurd, except in a thoroughly figurative sense, to ask how big is my mind. To speak of a 'small mind' is sheer metaphor. Minds are neither big nor small. If anyone denies this let him give me the approximate length of his mind, or any other, and say how he measures it. Is it six inches, or a foot, or a mile, or what? Clearly it is none of these. The question is absurd, for tallness and so on has nothing to do with my mind, but only with my body. The much maligned Descartes was obviously right in maintaining that it was distinctive of minds not to be extended.

When this view is advanced an objection is sometimes raised in the following terms. 'You know quite well where you are now, you are not in France, not in Oxford. You are in London, in this room, and you are standing at the desk in front, not sitting at the back.' This sounds plausible, but again that is only because the essential distinctions are not drawn for ordinary purposes. It would indeed be absurd and misleading for me to deny that I was not in France, or to seem to wonder whether I was in London. I know quite well where I am, when the question is put to me. But as philosophers we can also quite properly ask, 'What does this mean?'. It means, in the first place, that my body is 'here in this room', and the location of that can be quite precisely specified. It is the space which my body fills. But, secondly, the experiences which I have now are conditioned in certain ways by where my body is. If my body is up at a desk where I am speaking I can only have, as visual experiences, the seeing of these particular walls, of the furniture and occupants of this room and so on, my sense of being warm and cold depends on the temperature of this particular room, the pressures on the soles of my feet depend on the hardness of the boards, and my mental activities are affected in kindred ways. I am thinking these particular thoughts now because I am giving an address to a specific audience now. If the room were empty I should not be thinking just these thoughts, or at any rate I should not be thinking them in exactly the same way as in trying to explain my ideas to this audience. In all these regards, and in other similar ones, I am in this room. But it still does not follow that my mind is strictly in the room. Neither of course is it outside, or in France (except in a metaphorical sense if my thoughts *stray*, as we say, to a holiday in France). To deny that I was here, in any sense that implied that I was elsewhere, would be absurd. But the strict truth is that my mind is nowhere, location simply does not apply to it. My thoughts are not extended, although they are affected in many ways by extended substances, including specially my body.

To some extent Strawson takes account of this. He agrees with Descartes that 'I am not lodged in my body like a pilot in a vessel', and he goes on to refer to the ways in which my perceptual experiences are dependent on my body, on my eyes being open, on the direction of my head and so on; he toys ingeniously[1] with the possibility of one's being dependent in these ways on more than one body. That is not in fact our actual situation, and thus 'there is for each person one body which occupies a certain causal position in relation to that person's perceptual experience' and which is unique to him also 'as an *object* of perceptual experience'. These considerations seem, however, to Strawson, to leave the central question unanswered. They show why I should have a special regard for one body, 'But they do not explain why I should have the concept of *myself* at all, why I should ascribe my thoughts and feelings to *anything*. Moreover, even if we were satisfied with some other explanation of why one's states of consciousness, thoughts and feelings and perceptions, were ascribed to *something*, and satisfied that the facts in question sufficed to explain why the "possession" of a particular body should be ascribed to the *same* thing (*i.e.*, to explain why a particular body should be spoken of as standing in some special relation— called "being possessed by"—to that thing), yet the facts in question still do not explain why we should, as we do, ascribe certain corporeal characteristics not simply to the body standing in this special relation to the thing to which we ascribe thoughts and feelings, etc., but to the thing itself to which we ascribe those thoughts and feelings. For we say "*I* am bald" as well as "*I* am cold", "*I* am lying on the hearthrug" as well as "*I* see a spider on the ceiling" .'[2] But it is just here that linguistic usage is made to carry far more weight than it can. We have Strawson admitting that any dependence on my body in perceptual and kindred ways does not prove his main point. It only explains why the '*possession*' of a particular body should be ascribed to the 'something', whatever it may be, to which my thoughts and feelings are ascribed, in other words, it explains why I say that I *have* a body, it does not

[1] *Op. cit.*, p. 91.
[2] *Op. cit.*, p. 93.

account for the fact that my thoughts and feelings are ascribed to the same thing as my physical characteristics; and to substantiate the latter claim, the crucial one for Strawson, all we have at this stage is the reference to the fact that we say 'I am bald' and so on. But a phrase of this kind is capable of further analysis and cries out for it; it can quite properly be analysed in terms of the notion of my *having* a body, that is being peculiarly dependent on a certain body and so forth. The strict truth is not that *I* am bald, although that is a perfectly clear way of putting it for normal purposes, but that my *head* is bald. It is my *own* head, part of a body to which I stand in a very special relation, but my mind is neither bald nor covered with hair, it cannot be; and if the baldness is ascribed to me that is only to me as a complex being having a mind as well as a body or being dependent on a body; it is not ascribed to me in any further sense which requires physical and mental characteristics to belong strictly to the same entity.

I should also wish to add that my real self is my mind, and that it is only in a derivative and secondary sense that my body is said to be myself at all. In other words, in the strict sense I am not bald at all, and cannot be; it is only part of my body that can be bald, my body is not something that I *am* but something that I *have*, and here linguistic usage, if that were what we should appeal to, is on our side. The appeal to ordinary language is apt to cut disconcertingly both ways.

One wonders also why it should have been thought to be initially so plausible to suppose that my dependence on my body in percep-tual experience and so on might be the explanation of 'why I should have the concept of myself at all'.[1] Strawson is indebted in some ways to Kant, and one would have expected this to have left on him a firmer impression of at least the greater initial plausibility of an explanation of my having 'a concept of myself' in terms of some inherent feature of consciousness itself.

Strawson is not, however, unaware of the sort of objection I have brought against his main argument. He refers to two positions which might be alternatives to his own. One is the 'no ownership' view which it is thought might have been held by Wittgenstein or Schlick. On this view it is perfectly proper to refer to the depen-dence of my experiences on my body, and it is not very inappropri-ate to say further that my experiences 'belong' in this sense to my body. But, it is contended, we are apt to slide from this to the

[1] *Op. cit.*, p. 93.

wholly inadmissible position that experiences may belong to something else not a body at all, an 'Ego, whose sole function is to provide an owner for experiences'. We fall victims in this way to 'a linguistic illusion'. This theory, however, fails, according to Strawson, because it cannot be stated without 'internal incoherence', for the exponent of it can only refer to the facts which give rise to the illusion of the ego in some such form as: 'all *my* experiences are had by (*i.e.* uniquely dependent on the state of) body *B*'. In this way ownership in some sense is implied.

It is not for me to defend the 'no ownership theory', and that theory is, in fact, as far removed from what seems to me to be the truth as anything can be; and yet I am not sure that it is as conclusively refuted as Strawson supposes in terms of this alleged internal incoherence. The present mode of settling arguments seems to me deceptively simple, and it does not take us very far beyond the appeal to established usage. I should not place it beyond the ingenuity of a sufficiently determined advocate of the 'no ownership theory' to find a reasonably satisfactory statement of his position. Strawson observes that the reference to experiences as mine, in the sense solely of belonging to my body, is analytic inasmuch as it adds nothing to the assertion that the experiences depend on this body. But is it quite obvious that the no ownership theory could not get along with that? Does it have to bring in the word 'my' in a way that would expose it to incoherence? In other words, is Strawson's present point a bar to *any* statement of a no ownership theory on the basis of an alleged linguistic confusion due to ways in which we refer to the dependence of certain experiences on a certain body?

The real objection to the no ownership theory is that it is out of accord with the facts about consciousness. There is something left out of the account, and the incoherence arises only if the advocate of the theory assumes this further factor in his statement of his own position. I am not altogether convinced that he is bound to do so, but Strawson's ascription of essential incoherence to him does involve also stressing that the sponsor of the theory does leave something out. But what then, in Strawson's view, is it that the no ownership theory overlooks?

It overlooks something, we are told, which is also neglected in the other alternative entertained by Strawson, namely, the Cartesian position. Both these mistaken positions, it seems, overlook what Strawson rightly describes as 'a very central thought' for him, namely, in his own words that 'it is a necessary condition of one's ascribing states of consciousness, experiences, to oneself, in the way one does, that one should also ascribe them, or be prepared to ascribe them, to others who are not oneself. This means not less than it says. It means, for example, that the ascribing phrases are used in just the same sense when the subject is another as when the subject is oneself'.[1]

In one sense this statement is true—at least in the main. When I say that someone other than myself is thinking about philosophy or planning to go for a walk, I am ascribing to him the same sort of mental state as I should if I claimed to be doing these things myself. In other words, for me to be thinking about philosophy is the same thing as for you to be thinking about philosophy. Whether this holds at all points is less certain. It has been suggested, I think with justification, that when one person claims to see red colour there is no absolute certainty that his experience is strictly the same as that of some other person who makes the same claim. If red appeared consistently in my experience when others had experience of yellow colour I should never know of the difference and should use the word red in these situations in the same way as other people. There are stock replies to this, some of them taking the short way with the dissenter common in linguistic philosophy and identifying the meaning of the word red with its use. But these objections seem to me to proceed on unwarranted assumptions, and I think there is a good case to be made, although I shall not make it here, for the view that there may be many radical differences between our experiences such as the one contemplated in the standard problem about seeing strictly the same colour. I have hinted at the very far-reaching character of these possibilities in my paper on 'Public and Private Space'.[2]

These are not, however, matters that I wish to press now. I have admitted that, in the main, to ascribe states of consciousness to one person is the same as to ascribe them to others in the sense noted hitherto, namely, that what is ascribed is the same. If there are exceptions to this they require to be considered carefully as a separate problem and need not worry us now.

But what about the process of ascription itself? Does not this come about in a radically different way in my own case from that of another? At this point Strawson refers to an alleged difficulty

[1] *Op. cit.*, p. 99.
[2] Reproduced below p. 329.

concerning the difference in the method of verification. 'How could the sense be the same', so Strawson puts the philosopher's difficulty, 'when the method of verification was so different?'. Strawson himself does not think there is real cause for anxiety here. But this is not because he questions the assumption about meaning and method of verification from which the supposed difficulty arises. On the contrary, it is the acceptance of that assumption that mainly underlies his own contentions, and it is an assumption for which little justification is ever offered. On what grounds, other than the dogmatic acceptance of a certain philosophical method, can it be maintained that the same sort of situation could not come to be known, in different cases, in radically different ways? We are surely not to be told at this time of day that the meaning of a statement *is* its method of verification. But what substance is there in the alleged repudiation of the original forms of logical positivism, and in the supercilious contempt shown towards them, if we are to retain the present form of the principle of verification as a basic one in philosophical procedure?

Professor Strawson, as I have said, does not repudiate this principle; his position seems to be that if we ascribed states to ourselves in a different way from ascribing them to others, there would be an insuperable difficulty arising directly from the view about 'verification' and 'sense' to which I have just alluded. It seems also somewhat partisan of him to describe this as a difficulty which gives 'trouble to the philosopher' as if it were a trouble which had generally worried philosophers in this context. It is, in fact, only a trouble to those who follow the prevailing linguistic and empiricist fashion in philosophy. Not that philosophers have not had troubles here. They have had indeed many well-known troubles about our knowledge of other minds, and it is these troubles which Strawson, in common with many others to-day, tends to thrust altogether aside, as happened in Strawson's initial reference to solipsism, as if they had no substance but were on the contrary the bogus and unilluminating problems of stupid philosophers.

Strawson believes, however, that the trouble to which he refers can be effectively eliminated. It does not really arise, not as I have observed because we must modify our views about verification, but because we are bound to ascribe states of consciousness to ourselves in precisely the same way as we ascribe them to others. We can, indeed, only identify ourselves when we also identify others. Strawson in fact puts the initial 'trouble' about ascription and verification in the alternative form of questioning the right 'to talk about ascribing in the case of oneself'[1]; there can be no question of identifying oneself. We only identify other persons and it is only in an elliptical sense that we may be said to identify ourselves when we do so *for* other persons—to tell someone else who is in pain and so on. This argument is again severely, if subtly, linguistic. It is quite true that, for normal purposes or in ordinary usage, there is no point in trying to identify ourselves or tell who we are. In practice it is always, or nearly always, a question of informing other people. But the philosopher is not concerned with ordinary aims and practices, and at the philosophical level there is a very proper problem of how it is that we know or identify ourselves. It may be that we never are in doubt, except in subsidiary senses,[2] but even so it is proper and important in philosophy to indicate the mode of awareness involved. Knowledge, notwithstanding what many have assumed to the contrary to-day, is not less genuine if it happens to be the sort that cannot in fact be doubted.

It is this, however, which Strawson seems to query; and it is for such reasons that he comes in due course to declare that 'one may properly be said to ascribe states of consciousness to oneself, given that one can ascribe them to others'. The point he is making is not the one that has often been made in the past by philosophers, namely, that we are essentially social creatures and could not as a matter of fact have the sort of awareness of ourselves which we have as human beings, or indeed be at all the sort of persons we are, were it not for the very intimate relations we have with one another. No one would seriously dispute this point, and it is not anything so trivial that Strawson is affirming; he is concerned with a much more subtle logical difficulty about the very meaningfulness of ascribing states of consciousness to ourselves independently of ascribing them to others.

The obverse of this difficulty for Strawson is that the problem of ascribing states of consciousness to others would be insoluble if the things (*sic*) to which we ascribe them were 'a set of Cartesian egos to which only private experiences can, in correct logical grammar, be ascribed'.[3] For there would be no way 'of telling that a private experience is another's'. But here again there are

---

[1, 3] *Op. cit.*, p. 100.
[2] As seem to me to be those involved in the case of loss of memory, and so on. See below p. 235.

unwarranted assumptions, in particular the assumption that if experiences are such that in themselves or directly they are private to those who have them there can be no other way in which they can also be made public or known about indirectly. We have met this already in *The Concept of Mind*; and we must give the same reply to Strawson as to Ryle. To affirm that we have private access to our own experience does not preclude us from insisting also that there are ways in which these experiences may be disclosed, deliberately or in other ways, to others. How that comes about is the traditional problem; in one sense we are in a world of our own and in one sense we are not. But Strawson rules this out on the ground that there can be no sense in which an experience is mine unless this *expressly* involves the contrast with those of others. This seems to be the point of his saying that, on the view he opposes, 'All private experiences, all states of consciousness, will be mine, *i.e. no one's*'.[1] Here, again, we must admit that 'mine' normally implies the contrast with 'thine' and 'theirs'. This is because the words 'mine' and 'thine' usually refer to a claim, to a right or property, and this involves excluding others or limiting their rights. But, unless we are to be the slaves of ordinary usage, there is nothing here that in any way precludes my being aware of my own experiences, and thereby knowing them to be mine, in a way that does not directly involve the very different awareness I have of the experiences of others. I know that a private experience is mine in having it. I could not, admittedly, have the private experience of a human being, or reflect expressly upon it as being mine, without association with other persons. But that is quite a different matter from the curious logical point which Strawson is attempting to make.

Strawson sums up his argument up to this point as follows:

'One can ascribe states of consciousness to oneself only if one can ascribe them to others. One can ascribe them to others only if one can identify other subjects of experience. And one cannot identify others if one can identify them *only* as subjects of experience, possessors of states of consciousness.'[2]

The last statement in this quotation is important as providing the link with the other main features of Strawson's central thesis. That is the insistence that we can only identify other persons and

[1] Italics mine.
[2] *Op. cit.*, p. 100.

come to know about them through observing their bodies. Of human beings situated as we are in this life that is largely, if not entirely, true. We know other persons normally through the movements of their bodies, the sounds they utter, and so on; and even if there are further paranormal ways of learning about other persons, it is exceptionally hard to see how this would be possible for us if we did not have also the knowledge of other persons obtained in the ordinary way. But if we allow this, and if it is also asserted, as is done by Strawson, that we cannot identify or know ourselves except in a process which essentially and directly involves the identification of others, then it seems impossible to ascribe experiences to ourselves at all except in ways in which our bodies have an indispensable part. The basic unit, what Strawson calls the 'logically primitive' concept is thus, 'a type of entity such that *both* predicates ascribing states of consciousness *and* predicates ascribing corporeal characteristics, a physical situation etc. are equally applicable to a single individual of that single type'.[1] We cannot, in other words, conceive of ourselves at all except as beings with physical characteristics.

This is much more drastic and radical than saying that in point of fact it is very hard to see how we could function independently of our bodies, that it would be difficult to identify ourselves without the sensations and experiences which are most directly related to our own bodies, that the causal dependence of mind on body is so close that it is implausible to think that the mind can function independently of the body. These are very substantial, though not to my mind insuperable, difficulties, and it is easy to see why people are daunted by them when they consider any kind of disembodied existence. But in Strawson's view, discussion at this level is quite superfluous and indeed improper since, in terms of his own very radical position, it is out of the question to conceive of ourselves independently of our bodies; the attempt to do so stands condemned on logical grounds at the start.

To sum up the main theme in Strawson's own words: 'The point is not that we must accept this conclusion in order to avoid scepticism, but that we must accept it in order to explain the existence of the conceptual scheme in terms of which the sceptical problem is stated. But once the conclusion is accepted, the sceptical problem does not arise.'[2] As it used to be put, the traditional

---

[1] *Op. cit.*, p. 102.
[2] *Op. cit.*, p. 106.

problem is a pseudo-problem, and when Strawson presents his own work as 'descriptive metaphysics' one wonders whether the vaunted new metaphysics is but the old anti-metaphysical philosophy in disguise.

Let me note now two supplementary arguments used by Strawson in the same context.

The first is his reply to a possible defence of Cartesianism. It might be argued, he supposes, that we do not find it difficult to identify bodies and that we could thus identify a subject as the one that stands in the same special relation to a particular body as I stand to my own. This is wrecked, however, on the rock of the assumption implicit in it that I have already identified myself in terms of my relation to my body—what, so it is put, 'is the word *my* doing in this explanation?' 'Uniqueness of the body does not guarantee uniqueness of the Cartesian soul.' I do not know whom Strawson believes he is tilting against here; it could hardly be Descartes himself. He certainly did not claim to know himself in terms of any relation to his own or any other body. His well-known contention is that consciousness of oneself is prior to any awareness of the external world. If he, or someone else defending substantially the same position, claimed to know his own existence, and to distinguish between himself and others, on the basis of his special relation to his own body the argument would certainly involve the absurdity[1] of assuming at the start a knowledge of the self which is also alleged to be known only through a special relation to a particular body. This is not, however, an absurdity of which Strawson's opponents are guilty—it is a Cartesian man of straw set up as a sitting target. The 'my' gets into the real argument on the basis of one's experience of oneself as a conscious being, and if Strawson wants to argue that this cannot be allowed independently of the special relation to bodies for which he holds a brief, then that has to be established on its own account and cannot be presupposed in an argument that is meant to support it.

In the second supplementary argument, Strawson again presents the alternative to his own position in another very misleading way. He declares that, whereas we should ascribe states of consciousness and corporeal entities to '*the very same things*', 'we are tempted to think of a person as a sort of compound of two kinds

---

[1] Ascribed also, we have seen, with more plausibility to the 'no ownership theory'.

of subjects: a subject of experiences (a pure consciousness, an ego) on the one hand, and a subject of corporeal attributes on the other. Many questions arise when we think in this way',[1] and in seeking to cope with them we are 'apt to change from the picture of two subjects to the picture of one subject and one non-subject'.[2] I find it, again, hard to discover where this movement of thought is in fact found. Who are the philosophers who start in this way with the idea of two subjects? Is not the reference always and from the start to one subject and one non-subject, although these are not quite the terms I should like to use? I certainly ascribe corporeal attributes to my body, but it is only in a highly elliptical sense that this may be described as ascribing them to myself. My body is not strictly myself, or some part of me. It is something to which I am very specially related, no more. One does not think of it as a subject, it is just not a starter as a candidate for the status of 'ego' or 'subject' as the terms are used in the phrase 'subject of experiences', and if the contrast of subject and non-subject is not to be understood in this way Mr. Strawson gives us no indication how then it is to be understood.[3] He simply repeats his earlier argument against the notion of a subject of experiences as such. 'For', he observes, 'there could never be any question of assigning an experience, as such, to any subject other than oneself; and, therefore, never any question of assigning it to oneself either, never any question of ascribing it to a subject at all. So the concept of the pure individual consciousness—the pure ego—is a concept that cannot exist; or, at least, cannot exist as a primary concept,[4] in terms of which the concept of a person can be explained or analysed'.[5] But this is a reaffirmation of the original argument, and if the additional argument presupposes the earlier one, what point is there in the reference to the 'two subjects' and so on beyond saddling those who sympathize with Descartes with an impossible, and perhaps ridiculous, position very far removed from what they really maintain?

The core of Strawson's own position is well exhibited in the account which he gives, in illustration of his main thesis, of the concept of depression. I may feel depressed and I may behave in

---

[1, 2, 5] *Op. cit.*, p. 102.

[3] It has been put to me that he is thinking of the logical or grammatical subject. But clearly this would not serve his purpose at all, and the phrase he uses is 'subject of experiences'.

[4] There is no real concession here.

a depressed way. The behaviour, we are inclined to say, can be observed but not felt and the feeling can only be felt. There seems thus to be 'room here to drive in a logical wedge'.[1] But Strawson contends that in fact the concept of depression must cover both what is felt by me and what is observed by others. '*X*'s depression *is* something, one and the same thing, which is felt, but not observed, by *X*, and observed, but not felt, by others than *X*.'[2] This argument I must confess, I find very mystifying. It is true that for rough and ready requirements of every day we can say that we observe the depression that *X* feels. But this, for a philosophical purpose, allows of further analysis and much needs it. What we strictly observe is the physical behaviour of *X*, his demeanour and so on, and we infer his sadness from this. His sadness does not belong to his behaviour in the sense of that which we can strictly be said to observe. We observe the physical movements and infer from these the further different process of *X*'s feeling sad. The logical wedge is unavoidable and it only seems hard to drive because it is obscured in the language we use for ordinary purposes which do not require special heed to the distinction in question. Unhappily, it is to language that Strawson wishes to appeal, the linguistic convention becomes the head of the corner in his argument and is made to bear the weight of all the far-reaching contentions he makes in his book. 'To refuse to accept this' (the argument I have just reproduced as he put it) is, he adds, 'to refuse to accept the *structure* of the language in which we talk about depression. That is, in a sense, all right. One might give up talking or devise, perhaps, a different structure in terms of which to soliloquize. What is not all right is simultaneously to pretend to accept that structure and to refuse to accept it; *i.e.* to couch one's rejection in the language of that structure.'[3] This may not appear to be quite what was meant by the appeal to ordinary language, but is there any difference of substance here between the old linguistic veto and the new?

In the closing stage of his discussion of 'persons' Strawson turns to the 'residual perplexity' of why, in view of his thesis, we ascribe to persons predicates implying states of consciousness at all. He does not claim to give an exhaustive answer but only to indicate the main clue. It is found in the nature of predicates 'which involve doing something',—going for a walk, coiling a rope.

[1] *Op. cit.*, p. 108.
[2], [3] *Op. cit.*, p. 109.

These predicates have the 'interesting characteristic' that 'one does not, in general, ascribe them to oneself on the strength of observation, whereas one does ascribe them to others on the strength of observation. But, in the case of these predicates, one feels minimal reluctance to concede that what is ascribed in these two different ways is the same. This is because of the marked dominance of a fairly definite pattern of bodily movement in what they ascribe, and the marked absence of any distinctive experience'.[1] There seems thus to be a case, our own, where we learn about 'the bodily movement' without either observation or private experiences. This releases 'us from the idea that the only things we can know about without observation or inference, or both, are private experiences; we can know, without telling by either of these means, about the present and future movements of a body'.[2] This, again, seems to me highly questionable. In the first place, do I ever strictly know that I am going for a walk without observation? I do know without observation that it is my intention to walk, but do I ever know that I am actually managing to do so without noting the position of my limbs and so forth? On the other hand do I learn about my intention without living through the experience of intending? But what follows if we allow Strawson his point? It follows for him that, in the case of bodily movement we have something which can be known by observation and also without observation, and from this it is deduced that in observing the bodily movement of others we 'see such movements as *actions*',[3] the force of this being, apparently, that in observing the actions of others we observe what they themselves know without observation. But again we must ask what is meant by 'see' in this argument. All we strictly see or observe is the physical movement, and we then learn about the private intention by inference from what we observe. There is nothing in the situation to suggest that there is some one thing which is both visible movement and intention.

On these slender bases, and by tortuous arguments which overlook fundamental distinctions which we need to draw, Strawson sets up his final conclusion. It is that his 'remarks are not intended to suggest how the "problem of other minds" could be solved, or our beliefs about others given a general philosophical "justification". I have already argued that such a "solution" or

[1], [2] *Op. cit.*, p. 111.
[3] *Op. cit.*, p. 112.

F

"justification" is impossible, that the demand for it cannot be coherently stated'.[1] Implicit in this wholesale disposal of 'the familiar philosophical difficulties' is the further notion that just as we dispose of the usual distinction between mind and body, so we might also find the distinction between self and others not quite as ultimate as we are apt to assume. A 'technique' is available by which we might 'construct the idea of a special kind of social world in which the concept of an individual person is replaced by that of a group'.[2] We do already speak of groups of people engaged in corporate activities. Strawson does not develop this hint, but the mention of it is an ominous indication of where we end when, in seeking to understand human life, we resort to techniques and linguistic procedures which do not take close account of what we find the facts about ourselves to be in our own experiences. Professor Strawson says that those who find the idea of group personality absurd show nonetheless that they know quite well what it means. But do they show that they understand more than the *metaphorical* notion of group personality and the usefulness of this in certain legal and similar contexts?[3] The distinctness of persons seems to me ultimate, and while I do not go further into that question at present, I should like to express here my conviction that few notions have done greater harm in politics or theology than that of group or corporate personality taken strictly.[4] Recent history, in matters of thought and practice, provides abundant and appalling support for this conviction. It behoves us, therefore, to consider carefully how we build when we sweep aside, on flimsy and highly dogmatic grounds, the distinctions which men have usually found deep and important in their attempt to make sense of themselves and their situation.

NOTE

Professor Strawson refers also, very briefly, to the possibility of disembodied existence. He seems disposed (not, it seems to me, at all consistently with his main arguments) to allow this in an

---

[1] *Op. cit.*, p. 112.

[2] *Op. cit.*, p. 113.

[3] In any case, to understand roughly what is meant by a theory is not tantamount to endorsing it. Or is the 'short way' with the philosophical dissenter to become now very short indeed? Thus: if I understand my opponent's view I concede it; if I do not I am not entitled to criticize it.

[4] *Cf.*, my *Morals and the New Theology*, chaps. VI, VII, VIII and my *Freedom and History*, chap. 3.

'attenuated vicarious' form restricted to memories of present existence and 'interest in the human affairs of which he is a mute and invisible witness. . . . In proportion as the memories fade, and this vicarious living palls, to that degree his concept of himself as an individual becomes attenuated. At the limit of attenuation there is, *from the point of view of his survival as an individual,* no difference between the continuance of experience and its cessation'.[1] This would hardly content the religious believer, or anyone else who is seriously concerned about survival. Strawson adds that 'the orthodox have wisely insisted on the resurrection of the body'. I much doubt in fact whether they have done so in senses which Strawson would intend, and the matter is certainly too complicated to be disposed of in a somewhat cryptic allusion. The believer should, in any case, be wary how he accepts advice from quarters very alien to his own. This I shall not pursue further. But there is one point I should like to mention.

It is that, in discussing these questions, closer heed should be paid to a distinction between partial and absolute disembodied existence. In the latter case there would be nothing even resembling bodily existence and perception. There could be many varieties of the earlier case, and there is no obvious reason why survival, if accepted, should not be one of them. But the other possibility should not be ruled out. Obvious difficulties here would be identity and communication, and of these, as I understand personality, the latter would be much the more formidable. A possible solution might be in terms of significant patterns of unexpected changes in our own thoughts which might warrant their ascription to influence by some other mind. But the religious person will remember that he is dealing here with matters affected in some ways by the radical mystery of God and our dependence on Him. His faith is certainly not upset but rather strengthened by the thought that 'it has not yet been disclosed what we shall be'. If the body enters into his expectations will it not be a 'spiritual body?' That would take us very far from Strawson's *M* predicates involving, as we are expressly told, a 'physical situation'.[2]

---

[1] *Op. cit.*, p. 116.
[2] *Op. cit.*, p. 102.

CHAPTER VIII

SOME CONVENTIONAL OBJECTIONS
TO DUALISM

The rejection of Cartesian dualism is not confined today to those who make most use of the techniques which have become fashionable in Anglo-Saxon Philosophy. William Temple declared many years ago that our major errors seemed to stem from Descartes. This misgiving reflects the more straightforward difficulties which many are inclined to feel when they begin to reflect about the sort of interactionist thesis which I have been defending hitherto. Such difficulties are presented very neatly and forcibly by Professor R. J. Hirst in his book, *Problems of Perception;* and I should like now to turn to some of these more conventional objections to the dualist position. I shall keep fairly closely to Professor Hirst's account of them.

He begins, in chapter VII of his book, with a clear presentation of the position he proposes to examine. Although this is now familiar to us, I should like to reproduce Hirst's admirable statement of it. He writes:

'The essential notions seem to be: first, that there are two distinct orders of being or substances, the mental and the material. Mind or mental substance is neither perceptible by the senses nor extended in space; it is intelligent and purposive and its essential characteristic is thought, or rather consciousness. The body on the other hand is part of material substance, perceptible and extended; it lacks purpose and consciousness and, at the macroscopic level at least, is governed by rigid laws of cause and effect. Secondly, the person or self is strictly to be identified with mind and to be regarded as a mental substance; each one of us is primarily and in reality a mind or soul, though in some ways associated with a body. Hence one can legitimately think of the mind as the entity that experiences, wills, and thinks.'[1]

Hirst also declares that perception only shows a person as a body. But, he adds, it will be maintained, on the traditional view, that we know by introspection 'mental activities which can be observed

[1] *Problems of Perception*, chap. VII, p. 181.

only by the person concerned. I may infer what another person is thinking from his words and expression but only he can know by direct action what is going on his mind'.[1]

These seem to me quite adequate statements of the traditional view, and I believe they give us the truth of the matter. Hirst objects to it, not on linguistic grounds, although he comes close to that at times, but on considerations like the following: He declares:

'We only have evidence of certain experiences and activities, of ourselves thinking and seeing. There is no revelation of the onto-logical status of these activities or of the self which performs them. We may see a red glow and be aware that we are seeing it, but we cannot be aware that it is a sensation in the mind, for that is pure theory, a hypothesis to account for the experience of the red glow after certain brain activity. Or we may catch ourselves day-dreaming and find that we are thinking of palm trees on the Riviera, *i.e.* some other material thing. But we are not then intro-specting that we are aware of mental images as private mental representations of palm trees. That is not revealed to us, it is a supposition to explain the absence of actual palm trees.'[2]

This seems to me confused. It is true that we only think of the 'red glow as a sensation in the mind' when we theorise. But in being aware of the glow, whatever at the time we take it to be, we are also immediately aware that we are aware of it. The awareness and the glow are not the same thing. We may not stop to reflect on this—or put it to ourselves in any way; we do not normally do so, nor is it merely on special occasions of deliberate introspection that we are aware of the awareness. We are all the time aware of being aware; self-awareness is the obverse of our awareness of things. It is not the result of philosophical theorising, and it is not confined to anything we may be prone to regard as 'sensation in the mind.' It is not because of Berkeleyan or other reflections about sense experience that we claim to know our private mental activities—the issue is not affected in this way by theories about perception. We may take a subjective or a more realist view of perception and in *either* case have to distinguish between that which we apprehend—even an after glow or some colour patch

[1] *Op. cit.*, p. 182.
[2] *Op. cit.*, p. 183.

private to ourselves—and the apprehending of it. It is the latter that introspection discloses.

Such introspection, it must be added, is not an act of observing our awareness that is quite distinct from that awareness or performed upon it. If it were we might be exposed to an infinite regress—must not the awareness of the awareness involve awareness of that etc., ad infinitum? It is rather that in being aware of objects we are aware of being so aware, and it is the failure to appreciate this peculiarity of cognition that lends plausibility to arguments like those of Hirst. This is how he comes to say that in introspection we have only evidence 'of ourselves thinking or seeing'. The statement is quite sound in itself but it is understood by Hirst to mean solely the presentation of 'the red glow etc.', whereas in fact there is the living through of the experience of having the red glow presented to us. Hirst seems to leave out the distinct mental side of seeing altogether and to assume that 'thinking or seeing' as such are neutral and that the alleged dualism is only the result of theorising about them. But there can be no thinking or seeing that does not involve the dualism of our own experiencing and an entity of some kind confronting us.

Likewise in the case of the palm trees of which I day-dream. We only think of these as private mental images etc., we are told, as a supposition to explain the absence of palm trees. This may be true, but to be aware of our experience as a private mental activity is not the becoming aware of the images as private mental images. It is the inner side of the experiencing of the images—whatever they are taken to be, and is quite independent of any theory about them. Hirst seems here to be confusing the two senses in which we may speak of a private or inner world—(1) that in which sensation or sense presentations are private although providing a means of inferring to some public world—the dualism involved in some theories about perception—and (2) the sense in which experiencing as such, whether of sense contents or of anything else, is essentially private and known in the first instance directly only to the person concerned.

Hirst goes on: 'The self that we discover to be thinking or seeing is not, thereby, discovered to be an immaterial mental substance. Indeed, to judge from our language, we suppose that it is persons, you or I or John Smith, who think and perceive as well as eat, and that these same persons can be seen or observed by the senses. Thus: "I saw you yesterday. You were walking along High

Street day-dreaming as usual," but we would find it odd to say: "my mind saw you" or "I didn't really see you, I only saw your body walking".[1]

Now these would certainly be odd ways of talking and absurd for ordinary purposes. But here we are back again at the appeal to ordinary language as we find it in Ryle and Strawson. The oddity only comes about because we do not, in ordinary discourse, draw the distinctions which are implicit in what we find it useful to say. It would indeed be improper to say 'I only saw your body walking', because I have every reason to believe that more than a body is involved. But this experience of seeing someone walk does nonetheless admit of analysis; and on this analysis we may find (as I have already stressed) that, in the strict sense it is a body that I see and that I only infer (certainly and instantaneously) that the bodily movements are intended by a mind able in these ways to control the body and will these movements.

It would likewise be odd to say—'my mind saw you', for there can be no seeing normally without the bodily changes involved in the stimulation of our senses. Seeing is a complex activity, involving mind and body, but it is the mind and not the body that strictly has the experience of seeing, and in this sense it is correct, though not perhaps the best way of putting things, to say 'My mind saw you'.

Indeed Hirst is himself a fairly stern critic of the attempt to settle philosophical questions by appeal to language, and he adds here the caution:

'These linguistic preferences of course carry no guarantee of philosophical truth, but they do at least show, that despite centuries of effort by philosophers and theologians to persuade us that we are really minds lodged in bodies, the commonsense assumption is still that the same person who walks and thinks can be publicly observed, even if many of his activities, including the thinking, can only be inferred by others.'[2]

This appeal to common sense, even as a means of establishing an initial presumption of truth, seems to me ill-conceived. The relation between mind and body is so intimate in many ways that it would become hopelessly cumbersome to be always taking account

---

[1] *Op. cit.*, p. 182
[2] *Op. cit.*, p. 183

of the distinction between them. No one would normally dream of saying—'I saw your body moving and judged you were intending this'. But this proves nothing, even in the way of setting up an initial presumption, about the true relations of mind and body. It only shows that for certain purposes express account of the distinction need not be taken.

Moreover, if we are to appeal to common sense, I think its verdict would usually be on the side of the dualism which Hirst opposes. If the introductory passage of the chapter, as quoted above, were read to a reasonably intelligent person, not very familiar with philosophy, I think he might well say—Yes, something like that seems to me to be plainly the truth of the matter. Common sense has been invoked far too readily in support of fashionable views today, and the upholders of the more tradition-alist views have been much too ready to allow this when in fact they themselves have a much stronger claim to common sense as an ally.

For this reason I find myself quite unconvinced by Hirst's contention that 'introspection is neutral between monism and dualism'. He declares: 'I am aware of myself thinking or imagining, but, for all this awareness can tell me, "myself" may be a mental substance lodged in a body, or may equally be a self-conscious physical organism.' It seems to me, however, that introspection directly apprises me of myself as some mental reality distinct from my body. This distinction is not the result of subsequent theory. Hirst himself continues: 'It is difficult to put this point without begging the question, for the use of "mental" and "physical" and similar terms in philosophical contexts tends to imply dualism; the terms can ordinarily be used in a neutral way *e.g.* "mental arithmetic" or "physical training," to classify types of activity, but as soon as the distinction is applied to actual or supposed entities it is "theory-laden".' I do not agree that 'mental arithmetic' or 'physical training' are neutral terms. 'Mental arith-metic' does not imply that there is some arithmetic which is not mental; all it means is that we count without using an abacus or pencil and paper or their equivalents. When we do use the latter the counting is still, in essentials, mental. The physical counting, by touch or utterance etc., is an aid, no more. And the reason why the 'distinctions' in question are theory-laden when applied 'to actual or supposed entities,' is in my opinion, that the distinction is fundamental to all our experience of the world.

In further support of his view Hirst invites us next 'to turn from the individual to the world in general.' He observes that it is very difficult here to draw a rigid distinction between mental and material orders of being. It was easier in Descartes' day to regard 'all animals as mere automata bound by rigid mechanical laws'. But no one conversant with modern biology would be prepared to mark the boundary of mind and matter as rigidly as that. With this I entirely agree, as far as it goes. Indeed, I do not think we need modern biology to assure us that animals share with us the exercise of intelligence in some form. We have only to look at a dog penning sheep, or in fact, just gambolling about. The strange thing is that anyone should have doubted that animals have intelligence (and, as we have also seen, Descartes was not nearly as much the villain of the piece, in this matter, as many have supposed). But if we allow that there is intelligence lower down the scale of animal life than human life, what follows?

Hirst seems to think the admission fatal to the dualism he opposes. But this would only hold if such dualism were supposed to characterize merely human life. If we had to deny any continuity between human intelligence and the intelligence of brutes, or if we were maintaining that a distinction between mind and body is obvious in the case of human beings and equally obviously absent in all other living things, then we might seem to be in desperate straits. But what need have we of this embarrassment? The difficulty only arises because Hirst, like many others, takes it to be plain that the life of brutes must be described in unquestionably monistic terms. That makes it seem odd and artificial to insist that human life which has much continuity with the life of brutes involves a radical bifurcation of mind and body to be found nowhere else.

But the simple truth seems to be that the distinction of observable bodily activity and private inner experience appears, not only in the life of higher animals like dogs or chimpanzees, but also much lower down the scale, indeed wherever there is any kind of sentience. It is in truth surprising that Hirst, and other opponents of dualism, should have overlooked the fact that the case for private mental experiences, distinct from physical occurrences, is in many respects as strong in the case of animals as it is in the case of human beings, and that it is in these terms that the position would normally be defended.

Consider the case of an animal in pain. A dog yelps and holds up his paw. This is a sign that he is in pain, he behaves in this way because he is in pain, but the observable behaviour is not the pain. Nor is the laceration of his leg, if he has caught it on a sharp instrument, the pain. We may see his bleeding leg, but we cannot see his pain. The pain is just something he feels, and it would be as absurd to describe the pain itself in terms of what we can inspect or see, in the case of a dog, as it would be in the case of a man. The pain is private in both cases.

If this were not the case we should not feel so badly about cruelty to animals. If I beat a dog or starve it or let its leg be caught in a trap this does certainly mar it as a dog, in the way a spade would be marred if I dashed it against a rock until the blade was bent or the handle torn. But we do not speak of cruelty to implements, except in an obviously highly metaphorical sense. It is the owner who is really hurt, the spade is only spoiled. But we speak of cruelty to animals because of what they themselves experience, not because their utility is lessened—though that is a further objection to harming them. If anyone argues that the animal does not really feel anything, or that the pain is just the twitching of his muscles or his yelping or (with Ryle) his disposition to yelp, then we would usually consider this as absurd as it would be if we were thinking of a human being in pain, notwithstanding that human beings can suffer mental agonies not possible for brutes. The case of pain is a particularly good one for the dualist to choose. This is where it is most preposterous to deny that there is something felt by an agent which is not open to direct public inspection or describable in terms of witnessable behaviour. But the same holds, in substance, of all an animal's behaviour. When the dog rushes around with his nose to the ground we may say that he is following a scent, but the smelling is not the twitching of the nostrils or the running about with nose to the ground; there is also the smelling in the strict sense, that which the dog enjoys and which induces him to continue on his course. Likewise with the sheer enjoyment of his bodily movement. There is the inner as well as the outer side of this too.

In short, the distinction of inner and outer, of private experience and observable behaviour, does not arise directly from the distinction between the more specifiable rational and reflective experiences of human beings, on the one hand, and on the other, the more limited experiences of beings who have not, as we say, the use of reason. It has not to do with the sort of things which distinguish us especially as men, but arises rather at all levels of our experience, including those which we share more obviously with brutes. It is a characteristic of experience as such to be private in the sense in question, whatever the degree of rationality which the experience involves.

This is, moreover, why we can take our distinction (and must in consistency take it) much lower down the scale than the lives of higher animals. The question then arises—where do we stop? The simple answer is that we stop where sentience stops; insects, worms, jellyfish are obviously sentient to some degree. We would think it cruel to mutilate an insect, and if we are perhaps thoughtlessly callous about the worm we put on a hook, and have little compunction about the way we destroy a jellyfish, this is partly because we believe their nervous system is such as not to give them very intense sensations of pain. But they clearly do have some feeling, and this is private to them as subjects or centres of sensation, although their response and other behaviour is all in principle observable. This would hold even lower down the scale to the simplest form of animal life there is. Presumably plant life would be excluded. Plants are indeed in one sense very much like animals. They grow and respond in an organic way to their environment. But it seems on the whole unlikely that they are sentient. We have no compunction about lopping off the branches of a tree (beyond our reluctance to spoil a thing of beauty and so on) although we would think it brutal to butcher an animal in that way without first making sure that it had been killed in the most humane way possible. This is because, as we say, we do not suppose that the tree *feels* anything. Anemones close as we touch them and daisies open to the sun, but it is a moot point whether they can be said to do this because they really feel our touch or the kiss of the sun. It does not follow that the account of their responsiveness must be in purely mechanical terms—far from it. But it is not likely that there is any, even the most rudimentary, experience involved here. It is not for the philosopher, however, to indicate where the line should be drawn between sentient life and other forms of animate being, or between animate and inanimate things. In the light of recent biophysics the line is increasingly difficult to draw; and it may not be possible, in respect to certain forms of being and activity, the very lowest levels of animal life, for example, to do more than hazard a rough guess. The philosopher can, of course, help in providing the right concepts, and the main consideration, so far as he is concerned, is that mere responsiveness, however much it simulates sentient life, is not as such rudimentary experience. The machine, which we know from its construction to be a machine, does not think or feel, however convenient it may be for certain purposes to speak of it metaphorically in such terms. But the question of where it is plausible to draw the relevant demarcations is ultimately a question of fact, and one which it would not be profitable to pursue further now. The main point for the moment is that, wherever the line is drawn, a distinction of private or inner experience and outward behaviour must be made whenever we are dealing with any sort of sentient life.

If I am pressed to say how I would conceive of sentient life or define it, if not in terms of certain kinds of responses and so forth, my reply is that I understand it, in the first instance, in terms of what I feel and am aware of myself. I ascribe a low degree of this to creatures whose reactions, however simple, seem to suggest it.

It does not follow that we must ascribe a soul, in the sense in which this term is used in religion, to sub-human beings. The question here is partly one of terminology. There is high precedent for speaking of animal soul and of plant soul, and some cultures and religions are not at all averse to supposing that animals as well as human beings may be reincarnated. But the distinctiveness of properly rational, reflective, responsible beings such as men remains, and that has, of course, prime importance when we think of ourselves as beings with souls to be saved and destined to know and worship God.

I return then to the main point at the moment, namely that the upholder of the dualism which Professor Hirst opposes need not be embarrassed at all by the continuity of human and animal life. For the sharp distinction of mind and matter which I am commending is not to be equated at all with the distinction between human and sub-human creatures. It cuts across this, although its main significance appears in its application to human beings, or to superhuman beings which are in some ways like us, if there are any.

Professor Hirst mentions briefly two further objections to dualism of mind and matter. These are more familiar and traditional and he does not present them in detail.

The first concerns the possibility of causal action on one another by processes or substances of such radically different nature as mental and material ones are alleged to be by the dualist. Must there not be some community of characteristics in cause and effect? This is not, in my view, a very grave difficulty. Hirst himself does not press it very hard, admitting that we now have 'doubts about the dogma on which it rests'. It seems evident that we do not expect causes to be normally like the effects they produce, and we are able to say little in the last resort about the causal relation itself. Having learned Hume's lesson we realize that, however we account for the factor of necessity in causal relations, we have no *a priori* way of determining causal relations. We find that effects are produced in a certain way and that there is consistency and concomitance in this. Knowledge of the world and science are made possible in that way. But why it should be this kind of world, and why entities in the world should have the properties they do have, is something we have to accept in the last analysis without providing any explanations. This situation may point beyond itself to something of a religious nature, but so far as our ordinary commerce with the world is concerned we must just take the world as we find it.

There seems, therefore, to be no limit to the disparities we may find between causes and effects, and there is no reason at all to rule out *ab initio* the possibility of interaction between mind and body when these are affirmed to be distinct and radically different in nature. We do find in experience that, if a person seriously intends or 'sets himself' or wills to move his arm, he is normally able to do so. We find also that when certain effects are produced on our bodies, culminating, as in more sophisticated thought we learn, in certain states of the brain, we have certain experiences. It may not be possible to explain at all how this comes about. We may just have to accept it, but this interaction of mind and body is not, in this respect, radically different from any other. We find that certain sorts of things happen, others not; and it seems perversely conceited on our part to deny the facts as we seem patently to find them, namely that mind is distinct from body and that these do affect one another, simply because we are not able to say how this comes about or is possible.

It is worth noting a somewhat curious way in which Professor Hirst at one point puts the objection I have just been considering. He asks: 'How can the spatial characteristics of physical things be reproduced in the unextended non-spatial mind, as the traditional representative theory supposes?'.[1] I hold no brief for the representative theory of perception, although I do not think that it is bound to carry the implication ascribed to it here. But the dualistic

[1] *Op. cit.*, p. 185.

view of mind and body, whether or not accompanied by a representative theory of perception, does not imply in the least that spatial characteristics are 'reproduced' in the mind. They are known by the mind, but the mind does not have to become in some way spatial in order to accommodate spatial reality in the sense of *knowing* it. Knowledge of space or matter need not be itself spatial or material in any sense.

The final objection adduced by Professor Hirst is that 'all the scientific evidence shows that without a properly functioning body and brain the human mind cannot exist and act at all'.[1] I do not see that the detailed scientific evidence is particularly necessary or relevant here. Everyone knows that normally the functioning of my mind depends on the proper functioning of my body. Hit me on the head and I become delirious or unconscious, close all the windows and I become duller from lack of fresh air. All these are matters of common undisputed observation and they hardly need the elaboration of the scientific explanation of the details of the process. But this does not reduce the mental activity itself to a functioning of the body. Nor does it prove an absolute dependence of mind on body. There are, no doubt, other difficulties in the notion of disembodied existence,[2] and we may need very strong reasons to fortify us in any expectation that the mind could function without the body. But all that we can strictly conclude, from the causal relationship itself, is that,under the conditions we normally find in the world, the dependence of our mental activities on the proper functioning of the body, and of the brain in particular, is exceptionally close and constant. It does not follow that the mind could never function independently of these conditions.

Professor Hirst virtually concedes the last point. He declares: 'Even if one believes that in some way the human mind survives death without the resurrection of the body, one cannot deny that, *during life*, if some person suffers from serious brain injury or disease, if he takes certain drugs, or if the blood supply to the brain is interrupted, then unconsciousness supervenes and he cannot think at all.' No one denies this—as an account of the conditions we normally encounter in the *present life*. All that is contended is that there may be a state of things in which these conditions do not hold, and Hirst seems disposed to admit that in the first part of his statement.

[1] *Op. cit.*, p. 185
[2] *Cf.*, below chap. X.

Professor Hirst does seem to think, however, that it is somehow inconsistent for a Cartesian to recognize the normal dependence of the mind on bodily conditions. If mind is a distinct mental substance it 'needs no aid from the material brain'. But it is not clear why the distinctiveness of mind should preclude a causal dependence on something else—just as other substances are taken by Descartes to act on one another. We cannot determine in this *a priori* way what causal relations there can be; and if we think, as Descartes did, of mind and matter as being created by God and sustained in being by Him, it must surely be for Him, in His wisdom, to set the conditions under which they may operate— and, one may add, to suspend these.

Despite his strictures on dualism, Professor Hirst is all the same very anxious to maintain the reality of mental events and our privileged access to these by experiencing or introspecting them. This is where he differs sharply from Professor Ryle and from more explicit forms of behaviourism and materialism. Hirst is quite emphatic about this. The mental acts known directly only to the subject or agent himself must not be jeopardized. But how can we preserve them without resorting to some form of dualism? The answer is given us in the theory described as 'the Identity Hypothesis.' Mental acts are as real as material processes, but these two are not eventually distinct. They are different aspects of the same events. There is only the one reality which is both mind and matter, the main difference being in the ways the one reality is disclosed. The same event is thus, in one aspect mental, in the other material, a process in the brain. The brain is thus both mind and matter.

If this thesis could be sustained, it would appear that many of the objections to materialism, as normally advanced, could be removed. We would seem to be preserving the main things that the dualist is anxious about without the embarrassment, as it seems to many, of two substances or two quite distinct sorts of processes.

Even so some difficulties would remain, notably those which concern our freedom and the genuineness of the difference which thinking makes to our conduct. If we identify our thoughts with the course of events in the brain it is hard to see how our thoughts could ever make a difference on their own account to the course of our lives, and if they do make a difference they must have some status of their own.

This difficulty is met, by some thinkers, in terms of the principle of complementarity. I shall not pause here to consider this principle closely, as it has more relevance to the themes to be discussed in the sequel to this volume. All I will say at present is that, in spite of the flourish with which this principle was first advanced in some quarters and the confidence in it as an easy solvent of traditional problems, it seems to me to be little more than a daring affirmation of impossible paradoxes.[1] For the present, however, I content myself with noting in the simplest way how difficult it is to regard mental processes as effective in any distinctive way in the world if they are no more than aspects of the activity of my brain.

To put this as forcibly as possible, it may be noted that, on the theory in question, it becomes inevitable, from the state of my brain alone and other physical conditions, that I shall get up, let us say, and open the door in five minutes time. There is no avoiding the course of events prescribed in this way, and someone who had, *per impossibile* at the moment and perhaps at all times, the requisite full knowledge of my brain states and my physical environment could, on this basis alone, predict what I shall do. But in that case my belief that someone is waiting for me, that it is time to give a lecture, or that I am getting stale and had better have some fresh air—all this seems to make no difference. Indeed I might have thought the opposite, except that advocates of the identity theory could maintain that if my thoughts were different this would imply that my brain states were different. We would certainly have to say that what seems to me the natural course for my thoughts as such to follow is quite illusory and that my assumption (obviously our normal one) that I am opening the door because I believe that my work has reached a point where I need a break is itself determined by the processes that go on in my brain, and by nothing else. This, quite apart from the special question of morally accountable action, seems very far removed from all that we normally think, and the difficulty calls for far more attention than is usually accorded to it by sponsors of the double aspect theory.

Professor Hirst, in fact, hardly attends to this difficulty at all. But even if we waive this difficulty for the present, the view commended by Hirst is only made to seem plausible by boldly affirming

---

[1] The reader will find some extremely pertinent critical observations on this topic in Mr. Peter Alexander's article "Complementary Descriptions", *Mind*, April 1956.

that two things which seem plainly distinct are in fact one. If we can accommodate mental acts within the Identity Hypothesis then of course the more obvious difficulties are removed and the sting seems to be taken out of monism. This is what enables Professor Hirst to write as confidently as he does about the ability of his theory to survive obvious difficulties. He is not denying what we might take him to deny. But the real question to put to him is whether he is entitled to take up this position at all.

To clarify Hirst's position a little let it be added that he takes the double aspect feature of his theory quite seriously. The word 'aspect' is a metaphor and it could be taken in such a loose way that no one would object to it. We might speak of different aspects of a house in the sense of quite distinct parts of it, and of the different aspects of a character, the kindly and the more malicious. These are aspects of the one building or the one person, but they are far from being strictly identical. The dualist might thus say that my intention is one aspect of my behaviour and the movements of my limbs another. But Hirst wishes the word 'aspect' to be taken in a much more serious sense and one which is not 'akin to view.' Mental and bodily events are really identical and only appear different owing to different modes of access to them. He writes:

'The suggestion then amounts to this: that the various experiences of imagining, remembering, and thinking, *e.g.* images of various kinds whether vivid or vague, are the inner aspects of these various episodes and activities in a person's life and are what the person concerned experiences as an actor and not spectator in these situations, whereas brain activity is an outer aspect and is what can be observed or inferred scientifically by others. These experiences, particularly in thought, may be rather vague and nebulous, but I do not see how they can fairly be denied, and reluctance to admit either them or privileged access to them may be dispelled if it is realized that the access is not to a ghost world but to the same events or activities as neurologists may observe from without.'[1]

The plain difficulty that I feel about this is that, except in a very broad metaphorical sense, the activities the neurologist observes just are radically different from those of imagining, remembering,

[1] *Op. cit.*, p. 195.

etc. The mode of disclosure is indeed different, but, in this case, the mode of disclosure is different and has to be because of the total difference of nature of the processes involved. The main argument which Hirst brings against this turns on the very close correlation of mental and neurological processes. No one denies this correlation and it is rather pointless, in this context, to emphasize, as Hirst does, those features of it of which the scientist provides more detailed and precise information. No one need question these facts. But correlation is one thing, identity another, and the closeness of the correlation we can in fact establish does not in the least imply that only terms in one sort of process are effective; much less does it help to establish the identity of processes which, in direct inspection of them, are seen to be altogether different in nature. In acknowledging the reality of mental acts, and the patent difference between them and physiological events, Hirst appears to have removed altogether the possibility of strictly identifying the two in anything other than name. If the battle is a merely verbal one then there is no great point in joining it. If it is not verbal, then we have to insist that the difference between what we encounter in the processes of our own thought and what we observe in our bodies, including the brain, is so fundamental that it can only be by a resolution that flies in the face of the obvious facts that we can pronounce them to be also strictly identical. But we are far from having done, as yet, with the identity thesis.

CHAPTER IX

THE IDENTITY THESIS

I turn now to some further versions of 'the identity thesis', as it has come to be generally named. These draw away yet further from the position and method of argument we find in Professor Ryle's work, although at certain points they have at least a formal indebtedness to him, as will be indicated from time to time. The position I wish to examine most closely is that of Professor Herbert Feigl. He has wrestled with the position of the relation of mind and body in more than one place, but we find a fair and sustained presentation of his view in a much discussed essay contributed to *Minnesota Studies in the Philosophy of Science*, Vol. II, under the title 'The "Mental" and the "Physical" '. As the title of the volume suggests this purports to be a severely scientific treatment of the problem, but it is also hard to avoid the impression that what we have in the final result is a rather bold form of metaphysical speculation using arguments which we may not immediately associate with metaphysics. The return to a metaphysical treatment of the problem will be noted in the work of other writers to be mentioned in this chapter.

Professor Feigl rejects what he calls 'the clear-headed phenom-menalism of Hume'[1] and of his followers at later times. This in-volves in particular the rejection of 'neutral monism' and of kindred forms of positivism and reductionism, such as the early work of Carnap. On these theories, all that we have ultimately is 'the raw material of immediate experience' or 'a set of neutral experiential data'.[1] Everything else that we mention, on the mental or physical side, is some kind of logical construction out of these data. But this kind of reductionism fails in particular when we consider how impossible it is to reduce what we find in direct experience and introspection, having a pain or feeling gloomy and so on, to what can be observed as our behaviour or our neurophysiological states. There seems to be some radical distinction to be drawn somewhere, and in acknowledging, in a most firm and uncompromising way, the distinctive and irreduc-ible character of 'the direct experience itself, as lived through,

[1] *Op. cit.*, p. 371.

enjoyed, or suffered',[1] and even more in speaking of 'the privacy of immediate experience',[2] Feigl seems set on a course which does not very obviously lead to monism; we are, in Strawson's words, driving in a 'wedge' of some kind; we have irreducible experience, on the one hand, and, on the other, observable and physical reality. Those who question this are bluntly confronted with the question 'Don't you want anaesthesia if the surgeon is to operate on you?'[3]

We are very far here from the sort of repudiation of private experience and private access which we found in Ryle and those who take his lead. There is no question of an easy dissolution of the problems of mind and body by simply denying that there is any reality which is not in principle observable. The mind-body problem is not a pseudo-problem. The author is insistent that 'statements regarding the correlation of psychological to neurophysiological states' must be synthetic or empirical in character.[4] At one time Feigl had been attracted to the 'double-language theory of the mental and the physical', but he now declares firmly that 'this will certainly not do'.[5] 'The equivalence must be construed as logically contingent.'[6] This rules out any strictly reductionist programme.

It is also insisted with equal firmness that we must give 'an adequate account of the efficacy of mental states'. 'Admittedly, the testimony of direct experience and of introspection is fallible. But to maintain that planning, deliberation, preference, choice, volition, pleasure, pain, displeasure, love, hatred, attention, vigilance, enthusiasm, grief, indignation, expectations, remembrances, hopes, wishes, etc. are not among the causal factors which determine human behaviour, is to fly in the face of the commonest of evidence, or else to deviate in a strange and unjustifiable way from the ordinary use of language. The task is neither to repudiate these obvious facts, nor to rule out this manner of describing them. The task is rather to analyse the logical status of this sort of description in its relation to behavioural and/or neurophysiological descriptions.'[7]

The course which the proposed analysis takes may not convince

---

[1] *Op. cit.*; p. 404.
[2] *Op. cit.*, p. 398.
[3, 5] *Op. cit.*, p. 390.
[4, 7] *Op. cit.*, p. 389.
[6] *Op. cit.*, p. 391.

us, but the firm insistence that mental states are among the causal factors which determine our behaviour is reassuring and implies a very different approach to the problem from the translation of mental activity entirely into behavioural and dispositional terms.

It could, of course, be the case that grief, indignation, expectations, etc. were understood solely in their dispositional sense or as a mood in the manner of Ryle. But in that case it would be odd to call them mental states or speak of the way they influence conduct as a causal one. There seems, in short, to be some 'immediate data of first person experience'[1] or 'conscious events or processes (*e.g.* directly experienced sensations, thoughts, feelings, emotions, etc.)'[2] These are also described in many places as 'raw feels', a somewhat inelegant but suggestive term made popular, I believe, by Professor R. W. Sellars. Every person has these raw feels initially in a quite private way himself, he alone has access to them, but they can be ascribed by analogy to other persons and even to sub-human beings.[3] They could not be ascribed to machines, and however the functioning of the latter may resemble the responses of conscious or sentient beings, we must not forget that 'it is ourselves who have built them in such a way'[4] that they do so. A machine has no sort of experience.

In the light of these and kindred considerations Feigl concludes that 'the central puzzle of the mind-body problem is the logical nature of the correlation laws connecting raw feel qualities with neurophysiological processes'.[5] But his own approach to the problem is further defined in reflections like the following.

The main issues must be capable of settlement, in the last analysis, in a scientific way, provided this is understood in a fairly broad sense of providing a 'coherent and adequate descriptive and explanatory account of the spatio-temporal-causal world'.[6] Our answers must come within 'the intersubjective observation language of common life'[7] and they must thus be answers 'to which empirical evidence is ultimately and in principle relevant'.[8] This is not quite as restricted as it may seem. For allowance must be made for direct experience or raw feels. It is not a matter of

---

[1] *Op. cit.*, p. 438.
[2] *Op. cit.*, p. 446.
[3] *Op. cit.*, p. 399.
[4] *Op. cit.*, p. 418.
[5] *Op. cit.*, p. 416.
[6], [7] *Op. cit.*, p. 377.
[8] *Op. cit.*, p. 374.

wholly unrelieved physicalism. The main point is rather this. We must indeed take account of what is known in direct experience, and this is how we come to ascribe 'raw feels' to other persons by analogy. But once we have got thus far, we have to settle questions like that of interactionism versus some kind of monism on the basis of the correlations we find between subjective states established by observation and neurophysiological states which we also observe. This is how the enterprise becomes respectably scientific.

But this programme at once invites two comments. In the first place it is much more obscure than may appear at first. For how are the neurophysiological sequences to be established in relation to the relevant mental states? The task is not wholly daunting when we think of very simple sensations. We associate a wince with a certain sort of painful sensation. But our mental life is rarely, if ever, restricted to discrete simple items of that sort. It is much more elaborate, alive, and subtle. It is constantly changing. How do we establish the full rich character of mental states with sufficient precision in a variety of situations to examine the close correlation between them and the concurrent physiological states? The controlled observation and experiment of science would seem to be peculiarly hard to attain in this case. That there are close relations between mental and physical states is a matter of common experience. But to determine the extent and precise form of this on the basis of sustained exhibition of states confirmed by observation sufficient to decide between interaction and other views requires the sort of exactitude we can hardly expect here. On the physical side the situation is also immensely complicated.

Indeed, so much is this the case that Feigl himself seems to be looking to a very distant future, '3000 A.D.'[1] in one place and 'a thousand years hence' as it is repeated later,[2] for the proper completion of his programme. The nearest we could get in the meantime would be by autocerebroscopic evidence which would determine, for example, whether experience of volitions as directly introspected could be strictly correlated with simultaneous cortical states as observed by looking upon the screen. If the idea of interaction is sound there should, it is argued, 'be sensations (produced by the chain of processes usually assumed in the causal theory of

[1] *Op. cit.*, p. 442.
[2] *Op. cit.*, p. 450.

perception but) not strictly correlated with the terminal cortical events'.[1] Why we should just speak of sensations in this case is not clear to me, and I should have thought that, even in the case of observing one's own cortical states, the sort of vastly complicated information required initially (and held in mind at the time) to establish that our direct awareness disclosed nothing which could not be read off from the cortical states, is daunting to the utmost degree. Is this not also a programme for some very distant date? We are nowhere near it now, and, if any importance is to be attached to it, a great deal more requires to be said about the precise form which such an investigation should take than the very general allusions to it in Professor Feigl's paper.

The most that we have, in short, is a programme, conceived in rather general and not too clear terms, and a pious expectation that all truth will eventually be found to be conformable with what is 'scientifically defensible' and most in accord with the require-ments of scientific prediction. As the writer very frankly admits— 'I just place my bets regarding the future of psychophysiology in the "Victorian direction",'[2] that term here indicating the belief in 'the predictability of mental events from neurophysiological states of the organism'.[3] But why should such a bet be placed at all? The appropriate experiments are only dimly conceived and the assumptions on which we act from day to day seem to be all against it. Is not Feigl himself here guilty of the sort of prejudice and dogmatism of metaphysicians and theologians of whose 'emotionally and pictorially highly charged phrases'[4] he himself complains?

This again, I must stress, does not mean that there are not very close correlations between mental and physical states, and this means that with greater knowledge and finer equipment we may well be able at some future date to infer far more than we do now about mental states from observations of the brain and so forth. The question is whether the circuit could ever be closed at the physical level. Feigl himself provides an interesting analogy for us when he refers[5] to a mischievous boy interfering with the move-ments of billiard balls otherwise predictable on the basis of mechanical laws. We may recall Nicolai Hartmann's 'plus of

[1] *Op. cit.*, p. 382.
[2] *Op. cit.*, p. 379.
[3] see *Op. cit.*, p. 376.
[4] *Op. cit.*, p. 386.
[5] *Op. cit.*, p. 378.

determination'[1] which modifies without wholly suspending a process already subject to some determination. Feigl allows that something of this sort is conceivable in the relations of minds to bodies, and that interactionism can thus be properly stated and considered. He is simply confident that future experiments will rule it out; and it is this confidence which seems to me so misplaced at the present state of such experimentation and in the light of common experience and all it implies.

The same impression is deepened in two further observations made by Feigl at this stage of his discussion. He declares that if there should be any mental states 'not inferable on the basis of intersubjectively accessible' neurophysiological states, 'then their role is suspiciously like that of a deus ex machina'.[2] But why should it be? Only, it seems to me, on the dogmatic assumption that there is something essentially suspicious and baffling about any process of which it is not possible to give a strictly scientific explanation. There is nothing inherently improper or defeatist about a notion which accords so well with what we find the facts of experience as a whole to be. It only seems so if we dogmatically rule that there can be nothing which is essentially 'excluded from the scope of science'.[3]

Likewise in the reference to the type of interactionism which requires, not merely 'raw feels or passing states of mind', but some kind of permanent soul or substance to which these belong. This idea gets very short shrift indeed. We are simply told that 'there seems little scientific evidence that would support it'.[4] There are no 'good cognitive reasons' for it. But what is wrong with the 'cognitive reasons' adduced by a host of thinkers from Plato through Descartes, Berkeley, Kant to Ward and Tennant and many today like H. J. Paton, Brand Branshard and C. A. Campbell (to name some that first come to mind) we are not told at all. Feigl is just content to note, without further argument, that any 'role the self' may have here 'may very well be explained by a more or less stable structure of dispositions' due to the 'continually modulated structure of the organism (especially the nervous and endocrine systems)'.[5] But this is just a further pious hope backed by no argument or any examination of the arguments of others.

---

[1] Nicolai Hartmann. *Ethics* Vol. III.
[2] *Minnesota Studies in the Philosophy of Science*, Vol. II., p. 383.
[3] *Op. cit.*, p. 385.
[4, 5] *Op. cit.*, p. 386.

A very casual reference to the freewill problem takes the same course. Feigl sides with those who hold that freewill involves determinism, and offers no comment on the arguments of these (notably C. A. Campbell) who take the opposite view today. The idea of an indeterminism which would 'require "spontaneously" arising mental states', by no means the form of words which all indeterminists would favour, is dismissed as 'neither supported by empirical evidence, nor advisable as a regulative idea for research'.[1] Related views are dismissed by just invoking the rule of parsimony which 'warns us not to multiply entities (factors, variables) beyond necessity'.[2] But the only necessity recognized is that which might 'become evident in the progress of research'. Feigl can 'cheerfully accept this enrichment of the conceptual apparatus of science; or, ontologically speaking, this discovery of new entities in our world'.[3] But why should it be assumed that entities can only be found to be necessary in this way?

Proceeding on these assumptions, however, Feigl sets out in greater detail his list of the conditions to be satisfied for the solution of his main problem, namely that of the correlation of our 'raw feels' with neurophysiological processes. One of these conditions is surprising, but indicative in a significant way of Feigl's approach to the subject. In sorting out the various meanings of 'mental' and 'physical', he refers to the alleged non-spatial character of mental events as one of the 'most powerful arguments in favour of a radical dualism'.[4] He has thus to dispose of this notion while holding to the view that we have some direct or private acquaintance with our own mental states. He does so in this way. Firstly, the 'rhetorical questions asked by dualists' about the location of the feeling of motherly love—and 'how many inches long is it?' etc.—are exposed to scorn as 'a category-mistake of the crudest sort', the influence of Ryle being evident here as in the earlier reference to the dispositional account of the self. The category-mistake in this case is a confusion between universals and particulars. 'The feeling of motherly love is a universal',[5] and the question of location does not arise. But surely this is itself the worst type of confusion. There are also actual manifestations or cases of motherly love, what goes on in the experience or mental life of the mother, and this is said to be non-spatial because in fact it is so, not because the question does not arise. In his

[1, 2, 3] *Op. cit.*, p. 386.
[4, 5] *Op. cit.*, p. 406.

second point, Feigl admits that concepts may be applied to individuals. There is the case of someone feeling depressed. 'In this case there is quite clearly a location for the feeling of depression. It is in the person concerned.'[1] But this is extremely odd and unhelpful. What does 'person' mean here? Is more implied than that it is X who is depressed? Feigl anticipates this comment and allows that there is 'a more delicate' question about 'individual mental states'. He seems prepared to admit that these may not be in physical space, but they are nonetheless not wholly immaterial. Physical space is a 'theoretical construction', and it is made possible by the 'phenomenological space of our experience'. My 'feelings and emotions' have a place in the latter since they can be said, as William James had claimed, to 'pervade large parts of my body-as-I-experience it'; they 'may be located at least vaguely or diffusely in some not very sharply delineated part of the organism', elation or depression, for example, 'in the upper half or two-thirds of my body', sounds and smells 'partly outside, partly inside the phenomenal head'.[2] There seems to be thus a location of some kind at least for individual mental states.

There is much here, however, which invites comment. I should wish myself to draw some distinction between public space and space as each one experiences it.[3] But this is a distinction which needs to be very carefully drawn. Feigl tells us little about the precise way in which he understands it. But even with the distinction allowed, it is a very moot point how far any mental state can be said to pervade even 'the-body-as-I-experience it'. The hard case here is that of so-called 'physical sensations' like pain. We seem to locate these in parts of our bodies. On the other hand, many contend that we do not do this directly, but only by some kind of judgment. But, however the issue is settled in the case of 'physical sensations', this seems to give little warrant to the locating of feelings of elation or depression within the body. Such feelings may be accompanied by sensations which pervade some part of the body, but that is not what they are in themselves. In essentials they involve thoughts, hopes, expectations and so on, some of which are actively entertained. In no sense have these any sort of spatial location. Why, in any case, should the issue be restricted, as it is by Feigl, to feelings of depression and kindred 'feelings and emotions'? These do not exhaust our mental life.

[1, 2] *Op. cit.*, p. 407.
[3] See addendum p. 329.

What about solving a problem? Or is there nothing we directly experience here? Are the admitted raw feels just matters of emotions and sensations? Why should they be? Whatever may be said for direct acquaintance with our own mental states in the one case may be said for it in the other. If not, some justification should be offered for the restriction. None is attempted by Feigl.

There appears to be thus little justification for the view that 'mental events as directly experienced and phenomenally described are spatial'.[1] The further main conditions for the solution of the central problem cover mainly matters of which mention has been already made. There is the insistence that experiential events are private to each person, although confirmable intersubjectively on the basis of analogy. It is also urged that the ideas of quality and quantity cut across the distinction of mental and physical, and in some of the many uses of such terms this is plainly true. We are reminded that 'purposive' is a term which has ambiguous uses but that in the sense in which 'mentality', as involving purpose, is the prerogative of man, it involves also sentience and raw feels. Again the mnemic and holistic aspects of mind, including the storage of information, while they have parallels or, one might perhaps say, manifestations, in nonmental spheres, are only relevant in the case of mental life with 'the addition of the criterion of immediate experience'.[2] Finally, we are reminded of the intentional character of thought, it is 'about something', this being thought to be implied especially in the fact that we may not only 'have an experience' but 'be aware of having it'. Such 'aboutness' cannot be given a merely 'behavioural or neurophysiological description',[3] but in saying this Feigl tends also to imply that this side of the question can be handed over to logic, it is a question for the study of meaningful content and not of fact. That, of course, overlooks the process of entertaining a meaningful content. But nothing is specifically said here by Feigl to repudiate the admission of the direct awareness of our own experience. That is the crux of the matter.

The main move now made by Feigl is to indicate how identification comes about in scientific theories. It 'consists simply', we are told, 'in the recognition that one and the same individual (or

---

[1] Op. cit., p. 408.
[2] Op. cit., p. 413.
[3] Op. cit., p. 417.

universal) may be designated by different labels or described by different characterizations'.[1] This varies from logical synonymity to extensional and empirical identification. In the factual sciences identities are 'confirmed on the basis of empirical evidence'.[2] It is simply a case of individuals 'uniquely described in two or more ways'. The author of Hamlet is identified in this way with the author of King Lear, table salt is NaC1 and 'a metal characterized in terms of its thermal conductivity may be identical with the metal characterized by its electric conductivity'.[3] The descriptions are not of course identical in these cases but 'the referent' is. We may describe a city as the one which is the seat of the United States Government and the one where there is a certain degree of humidity, pressure, temperature at a certain time. 'The referent of these descriptions is the one city of Washington, DC.'[4]

Mention of 'the referent' is of great importance here. We are indeed told that it is 'a matter of convenience in epistemological reconstruction' just where we decide to put the boundary (or 'partition') between the data of observation and the inferred state of affairs. 'But somewhere we must put it, if we are not to lose sight of the empirical character of the relation between the data and the illata.'[5] I am not sure just what this means. But it does become clear that Feigl is not content with any kind of 'phenomenalistic translatability doctrine'. 'The practice of scientific thinking clearly demonstrates that theoretical concepts (hypothetical entities) are never reducible to, or identifiable with, observable data (or logical constructions thereof).'[6] 'Theoretical concepts are "anchored" in the observables, but are not logically (explicitly) definable in terms of the observables.'[7] Nor is Feigl merely content with the unavoidability of 'thing-language' in ordinary parlance and science. He takes his objections to phenomenalism further than that. He commits himself firmly to ' "the causal theory of perception" so much maligned by phenomenalists'.[8] On the other hand the form which this takes remains obscure, since Feigl seems also to be very sensitive about the objection that 'there is no sense in talking of a thing existing over and above the actual and possible "evidential" data and their important correla-

[1, 2] *Op. cit.*, p. 439.
[3, 4] *Op. cit.*, p. 440.
[5] *Op. cit.*, p. 443.
[6, 7] *Op. cit.*, p. 444.
[8] *Op. cit.*, p. 452.

tions'.[1] 'Far from requiring an unknown or unknowable "third" or "neutral propertyless substance", ordinary knowledge and especially scientific theory contains a great deal of information about the nature and structure of stimulus objects.'[2]

The conclusion which I feel must be drawn from this is that Feigl has not sufficiently thought out the precise form of his alternative to phenomenalism and relies on a rather vague form of realism based upon the intersubjective confirmability of what we learn about the world around us and the well-known difficulty of reducing this to exhaustively phenomenalist terms. We may indeed know a great deal more through science about a bell, for example, than we have in mind at the common-sense level, but that in itself does not show that the detail and system provided by science is different in kind. It is certainly not enough to assume dogmatically, as so many do today, that 'the phenomenalist thesis of the translatability of physical object statements into data statements is untenable'.[3] We must be shown more clearly where this breaks down in principle, and what, in the light of this breakdown, is the nature of the referent which is thus required. It will not suffice to remind us how much we know about the referent from the data when the question is just what is the referent over and above the data. I will not press the point further here, but merely say that the sense in which a referent is required in the present context calls for a great deal more clarification. But the upshot of what I at least find to be a rather obscure position is that some very close identity is affirmed between the observables and the referent about which they tell us. The latter is neither a phenomenalist construct nor a further unknown 'reality-in-itself'. It is more than the observables and yet one with them in some very strict, but unspecified, sense.

The next move is a crucial one, although by no means easy to follow. It seems that there are referents, not only for the observables by which the world around us is known, but also for raw feels or the acquaintance terms used by the 'subject in introspective descriptions of his (the subject's) direct experience'.[4] What does this imply? One is led to think at least of some substantival view of the self as some reality over and above its passing states, and at one point at least we come very close to a Kantian style of

[1] Op. cit., p. 451.
[2], [3] Op. cit., p. 452.
[4] Op. cit., p. 436.

argument. 'In the directly given data', we are told, 'there is a
certain feature of centralization' based 'on the ever-present
potentialities of recollecting a great many events or sequences of
events'.[1] But we have already seen that we must not invoke the
idea of some ulterior 'reality in itself' or 'unknowable third'
altogether distinct from the evidential data. And with this I would
have much sympathy, as I am certainly not drawn to the notion
of an utterly unknown self merely presupposed to explain other
things. The self which is more than passing states is also given
with them in what our experience as a whole is like, as I shall stress
again. But it is to neither of these ideas, or any kindred variation
on the notion of the self as an abiding entity, that Feigl turns. The
referent is understood here as elsewhere in terms of the object
that comes in sight in the process of inter-subjective confirmation,
including what I learn about myself beyond my immediate experience. Other persons learn about me by analogy, and there is
a referent in this process, and in kindred indirect knowledge I may
have of myself, which goes beyond the immediate data, as in the
causal theory of perception, but is also in some way continuous or
identical with them.

This seems to make it possible that in some cases the referents
of what is directly presented in experience, raw feels or 'acquaintance terms', are identical with the referents of 'objective' or
physical terms having to do with 'a state of affairs in the world
outside the observer'.[2] The absence of a radical discontinuity
seems to make this possible, and this possibility seems to be very
much heightened when we learn that the immediate data of
experience, and whatever regularities these exhibit, can themselves be objects of knowledge or referents in the sentences which
just describe what they are in themselves. They can thus 'function
either as verifiers or as referents of knowledge claims'.[3] But where
the identity is firmly established, according to Feigl, is where the
referents of 'molar behaviour theory', which deals in concepts like
'habit strength, expectancy, drive, instinct, memory trace,
repression, superego, etc.', 'are empirically identifiable with the
referents of some neurophysiological concepts'.[4] For the raw
feels of direct experience can themselves be identified with 'the
referents of certain specifiable concepts of molar behaviour

---

[1] *Op. cit.*, p. 460.
[2], [3] *Op. cit.*, p. 438.
[4] *Op. cit.*, p. 445.

theory'.[1] In other words, 'what is had-in-experience and (in the case of human beings) knowable by acquaintance, is identical with the object of knowledge by description provided first by molar behaviour theory and this is in turn identical with what the science of neurophysiology describes (or, rather, will describe when sufficient progress has been achieved) as processes in the central nervous system'.[2] 'The data of experience are' thus 'the reality which a very narrow class of neurophysiological concepts denotes'.[3]

There is, however, one gap, at a vital stage of this very intricate argument, which Professor Feigl does little to fill, and I am much at a loss as to how it might be filled. This concerns the ascription of what goes on in immediate experience to the so-called concepts of molar theory. For it seems to be just taken for granted that this can be done in a quite exhaustive way. In other words what I think and do, and so on, can be completely explained in terms of dispositions or kindred sets of my character or nature—my 'make-up' as we sometimes put it. The way these themselves function and belong together is thought to require nothing beyond themselves at the properly mental level. To that extent they account for our experience and the course of our thoughts exhaustively. Many would think that more is required here, especially as the explanatory power of dispositional traits is severely limited. But what seems most patently overlooked is the way thoughts themselves, and thus our experience as a whole, determine the way they should go. The nature of thought itself seems to be left out of account. Admittedly Feigl does refer to 'intentionality' and may seem thus to do justice to the importance of meaningful content. But for the most part he seems content to leave this to logic and semantics, although he does refer at one point to intentional acts as 'occurrents in direct experience'.[4] For the most part, under cover of the curious term 'raw feels' which is here peculiarly misleading, the whole problem is transferred, together with fleeting sensations, to the field of molar explanation as described above. This seems to me to leave a fatal gap in the argument, to say nothing of the rejection of all possibility of the sort of undetermined choice which many thinkers take to be involved in moral action.

[1, 4] *Op. cit.*, p. 445.
[2] *Op. cit.*, p. 446.
[3] *Op. cit.*, p. 453.

But even if we remain content with the exhaustive ascription of thought and experience to these 'concepts of molar behaviour', and they certainly have importance, there remains a very hard problem about the identification of these, or their referents, with neurophysiological patterns and their referents. Granted the notion of a referent as it stands, and it is by no means beyond question, why should we assume that the referent required or appropriate in the one case is identical, or even of a like nature, with that which has place in the other? In its simplest and bluntest terms the position is this. We explain thoughts and experiences in terms of dispositional traits of various kinds which in turn have their referents. The latter are not a set of unknown 'third' things or characterless substances, they are known through the molar concepts though distinct from them, and there is here a nest of problems I shall not stir up further. We also learn by observation about neurophysiological processes, and these in turn have a referent likewise involved in inter-subjective confirmation. But why, even if all this were altogether plain and beyond dispute, should it be supposed that the referents could ever be identical in these two cases?

It will not suffice here, although it seems to be hinted at one point that it will, to claim that we do know the raw feels themselves as referents in one limited way. For it does not follow from this that a further very different sort of referent is not required when the picture comes to be completed with the account of the neurophysiological processes involved. To have established the raw feel as a referent does not prove in the least, except by a gigantic begging of the question, that it is the only referent involved. Nor does any alleged continuity of the referent and the patterns in which it is involved preclude a discontinuity of types of pattern and their referents, unless again it is assumed that in getting at a referent we have reached the only one involved.

Feigl is not unaware of this difficulty. Indeed if he were to overlook it he might be well on the way to some kind of panpsychism or a view of the coextensiveness of mental and material reality such as we find in the work of G. F. Stout. Feigl certainly wants to avoid this kind of metaphysics. His view is that the referents of mental and physical processes are identical in *some cases only*. It is only neurophysiological processes that have 'internal illumination'. But how then do we establish the identity in the cases where it is claimed?

We do so on the empirical basis of an 'extensional equivalence'. This is obtained from the close correlations between certain neurophysiological processes, cerebral ones especially, and our behaviour. The correlations indicate an identical referent, they are what counts, it seems, in the process of inter-subjective confirmation. And if we are told that this procedure crosses 'an ontological barrier', we need not be perturbed, for there is in fact no 'unbridgeable gulf' and 'no occasion for metaphysical shudders'; for 'private states known by direct acquaintance and referred to by phenomenal (subjective) terms can be described in a public (at least physical) language and may thus be empirically identifiable with the referents of certain neurophysiological terms. Privacy is capable of public (intersubjective) description, and the objects of intersubjective science can be evidenced by data of private experience'.[1]

An initial and, it seems to me, radical, weakness in this procedure is the slender and incomplete nature of the correlations that are firmly established. We can establish these with some precision in respect to fairly simple stimulus and response conditions and indicate certain general ways in which brain conditions affect our mental life. Even with modern techniques and refinements such as the use of an autocerebroscope, the information at present available remains very meagre. Feigl is himself well aware of this and he himself reminds us that 'our psychophysiological ignorance is still too great to permit anything more than bold guesses on the scientific side'.[2] We need 'further clinical, experimental, or statistical studies'.[3] 'Any detailed account' is 'a matter for the future progress of psychophysiological research'.[4] 'In the light of the scanty knowledge available even today' a "psychological physiology" which frames hypotheses about neural structures and processes on the basis of a knowledge of the characteristics and the regularities in the changes of phenomenal fields must, therefore, always remain extremely sketchy'.[5]

This is in line with the point I made earlier, namely that the weight of a very bold theory is made to rest on very scanty evidence and the wishful expectation that it will be confirmed at some future date, in all likelihood a very remote one. A view that is odd

[1] *Op. cit.*, p. 448.
[2] *Op. cit.*, p. 458.
[3] *Op. cit.*, p. 437.
[4], [5] *Op. cit.*, p. 457.

G

almost to the point of paradox ought to have a firmer basis from the start, or at least to be put forward in an extremely tentative fashion. But even if the appropriate correlations could be effectively established, what would we have gained? It could be shown that the idea of interaction was out and that we could move, in the process of trans-subjective confirmation, with complete ease and confidence from one level, mental or physical, to the other. There could be a uniform notation or symbolism for the two processes, but this seems still to fall very far short of identity—in either the processes themselves as observed or the purported referents. If there is to be a referent in the two cases, however precisely this is to be understood, we should expect it, in each case, to reflect the initially very different nature of the processes from which it is posited, that is mental states and the presentations from which the world of nature is known.

This suggests that, even if the evidence should eventually take the course which Feigl himself so confidently anticipates, the most that we could affirm is some kind of psycho-physical parallelism or epiphenomenalism. The mental would not have been eliminated in favour of material reality, and why should we not at least leave the issue open so far as monism or some form of parallelism are concerned? Feigl is again very sensitive about this difficulty. It presents itself sharply in the very need for empirical confirmation of his thesis to which he himself attaches great importance. The required identity cannot be obvious if such confirmation is needed, and Feigl himself brings this out in a somewhat oblique comment on Leibniz's principle of the identity of indiscernibles.[1] His reaction is to admit that parallelism or isomorphism is a possible position, even if the appropriate correlations were exhaustively established by a 'compleat autocerebroscopist', and that the question cannot, therefore, be settled finally in scientific terms. A parallelistic account is at least scientifically feasible.[2] But 'the scientific evidence for parallelism' has to be 'interpreted as the empirical basis for the identification. The step from parallelism to the identity view is essentially a matter of philosophical interpretation'.[3]

How then does philsophy come to the rescue here? It does so in terms of a principle particularly dear to those who claim a scientific orientation to philosophy, namely the principle of

[1] *Op. cit.*, p. 456.
[2,3] *Op. cit.*, p. 461.

parsimony. Entities are not to be multiplied without necessity, this famous rule being taken to be 'in the spirit of normal procedures of scientific induction and theory construction'.[1] But valuable though Occam's razor may be to snip off unnecessary metaphysical encumbrances, it has also to be used with restraint and discernment. It is not a way of being rid of just anything we do not like or which does not suit our theory. Let us by all means prefer simplicity, but not at the expense of the facts, or as our sole principle on crucial issues. The fact is that we are aware of our own mental processes directly, as Feigl himself handsomely allows, and we are aware of them as being different in nature from what we encounter otherwise of the world around us. If we are to have second thoughts about this and call into question what seems to be a plain fact of common experience, it would also seem necessary to invoke something more for the purpose than a very arbitrary use of the principle of parsimony.

For all we know there may, in fact, be many orders of being or types of reality in the universe besides the two with which we are familiar. Spinoza and others have made suggestive use of this possibility. We certainly cannot rule them out of court from the start on the grounds that it makes things complicated if they are right. Least of all can we go against what in fact we find to be the case on the ground that it is simpler to have one rather than two sorts of things. Simplicity can hardly be given that sort of dominion over thought. And yet that seems to be all that Feigl offers us at what he himself describes as 'the philosophical or logical crux of the identity thesis'.[2]

It makes little difference here to be assured that the reality of our brain processes is not to be confused with the grey mass we observe on opening a skull. For whatever may be said in these terms about the true nature of our brains and other parts of our bodies—and we may well be on to very doubtful metaphysics here and a *naïveté* of speculation little in accord with the much vaunted scientific spirit—we have no reason to posit anything akin to mental reality without evidence of the sort of response by which the latter is detected. But Feigl offers us nothing of that sort, putting his trust entirely in the correlations which he hopes will eventually be established and the principle of parsimony.

The issue is, in short, prejudged at the crucial points, and this

[1] *Op. cit.*, p. 386.
[2] *Op. cit.*, p. 461.

becomes yet more plain in the sorts of comparison Feigl uses to illustrate his main thesis. Some individuals, like Anthony Eden, have direct acquaintance with the Queen while others can only lay claim to some knowledge about her. 'It is surely the same person that Eden and I know, each in his way.'[1] The knowledge a cartographer has of a jungle from the vantage point of a balloon is more complete and accurate than that of a person lost in the jungle. But it is the same jungle. The author himself admits that this simile is misleading, since the appeal in both cases is to sensory perception.[2] But he does not seem to take the full force of his admission. It makes no difference, he thinks, when we identify the referents of a feeling of anxiety as I report it and that of the symptoms or the cerebral processes which scientists observe. But it seems to me that this is just where a radical difference is found. We have to move by inference from the scientific description to a totally different type of reality to get to the feeling of anxiety. It is not a case of extending our knowledge simply at the same level of discourse.

The elaborate structure of Professor Feigl's arguments is, therefore, inclined to be deceptive. So is the impression it first conveys of having a formidable scientific character. For, on examination, it seems to reduce to a confident assumption that whatever is most consistent with scientific procedure must be sound in philosophy. It is assumed that dualism cannot be a respectable view for someone who also wishes to have proper regard for science and the scientific spirit. This is how the major issues come to be begged at the crucial stages of the argument. But for that there is as little warrant as for the dogmatisms of religiously minded persons who are accused of substituting emotionally highly charged phrases for reasons. Theologians have no monopoly of such error, and the counterpart of their lapses seems on occasion to be most marked among those who chastize them in the name of a liberal and open scientific spirit. One admires the determination of Feigl to recognize the genuineness and inwardness of mental states and his frank admission of the sense in which they are initially private. That compares well with the rude dismissal of private mental states. But, in the attempt to accommodate this within a monistic framework thought to be the most consonant with the scientific temper, there appear

[1] *Op. cit.*, p. 462.
[2] *Op. cit.*, p. 463.

to be many of the limitations of those who seek an expressly religious answer to every question.

A position very similar to that of Feigl, and in some ways, it seems, much indebted to it, is that of Professor J. C. C. Smart in his *Philosophy and Scientific Realism*. He starts his discussion of consciousness, in chapter V of this book, with substantial concessions to Ryle. Much that we say about alleged inner processes can, on his view, be understood in terms of 'characteristic behaviour pattern'[1] and avowals, provided we also take some account of the causal conditions of behaviour patterns. But he does not want to deny altogether that we do have experiences of which 'genuine reports' can be given. It is significant that the examples he offers us here are those of being in pain or having an after-image. For these are the sorts of experiences which can be most directly correlated with physiological processes. But I should argue that there is as much an element of 'neat experience'[2] in solving a mathematical problem or writing a poem as in undergoing physical pain. I will not, however, follow this further now, as I would have nothing to add to what has been already said about the Rylean arguments which Smart would invoke here. The important point is that Smart does allow that 'there seems to be some element of "pure inner experience" which is being reported, and to which only I have direct access'.[3] We do have neat or immediate experience.

This is a frank and welcome admission, and there is no prevarication about it. But one is startled to read in the same context that these 'conscious experiences are simply brain processes'.[4] How does this transformation come about? How can an undisputed 'inner experience' be also an observable physical process in the brain? The arguments in support of this curious position are somewhat circuitous; they consist largely of refutations of alleged objections, and it is thus not easy to discover what positive submissions Smart has to offer for a view admitted to be so paradoxical that 'almost every first-year student of philosophy would claim to be able to refute it'.[5]

One objection to his view which Smart considers is that a person (an 'illiterate peasant' perhaps) can report 'his images and

[1] *Philosophy and Scientific Realism*, p. 89.
[2], [5] *Op. cit.*, p. 91.
[3] *Op. cit.*, p. 89.
[4] *Op. cit.*, p. 88.

aches and pains, and yet nevertheless may not know that the brain has anything to do with thinking'.[1] The reply is that brain process is not 'part of what we *mean* by "experience" ',[2] although it is what experience as a matter of fact is. We do not mean by 'the author of Waverley' 'the author of Ivanhoe', but the author is in fact the same person in both cases. 'The true nature of lightning, what lightning really is', is 'to be a motion of electric charges'.[3] But we do not need to know this to recognize lightning in the ordinary way and know the meaning of the word.

These analogies seem to me extremely misleading. When we say of the author of Waverley that he is also the author of Ivanhoe we are affirming something further of a specific nature about him, and the question then arises of how far this assertion is in the same vein and what is the relation between these two attributes of the same person. In the same way we may recognize lightning as a flash of light of a certain sort heralding a clap of thunder and so on, and we may also learn what is not obvious at first, namely that this is brought about by electric discharges of a certain kind. This is a causal relationship, and if we are to go on to identify the flash and the electric discharge this must be on the basis of a clearly formulated view of the relation of cause and effect in such cases and the justification this offers for the affirmation of identity we proceed to make. For rough and ready purposes we may say that the lightning is the electric discharge, but this leaves it very open what sort of relation we are to affirm eventually between the flash and its cause.

We have to be even more cautious in the case of a sensation of pain or an after-image and the brain processes which cause it, for the difference between cause and effect here is of a very radical nature. We may say, in a very rough and ready fashion indeed in this instance, that the ache is the brain process; but that would only be a very elliptical way, legitimate perhaps, if also very risky, for some pedagogic purposes, of indicating the close causal relation involved. We may indeed say that the person who sees the flash is also the person whose brain undergoes a certain change. But this, as we have seen earlier, is in line with much that we find it convenient to say in a rough-and-ready way for ordinary purposes. It does not imply that anyone, in ordinary discourse or in sophisticated thought, considers himself to be strictly identical with his brain. There are distinctions to be

---

[1, 2] *Op. cit.*, p. 92.
[3] *Op. cit.*, p. 93.

drawn, relationships to be considered, and this is what is hopelessly obscured in comparisons like that of the lightning being said to be in fact an electric discharge.

Undaunted by this sort of consideration, Smart goes on boldly to reject a version of his thesis which might afford some amelioration of its difficulties, namely the double-aspect theory in a form which allows of some non-physical properties. He wants the identification with the physical process to be more complete than that; and, to substantiate this contention, his next main move is to insist that one's report of 'what is going on in me' when I have an after-image or an ache is 'topic neutral'. It does not imply that it is brain or heart or wholly non-physical. It is like the word 'somebody' in 'somebody is coming through the gate', a 'colourless' word little indicative of what real flesh and blood person is coming through the gate. This seems to me again altogether misleading. In becoming aware of my ache, in having the ache, I am aware of it at once as something different in nature from anything I come subsequently to understand as a process in the brain or any other functions of my body, however close I take the causal dependence of the one on the other to be. There is no neutrality about it on this score. The status of the after-image itself is not, of course, what is in question here, although that is also in some sense very private; the having of the image or feeling the ache (or, I would add, following the arguments in a discussion) simply cannot be conceived as anything other than distinct mental occurrences radically different in nature from anything we can observe through our senses.

Smart adds that we classify an experience of an after-image as being like, let us say, the experience I have when I see an orange. But this likeness, he contends, 'must consist in a similarity of neuro-physiological pattern'. It is tempting 'to suppose that reports of similarities can be made only on a basis of the conscious apprehension of the features in respect of which these similarities subsist', but this is unwarranted when we 'think objectively about the human being as a functioning mechanism'.[1] But why should we think in this way? Why not think in accordance with what we find the facts to be? The procedure derided by Smart is said to be metaphysical and *a priori*, but could anything merit these descriptions more than the assumption, as the basis of an argument, that we can only view ourselves objectively if we take ourselves

[1] *Op. cit.*, p. 95.

to be merely 'functioning mechanisms'? On that basis the similarities
in question could only be some physiological pattern, but in
actual fact what they are initially or as a feature of the inner
experiences we report are resemblances only intelligible in the
light of what these experiences are in themselves and quite independently of any neurophysiological processes that may occasion
them. Having an after-image is like seeing an orange for the simple
reason that the two experiences are similar. No one, in such a
case, reporting that his experience is like seeing an orange, is
thinking, in the first place, if indeed at all, of processes in his
brain or any part of his body.

It is also urged that we only learn how to use a word like 'pain'
in some environmental situation. This is true, but it does not
follow that we are referring to such a situation when we assert
that we have a pain, much less that we are thinking of the neurophysiological factors of the situation. Smart also holds that there
is no such entity as an after-image. This, I believe, is doubtful,
although I shall not pause now to consider the status of after-
images. But I agree that it is the having of the after-image that
matters at the moment. Where I fail to follow Smart is in the
assumption that, if we think expressly of having the image, and
not of the image itself, all we have left is a brain process. What we
have in fact is an experience, although it could not be the sort of
experience it is except in having a precise character of our having
a particular sort of after-image.

To the objection that the experience of having the ache or the
after-image is not in physical space Smart replies that the experience is not reported as something spatial, but only in a quite
neutral way as 'what is going on in me' which we learn in due
course is spatial and physical. To this I can only reply again that
the experience does not seem to me to be neutral or open at all in
this particular way.

The reply made to yet another objection is, I think, very
revealing. Suppose it were affirmed, through the use of an electro-
encephalograph, that I did not have the brain-process that goes
with the experience (of seeing something yellow perhaps) which
I actually and sincerely report. In that case we could hardly
identify the experience with the sort of brain-process that normally
goes with it. Smart frankly admits this—'if it did happen', he
declares, 'I should doubtless give up the brain-process theory'.[1]

[1] *Op. cit.*, p. 99.

Should he not give it up even by just having to entertain the possibility? What he does say is that 'I can still believe *that this will never in fact happen*'. But this is indeed to throw a considerable hostage to fortune. Might it not be discovered that the correlation of mental and physical processes is not as complete as we actually take it, even apart from all that interaction may require? Could we not, perhaps, have paranormal experiences which do not have the usual brain conditions? May we not somewhere come across creatures whose experiences resemble our own in spite of their having a very different physical make-up? May we not indeed, scandalous though it may seem to a hard-boiled materialist, wake up some day to find ourselves having various sorts of experiences without our bodies in their present form at all?

As in the case of Feigl, Smart is basing his initial assumption on what he takes will be the invariable scientific evidence when it is more fully available, and for this there appears to be no better foundation than the dogmatic determination to take a certain side whether properly confirmed or not. It is to substitute dogmatic optimism for rational enquiry, no less reprehensible in a scientist than in a religious believer.

As another line of defence, Smart, while granting to his critic at one stage the incorrigibility of first-person sensation reports, holds that, in fact, it is 'logically possible that someone should sincerely report an experience and yet that the experience should not occur'.[1] There is nothing we need question here so far as correctness of description is concerned. Colour-blind persons report experiences they do not have. But this hardly affects the present issue. One knows oneself what sort of experience one is having, whether or not we can label it or describe it correctly in relation to other things, and for the most part we do in addition take one another's reports to be quite reliable. Our experiences cannot be other than we find them to be, and we certainly find them to be other than externally observable reality. Smart's point, but I also find him very obscure here, is that, as we can be mistaken about our experiences, we can in fact suppose that they are anything. They could be 'some sort of non-physical ghost stuff'. This, he observes 'is a possible hypothesis to set against mine'.[2] He argues for his own 'on the grounds of Occam's

[1] *Op. cit.*, p. 100.
[2] *Op. cit.*, p. 101.

razor and scientific plausibility'.[1] But here again we seem to have recourse to Occam's razor in a very arbitrary way to go against the plain facts of experience which are, not only that it is possible, but inevitable in the nature of what we find experience to be, that they should consist of something non-physical, whether we elect to describe it as 'ghost stuff' or not.

Smart alludes also to the problem of the way we locate pains and other sensations. He rejects, without argument, the 'local signs' theory and similar accounts. He thinks we may 'just locate them immediately' and he even makes the curious suggestion that there may be some cerebral mechanism by which 'the pain may touch off the words'.[2] This is supposed to show further the alleged openness or 'topic neutrality' of such sensations; and this leads to the challenge with which the discussion closes, namely that if we are to dispute the brain-process theory we must 'produce experiences which are known to possess irreducibly "psychic" properties, not merely topic neutral ones'. But if this means that we must single out some experiences which are 'psychic' in some quite distinctive way, it is a challenge that no one can take up, not because there are no 'psychic' experiences but because they *all are psychic*—and inevitably so, for they could be nothing else.

A peculiarly interesting light is thrown on the 'identity thesis', and the plight to which its sponsors are reduced today, by the main defence offered for it by Mr Anthony Quinton in a paper on 'Mind and Matter' in a volume of essays entitled *Brain and Mind* edited by J. R. Smythies. Quinton's position, like that of many who set out today with the same general aim, is that room must be found, in any adequate theory, for that consciousness of ourselves which it seems certain, as a matter of common experience, that we all enjoy. There are at least some mental states which are private and of which each one has 'direct awareness in the psychological sense'.[3] How then can it be held, in the light of this admission and kindred departures from out-and-out behaviourism, that mental states are also physical and observable? Only by insisting that the identity in question is a *'contingent'* one. This is in line with Feigl's insistence on empirical confirmation of his own theory. The impression we have is that some distinction has

[1] *Op. cit.*, p. 101.
[2] *Op. cit.*, p. 104.
[3] *Op. cit.*, p. 233.

to be drawn between mental and physical reality, in the way in which common sense would draw it, but that, in seeming defiance of all we seem forced to admit, we must also represent this distinction as a misleading or provisional one. This is, I think, the point of defending a merely contingent identity of mind and matter. It seems to allow to common sense a great deal, if not all, that it requires. Mental reality is not *ipso facto* material, but it can be shown in a further way that mental and physical reality are the same.

Two main considerations are advanced in support of this conclusion. The first concerns the alleged non-spatial character of mental reality. Quinton agrees with Feigl about many of the characteristics which must be taken to belong exclusively to mental processes, such as mnemic causation and purposiveness. For although analogies to these may be found in the external world, the meaning they have in their proper application to our minds is distinctive and incapable of extension in the strict sense where there is no sort of consciousness, so that, as far as these considerations are concerned, 'we are back once more with Descartes'.[1] But this does not hold where spatial characteristics are concerned. For these can be applied without ambiguity to minds and bodies alike.

This might be thought to be most apparent in the case of bodily sensations, on their own account or as constituents of powerful emotions, which seem apt to be at or pervade regions of the body. But in these cases, as also in dreams and vivid imaginings, the spatiality is of an ambiguous or 'marginal' kind. A pain is not 'literally in my right ankle in the way my right ankle-bone is'.[2] Impressions 'have size and position only relative to one another'. This would require, in my view, some qualification, but then I would also distinguish between the impressions and the experience of having them. I shall not, however, follow this further now. Suffice it to note that Quinton is not quite as happy as others in straightway taking physical sensations to have bodily extension. In some ways also he thinks the categorization of them as mental is suspect. We have, therefore, to look for 'a further reason for saying that mental states and events must have a real position. This is,' according to Quinton, 'that unless experiences have a position in space they cannot be individuated.'[3]

[1] *Op. cit.*, p. 208.
[2] *Op. cit.*, p. 209.
[3] *Op. cit.*, p. 211.

The main idea here is that if two experiences have exactly the same content, or are 'qualitatively indistinguishable', there is no way in which we could distinguish between them except on the basis of spatial location. This raises difficult questions about the senses in which experiences could be qualitatively indistinguishable. Unless they are very simple experiences they are bound to be affected by the context of other experiences in which they appear, by my past history, my dispositions and so on, and the argument would then have to be moved to the somewhat different ground that the required continuity of experience presupposes bodily existence. But apart from this sort of consideration, it does not seem to be in the least evident that an experience could not be distinct or individuated by just being the experience it is, even if no reference is had beyond it to any other reality. If that is not so, the point at least requires consideration and defence which Quinton does not supply.

There is, however, a distinction we ought to draw here, and I think that it is the failure to draw it that makes Quinton's argument seem more conclusive than it is. We have to distinguish between the way in which we identify or recognize some experience in its particularity, when it is the experience of someone other than ourselves, and the identification of some experience as an experience of one's own, or the 'individuation' of it in a particular person's experience. We learn about other people's experiences, and discover that a particular experience is had by some individual at a special time in a certain way, normally through observation of people's bodies. Even if there should be paranormal communication in particular instances we can only recognize and identify the experience as one that emanates from a certain source, and being this experience and not any other, in terms of what we have learnt already in communications that involved people's bodies. Whether or not it would be possible for us to exist in a wholly disembodied state and recognize one another's communications from some pattern of experiences themselves not determined by bodily existence at any stage—all this is indeed doubtful and difficult. I should not myself despair of overcoming the difficulty, and we should retain an open mind about possibilities of communications through media of which we have no conception in our present existence. But even if all these possibilities are waived, the most that we have is the difficulty, or impossibility, of singling out one experience from another when it is a case of the experiences of other people. Nothing is proved about the situation when it is one's own case.

That Quinton takes little heed of this distinction seems to me due to the approach to the subject which he shares with so many other philosophers today, including the assumption that there must be some kind of observable criteria for all meaningful claims. He puts to the dualist the challenge—'Can the dualist attach any sense to the idea that two experiences of disembodied persons that are strictly contemporaneous and indistinguishable in introspective content are really distinct and not one and the same experience?'. He thinks it likely that the dualist will in fact 'attach the experiences in question to some ghostly but really located surrogate, a shade or spectral voice, to carry out the indispensable positioning work ordinarily done by the body'.[1] But why should Quinton assume this when quite the opposite procedure has been adopted by a number of outstanding thinkers such as Kant, Berkeley, James Ward and their successors today? Is not Quinton simply adopting in a quite uncritical way here the dogma that there can be no conception of an inner reality that is not some impossible duplicate of observable things?

Quinton does, however, make one brief allusion to the idea of a mental or spiritual substance, but he dismisses it, at least as an answer to the present problem, with the curt insistence that it could never be 'shown that a single experience cannot be owned by two such substances'.[2] This may seem plausible again if our thought is coloured by considerations of what is intelligible as some kind of duplicate of the external world. If there is no spatial identification, then, in the event of our looking for something else like it, we are bound to be baffled. But the Kantian arguments suggest one way in which experience might be found to belong to one abiding subject, and I should go further and maintain that, in having any particular experience, I am bound to be aware of it as belonging to myself, as an indivisible being, in a way that is unavoidable and indissoluble in a fashion to which no proper parallel is found in the relations of external things to one another. There is, in other words, a finality and ultimacy about the way an experience is *ipso facto* known to be the experience of an agent who has it,[3] though few reflect on this philosophically or have the

[1] *Op. cit.*, p. 211.
[2] *Op. cit.*, p. 212.
[3] *C.f.* below chap. XI.

means of expressing it without conceding more than one should to the metaphors in which we are bound to speak about mental reality. This holds, in my view, for all sentience as well as for the experience of reflective beings. But phrases like 'owned' or 'belonging', or 'being related to', obscure the peculiarity of this situation and the exceptional difficulty of handling it philosophically which encourages the less patient quasi-materialistic treatment of the subject which makes considerations like those adduced by Quinton seem so conclusive.

But even if we granted to Quinton the substance of what he maintains, we would be still very far from a proper identification of mental and physical processes. We would have shown that there could be no mental processes in detachment from physical ones, but this is very far from saying that they are the same. No one denies, as I have often allowed, that there is in our experience a close dependence of mind on body, and if this were shown to be invariable or unavoidable, something important would no doubt be established. Most religions would find it difficult to come to terms with it. But it would still be misleading to conclude that mind and body were essentially of the same order of being. It would not have been shown that minds as such were spatial.

Further arguments adduced at this point by Quinton show again how easily he passes from the recognition of some kind of spatial condition of various experiences to a strict identification of them with a physical existence. He lays it down, for example, that 'a disposition cannot exist in a disembodied way. It must have a bearer'.[1] But why should the bearer be physical? Even if it should be thought inevitable that there should be physiological conditions of our dispositional make-up, this does not show that we can dispense with a further mental 'bearer'. Quinton notes again how smells can pervade a certain locality. We give them at least a 'rough, indeterminate location'. The smell, we say, is in the cellar or along the river-bank. But do we seriously think that smells (or heat or noises) strictly fill the area in which we roughly locate them? Is it not more correct to say that the cellar or the river-bank is the locality in which our bodies receive the stimulus which causes us to have the experience of smelling (or feeling hot or hearing a sound)? The physicist can locate these phenomena more precisely, but what he determines is the more exact nature of the physical conditions of the sort of experience we have.

[1] *Op. cit.*, p. 212.

The special point of examples like those of smells and noises is that these are not located initially with precision. This is what is meant by saying that they are 'weakly spatial' although we can discover their 'strong spatial characteristics'. The suggestion, I take it, is that any reluctance we may have to acknowledge the spatial character of our other experiences must be ascribed to the fact that they also in the first instance are only weakly spatial. They have at least a rough position in space which science may render more precise. To the demand for a criterion of identity of mind and body, therefore, we find that 'the answer is spatio-temporal coincidence (which if perfect would, of course, be an entirely sufficient criterion of identity) supported by concomitant variation of properties'.[1] But nowhere, in the substance of this argument, do we get beyond the recognition of certain physical conditions of mental phenomena. These can indeed in principle be made very precise. But the difference between vagueness and precision has little to do with the radical difference between experiences and material processes.

In his second main attack on his problem Quinton concentrates on the 'irreducible intentionality' which he considers to be an essential feature of mental reality. Even 'animals have thoughts even if they cannot express them in words'.[2] These cannot be described entirely in terms of behaviour. 'Mental states exist in addition to behaviour. As well as the behaviour that manifests them there is belief, intention and understanding.'[3] Some have taken these to be the objects of incorrigible awareness. 'Nothing physical,' it is argued, 'is the object of awareness of this kind. Though we often have knowledge of physical existences our beliefs about them are never incorrigible in the sense that they could not be false.'[4] This gives us, it is claimed, 'the most favoured current criterion of the mental'. If it is accepted, it seems to tell heavily against the identity theory. For 'the objects of direct acquaintance must be what they appear to be and must appear to be what they are. Since they do not generally and unreflectively appear to be states of the brain they cannot be identical with states of the brain.'[5]

To counter this argument, Quinton is content for the most

---

[1] *Op. cit.*, p. 214.
[2] *Op. cit.*, p. 223.
[3] *Op. cit.*, p. 224.
[4, 5] *Op. cit.*, p. 229.

part to refer his readers to arguments set out by Mackie and Armstrong in other writings. But he does mention, very briefly indeed, the stark difficulties about the fallibility of memory and the logical difference between having an experience and being aware that we have it. I should not wish, in reply, to defend the view that incorrigibility is the best criterion of the mental, but I do maintain that there is a way in which we are unfailingly aware of our experiences in having them, notwithstanding that we may misdescribe an experience or fail to get the true flavour of it in considering it reflectively at some remove, even a very slight one. But I shall not join issue with Quinton on this particular question here. For he does seem disposed to agree that, whatever may be said about incorrigibility, experiences do have a meaning content or intentionality in some way which seems to set them quite apart from material things. How does he deal with this difficulty?

He first concedes that intentionality is fatal to behaviourism. 'There is more to thinking and meaning than verbal and other behaviour', but, Quinton argues, 'the identity theory does not deny that mental events and states are introspectible nor that they are distinct from mental and other behaviour.' It 'does not regard the physical and mental descriptions of states of mind as *logically* equivalent. Only a contingent identity is claimed for physical states of the brain and introspectible states of mind'. But in that case we have learnt nothing which substantially alters the position as it defined itself in the discussion of the alleged spatial quality of mental events. Everything depends on how the idea of a contingent identity is to be understood and how far it is plausible.

This idea, like most current versions of the identity hypothesis, is an important advance upon Ryle in one respect. It does not deny private access or reduce all mental reality to dispositional terms. But has it the advantage in greater consistency? What sense can be made of it? Can it be more than relational? We have seen that, for Feigl, the main considerations he adduces leaves the issue ultimately open at least so far as some kind of psycho-physical parallelism is concerned and that nothing avails to close the gap further besides the exercise of Occam's razor. It has not been shown that mental and physical reality are truly the same, and Smart was also anxious to insist that we do not *mean* the same by experience and physical occurrence. The most that seems possible, therefore, is some causal dependence or close correlation which leaves the inherent nature of the two realities quite distinct. The motive behind the notion of a contingent identity is thus fairly clear. It is assumed that one cannot be philosophically respectable in a scientific age without regarding all reality as somehow capable of scientific investigation. Hence we must insist on the ultimate identity of mind and matter. But by making the identity contingent we seem also to come to terms with the patent facts or experience which a more ruthless reduction like that of Ryle seems to disregard.

The idea of a contingent identity, however cries out for analysis. Indeed it could be understood in so wide a sense that hardly anyone would wish to question it as an account of the relation of mind and body. Descartes stressed the peculiarly intimate relation of the two, and other thinkers who defend a dualist position would almost invariably insist on the close interdependence of minds and physical bodies in any condition of existence that we know. This is why much that we say about ourselves in ordinary parlance makes specific reference only to our bodies— 'I am writing in this room', 'I am walking down the Strand', and so forth. We think of ourselves, in fact, as composite beings, having a body as well as a mind, even if on stricter analysis we identify ourselves with our minds. In all normal situations at least my body is indispensable to me in the present life, and any malfunctioning of my body affects my experience and mental life at once, usually in a seriously inhibiting way. To this extent I am one composite being and very closely identified with my body. Hardly anyone short of an out-and-out illusionist, if that is a proper term for those who would wholly deny or discount our bodily existence and subjection to physical laws, would deny the sort of relation instanced between mind and body. We may also of course hold, as I do, that it is conceivable that we should exist without the present body or any strictly like it, and we may wish to stress the influence of the mind upon the body as well as the physical conditions of mental processes. But this would be within the framework of a peculiarly close relationship of mind and body. The idea of contingent identity might be wide enough to apply to this situation. In some sense almost everyone is prepared to identify himself with his body, and for rough-and-ready purposes we do so all the time. But in that case the idea is almost useless. It will certainly not suit Quinton's purpose if it is interpreted in so wide a sense that a consistent Cartesian could readily subscribe to it as a description of the true relations of mind and body.

It is essential, therefore, to indicate at least the degree of contingency involved and explain how it operates. If this is attempted, I suspect it will make it very hard to exploit this idea as a way of upsetting the radical nature of the distinction we draw between mental and physical reality as we find it in actual experience. It is only the vagueness of the idea of contingent identity that makes it seem a possible means of reconciling the demands of common sense with materialism. Quinton himself does not help us by providing any careful indication of how precisely this central idea of his paper is to be understood. In the absence of such an analysis we can hardly conclude that he has advanced the subject in his main contention, although he has done a great deal unwittingly to disclose the state of the problem as it is handled by sponsors of the identity hypothesis today.

CHAPTER X

MEMORY AND SELF-IDENTITY

I have been concerned with various forms of the identity hypothesis. These have been affirmed with great boldness, but it seemed also plain that the substance of what was being maintained became increasingly more tenuous, almost in proportion to the confidence with which the thesis was advanced. Handsome concessions were made to the dualist in the matters in which he has a particular interest. The privacy of experience was allowed to such an extent as to make it difficult to see what difference of substance there could be between the positions in question and at least certain forms of psycho-physical parallelism. This is even more evident in a remarkable work on which I wish to comment now. It is *Self-Knowledge and Self-Identity* by Sydney Shoemaker. I think this could also be described as a defence of a form of identity hypothesis, but the way the position is maintained and defended by Shoemaker makes it far less disturbing to the dualist than the usual forms of the identity thesis, and I shall argue in due course that it is questionable whether the arguments finally adduced by Shoemaker, important and impressive though they are in themselves, prove any identity of mind and body in a way which a sensible dualist would wish to dispute. In the meantime, in approaching his final position on this question, the author says a great many things which substantially advance our understanding of the subject and point us firmly in the direction in which further progress may be made. I shall not accept all that he says, at crucial points, as it stands. But he does seem to me very close to saying just the sort of thing which most needs to be said at the present stage of the discussion of the mind-body problem and it seems highly instructive that the controversy should be taking the course typified by this ingenious study.

Let me first note those features of Shoemaker's views which I take to be illuminating and suggestive. It will then be possible to consider more expressly what he holds about the mind-body problem.

Shoemaker holds that philosophers have often missed the way and been at cross-purposes with one another, in discussing the questions of self-identity and mind-and-body, because they have had a picture or model in their minds of the person as an entity not very radically different from what we observe in the world around us. Many of us have the feeling 'that we do not really understand the nature of a thing unless we can imagine or picture it. The ordinary way of picturing a person is by picturing the human face or the human body'. But once the person is thought of as logically distinct from his body 'this way of picturing a person no longer seems to do. It is, among other things, the apparent lack of a philosophically suitable way of picturing a person that makes persons seem a mysterious sort of objects'.[1]

I am not sure how far we tend to picture the soul or person by strict analogy with the human body. On the whole I doubt whether we do so, although we certainly do think of other persons, in their absence, by calling up some picture of what they look like. In these cases we are thinking of the person, as we normally encounter him, as a composite entity of mind and body whose mind we know almost wholly from its bodily manifestations which we thus associate very closely indeed with the person himself. But when we reflect philosophically I do not think we conjure up this kind of picture of the soul or self which inhabits the body. We do tend, however, to have some kind of mental picture, usually of a rather vague sort; and if we take this too seriously we are at once on the wrong tack, some affirming that they find some corresponding entity within themselves and some strictly denying it, as in the famous case of Hume. The mistake is to think, at this point, in *any* quasi-physical terms.

In the case of Professor Ryle we have found, I suspect, the extreme example of the error in question. He certainly tends to ascribe to his opponents the idea of a little man inside me or of rehearsals of overt behaviour, but I do not think this can be the initial source of his errors, it is more an extension of them due to the policy of lampooning and deliberate abusiveness. Except for extreme cases of this kind, I believe that what leads us astray is less an explicit picturing of the mind in forms like a human body and much more the presentation of it in a more subtle and elusive physical way which sober reflection refuses to countenance as any true reality.

I certainly agree with Shoemaker in general in his view that some pictures we have 'as representations of psychological facts',

[1] *Self-Knowledge and Self-Identity*, p. 40.

pictures encouraged by the way we talk though not wholly due to that, are apt to lead us badly astray. Some philosophers have failed 'to find a subject by introspection' 'because it seems to them, even before they "look" into themselves (if, indeed, they bother to make a show of looking), that *whatever* they find will inevitably be something other than the subject of awareness'.[1] In this respect it may be that those who have warned us most consistently of the danger of being misled by language, and by 'certain pictures and analogies',[2] have themselves been the worst victims of the peril they warn against.

This points to the view, of which more than one indication has been given already in this book, that the mind is some kind of reality that is radically different from anything we can conceive in material or quasi-material terms. This may not be the conclusion that Shoemaker would finally accept, for, as he warns us, in line with many famous precedents, what it is natural or plausible to say 'is often not what I would have us say in the end'.[3] But he does not wish to go back on the warning, made at many points, not to understand what we say about minds or selves in expressly physical terms; and much that he says in the first part of his book is in exemplification of the thesis that the properly psychological statements we make about ourselves (by contrast with remarks like 'I am out of gas' or 'I am six feet tall') are such as 'I can know to be true quite apart from knowing anything about my body'.[4]

This is found to be especially significant in the intriguing case of an imagined transfer of brains. Suppose it is possible some day for clever surgeons to remove a brain and operate on it. By some mishap the brain of one person is put back in the skull of another. Whom in that case would we take a person to be? The one whose body we recognize as that of A would presumably think and act and remember as B. We would not say that he was A simply because he had A's looks and physical manner. Nor if he continued to act like A would we say that he was B because he had B's brain. We would have to say, on the contrary, that what seems normally true about brains and psychological states is no longer operative, for 'whatever relationship there is between the state of one's brain and the state of one's mind (*i.e.* one's psychological features)

---

[1] *Op. cit.*, p. 75.
[2] *Op. cit.*, p. 72.
[3] *Op. cit.*, p. 2.
[4] *Op. cit.*, p. 18.

is surely causal and contingent, not logically necessary'.[1]

It would still of course be possible, though it seems to me with extreme desperation, to give a behaviourist account of this situation. We would have to note, in that case, that we start from the behaviour of the person concerned and reduce all we have beyond this to dispositional terms, allowing 'the same set of dispositions to exist in different bodies at different times'.[2] Or we could say, Shoemaker suggests, that questions of identity in the present case as in all others are ultimately a matter of definition, of what for convenience we call identity. As in deciding whether a bridge which has undergone drastic reconstruction is the same bridge, we can say what we like about identity so long as we are clear about the facts, our decision being 'arbitrary or made on pragmatic grounds'.[3] But whatever may be said of these submissions there seems at least to be one case where they do not hold, namely when we are not thinking of a third person but of oneself. What is A himself to say when he wakes up? He will, no doubt, be surprised and alarmed to see the change in his body, but he would have no serious doubt about his identity. This is because he is not dependent on inferences from the way he acts and talks, he has some more immediate consciousness of his own identity, namely, for Shoemaker, his own remembrance of doing the things he did before his operation.

This is a bold conclusion. For it seeks to establish, by the same stroke, not only that there are some psychological statements we can make without observable data, but also that I am the same person in the course of several experiences. The problem of self-identity is being settled as well as, in one respect at least, the problem of mind and body. I strongly sympathize with this, as it seems to me that, in the last resort, we do make the same sort of move in the two cases, and I hope shortly to explain this further. But in the meantime the procedure of Shoemaker is a little perplexing. It is certain that, if it can be said that I remember something, that event must have happened and I must have been a witness to it, perhaps as the person who brought it about. I cannot remember that I saw a tree in the garden yesterday unless there was a tree there and I cannot remember cutting it down unless in fact I did this. If I do remember cutting the tree, then I must be

[1] *Op. cit.*, p. 24.
[2] *Op. cit.*, p. 26.
[3] *Op. cit.*, p. 30.

the same person now as was cutting the tree yesterday. But this is, of course, only true if the word 'to remember' is taken very strictly, that is as being by definition remembrance of the past event in question, and if it is clear that we do remember things in this way. If there is no doubt that I remember doing something yesterday then I must now be the person who did what I remember doing.

It is not, therefore, merely in our immediate experiences, as in having pain or in thinking about philosophy now, but also in respect to my continuous identity that I seem to have some assurance that is not based on observations of my body. I remember shutting the door and I must, therefore, be the person who did so. All this depends, however, on how we understand memory, and whether it is fallible or not. Do we not in fact seem to remember things which never happened or which we never did?

Shoemaker wrestles with this difficulty at many points and only gives his final answer late in the book. In one place he draws a distinction, legitimate enough it seems to me, between memory statements which are express reports of what we remember and those which are based on memory in the sense that they are 'conclusions *from* what is remembered'.[1] Such conclusions can be false, and, if our identity were thought to depend upon them, it would require a justification very different in principle from the account which Shoemaker himself offers. He rests his case on memory statements proper. And if these state what in fact I do remember and are not fallible in the way an inference from what I remember is, then we seem able to establish our self-identity from 'the meaning of the word "remember"'[2] and thus in a way that has not to run the gauntlet of empirical justification in the ordinary way or anything resembling it. We seem right out of the ordinary dangers and difficulties. The question is settled with a finality that brooks no doubt or further debate. It is not a matter of providing any grounds or criteria of self-identity, and being perhaps mistaken, or involved in argument, as to what these could be. There are no such criteria. Self-identity is expressly involved in what we understand by memory.

This seems to me to be another very 'short way' with philosophical difficulties, and it is, of course, evident to so ingenious a thinker as Shoemaker that the matter cannot just rest as it stands. The argument is—if what someone 'remembers is that *he* broke

---

[1] *Op. cit.*, p. 133.
[2] *Op. cit.*, p. 134.

the front window, then for him the question "Am I the person who broke the front window?" cannot arise'.[1] This certainly establishes identity in some sense. For I would contradict myself if I said that I remember breaking the window and that it was not I who did it. But this leaves it open just what we are to understand by 'person' here, and it also presupposes that we do remember in the sense in which remembering implies that what I remember doing I must have done; and it is here that the question of the fallibility even of memory statements proper becomes insistent. How certain am I that I do remember doing something in the sense of 'remembering' involved here? Must I not offer some justification for the confidence I have in my memories, and in that case are we not, in essentials, in the same position as we would be in if we started with the statements grounded upon memories? In short are not memories also fallible, and in that case what happens to the particular argument which is based, in the way noted, on the meaning of 'remember'?

Shoemaker certainly does not claim that our memories are infallible. He refers more than once to cases where we misremember and to 'the ostensibly remembered event'.[2] 'A person can be mistaken in claiming, and in believing, that he remembers something. How then, can we establish whether a person does in fact remember something?'[3] Only, it is held, by showing that he is the same person who actually did or witnessed what he claims to have done or witnessed. But for this we need independent justification and are no longer moving in the rarefied way with which we began. We must indicate what we mean by 'same person' and why the claim of identity is made in this case. Otherwise we beg the issue we are trying to settle. 'If we are not relying on the person's memory claim, but are trying to check up on it, we cannot use memory as our criterion of personal identity.'[4] But in what other way can we deal with the question?

We must certainly not try to deal with it by going back in any way on the admission that the truth of a particular memory claim is a contingent matter. But we can, however, insist that 'it is a necessary (or logical) truth, rather than a contingent one, that memory claims are generally true'.[5] If this can be shown, then it follows

[1] *Op. cit.*, p. 135.
[2] *Op. cit.*, p. 141
[3], [4] *Op. cit.*, p. 200.
[5] *Op. cit.*, p. 201.

that there is much which we can rightly claim to remember. Even if particular items are in doubt, there is no question that we do in fact remember a great deal, and if this is known in an *a priori* or logically necessary way, there must be many occasions (indeed most of the occasions when we seem to remember something) when I was the person who subsequently remembered certain things— the things I did or witnessed. My continuous identity, or self-identity, seems thus to be something we establish from what we find is bound to be the case about memory. No other sort of philosophical considerations are needed. We have only to reflect on the fact of memory in the way indicated.

All this presupposes, however, that it is sound to maintain that it is a necessary truth that memory claims are generally true. How is this warranted? Shoemaker begins his reply with a 'minimal claim' that the mere fact that a memory statement is confidently and sincerely made 'gives *some* reason for believing it to be true'.[1] But it is not very clear that this will do the trick, and the claim in question is in any case one that is not to be detached from much else that we believe—about ourselves and the world around us. It cannot just be accepted neat, and for that reason the element of necessity seems to go out. But Shoemaker thinks that he can proceed to a stronger claim. He declares that 'to suppose that it is only a contingent fact, which could be otherwise, that confident perceptual and memory statements are generally true is to suppose that we have no way of telling whether a person understands the use of words like "see" and "remember"'.[2] In that case we could not go on using these words, and that would be absurd. We could not even say that memory statements are contingent. As it is also put: 'Anything that might seem to show that the confident and sincere perceptual and memory statements that people make are generally false would in fact show that we are mistaken in regarding certain utterances as expressing certain perceptual and memory claims.'[3] This seems to be, however, a very uncertain foundation on which to rest such bold and elaborate claims as the main thesis which Shoemaker defends. It is indeed a familiar move and not unlike the appeal to the paradigm case that philosophers have sometimes made. The trouble with it is that while it shows that we have a use for words like 'see', 'remember', 'freedom', etc., we

[1] *Op. cit.*, p. 230.
[2] *Op. cit.*, p. 231.
[3] *Op. cit.*, p. 232.

have yet to consider properly what these involve. It is possible to be rid of all manner of doubt and perplexities by these appeals to what we generally say. But this leaves us with the nagging feeling that we have neglected to play the main moves in the game.

There is, certainly, something we would all describe as seeing, and we would have no use for a word like 'see' unless people generally had such experiences. But this does not rid us of the problems of perception. What is it that we do see, a material object or a sense presentation or a field of vision? To what extent are the perceptions of various persons similar? We settle none of these or kindred problems, we do not determine whether perceptual statements are ever more than probably true, by simply noting that in some sense or other we have experiences like seeing. Likewise it is a very strained argument to move from the fact that we do make memory claims, and understand one another well when we do so, to the conclusion that there is some necessity about the general dependability of memory claims. Perhaps the basic thing is that we find our memory claims consistently confirmed in experience, and if this is the case we cannot rest our ideas about self-identity 'on the meaning of the word "remember"' without going behind this to consideration of the sort of experience we have. In that case we would have a much less *a priori* argument than the one which Shoemaker offers us.

A supporting argument used by Shoemaker invites the same comment. He notes that we could not regard our own confident memory claims as generally true without allowing that this must hold for all other persons also. But no one can have confident memory beliefs and at the same time hold that, for all he knows, most of them may be false. To do that would be to confess 'that the beliefs in question are completely irrational'.[1] 'It is not a psychological fact, but rather a logical fact, that one cannot help regarding one's confident perceptual and memory beliefs as constituting knowledge.'[2] This seems to be another suspiciously easy way of settling major disputes. Much turns on how the word 'knowledge' is used and what degree of certainty it connotes. We could speak of knowledge, for ordinary purposes, without implying that, in the case of perception, we ever get beyond an overwhelming degree of probability. This is consistent with holding confident beliefs while admitting some, no doubt remote, possi-

[1] *Op. cit.*, p. 233.
[2] *Op. cit.*, p. 234.

bility that most of them are mistaken. If this is not the case, the issue ought to be argued out in some more comprehensive way than by noting that it is precisely of one's confident perceptual and memory beliefs that one uses the word 'know'.

Shoemaker seems to think that we could not begin to establish the general soundness of perceptual and memory beliefs without presupposing what we set out to prove. We could not get started unless we had some sound perceptions and memories to go upon. But this again depends on what sort of claim we make about perception and memory and on whether it may not be the sort which could be established on the basis of mutual confirmation of otherwise uncertain claims through some pattern or other feature they manifest in relation to one another. It is not necessary for our purpose to go more exhaustively into the question of the dependability of perception and memory. The comments I have made on Shoemaker's arguments hold irrespective of whether we hold some inferential or 'direct' view of the nature of memory. Some have argued that, in memory, we look back in some direct way to the past event. At one level this is very plausible. When I remember shutting the door half an hour ago, I am not drawing a deduction from the present appearance of the door, the disposition of the furniture in the room and of my own body and so forth. I seem just to remember. But this leaves it very open whether or not more subtle inferential factors come into my confident remembering. The appearance of some kind of immediacy may be deceptive. At times Shoemaker seems to be taking up the position of those who have maintained from time to time that memory is immediate in the sense indicated. But his procedure and style of argument is, in fact, different. It is true that for him also questions of justification do not arise, in the sense that, if I remember something, that is *ipso facto* the case. I do not ask for evidence that P if I remember that P. My remembering 'that P entails that P'.[1] But this is a severely logical contention based on the meaning of 'remember'. It leaves it open, as has been stressed, how far we do remember in this strict and infallible way. Those who claim an immediate element in memory in the more usual senses almost always admit that we may misremember and try in various ways to cope with this. If their views were sound it would still not provide a basis for Shoemaker's argument, and I suspect he would have little use for that support, without the further way in which the difficulties due

[1] *Op. cit.*, p. 134.

to the corrigibility of memory claims are met; and this, as involving certain *a priori* ways of establishing the general dependability of memory, I have tried to show to be suspect.

It does not follow that memory has nothing to do with self-identity or that the Kantian arguments based on the unity and continuity of our experience are without significance. I believe that, in essentials, the Kantian argument holds and I am much impressed by recent presentations of it such as those of H. J. Paton and C. A. Campbell. I believe, however, in addition that this particular approach to the problem itself presupposes a more fundamental way in which we are aware of ourselves[1] and which is present in at least a rudimentary way wherever there is sentience. This is where I find Shoemaker's procedure most significant. The precise way in which he seeks to establish our self-identity directly from consideration of the meaning of 'remember' does not seem to me satisfactory for the reasons indicated. But I think he is on the right lines all the same in contending that we are aware of ourselves and of our continuous identity in a way that is not dependent on any particular feature of our experience and that in the sense he has mainly in mind, though not always for his reasons, we have thus no criteria, or need for criteria, of self-identity. We just are aware of ourselves, and this is almost all we need say.

In spite of this, however, we find that Shoemaker also maintains that we could not be conscious of ourselves, in the way he describes, without bodily continuity. This is the reverse of what we would expect. For the insistence that we are aware of ourselves and of our self-identity in a way that is logically independent of observation of the state of our bodies, or of our behaviour, tends to suggest more the mind's independence of the body in the activity which is distinctive of mind. It seems to be grist more to the mill of the dualist than to that of the monist. How then does Shoemaker come to adopt this unexpected and almost paradoxical position? He does so mainly because of the peculiar style of linguistic argument by which he defends his position and which hinders him here, as elsewhere, from grasping fully what is most distinctive and significant in the drift of his own argument. Let me now pause to bring this out before taking up further the theme of the absence of criteria for consciousness and self-identity.

The first move which Shoemaker makes, in his insistence that

[1] *Cp.* chap. XI.

the mind and its identity cannot be logically independent of bodily continuity, is a familiar one, namely to urge that 'if *all* relations between physical and psychological facts were contingent, it would be impossible for us to discover such correlations'.[1] This argument seems to me not to take account of the complexity of the situation in which the relation of mind and body is established. It is assumed that we can only proceed by proving firmly and independently a relation between some detached mental event and a physical fact. This is, of course, out of the question, and if some initial independent link of this kind had to be established in the first place, or as a basis for setting up further correlations, the position would be lost from the start. I shall not go further into this argument here.

It is worth noting, however, how confidently Shoemaker claims that a person cannot declare himself to be in pain with the intention of making a true assertion unless he is in pain. This would normally be taken to show that we can know that we are in pain without having a correct view of the state of our bodies. But Shoemaker deals with it in the same strained linguistic way as his handling of other related problems. He observes that no one could be said to understand the word 'pain' unless he used the words 'I am in pain' seriously only when in fact he was so. But to be sure of this we must sometimes be sure that people are in pain. The word 'pain' has, however, an established meaning. It follows, so the argument goes, that we do sometimes know that people are in pain. This is again the linguistic short way. It by-passes questions which need to be considered, in particular how the established usage is itself warranted. Is that possible apart from certain facts we discover about ourselves and the world around us?

Shoemaker follows up this first skirmish with a heavier attack on the main front. He admits that we do not use facts about our own bodies as evidence in making psychological statements about ourselves. I do not say 'I am in pain' because I find that my face is contorted etc. My headache is not something I learn about through my behaviour, although that is what other people go upon. Such correlations I discover empirically, and I might find that they had ceased to hold. We might even do this in the case of other persons, for example if we found that a person could see behind his back. It would seem to follow that the correlations of psychological and physical facts were contingent.

[1] *Op. cit.*, p. 167.

To this, however, Shoemaker replies, in the first place, that if someone reported correctly what went on behind his back, and did not have a mirror or kindred device, or if, without radio contact and so on, he could describe events going on at the time in a distant place, we would not usually describe this as seeing. It would be clairvoyance. On the whole this seems to be true. But something would depend also on the form the clairvoyance took. Suppose I saw in a dream events which were found to have happened in Moscow, we might not, as the words already used imply, be averse to describing this as seeing. This would be especially so if, as usually happens, the dream involved mainly having visual images. On the other hand this would be an odd use of 'seeing'. It would be quite detached from the ordinary world of perception. But suppose it were a case, not of dreaming, but of having dream-like impressions, in waking consciousness, which tallied closely with events far away. Would we say that we saw those events? Perhaps not, but the difference between clairvoyance and ordinary seeing is much thinner here. If the phenomenon became common we might well find ourselves speaking of seeing at a distance and so on, as we speak of seeing someone on television. And if we could report, in the conditions described, what went on behind us, we might well find it a matter of common parlance to say that we saw things in this way. Extended uses of words are common, and whether we would in fact extend the word 'see' in these ways, and whether this would be advisable, is a very moot point.

But what turns on this? Not a great deal, it seems to me. For whatever words we used to describe such occurrences, that would not alter the fact that they happened. There is much to suggest that some of them do, and even if we did not have evidence to suggest this, it is plain that we can quite properly entertain the possibility; and that is all that seems to be required to make certain kinds of experiences logically independent of certain states of our bodies. We could conceive of further variations in the present causal dependence of psychical facts on physical facts.

It would be wrong to suppose, however, that Shoemaker rests his case entirely on our use of the word 'see'. He argues further that nothing in line with the experience we call seeing is possible unless the body is involved. His main consideration is that, in the absence of a body, there is no way of locating an object. For the object is located in relation to a point of view, this being the place on one's body from which one sees, normally the eyes. Short of this we can never be certain that a person does see what he claims to see. We can only check on his statement if we can locate objects in relation to where he sees from. He might see from the back of his head, but in that case he must do so with consistency. We would have to find for example that his vision from where he claims to see could be blocked. Short of this we could not even locate things in a field of vision. For how would we find the middle or the edges of such a field, or directions within it in other ways, except in relation to, in front of and so on, the point on his body from which his vision can be blocked? This is ingeniously worked out, and in substance the point can well be accepted. I am not altogether convinced that the point about blocking the field of vision to determine the point of view is essential. Would it not suffice if someone described correctly and with consistency the objects which could, in normal vision, be seen from a certain point? But I will not press this or kindred matters. For it is not on questions of this sort that I differ substantially from Shoemaker.

I am prepared to concede that conditions in substance like those he describes are involved in anything which closely resembles what we normally find perceptual experience to be. But is our experience bound to be like that? What would happen if we had a shifting point of view? For Shoemaker this would be equivalent to not having a point of view at all, at least if the point of view were thought to be constantly shifting. Admittedly it would be very hard, perhaps impossible, for anyone other than myself to make sense of my alleged perceptual experience if there were no fixed point of view located on my body. For there could be no way of relating what I describe to what is otherwise found to occupy various spaces. As Shoemaker puts it, 'what could possibly show us from what point a person sees *now*?'.[1] But might I not at least know it myself? The answer is that this would only be possible in slight or occasional ways and that I could not make sense of it without reference to what could be established independently and involving a fixed point of view. And even if it were allowed that I might seem to myself to be seeing things from a constantly shifting point of view, there could be no way of determining whether any of this 'was actually happening'.[2] We would 'obliterate the distinction between egocentric statements and other kinds of statements'.[3]

[1] *Op. cit.*, p. 180.
[2] *Op. cit.*, p. 184.
[3] *Op. cit.*, p. 181 f.

To avoid obliterating this distinction we must, according to Shoemaker, have recourse to what can be established from evidence to which other persons contribute. For I cannot make sense even of my private experiences unless I can put some reliance on what I remember. But I cannot put reliance on my memory without checking up on it by considering 'evidence that other persons could also examine'.[1] That could not happen without some correlation of my own experience with that of others, and this in turn involves some identifiable point of view from which my own experiences can be established.

But, granted the substance of this point again, what is it that we really prove? We prove that the identification of sensible objects or of some identifiable order of external events is not possible without the sort of communication which is only possible when we have our visual experiences from an identifiable point of view on our bodies. I am not quite certain that this is proved as conclusively as Shoemaker thinks, and we obviously could not rule out the possibility of a visionless world or of communication between creatures none of whom had a sense of sight. I will not, however, press this sort of issue. I am prepared to grant most that Shoemaker claims in that context. But it does not seem to me to take us as far as he supposes.

For while it could be granted that we could not, in the conditions of shifting points of view he envisages, know that certain things were happening, in the sense of events in an external public world, this would not preclude their happening in the sense of our having some private experiences. Is not this what happens in a dream? Events in a dream are not real, and they could not be proved to be real, in the ordinary sense. But they are real in the sense that we have certain experiences, including visual ones, and that, while we are in the dream, we often make very good sense of them. This involves no express reference to a point of view on my actual physical body. There are no doubt other physical conditions of my dreaming as I do, but these are clearly causal and logically contingent, as Shoemaker would allow. There is no inherent reason why I could not have the experiences I have in a dream without a body at all. The most that could be allowed to Shoemaker, therefore, is that we could not have some experience like our normal perceptual experience without a body somewhat like our present one. And I do not know that anyone would want to dispute that.

[1] *Op. cit.*, p. 190.

We can, moreover, envisage conditions in which our bodies would function very differently and where many of the physical conditions to which we are subject now were altered or suspended. I might acquire a ghost-like, intangible body, which could pass through otherwise solid objects, but which behaved in other respects like my present body. It is not obvious that creatures so constituted could not communicate and identify one another. It follows that we can at least conceive ourselves functioning with very different bodies.

Furthermore, even within the context in which Shoemaker's arguments have their main force, the most that seems to be established is that we could not, in fact, identify objects and one another without our present bodies. It would not follow that the minds which were so identified had themselves to be identified in turn with their bodies. Mind would still remain distinct from body in its own nature, even though it could not be conceived to function without the body. Mental processes do not become physical processes by being dependent upon them in a peculiar way. The identity of the person would characterize him as a mental being, however it may be thought to be also conditioned by his body. I do not become my body by not being able to function without it.

Nor must it be overlooked that we have many experiences besides perceptual ones. Shoemaker concerns himself mainly with perception. But what about thoughts that are not directly about the external world, like my thoughts about my friends or mathematical thoughts? To what extent are these conditioned by perceptual experience? It might be thought that they must be so conditioned to the extent that they involve communication with other beings. But may it not be possible for us to communicate in other ways than the present ones? Some people appear, even in this life, to have clairvoyant and telepathic experiences. Shoemaker does not take as much account as he might of quasi-perceptual forms of clairvoyance, as when I have a vision like what is happening elsewhere. Telepathy could take the same form, and it has yet to be shown that we could not manage to communicate and make the necessary identifications solely in terms of characteristics of experiences of this kind. Shoemaker dismisses clairvoyance as just our being able to make true statements without knowing them in any of the normal ways. But examination of the modes it seems commonly to have would be most relevant to his own investigations and might cast doubt at least on the indispensability of our present bodies and their role in communication.

H

But there could be forms of clairvoyance and telepathy which did not involve visions or other quasi-perceptual experience. I might just have the thought of something happening, and so on. Suppose all our experience were of this kind. Is it altogether plain that this is impossible? It is very hard indeed for us to envisage just how we could identify one another in such conditions and communicate. But perhaps this is because we have not tried hard enough. Peculiarities and patterns of our private non-sensible experiences might afford the necessary clues to what comes in some way from without. And even if we cannot, under present conditions and limitations, work out properly how this could be, does that entitle us to exclude the possibility in some very different conditions of existence?

One factor which severely hinders Shoemaker from entertaining these possibilities and investigating them is the place he rightly gives to memory in the co-ordination of experience by which we make sense of it and identify things and one another. For, as we have seen, he ascribes the reliability of memory in the last analysis to the fact that we have a use for the word 'memory', or 'to remember', on the basis of which any person's understanding of it can be tested. We could not speak of remembering unless some memories were sound. This I take, as intimated earlier, to be an inadequate and questionable procedure. We should look for our clue more in the nature of the experience we have. And in doing this we also find that the way that consciousness is found not to admit of characterization or criteria is essentially bound up with a distinctiveness of it which accentuates sharply the difference between conscious processes and physical ones. Had Shoemaker broken away more completely from the inhibiting linguistic method of his final approach to his problems, he might have grasped more adequately the sort of distinctiveness and elusiveness of minds to which his arguments point and which involve the sharp distinction of mind and body which he is forced to reject. The way would then have been open also for him to appreciate better just why it is that our own identity is also final and irreducible. It is to this theme that I next proceed.

CHAPTER XI

THE ELUSIVE SELF

I return now to the main theme of the distinctiveness of mental fact and of self-identity which is indicated in the insistence that there can be no criteria for either of these. For Shoemaker has still more to say that points us here in the right direction; and this we can now approach by noting that the position in question comes very close in some ways to that of writers who hold that we have some kind of direct acquaintance with ourselves. What is sound, or nearly sound, in that submission, however, can be seriously misrepresented by its sponsors as well as by critics, in a way which Shoemaker, in deploying his own arguments, helps to bring out. He also shows how much is mistaken in criticisms of various doctrines of the self because of a failure to grasp the peculiarity of our awareness of ourselves which he presents mainly as the absence of any criteria of self-identity. These are matters I now wish to bring out.

Shoemaker first takes objection to the view that the self can be some kind of entity other than the person 'that thinks, perceives, feels pain and so on',[1] in other words 'the subject of thought and experience'. It is a truism, he thinks, that we are all substances in the sense of a subject of thought, since it is pointless to speak of ourselves as if we had no psychological features—we obviously have or we would in no sense be the beings that we are. I feel, however, that the stance taken here by Shoemaker is deceptive and over-simple. He seems to be taking refuge first in the fact that everyone, philosopher and layman alike, will regard himself, in some sense, as a person who feels and thinks and so on—and talk accordingly. This proves nothing and is hardly a position in which a philosopher can rest, except in a somewhat Wittgensteinian sense (rather like what Malcolm tells us about dreaming) by which we come round in the end to what we normally and initially say. But those who speak of the self as a subject have usually meant more than this. That, in a way, is Shoemaker's point too. But he seems to think that, if they do mean more, that must be in the form of positing some substance which has a nature over and above the fact of being a subject who thinks and feels and so on.

[1] *Op. cit.*, p. 45.

This may itself seem a little cryptic; and we are, in fact, at the crux of our problem here. For there is, as I have stressed, something peculiarly elusive about the self, as there is about thought and all experience. It is not easy to say anything about the self as such beyond noting and recognizing it. But all the same we do posit in this way a reality which is certainly not external and observable and which is taken by those who speak of 'a subject' in this context as having some permanence which is not found in passing experiences as such. But the self so conceived is not some 'third thing' to which our thoughts and other experiences are attached. It is peculiarly involved with what experience is, and the supposition that this could be otherwise is a very grave mistake which Shoemaker does well to expose and resist. It is regrettable that he also supposes that the only alternative to the position he rejects is the truism which he considers to be falsified the moment we pass beyond it into further analysis.

In rejecting the notion of the self as some entity beyond what we expressly know in having our experiences Shoemaker has much in mind the position of Locke. He thought of a person's consciousness as 'annexed to' or 'the affection' of a substance, and while he thought it probable that the substance was, in the case of each person, 'one individual immaterial substance', he did not discount the possibility that our thinking should be done for us by different substances at different times, and even that they could be identical with material substances. To counter this Shoemaker draws attention to an inconsistency, arising out of Locke's own contention that a substance is a 'thinking thing'. This seems to rule out the possibility that personal identity, taken in the sense of subject of first person psychological statements, could be preserved in the change of immaterial substance; substance and person become identical. But rather than press this particular point of consistency, it would, in my view, be more effective to ask what a substance in the present case could be over and above the subject which thinks etc. What could we ever say about it? It is such a mystery as to be nothing at all, and the postulation of it serves no purpose, it is a quite redundant accretion in our theorising.

A similar mistake to that of Locke is made, so it is alleged, by Russell in the view he defends in *The Problems of Philosophy*. He urges that, in all experience, there must be something which has the experience, a subject as it is elsewhere called. We are 'acquainted' with this as we are with sense-data. But it could be quite momentary. There is no need to suppose that we are acquainted in this way with a more or less permanent person. But it is to the entity with which we are acquainted in all experience, the subject, that mental states are ascribed, it is this that thinks and experiences. As such, however, it must be the 'I' to which we commonly refer as persisting for relatively long periods of time. That contradicts the view that it could be quite momentary.

I am not sure how far Russell can be caught out in a contradiction in this way. If he can I doubt whether it is more than verbal. But Shoemaker seems to strengthen his case by assuming that the meaning of 'I' must be prescribed entirely by ordinary usage which makes it permanent in thought and experience. This is, however, an arbitrary ruling. We cannot in this way rule out the possibility that what we normally have in mind when we speak of persons should be found *on analysis* to involve no more than a series of momentary selves. At the same time Shoemaker appears to me to be again on the right tack—for the wrong reason. It seems certainly mistaken to suppose that we can postulate a self, some otherwise unknown entity perhaps, to account for some feature of experience, such as its unity, without such a self being known in the first place as the subject in all experience and thus identical with that subject. That, I am sure, is what is reflected most in ordinary usage. A pure self other than the self of the here and now appears to be a redundancy which leads to a needlessly perplexing bifurcation. This seems to me, moreover, expressly confirmed in the way the momentary knowledge we have of ourselves involves knowing ourselves in a more permanent way with which Russell does not reckon. I shall say more about this, but it is, in my view, that to which Shoemaker's arguments really point and which make his appeal to our use of 'I' seem a good deal more plausible than it truly is in itself.

It is worth noting very carefully here just what is wrong with the acquaintance theory as an account of the way we become aware of ourselves. For, as I think Shoemaker might allow, it comes very near to the truth. The theory is wrong if it implies that there is, in our knowledge of ourselves, something strictly analogous to the way we are alleged to have direct acquaintance with some content of our sense experience or with sensible objects in some other way—or on some views of memory with past events. For this suggests that we are able somehow to stand apart from ourselves and observe ourselves or to look in on ourselves; and that in turn suggests that the mind or self has some objective, identifiable character which is noted in our observation as we note this red patch in distinction from that. But this leaves us with a nest of problems, as Shoemaker is quick to point out—he devotes a chapter to it. The red patch, or whatever else we have in mind at this point, has some reality other than its being perceived and can be thought of apart from being perceived. But my perceiving the patch can hardly continue, or be thought of as some event in the world, in a way of which I am quite unaware. If it did, the question would arise of how, in becoming aware of it by acquaintance, I identify it and know it to be *my* perceiving or *my* self. This would need a further set of properties—and so *ad infinitum*. Shoemaker rings the changes at length on these and kindred considerations.

But the truth is that, in becoming aware of ourselves and of our own processes, we do not become aware of any specifiable content other than the characteristics of whatever it is that we apprehend or feel or do. A particular experience derives its distinctiveness from whatever it is an experience of—or in the case of action from what we specifically do. But there is no way of identifying the experiencing of the content in any way or ascribing peculiar characteristics to that in terms of which it is identified. There is just nothing we can say in that sense. Nor is any mind distinguished from any other in terms of peculiar ways in which it happens to be mind. Its distinctiveness at that level is entirely in terms of what happens to it and what it does. I have seen and done different things from you, but the distinctiveness of *my* seeing and doing them is not something that can be described or specified in a similar way. For that we must seek our clue in what is peculiarly ultimate and irreducible in having an experience as such.

This is where some thinkers who incline to a similar view to my own are apt to misrepresent their case when they declare that we become aware of ourselves through introspection—or as some would have it almost immediate retrospection. Not that there is anything wrong with introspection. It is just that we must not fall into confusion between two things. There is first the process by which I take some note of what I am thinking now, of how I am affected by what I observe and do and so on, of just how irritable I am if suddenly interrupted and how I cope with this and other reactions. In this sense we can certainly note and describe, in some cases, like that of a trained psychologist or novelist, most meticulously, what is distinctive in the kind of experiences I have and the things I do. It is in terms of these things, though not, of course, mainly on the basis of what I expressly report from deliberate or sustained observation, that I come to be known to myself and others as this particular person, having this particular history and a proclivity to do or feel certain things and so on. How important introspection is in this way need not be considered here. Nor need we go into the question of how the reports of it can best be checked and sifted.

For what matters here is that introspection, in the sense noted, has little bearing on the more fundamental question of how we know in the first instance that we are having the sort of experiences of which we take account in introspection. There is not here anything over and above the experience's being this particular experience, seeing this tree and so on, which could be isolated and described as this particular seeing. We do not look in on the seeing as something which could have a character and an existence of its own; and if the acquaintance theory implies, as on the whole it tends to do, that we look in on, or in some way observe, an isolable process of seeing to be noted and described on its own account, then it is plainly wrong. In other words, to be mental is not to be related to any further process or entity that is somehow beyond the experience we have; there is nothing that is not to be unpacked out of what we find our experience to be.

But we do have experience, that is what it is for us to be as mental creatures. And the point of Shoemaker's arguments, it seems to me, is just that we cannot describe what it is for an experience to be an experience or to be mental. No definition of 'mind' is possible in the last analysis; we just recognize what it is to be minds by being so ourselves, and mind requires nothing beyond itself for it to be itself—except of course in a sense not relevant here of some causal dependence. My experience does not, therefore, have to be referred to some quite mysterious entity outside it, or, as it were, over against it. I have no self, even a momentary one, in the sense of a detached entity of this sort. We can have no notion what it could be, nor is there any function it serves. It could not be the condition of our having unified experience without its being present to each experience as it comes. But we are not helped to understand particular experiences by thinking of an unknown somewhat that falls entirely outside them.

It is thus not through observing a particular content in the way noted that I become aware, in the first instance, of an experience as essentially my experience. It is not the course of my experience, in the first instance, that makes it mine, but the simple fact of my having it and being involved in this ultimate indefinable way in all my experiences. The self in experience cannot be prised off the experience and considered and described apart, the moment we try we expose ourselves to the objections which Shoemaker and others have skilfully marshalled with what seem at first to be devastating results. The self is not an entity like other entities but more diaphanous. Even that way of talking can be misleading. Being a mind is being something altogether different from being a describable entity, but it is not being nothing, or a mere form or 'focus' or further feature of what our experience more precisely is like. It is real but it is known as real in a way that is inseparable from having some precise experience. I could not be as a mental entity in some kind of splendid isolation aware of nothing and doing nothing. But in having an experience I am aware of it as being uniquely my experience, the experience is not just something which happens and which can be shown in some further way to belong to a person. It could not be without so belonging. I do not, to take a simple example, have a pain and then deduce that it must be my pain. There is no intervening stage, in fact or in logic, between having the pain and finding it to be mine. I can only have the pain as my own pain, and there just cannot be a 'floating' pain that belongs to no creature. But every creature, man or brute, is aware of a pain as its pain in having it. The 'belonging' of the pain is not something attached to it or needing to be sought in some way in which it is related to other pains and so on—there is not, and there cannot be, a justification of selfhood or identity in that way. The pain belongs to, is the pain of this individual, however short-lived, in the very fact of being a pain. And what it means for the pain to belong is something which is evident enough in itself although elusive in the sense that nothing further can be said about it.

This is, I admit, an awkward position for a philosopher to have to take up; and that is why philosophers have tried so desperately to provide some 'analysis of mind' or a justification of selfhood. The model for most of these is the Kantian one, and there is clearly substance in the Kantian claim that the sort of experience which human beings have requires that we should persist from one experience to another and be the same person in the varied facets of experience. But this is a peculiarity of the highly organized experience we have and which we share in some measure at least with the higher animals. There is no inherent reason why more rudimentary experiences should not be more detached or isolated— a passing show. But whichever it is, the awareness of a 'world of objects' or the mere 'flux of sense', there must be within the experiencing itself some kind of belonging or being the experience of some being, however short-lived, in which the privacy of the experiencing is much involved. This is not the uniqueness of place or quality, and that is why the usual attempts to establish it fail. It is given and ultimate, and it cannot be described in terms of any content of experience, it cannot be characterized. It is known in the first instance in having experience of any kind, an experience carries with it the kind of belonging in question; and each one recognizes this, in the first place, in his own case.

This is what we see very sharply in a fairly simple example like that of pain. There can be no experience that is not the experience of some being, and this is not a matter of verbal identification or of convenience in a relative or arbitrary classification, it is what each one finds experience as such to involve. One cannot, as I have said, characterize further what it is for experience to 'belong', nor can we find a wholly adequate term for what we find to be the case here. The uniqueness is not uniqueness of quality or relation in the first place, it is what each one finds himself to be, distinct and irreducible, in having any experience—not a thing or entity apart from or confronting his experience and requiring thus to be described or located in turn, but involved in having the experience and known peculiarly in each case in that way alone. It is only in mature or sophisticated consciousness that this becomes explicit, but just as no creature can have an experience without being aware, in the very process, that it has it, so it cannot fail to be aware of itself, in its irreducible distinctness, however little able to take express cognizance of this or reflect upon it.

This is where the word 'relation' is apt to be misleading, for I am not strictly related to my experiences in the way external things are related to one another. I am in my experiences in a much more inclusive way, and yet I am not to be reduced to my having this or that experience, or this course of experience. I am more than my having a particular experience, but no indication of this 'more' can be given beyond the awareness that everyone has of it in his own case in having any kind of experience.

This may be seen very clearly in a relatively simple experience like having a pain. No one learns by observation and inference that he is in pain. He knows that he has a pain in having it, and in precisely the same way he knows that it is he himself that is in pain. He could not for a moment suppose that it is someone else's pain. If a room is blacked out in an accident, and I hear someone scream, I may wonder which of my neighbours is hurt, and I may be mistaken in the judgment I form. But I cannot be in doubt or mistaken in my own case. It would be absurd to suppose that I could believe myself to be in agony and then find after all that it was someone else. This is not because the evidence is overwhelming and the inference practically spontaneous. There is no stage between having the pain and knowing that it is mine.

Consciousness of selfhood, in this irreducible sense, is gained for each, in the first place, in his own case. It is ascribed to others in ascribing experience of any kind to them. We can describe what is unique in the course of other people's lives, but the basic sense in which the experience is the experience of a unique individual is not found in that way but ascribed by analogy with our own case. On the other hand, we must not make more of a mystery of this than is warranted. The self is not mysterious in any transcendent way, as is the nature of God. It is not that we do not know what it is but that it is so much given in each case, for each one in being himself in his own experience. It is to this that Shoemaker's arguments really point, and the absence of any criteria of self-identity, which he rightly proclaims, is truly significant, not for linguistic reasons like the use of the verb 'remember', but for what we discover, in a way peculiar to this particular issue, to be the case.

The consciousness of oneself as a unique and irreducible being, or of self-identity in its most basic sense, is thus given with, is irretrievably involved in, the distinctiveness of having experience of any kind. The uniqueness and distinctness of persons is bound up with the uniqueness and irreducibility of having experience. It is thus not surprising that, in pointing to these conclusions, Shoemaker should be using arguments which, if successful, would prove equally the absence of any criteria of self-identity and of consciousness. He himself does not always make it sufficiently plain that his arguments have this double application. But this is not altogether strange, since that which makes his considerations initially plausible is the same in the two cases.

It should now be evident also why those who wish to substitute almost immediate retrospection for introspection, as the way we know ourselves, fail to grasp adequately just why it is that the self is elusive in a way that precludes strict observation. The argument, plausible enough up to a point, is that when the self tries strictly to observe itself, it is no longer itself that it observes; for it is seeking to make an object of that which is essentially subject. Alternatively, it is urged that in the process of seeking to observe one's own activities, the activity itself is altered. A mental process can thus never be strictly observed while it is happening. We have thus to be content with remembering and noting what an experience was like the moment it is over. This would be entirely sensible if what took place was some subtle kind of observing or watching ourselves. But, if I am right, we learn from Shoemaker, or are led by his arguments to realize, that we do not observe ourselves, in our initial awareness of ourselves at all, but rather find our knowledge of essentially non-material process in *having* such processes—and our knowledge of distinctness and identity we find in turn essentially involved in having any kind of experience. These are ultimate irreducible features of any experience and they are recognized for what they are without needing, or admitting of, any further description or indication of their nature.

For this reason also the idea of personal identity, in the basic sense I have noted, is not seriously affected by such phenomena as split personality or loss of memory or dreams. There is, of course, one important sense in which a person is uncertain of his own identity if he has lost his memory, just as we may also say that a man is not the same person when he is Dr Jekyll as he is when he is Mr Hyde. But these do not give us the primary sense of self-identity. When I lose my memory I am no longer aware of who I am—in one sense, namely that I do not remember my name, where I live, what I have been doing in the past and so on. I cannot place myself in the sense in which the outside observer would place me on the basis of what is known about me. But I do all the same recognize myself as the unique person I am. It is particulars of my past history and situation that I cannot recover. In a more basic sense I have no doubt who I am—I am myself, the being I expressly recognize myself to be in a way which is not possible for knowledge of any other.

In the same way, when I behave as Dr Jekyll there are certain traits in my nature which have become dominant at the time, to the

exclusion of other very different dispositions of mine. When I behave only occasionally out of character, perhaps through some
profound emotional disturbance, I am apt to say 'I was not
myself', 'this is not me'. That may not be a proper moral excuse,
as the question of the control we may exercise over our conduct in
such cases would have to be raised—are we capable of acting
contrary to the dominant strain in our natures at a particular time?
But, quite apart from questions of this sort, we do not find it hard
to understand what is usually meant by saying—'I was not myself',
and so on. We mean that we were subject to emotions and drives,
whether controllable in the last resort or not, totally different from
those we normally have. This is quite properly put in terms like
'I was not myself', but it is a figurative way of speaking not to be
taken too seriously. Our natures are in any case complicated, and
differing traits in our characters are elicited at different times and
in varying circumstances. What is myself in this sense is relative
and partial, and there is no difference in principle here between
the more extreme and disturbing cases of mental unbalance and
what we sometimes call dual personality. There is a sense in which
we are all many persons, the integration of our natures is never as
complete as it should be, we show many 'faces' to the world. In his
family a man may not be the same person as in his office. But in all
these variations he remains, in a more fundamental sense, the
same person.

Nor is this fundamental sense of 'the same person' to be found
by looking to what is more abiding and constitutive in his dispositional traits as a whole. That would also be one sense in which
we might think of what makes me this particular person; and
some, as we have seen, would look for the answer in terms of
bodily continuity. But what I am thinking of is the much more
radical and inescapable sense in which each person knows himself
to be the person he is, distinct and indissoluble, in having any
experience. He knows that his past history could be radically
different, and he could have a very different body, bewildering
though the experience would be—and shattering in some ways
perhaps. But more fundamental than this is the consciousness that
in all such variations he remains the being he peculiarly knows
himself to be. And it is of identity in this radical sense, an identity
which could be destroyed, but which could not be diversified or
split, that no description or criteria are possible. It is known to be
what it is by each in his own case.

The philosophical discussion of the problem of self-identity has, in my opinion, been much bedevilled by the fact that philosophers have had this sense of their own ultimate indivisible identity at the back of their minds but, not properly grasping just how peculiar and irreducible it is, they have sought, with varying degrees of ingenuity, to account for it in terms of other senses of 'being the same person', such as the ones instanced above.

Before I go further into the question of the two main senses of self-identity, I should like to pause to take up an objection which many will bring against the idea that we have some immediate consciousness of our own experience as our own, namely the objection that we could not be aware of our own experience as our own without picking it out from a number of claimants; there would be no sense in the ascription without such a picking out. But, it is added, the notion that we first inspect our own consciousness, and then certain others, in order to decide that one is our own, is absurd. We could not possibly inspect another consciousness in the same way as we do our own; it is plain that nothing of the sort happens. But then, I reply, the supposition that some picking out of this sort is required is itself highly questionable.

It is questionable partly because it is mistaken to suppose that the idea of an experience being mine involves expressly and in the first instance the idea of a contrast with the experience of other persons. This in turn is partly due to a subtle confusion between the use of 'my' in the epistemological or psychological sense and its use in an ethical sense. There is no 'mine and thine' in an ethical or legal sense without allocation of powers to various people. There is no point in claiming part of a desert island as mine if I am the sole inhabitant of it. But contrast is not present in the same way where an experience is said to be mine or to belong to me. This is matter of fact, not a claim. It holds in virtue of what is the case on its own account.

This does not imply that we could in fact make an ascription of this sort without any awareness of other people. For clearly we could not have the sort of sophistication which is involved in asking the question without close and highly developed social relationships. Only highly intelligent creatures could reflect upon their own status or make, even unreflectively, an explicit distinction of themselves and others. But this is a psychological, not a logical,

matter. It does not show that the consciousness we have of ourselves in itself directly involves the contrast with the consciousness
of others. We are aware of it in the first instance on its own
account, and I have also urged that some consciousness of the
experience as belonging in this way is present even in very rudimentary or low-grade experience, like that of a worm or some
creature to which we could ascribe little but sentience. In such a
case the contrast would not even be incipient. But the experience
would belong and be felt to belong all the same.

But, in any case, if the point is pressed that we cannot properly
speak of an experience as mine without a contrast with the experience of others, the reply may be made that we can in fact quite
properly make such a contrast without in the least implying that
we inspect the experiences of various persons before we conclude
that some of them are our own. We ascribe experiences to other
persons on the basis of what we see or hear or otherwise observe
of their physical movements. We speak of the consciousness of
which I am directly aware as my own and not that of another (and
in this way involving a contrast) on the basis of the experience
I thus ascribe to others in a way quite different from my consciousness of my own experience. There need be no question of
comparing experiences all apprehended in the same way.

Indeed, the idea of 'picking out' as the only way in which an
experience or consciousness can be claimed as my own is an
unfortunate legacy of fashions which have dominated so much of
recent philosophy. It has come to be widely held, mainly through
the prevalence of empiricism, that one sort of thing can only be
known in one sort of way and that the model for any sort of discrimination we make must be found in our knowledge of observable
reality. We identify things in the external world by picking one out
from others through some distinguishing features. But it is a wholly
unwarranted dogma to suppose that this is the only way in which
identification is possible. I do not pick my own consciousness out
in the way suggested. I have no need here of the diagnostic marks
by which other things are identified.

Some comparison may be made here with the way we speak of
our own visual fields. This is something we often do, and clearly
no one can cavil at such utterances as—'I see a black spot in the
corner of my visual field'. Note that we say *my* visual field. This
is clearly quite normal and unexceptionable. But it is also evident
that no one feels entitled to speak in this way because he has

inspected his own visual field along with a number of others and found reasons for claiming one of them as his own, as one might pick out one's hat from others on a peg. No one can inspect any visual field other than his own. I could never know that there was a spot in the corner of your visual field in the same way as I know that there is one in mine. But this does not in the least deter us from speaking of visual fields and of '*my* visual field'. I ascribe visual fields to others on the basis of my own experience and the presumption that they also have a sense of sight and whatever this involves. The argument against some immediate awareness of my own consciousness, namely that it would involve similar awareness of other people's consciousness, would preclude the reference to one's visual field which is quite common in writings where the objection under discussion is most confidently advanced.

Let me now return to the point with which I was already concerned a little earlier, namely that there are two major senses of self-identity. There is, in the first place, the sense of self-identity which I have described as the most radical or basic one. This is the sense in which one knows oneself as one ultimate indivisible being in the course of having any experience whatsoever. I know myself now as one being who just could not be any other. The question of my being or becoming some other person just could not arise, I am myself whatever my experience is like. But there is also a sense in which I am continually subject to change. Every instant I change; a moment ago I was the person who was looking at this tree, I am now looking at the lawn. My thoughts and sensations change all the time. In terms of what I undergo or experience or do I am never the same person. I may, moreover, from time to time, undergo drastic changes of interests or aptitude or other dispositional traits. These are sometimes so substantial that we are apt to say—'He is quite a different person'. But we also want to say that these changes happen to the same person, and we certainly do this normally in the absence of radical changes. An audience does not suspect that the person who is talking to them at one time is other than the person who started the lecture, and they may not have serious doubts that he is the person who was giving a lecture in the same course last week or last year. How is self-identity in this sense established, and what are the limits of it?

One could go a good deal of the way here by noting that it

would be absurd to suppose that I could have my present understanding and aptitudes without a good deal at least of the experience and history with which I am normally credited. My general understanding and knowledge could not come about without any antecedents, they could not just emerge out of nothing. They are only acquired through a certain continuous experience over a number of years, however much they may also presuppose hereditary traits or a certain natural endowment. My more precise and specific aptitudes and information require that I should have had precise experiences which make up the course of the life I would generally be thought to have lived. But when we pass beyond establishing the sort of continuity which my life must be thought to have involved in this way and ask what sustains the impact of one experience on another and makes possible the continuous course of a person's life, then we have to do more than note the relation of one experience to another, we must account for it. It does not seem to explain itself or be just an ultimate fact about our experience which we recognize. Philosophical analysis has to go further.

It is at this point that I, like Professor Shoemaker, have to have recourse to the facts of memory. But the idea of memory alone will not do the trick, at least not in the sense of noting that I am able to recall or in some other way be assured of some past event in my history. Memory does involve recalling, in a way that has at least the appearance of directness, something that occurred in the past. Whether this is some sort of direct contact or should be thought of as vivid impressions which we immediately and with justification take to be an assurance of a past event need not be settled. For the point I want to stress is that this could not be memory in the strict sense, (or, alternatively, could not afford assurance of our continued identity) unless the impression of the past event contains within it a recognition of its involving the same distinctive awareness of myself as a unique being which I have in my experience at this moment. It is this, and this alone, in the last resort, that guarantees the presumption I have that the past experience is an experience of the same person as I know myself to be now.

The guarantee in question cannot be obtained from any feature of the event which I do recall, however peculiar. For there is no inherent reason why I should not have vivid and dependable impressions of past events (however this dependability is constituted) without their being past events in which I have participated.

There could be clairvoyant knowledge of past events in which I had no part or which happened before I was born. This is why some have toyed with the possibility of more than one person having 'memories', in some after life or re-incarnated state, which are in all respects identical. Suppose, it is said, two persons come to life with the memories of Guy Fawkes. We could not in that case say that either of them was Guy Fawkes. I agree, although I would withhold the word memory, in such cases, and speak instead of dependable impressions or something of that sort. But this possibility cannot really arise if we think of memory proper, for this involves the recognition of the past occurrence as one in which I find the consciousness of myself as the person I am now. I re-live, as it were, the past event, or recapture it, in the form which involves the peculiar awareness I now have of myself as one unique being wholly incapable of being any other.

There is, in this way, a linkage with the past event, on its inner side as it were, independently of the sort of event it happens to be in other ways. We do not thus, in the ultimate analysis, look for linkages of content, for those could be fortuitous. Nor do we seek to rectify this by appealing to bodily continuity. For that is conceivably consistent with a change of occupant of a particular body. The essential linkage is not in extraneous matters of this sort. It is, usually at least, firm and more immediately dependable. I recognize myself in the past experience to be the person I am now, not, as I have stressed, because of any particular content of the experience it is, but more expressly in the proper reconstruction of the experience as a whole. I recall, in other words, not just what happened but its happening to me as the person I know myself to be now.

This comes very close, in some ways, to Shoemaker's argument that the way we use the word 'memory' is a guarantee of continuous identity. But I am not in fact appealing to the use of the word, nor would I wish to guarantee our use of it, in the sense that Shoemaker has properly in mind, merely on the ground that our use of it implies that it must sometimes be legitimately used. My appeal is rather to what, in fact, we actually find to be the case, namely that we are able to recall some past events in a reasonably dependable way and recognize the normal consciousness we have of ourselves as a feature of those events. This certainly goes beyond Shoemaker's position, as he presents and states it. But one also suspects in this, as in many similar cases of the appeal to our use of words, that more is involved than may at first be apparent. In that case the difference between what Shoemaker really wants to say and my own view may not be as wide as it seems. If my view is right, there can be no sense in which one person could acquire the memories of another. In a subsidiary sense we can all, of course, remember the same things. We can all remember things we have learnt, in a dispositional or some other way. We can all remember the date of the Norman Conquest, and a number of people may also remember things jointly in the sense of having personal memories of situations in which they were all involved. A group of people may remember jointly the holiday they had last year or some escapade of theirs in school. But no one in the strict sense remembers anything other than an experience or activity of his own. Such experiences will often be of situations in which others were involved and we may have good reason to suppose that they have memories of it as well. But what they can remember, in the strict sense, is what they themselves went through, linked very closely as it was with all that we were undergoing as well. Memory in the strict sense is essentially personal.

It is, moreover, memory in this sense that is involved in the first instance in establishing our continued identity. But once the initial linkage is established it can be supplemented in a host of other ways in which bodily continuity will play a considerable part. I can learn a great deal about my own history in other ways than through my own explicit memories. I can rest assured that I travelled to school and attended certain classes on some date in my boyhood in which nothing happened to me sufficiently eventful for me to remember. I have no recollection of this day, and it might be exceptionally hard to revive any. But I can be sure (from the school register if serious question arose) that I attended school on this day and and on many similar days when, as I may have good reason to know, my attendance at school was unbroken. I am sure that I was on those days the being I now know myself to be, but I know it now indirectly as a very strong presumption indeed from independent evidence.

This evidence is substantially the same as the evidence I have about other people. I have good reason to believe that my friends have certain thoughts and feelings when they are with me, and I may be fully justified in supposing that they and other people, some of whom I never encounter, have certain experiences at various times. I know about various people in the past in this way;

and I can learn from precisely the same sort of evidence that someone having my bodily appearance underwent certain experiences at some date in the past and responded in certain ways. This would, moreover, dovetail into further things known in the same way and forming the meaningful and continuous history of one person. It would be remarkable indeed if some slice of this history had another experient. For how would he know the things he would need to know to respond as he does if he had not been the being concerned in all the events that dovetail in this way into one another? One would need to presuppose some completely freakish exercises of clairvoyant power on the part of a number of agents having my bodily form in a succession without any crack at all to indicate it. This is such a remote possibility that no one takes it seriously. It is, however, around the central internal awareness of my own identity that anything I learn in other ways about the course of my own life is built. In the absence of it we could do no more than protest that mere association of ideas would not suffice as the explanation of continuous meaningful experience and presuppose some way, a wholly mysterious one, in which various experiences blend as the significant course of a person's life. The proper explanation comes from one's own inner consciousness of the unique being one finds oneself to be in any experience.

But once a continuous course of experience has been credited to me, together with the various aptitudes or dispositions which this involves, then it is possible to give me an identity in a subsidiary or secondary sense which does admit of, indeed requires, characterization or description. I am thus said to be the person who likes this or that, who is prone to be aroused in this or that way, who has witnessed certain scenes at certain times and so forth. This is the sense or level of identity we have in mind from day to day, and it is with this that philosophers have usually concerned themselves in the first instance when raising the problem of self-identity. But I am contending that we cannot give an adequate explanation of this kind of self-identity apart from the peculiar identification of myself as the unique being I am which I have expressly in any experience.

It would be a great mistake, however, to suppose that the two senses in which I may speak of my own identity presuppose two sorts of selves, as has sometimes been thought in speaking of a phenomenal and a noumenal self. The self which is characterized or described, on the basis of the sort of experience I have had and

so forth, is the self which I know, in a way that defies characterization, in all experience. Indeed it is not the self which is, strictly
speaking, described. What we can describe is the course of certain
events and the aptitudes or traits of character disclosed in these.
These are events which have happened to the person I find myself
to be, and they are the aptitudes I happen to have. To that extent
they are descriptions of me and they are the ways in which I would
be identified by other persons. Who am I? I am the person who was
born in a certain place, brought up and educated at various places,
who likes this or that and makes his living in a certain way and so
forth. There is no other way in which other persons can identify
me. But I could inwardly know myself to be the person I
am *if all these things were different*. They do not give the
uniqueness of my being the person I am in any experience
whatsoever. My experiences are indeed my own, and I must
not be thought to be divorced from them, as if I could just exist
in a vacuum—or as if experiences could be without being essentially someone's experience. But who the someone is can only be
properly known to himself.

There could thus be a radical change in the characteristics by
which I am known to others, and my history could have been
different. But if I became, or if I had been in the past, a very
different sort of person, or if I had lived at other times and places,
there would still be the basic sense in which I would know myself
to be myself. If, in the event of my having some other existence,
I retain no recollection of the present one, I would still have the
same sort of basic sense of being myself as I have now, although, of
course, I would not any longer know of my having it now.[1] This is
what is often overlooked in some criticisms of the idea of survival
which look exclusively for identity in terms of characteristics or a
history by which I could be described. I do not think in fact that
survival is at all probable in a way that is wholly divorced from my
present existence, but this is for further considerations in which
the worth and purpose of survival has a prominent place. It would
not, however, in my view be absurd to suppose that there could
be intermediate stages of a number of existences not related by any
consciousness of one another and culminating in some stage of
being to which they all contributed. This would be in accordance

---

[1] Some further telling arguments in support of this position may be found in
an article entitled 'Can the self survive the death of its mind?' by John Knox Jr.
in *Religious Studies*, October 1969.

with some notions of reincarnation. But I do not think in fact that it is likely to be the case.

It must be stressed at the same time, as I have done above, that the self which is not to be identified with its characteristics or the course of its experiences must not be thought capable of existing in a void without experience or a nature or character of any sort. I could not exist as pure being without some sort of experience, and I could certainly not have the sort of experience I have as a human being without some relatively stable nature which sustains the continuity of it and determines my responses. I will not stress this further, as the point has already been made above. But there is one consequential issue which should be noted, although it is not altogether peculiar to a position like my own.

Suppose that, in the course of one's life, one lapses into a state of total unconsciousness or insensitivity. This is what is normally understood by the idea of dreamless sleep. In dreamless sleep my body would still be functioning, but I would have no sort of dream experience at all. It is not to the purpose to ask how far it is likely that there is a state of total unconsciousness of this sort or how we would best settle the question. But it is conceivable that there should be dreamless sleep. In that case the question arises of whether I could be said to exist at that time at all. It could be said, of course, that I have a continued existence in the sense that when I begin to be conscious again my dispositional set-up will remain the same. It could be said to persist in the way dispositions normally persist, but unless we resort to a view of substance as a sustainer of dispositions which I do not hold, this would amount to little more than saying that, for some reason we cannot specify or for purely physical conditions, I would in fact continue to have the same dispositional nature, in essentials at least, on becoming conscious as before my lapse into total unconsciousness.

My own inclination, therefore, is to say that in a state of totally dreamless sleep (in the sense that we have no sort of experience while asleep) we simply cease to exist. I do not find this peculiarly disconcerting, although I believe many people find it so. It would almost be like dying and surviving except that my body would not have undergone clinical death—it would have functioned and nothing else. But this does not seem to me specially disturbing. Why should it, provided the normal continuities persist beyond the 'gap' and I have then the consciousness of myself which I normally have in any experience?

It should be evident now how important it is that there should be no ambiguity about the sense in which it is maintained that there is a certain distinctiveness and an elusiveness of consciousness and of our personal identity. This has not been defended in any esoteric way or as the invocation of some peculiar sort of mystery. It is not contended at all that we might, by some special sort of probing or by some peculiar disciplines or technique of meditation, manage to uncover some otherwise obscure element in our nature, some inner core of our personality of which we are normally quite unaware. I have not been suggesting any way in which we might peel off certain layers of our experience or our natures and reveal thus, to our amazement, some undreamed of treasure whose preservation takes precedence over everything else. The self is not alleged to be a mystery in that sense. Let me put it in this way.

It is held in some 'spiritualist' circles (or among some students of psychic phenomena) that our more manifest and gross material body is the outer wrapping, as it were, of finer bodies (more than one apparently) by which we may materialize, for suitable persons on suitable occasions, and function without the physical limitations to which we are normally subject. There may be more in such suppositions than we generally assume, especially if they were restated by people better suited to reflect on the available evidence than those who usually make such claims. But such ideas are obviously fraught with the utmost difficulties, and these by no means arise solely from the slenderness and imprecision of the evidence. But even if such difficulties could be overcome, they would not in any way help us to understand the sort of inwardness or elusiveness of genuinely mental existence with which I am now concerned. The suggestion of more and more ethereal wrappings of our gross physical body affords no proper analogy to the genuine inwardness of the self or person.

My concern at present is not, therefore, with obscure phenomena of the mental life. This is not because I wish to maintain that everything about us is perfectly transparent or evident, in principle, to ordinary or casual inspection. There may be various levels of mental life. Almost everyone would admit some kind of dispositional 'unconscious', that is the modifying of our dispositional tendencies through events of which we have no recollection —indeed something of this kind must be true of all dispositions. There may also be actual unconscious or sub-conscious processes, although the way we must understand this presents obvious difficulties—I shall not consider them here. If someone wishes to maintain that what occurs to us in this way could be superior to our normal conscious experience, that we have some entirely different richer life above or beyond the life we normally seem to lead, I should, indeed, be a good deal more sceptical. The repercussions of such a supposition would be very far-reaching and they would raise very grave problems about freedom and responsibility. I mention them here, however, to make it clear that, when I speak, in this book, of the 'inwardness' and elusiveness of persons and their experience, I am not alluding at all to some quality or level of our existence that is not open to us in the ordinary way and a feature of the experience of any person whatsoever. I claim to uncover nothing that is not there plainly for all to see.

All the same I am maintaining that consciousness and our continued identity are, in a very radical sense, mysterious and elusive. They are so in the sense that there is no special way in which they can be characterized. They are evanescent in the sense that they slip through our hands the moment we try to describe them or say what they are; and the core of the criticisms I levelled against influential contemporary thinkers was that they seem determined to look for some specifiable quality of consciousness, in some way akin to observable qualities (a ghost or shadow of them) by which consciousness could be picked out from other things we encounter in the world. This is just what we cannot do. We know what it is to be conscious *in being conscious*, we know quite well what it is to have an experience, but this is so radically different from the reality we find in the external or material world that we can only recognize the difference without saying anything further.

This holds quite independently of any view we may have about the external world or physical reality. We may incline, as I do, to a Berkeleyan or phenomenalist view of the world of nature. We would then hold that what we perceive, the choir of heaven and the furniture of earth, do not exist unless they are in some way experienced. But this would not in the least make them mental realities themselves. There would still be a radical dichotomy between extended existences (coloured or characterized in some other manner) which in some way confront us, and which we apprehend, and the apprehending of them or the setting ourselves to manipulate them. My view about the irreducible and distinctive nature of consciousness is in no way supported by inclining towards a phenomenalist view of material reality, although the latter view has importance in some other ways for our full understanding of what I can best characterize here as 'the human situation'. I require no support from a phenomenalist or Berkeleyan view of the world of nature for my insistence on the non-material *sui generis* nature of experience at all its levels. If I looked for such support I should not only weaken, but in fact quite undermine my position.

This was made very plain by Berkeley himself in his insistence that minds are not known by perception but in the altogether different way of notions. This applies not only to our awareness of conscious processes as such but also to each one's awareness of himself as a distinct irreducible entity which I have been specially concerned to stress in this chapter.

CHAPTER XII

SELF-IDENTITY AND
BODILY IDENTITY

The views which I have been advancing hitherto have one consequence which has curious ramifications in the work of thinkers who would normally be much inclined to subscribe to my main contentions about mind and body. It is that, if we have some kind of private or privileged access to our own experiences, there can only be knowledge of other minds in some indirect or mediated way, whatever that may be. This is the unavoidable corollary of all that I have been maintaining, indeed it is not so much a further point as another way of looking at the same point. But many writers of today find this feature of a dualist view very hard to digest. That is mainly because they seem convinced that no correlation can be established between the bodily movements of other persons and their mental states unless we can observe both together. There is not, to my mind, any substance in this misgiving. But those who are affected by it tend to surrender a dualist view, to which they might otherwise subscribe, in favour of some position, in the circumstances a rather ambiguous one, in which the body has still some indispensable part to play in the way our identity is established for ourselves and others. The idea of the person is thus thought to involve the body in an unavoidable way, and the wedge must thus not be driven too firmly between them. Professor A. J. Ayer provides an extremely interesting example of this situation, and I shall illustrate the main point I have been making by closer reference to his view in a moment. First let me add a general comment on current views about our knowledge of other persons.

The idea that we have communication with other persons, in some mediated way, through what we observe of their bodies or by kindred means, is generally much out of favour at the present day, even among persons who are not unsympathetic to some kind of dualism of mind and body. This is largely the legacy of the kind of reductionism, itself the offspring of various forms of verificationist theories, with which I have been much concerned earlier in this book. But it is difficult to deal with it, since what we usually have is a situation of simply taking it for granted, in a very dogmatic way, that any account of our knowledge of one another in analogical or similar terms is *naïve* and out for anyone abreast of the times in philosophy. The arguments are rarely presented except in the form of the behaviourist reductionism to which I have alluded.

One objection that used to be given much currency, but of which one usually hears less today, is that we are conscious of other people before we have any clear consciousness of ourselves. Psychologists used to press this point a great deal at one time. They poured scorn on the idea that a baby first became aware of itself and its own movements and then began to recognize its mother by analogy or deduction as another person also. This certainly is justified if any sophisticated process of reasoning is ascribed to infants. But the real point of it is that we have to be extremely cautious in any account we give of early development. Just how an infant begins to discriminate and note things, just when it is most aware of other people or of its own sensations, as the case may be, is a matter best left to the psychologist. The logic of the process by which we become aware of one another is not a problem for him, and he goes well beyond his book, as a psychologist, if he pronounces, on the basis of child psychology or any other branch of his subject, on the problem of what is essentially involved in our knowledge of other persons. The philosopher is equally at fault if he prescribes to the psychologist what he should do or hold on the basis of what he himself has to say on the more properly logical side of the question.

One thing seems certain. It is through our bodies, or through observation of these, that we normally do, as a matter of fact, come to know about one another. Hardly anyone seriously doubts that we do know one another. Nor is there serious doubt that we usually learn what other people are like, and what they are doing and thinking at any time, from what we see and hear of them and so on. If, therefore, we hold that what we learn about one another is not just about our physical processes or dispositions, but about some further quite distinct mental process, the obvious conclusion appears to be that we learn what these mental processes are like by inference from what we observe of bodily states. This seems so obvious, as a matter of general principle, whatever we may find it possible to say in expansion or supplementation of it, that I, for one, find it very hard to understand how it can be dismissed, not only in reductionist theses but by others, as a palpably mistaken, wrongheaded idea. If it is wrong it is certainly not obviously wrong, and I do not, in fact, think that it is wrong at all.

This leaves me very perplexed about the attitude of thinkers who, in other regards, approximate closely to my own position on this particular question, for example Professor A. J. Ayer. He firmly rejects the physicalist account of persons and maintains that what we know of other persons must be more than the states of their bodies; and he sometimes firmly declares that 'our knowledge of the experiences of others is inferential'.[1] If it is so it must, normally at least, be an inference from what we observe of their bodies. But Professor Ayer seems also hesitant about this conclusion, not merely in the sense that he is not satisfied with the analyses offered hitherto of the precise form the inference (or its logical justification) takes, but in principle. For, so he argues, there could 'always be room for doubt'.[2]

The core of this particular doubt lies in the fact that we can never inspect the experiences of others; and in being much impressed by this fact, in the present context, Ayer seems to me to be falling back to the sort of verificationism which in other respects he has abandoned. He concedes more than he should to the sort of argument which Professor Ryle, and others who share his kind of monism, are apt to advance with a sense of its being peculiarly irrefutable. It is that, unless we can in the first place establish that certain experiences other than our own occur, we can never get started with proving that there is any correlation between various mental processes and the processes we actually observe; the argument does not begin to get off the ground. In other cases correlations are established by noting concomitant variations of many sorts. But from the nature of the thesis involved we cannot do this in the case of an inferential theory about other minds.

This is the point of the much publicized analogy of the signal box. As Ryle himself put it: 'It is a process of inference analogous to that by which we infer from the seen movements of the railway-signals to the unseen manipulations of the levers in the signal-box. Yet this answer promises something that could never be fulfilled. For since, according to the theory, one person cannot in principle

[1] *The Concept of a Person*, p. 111.
[2] *Op. cit.*, p. 109.

visit another person's mind as he can visit signal-boxes, there could be no way of establishing the necessary correlations between the overt moves and their hidden causal counter-parts.'[1]

This argument depends entirely on the assumption that all our knowledge must take precisely the form of our knowledge of events in the external world. It amounts to little more than counter assertion or a dismissal of a position before it begins to be stated. For the theory to be attacked or defended is that we have knowledge of other minds without ever being able to inspect them. And the nub of the argument is as follows:

We do have awareness of our own experiences in having them. We know what it is to believe certain things, to perceive, to have sensations, purposes and so forth; and we find that we are able to carry out certain purposes through the control we exercise over our own bodies. When I wish to open the door I can will that my body moves accordingly, and normally it does so. I observe other bodies, constituted like my own, which behave in similar ways with infinite variations of seeming response and adaptation. There appears to be nothing, in the ordinary course of physical events, to account for what is thus extraordinary in the behaviour of certain physical bodies; but such behaviour becomes easily understandable if we ascribe it to the operations of minds with purposes and powers similar to our own. Is not this the obvious explanation to offer, and is it not plain that this is what we normally suppose?

It is not essential, for the purpose of the sort of communication we have with one another, that our bodies should have the close resemblance, in point of appearance and structure, which, in fact, they do have. There are, in any case, some considerable differences between our bodies, as human beings, and the bodies of other creatures to which we have no hesitation in ascribing certain experiences. And even if there were no observable body, we could still infer the activity of an intelligent being from other indications of it in the physical world. There might, for example, be a person of whom we knew nothing apart from a book he had left behind. We learn of the activities of ancient peoples from inscriptions, tombs, temples, pottery, weapons etc. This is on the presumption that marks and articles of this kind are most unlikely to have come about by any incidence of natural processes independently of purposeful intervention. In these cases one

[1] *The Concept of Mind*, p. 52.

presupposes that there were bodies involved not unlike our own. But the resemblance would not have to be as close as we take it to be for us to learn a great deal reliably about creatures remote from us in time or space.

Indeed, if the astro-physicist detected certain bleeps or kindred sounds that seemed to come from outer space, and if these formed a pattern suggestive of a code of some kind, this would create a reasonable presumption that these sounds, or some other modes the pattern might have, were intended as a communication. If it were found that the pattern changed in response to messages sent by ourselves in similar code, the presumption would be very much strengthened. At what point we would consider it confirmed is a matter I need not investigate now. For all that I am concerned to establish here is that some inference from physical media would normally be taken to afford us a clue to mental activity which is not itself reducible to processes of the same physical nature. We would conclude that creatures in outer space, perhaps at a point we could fairly precisely locate, had certain thoughts and purposes which they were thus communicating to us.

There might, indeed, be telepathic communication which did not involve any physical media. This, as I have noted earlier, would not be a case of having access to the mind of another similar to one's awareness of one's own mental state. That, in my view, is impossible in principle. But we might still be able to discover from the incidence of certain things that happened to ourselves that some communication was intended for us through some way certain other creatures were able to determine what happened to us. I need not here consider the possible limitations of this kind of communication or whether it is conceivable in a totally disembodied state.

The fact that human beings have bodies which are closely similar to one another is obviously a very great aid to communication, and it remains the case that much the greatest part of our exchanges take place through the bodily states of one another which we are able to observe. What is important, at the moment, is that there appears to be every justification for the inference involved and that in practice we do place every reliance upon it. This is not affected by the fact that we are sometimes mistaken and may even, in error, ascribe experiences to inanimate objects. For we place the utmost reliance on other inferences where we may also on occasion find ourselves in error. Occasional error will not upset our confidence where the evidence generally fits together in a quite overwhelming way. Why, then, should Ayer and others continue to have misgiving? What is there to occasion this special perplexity in the case of the inference to other minds?

What troubles philosophers here seems to be just the fact that we cannot in the case of other minds ever have direct confirmation by inspecting those minds. It is thus possible, so it is supposed, that we are subject to some colossal illusion. Perhaps it is an accident after all that bodies and other material objects behave in ways so markedly suggestive of intelligent activity. This may be a happening for which there is no explanation at all. Or perhaps some far superior being has contrived it that certain bodies behave in a seemingly intelligent way without there being, in fact, anything further involved. We would, in the latter case, still know something about the mind of another being, but we might not be in a position to settle for the alternative in question. And so Professor Ayer writes:

'So if my belief that other beings are conscious can be defended only as an inference from their behaviour, it is at least possible that I am the only person in the world. The short answer to this is that I know that I am not; but this still leaves the problem how I can have the right to be so sure.'[1]

I must confess that I do not share the perplexity of Professor Ayer here. For it seems to me to turn entirely on the requirement of a way of settling doubt which is just not obtainable in this particular case. We simply have no means of removing in a completely conclusive way the possibility that the persons we normally take to be real are not so in fact. This will always remain a theoretical possibility. We can never eliminate that. But why should this trouble us? For the possibility is not merely theoretical but also so remote that no one need take it seriously. There are, in other matters, high probabilities by which we must be guided, but if the probability is so high as to amount to what we usually call moral certainty, no one lets himself be bothered by a merely theoretical possibility of error. We go by the view to which the evidence most overwhelmingly points.

Ayer himself is not troubled in practice; and I do not think he would have been troubled philosophically—nor would others of our contemporaries—were he not still haunted by the ghost of his earlier verification principle. For he says, in a revealing

[1] *The Concept of a Person*, p. 109.

remark in this context: 'But what is the significance of a doubt which could never be allayed?'[1]. The suggestion seems to be, echoed also in *The Problem of Knowledge*, that if we can conceive no way in which an assertion could be properly falsified, then it is not a significant assertion. It is this legacy of Ayer's verification principle which has to be rejected, it being itself the result of an expectation of a kind of certainty which is not, in fact, available to us. It does not seem capable of a philosophical defence, and it is rare for any to be offered.

A subsidiary point made by Ayer is not without importance. It is that there must be some measure of realism in our perceptual experience for the inference to other minds to be warranted. 'There is,' he says, 'a special difficulty for those who think that one cannot conceive of physical objects except as logical constructions out of one's own private sense-data; for it may well be asked how I could possibly suppose that a logical construction out of my sense-data was endowed with a private world of its own.'[2] I do not find this point convincing. There appears to be no need to get out of my private world to a physical one before the question of communication could arise. For if we took a phenomenalist view, and thus supposed that, in the first instance, we had no experience of anything other than our own sense-data, there would be nothing to preclude us from supposing that the peculiar behaviour of certain groups of sense-data, those we normally think of in connection with other people's bodies, could only be accounted for on the basis of some influence which beings not unlike ourselves were able to exercise upon them. This seems to be as strong and justifiable a presupposition on a phenomenalist view as on a more realist view.

The reason why Ayer should doubt this seems to me to be just that lack of the courage of his convictions about the inferential view of our knowledge of one another which makes him also so concerned about the absence of a conclusive proof. He is still worried about the inference when we are not able to get behind the scenes and check up on it directly at some point, and he thus finds some consolation and a partial way of meeting the requirement he has in mind if we are shown at least to break out of our isolation to the extent of being confronted with physical entities existing in their own right and not in some private mind-dependent

[1] *Op. cit.*, p. 109.
[2] *The Concept of a Person*, p. 110 f.

way. But, of course, this does not do the trick, and if the requirement in question held we would have to pronounce it to be fatal
to the possibility of communication whatever view we held about
our perceptual experience.

The point is that it is the appearances of processes, not subject
to direct control by ourselves, taking a course overwhelmingly
suggestive of a purposive activity reflected thus directly or indirectly in them, that warrants the inference which is to be established. There is not at any stage, or in any form, any question of
any independent vindication of this. That is ruled out on principle, and no one need be worried that it is so.

This is what Ayer overlooks, and the misgiving which he has
in consequence leads him to seek an amelioration of it on the basis
of what he himself calls a 'middle way', middle, that is, between
outright dualism and the physicalism or behaviourism which he
also rejects. This middle way he finds by maintaining that, while
mental processes are distinct from physical ones, it is impossible
to give an account of self-identity except on the basis of bodily
continuity. The presumption thus seems to be that, since the
body plays an indispensable part, albeit in a somewhat indirect
way, in our personal existence, the sting is taken out of the difficulty constituted by our inability to pass beyond bodily processes
to direct inspection of pure experience.

This is a desperate expedient, and it should have been evident
to Professor Ayer that it will not avail him. For the inference
involved in our knowledge of other minds is not after all an
inference to them as bodily existences, or in virtue of bodily
existences, but to the mental realities which have to be admitted
on any but outright physicalist theories. It would have been
wiser to look again at the antecedents of the requirement which
prompts this expedient, for it might then have become apparent
that they are very questionable ones.

It is significant also that Ayer has not much of a positive
character to say in support of his view that the identity of persons
does, in fact, depend on the association of their experiences with a
particular body in each case. Most of the space he devotes to the
question is taken up with relatively minor modifications and
objections. There is, for example, the fact that our experiences
depend in some measure on the existence of bodies besides one's
own, those of one's ancestors for instance; and this objection is
met, adequately enough it seems to me within the limits of the

thesis in question, in terms of a distinction between mediate and immediate[1] causal conditions. The case of telepathy is met by narrowing our interpretation of what is to count as a bodily state to our nerves and brains. It would be hard to determine whether this covers the case. But what one seems to lack in the discussion as a whole is a more positive indication of how the proposed solution of the problem of personal identity is thought to meet the more direct and obvious requirements of the problem.

In an earlier work, *The Problem of Knowledge*, Ayer had propounded a somewhat different solution, one in better accord with his general position, it seems to me, and inherently more plausible, although I do not think it will do as it stands. Confronted with the problem of how our various experiences belong together as members of the same bundle, he had there fallen back upon the solution of a 'relation of which, perhaps, nothing more illuminating can be said than that it is the relation that holds between experiences when they are the constituents of the same consciousness'.[2] But, in *The Concept of a Person* he is loth to accept this because it is the postulation of 'an unanalysable relation' and this, for him, is 'to abandon the problem'.[3]

It is surprising that Ayer should concede so readily that the problem is abandoned the moment we invoke some item which is not analysable. For he has himself insisted that there are some ultimate terms in our experience of which further analysis is not possible and which he has not been averse to describing in some cases as intuitions.[4] I do not myself think that it will suffice to say that there is an ultimate unanalysable relation between our experiences. But this is a pointer in the right direction. What is not analysable, if I am correct in what I have maintained earlier, is the consciousness that each one has of himself as a unique being, and it is on the basis of this that we can account for the continuity of the experiences of a particular individual. Ayer is quite justified in not being content with a purely Humean account which offers us nothing but relations of the experiences themselves, and it is hard to see how anyone who has read Bradley's famous and devastating chapter on 'The Theory of Association of Ideas', in his *Logic*, Vol. I,[5] could ever suppose that we could avoid invoking

[1] *Op. cit.*, p. 120.
[2] *Op. cit.*, p. 226.
[3] *The Concept of a Person*, p. 115.
[4] See, for example, *The Problem of Knowledge*, p. 43.
[5] Book II, Part II.

I

some principle of unity which goes beyond the experiences themselves. Ayer is also right, like others, in rejecting the idea of the
self as an entity to be described in terms of its particular characteristics. It is ultimate and recognized in and for itself in each
case, and as such it is the core of our personal identity and the
condition of our experience in all its modes. The drift of Ayer's
arguments seems to carry him strongly in this direction, but he
seems also to suspect that such a move must be highly improper
and out of accord with his down-to-earth empiricist approach to
philosophy. Thus he turns to a very different solution in terms
of bodily identity, and it is not surprising that there is a hesitant
half-hearted air about his presentation of it. Nor do I think that
this would have come about were not Ayer so convinced that
there is something radically suspect in the notion of our mediated
knowledge of other persons, in view of the inherent impossibility
of checking up on this directly, and that the only alternative must
be to associate personality more explicitly than Ayer's arguments
otherwise warrant with states of the body. The real drive seems
to come from this source and not from the 'wind of the argument'
itself as Ayer is wafted by it; and I think it would have been
better if he had allowed himself to be carried by the logic of his
arguments even if it meant breaking further with his earlier
allegiances and admitting that the requirement of explicit verification is not indispensable in all the claims we make.

I return, therefore, to the view that there is no sacrosanct
philosophical principle which is being violated in the contention
that we know other persons indirectly through what we observe of
their bodies and in other mediated ways which do not require that
we ever become aware of the experiences of other creatures in the
same way as we apprehend our own. There is thus no avoiding
the fact that everyone is in a sense a world to himself, and this
appears also to be the view closest in accord with our ordinary
belief and reactions. We know we may be in error about other
persons, but normally we do not seek any check on this beyond
what may be observed, directly or indirectly, of their bodily states
and behaviour. This seems to some a rather bleak situation, a
position summed up well in Cook Wilson's famous complaint
that he did not want inferred friends. But there is no serious cause
for this kind of anxiety. The fellowship we have with other persons
is not less intimate and rich because it involves an unavoidable
element of mediation. Indeed our situation becomes more exciting

and colourful the more we appreciate the ultimate otherness of other persons and the strangeness which persists even in the closest and most intimate relationships.

I shall not go in fuller detail, in this volume, into the analysis of the mediated knowledge we have of one another. To draw out the logic of it in its fullness is an undertaking of considerable range and importance which I am forced to postpone for the present. I hope to take it up elsewhere and thereby confirm and extend the contentions of the present volume. For the present it must suffice to insist on the essential interiority of experience and the awareness that each person has of himself in being himself. In the present chapter I have only sought to remove a major obstacle and present in outline the essential features of the corollary to the main theme of this book, namely that everyone has an immediate awareness of himself and his own experience, and of no other. Before I close the present study I should like, however, to give some general indication of the bearing which my contentions hitherto have on further debates about the status of the finite person and on the implications of this for fundamental problems in ethics and religion. This will not be attempted exhaustively, and much will have to be postponed to a further volume[1] to be concerned more directly with the religious and theological aspects of the subject.

[1] Provisionally entitled 'The Elusive Self and God'.

CHAPTER XIII

THE ELUSIVE SELF AND THE
'*I-THOU* RELATION'

When we understand how the self is inwardly known to itself, not as an entity apart and capable of being characterized on its own account, but as a unique being identified for itself in having any experience, then we are able to see the point and importance of much that is said about persons in existentialist thought. This strain in contemporary culture has many forms, it is often hard to distinguish these and sort out the influences which they reflect. Existentialist writers have presumed much on the sympathy and understanding of their readers and have not always been sufficiently at pains to explain the unusual terms they use or to remove misunderstanding. Their work is sometimes notoriously obscure, and it is hard on occasion to avoid the conclusion that the difficulty of the subject and the complexities which invite unusual language and methods are being exploited by writers who should have taken much greater pains to sort out their own ideas and find more effective means of expressing them. But when every allowance has been made for these vexatious features of existentialist thought, one cannot but conclude that it draws attention to aspects of our situation and experience which we are much apt to overlook, in particular because they are so difficult to handle intellectually with the precision and clarity which those who are engaged in the pursuit of truth set as their aims and standard. Nowhere is this more apparent than in a short but remarkable work which has already become an established classic, namely Martin Buber's *I and Thou*. It is not, by any means, from this source alone that recent existentialist thought has drawn its strength, it has been fed by many other streams; and in some of its forms it owes a good deal less to Martin Buber than to other eminent writers. But there can be little doubt of the influence of Buber or of the extent to which his ideas have been formative in a great deal of recent philosophy and religious literature; his thought is not obscured by elaborate terminology and it affords a splendid example of the insights to be found in this kind of philosophy and also of the ease with which these may be misrepresented or distorted even by those who initially acquired them.

I propose now to look at some of the things Martin Buber has to say and bring out the bearing of it on the views already advanced in this book. I confine myself almost wholly to Buber and resist the temptation, for the course of the present work at least, of deviating into discussion of some of the illuminating things we find in kindred writers. For the most part I shall also keep to *I and Thou*.

Buber begins with his famous account of 'primary words'. These are '*I-Thou*' and '*I-It*'. These 'do not signify things, but they intimate relations'.[1] This seems formally obvious and one can easily see also why it is added that the two terms of these 'primary words' cannot be said in separation. If *Thou* is said the *I* is said along with it. At the ordinary level this would mean that we cannot think of others as persons without being aware of being persons ourselves. Likewise, if we say '*It*' we must also say '*I*'. We cannot think of the world or of things without being conscious of ourselves in contrast to them. But Buber also adds: 'There is no *I* taken in itself, but only the *I* of the primary word *I-Thou* and the *I* of the primary word *I-It*.'[2] This seems also understandable, but it is a little ambiguous and we are at the start of the difficulties many have felt in their study of Buber. It will be evident now in what sense I myself would agree that 'There is no *I* taken in itself'. There is no self as an entity apart, but only the self that is involved in having some experience. What this involves further in the way of an objective reality need not be considered. Neither is there need here to go into the question of solipsism. For these are not the matters with which Buber is now concerned. He certainly seems to be saying, however, the sort of thing I have been maintaining about the impossibility of prising the self off from any kind of experience and considering it as a thing apart. The trouble is that this is not all that he seems to mean, nor is it clear that it is the main thing he wants to say. But what else then does he mean? We get a further indication of his meaning when he adds: 'The existence of I and the speaking of I are one and the same thing.'[3] This is a strange remark, and, on the face of it, it is clearly not true. I do not exist just when I speak, least of all just when I involve myself in what I say. But clearly we have to probe deeper

[1] *I and Thou* (trans. Ronald Gregor Smith) p. 3.
[2, 3] *Op. cit.*, p. 4.

than this for Buber's meaning. I think he means, in part at least, that the self cannot exist without being aware of itself, and affirming itself, in the adoption of some posture towards the world. It thus takes its 'stand in the word', and this seems to mean that the 'I' is actually constituted by the adoption of an appropriate attitude. It has no reality at all in itself.

The latter seems to me to be Buber's main theme, although he is not as explicit about it in the case of *I-It* as in that of *I-Thou*. In that case he is going much further than I do in his presentation of the view that the self cannot be described or characterized. I have certainly no intention of denying that the self is real in itself. I simply hold that it is *sui generis* and known by each person in being himself and having the experience without which he would not exist. I believe Buber has this in mind too, or at least that this is what gives plausibility to much that he says and has made it attractive to others. But this insight tends to be overlaid or distorted by a different, and in my view quite mistaken, notion, that the self simply exists in certain relations. The mistake does not hinder Buber from bringing out important consequences of the general view that the self cannot be laid hold upon as a thing or entity apart. But he could have done better justice to his insights if he had not been so disposed to think of the self entirely in terms of its 'twofold attitude',[1] as he put it, or if he had paused before saying at the start that 'primary words do not signify things, but they intimate relations'.[2]

It is certainly the relation that counts for Buber when a man is alleged to 'say *Thou*'. Here 'the speaker has no *thing*, he has indeed nothing. But he takes his stand in relation'.[3] This is in fact the central affirmation of the book. And it appears that it has to be understood in a twofold way. When a person says 'Thou' he is not only not a thing himself but he is not involved with things. It is the relation alone that matters and the constitutive qualities of things drop out of the picture. Those matter only when we say *I-It*. As he puts it:

'Man travels over the surface of things and experiences them. He extracts knowledge about their constitution from them: he wins an experience from them. He experiences what belongs to the things.'

[1, 2] *Op. cit.*, p. 3.
[3] *Op. cit.*, p. 4.

'But the world is not presented to man by experiences alone. These present him only with a world composed of *It* and *He* and *She* and *It* again.'[1]

This is no different if we speak of inner rather than outer experiences. We are still learning what things are like. 'If we add "secret" to "open" experiences, nothing in the situation is changed.'[2] 'Inner things or outer things, what are they but things and things?'[3] If we set up 'a closed compartment in things', we have still only '*It*, always *It*'.

There is obviously an important point here, although not everyone would put it in the same terms. The distinction between inner and outer is indeed important, and most of this book has been concerned with the need to recognize the private or 'inner' character of mental processes. But I have also urged that the elusiveness of mental processes, in the sense that we cannot say what it is for them to be mental and not external or observable phenomena, is matched by the elusiveness of the individual person which is not found by his having this or that course of experience or history but rather in something plain to himself which beggars all description. This has at least much in common with Buber's view. For he is also anxious to avoid a characterization of what is ultimate and of most distinctiveness in the lives of persons in terms of the course of their lives or their experiences and aptitudes. But Buber himself achieves this end largely by treating the *Thou*, to keep to his own term, entirely in terms of the relation in which it 'takes its stand'.

He might have avoided this consequence, and some of the further disasters that follow from it, had he passed a little less lightly over the distinction between 'inner' and 'outer' things in his proper opposition of both to the ultimate reality of individual persons. For he might have found, in the elusiveness of inner things a clue to an elusiveness of the true being of persons that would not have involved their reduction to the tenuousness of relations or divorced them from the reality of the experiences in which they are essentially involved and which belong pre-eminently to them. This latter error is as serious as the first.

But, in the case of the *I-Thou* relation, it is not merely the *Thou* which is thought of entirely in terms of the relation in which it takes its stand; the same situation holds in reverse for some *Thou*

[1, 2, 3] *Op. cit.*, p. 5.

which is being addressed. Not even where entities in the world of nature are concerned should they be thought of, in their *I-Thou* relation, as things to be characterized or situated in the ordinary sense. Here also 'relation is mutual',[1] and there seems to be nothing but relation.

Buber is, of course, fully aware that we do not subsist entirely in this rarefied role of standing in 'mutual relation'. That only holds when we 'say *Thou*'. But there is also commerce with the world in its qualified and quantified form as object-reality. We learn about the world in this way, we manipulate it, we 'win' experience from it. In this way I can take in the details of a tree when I look at it. I observe its colour, shape, situation and so forth. I 'perceive it as movement; flowing veins on clinging, pressing pith, suck of the roots, breathing of the leaves, ceaseless commerce with earth and air—and the obscure growth itself'.[2] 'I can classify it in a species and study it as a type in its structure and mode of life.'[3] But 'in all this the tree remains my object, occupies space and time, and has its nature and constitution'.[4] It remains a thing, an *It*.

But while Buber allows that, in our ordinary commerce with the world, whether in the form of natural objects or of persons, we have to treat it as an *It* and take proper account of the characteristics of things as they confront us, yet, in the *I-Thou* relation, we have to think of even natural entities, including inanimate objects, in terms of the relation in which they take their stand. On no side does there seem to be anything other than relation.

We must be careful, however, not to misrepresent Buber here. He does not maintain that, once the *I-Thou* relation is established, we can simply disregard the characterization of things and persons. In his own example of the tree, he expressly declares:

'To effect this', that is 'to be bound up in relation to' the tree, 'it is not necessary for me to give up any of the ways in which I consider the tree. There is nothing from which I would have to turn my eyes away in order to see, and no knowledge that I would have to forget.'[5] 'The tree is no impression, no play of any imagination, no value depending on my mood, but it is bodied over against me and has to do with me, as I with it—only in a different way.'[6]

[1, 6] *Op. cit.*, p. 8
[2, 3, 4, 5] *Op. cit.*, p. 7.

On the other hand it is not any form of animism that is being commended to us here. It is not that there is something akin to the life of persons belonging to the tree in addition to its natural properties. Buber is quite explicit about this. He puts the question himself: 'The tree will have a consciousness, then, similar to our own?' and he replies, 'Of that I have no experience,' 'I encounter no soul or dryad of the tree, but the tree itself.'[1]

It seems clear then what are some of the things we are not to suppose. But this makes the position all the more mysterious. For although we do not set aside the properties of things, in the *I-Thou* relation, we somehow supersede them, they become 'united' in the 'mutual relation'. As the position is summed up:

'What, then, do we experience of *Thou?*
Just nothing. For we do not experience it.
What, then, do we know of *Thou?*
Just everything. For we know nothing isolated about it any more.'[2]

Knowledge which is 'everything' and involves no 'isolation' or particularizing is not knowledge in any ordinary sense, and we are expressly told that 'No system of ideas, no foreknowledge, and no fancy intervene between *I* and *Thou*'.[3] There is simply 'meeting' and 'All real living is meeting'.[4]

This is undoubtedly baffling, and it is not surprising that many are disposed to give up altogether at this point and treat utterances like the ones just noticed as of no account or at best a 'philosophical prose poem' which does not provide any helpful philosophical enlightenment. The irritation is increased when admirers of Buber echo his thoughts in distorted forms of their own, sometimes with little heed to what Buber himself may have meant. I believe, however, that Buber is saying something of the utmost importance at the point where his thoughts are most bewildering.

I believe that one of the things he has in mind, at the point where he speaks of 'meeting' or being in relation with natural objects, is that particular things, including here persons as well as other entities in the world of nature, can be significant in a profound and instructive way in virtue of their distinctiveness

[1] *Op. cit.*, p. 8.
[2, 3, 4] *Op. cit.*, p. 11.

and particularity. How this comes about cannot be easily explained, for an account of what is significant about things in the present sense cannot be obtained by just reviewing their properties. It is a work of artistic illumination which makes things articulate in their particularity. One of the reasons why Plato, himself a supreme artist who felt profoundly the lure of art, was apt to dismiss the artist as of no account was his preoccupation with form and universal truth. This is a tale that has often been told and I have myself attempted a variation on it in my essay 'On Poetic Truth'.[1] All art, I have there maintained, is concerned with the particular, and even universal ideas have to be invested with some kind of particularity by their context to be proper features in a work of art.

This is a theme which calls for elaboration on its own account. I shall not attempt that here, but simply draw attention to what many, myself among them, have maintained about the way the artist makes some particular object or event alive to us in its distinctness; he provides a confrontation or a means for things to make some peculiar impact upon us. We thus see natural objects as we do not normally see them, they become alive to us and have an interest well beyond our ordinary use and placing of them. They are a source of wonderment and fascination because of some newness with which the artist invests them, by unexpected associations perhaps, by exaggeration or distortion of some of their features, by presentation in an unusual setting of sounds or other harmonies. The world is made to speak to us, to become strange, alarming, delightful and so on in a variety of ways and by endless devices. This is the insight of the artist and the mode of illumination which he provides.

This is also what Buber appears to have in mind, in great measure, in what he says about confrontation and meeting. Nor are there many more suggestive sources for the study of this view of art, and of the world being made peculiarly articulate for us, than Buber's *I and Thou*. A poet speaks here about what poetry means to him. This, then, is one way of understanding what Buber is saying in this book. But if this were all, notwithstanding its importance and his grasp of it, he would be introducing needless encumbrances and complexities into his presentation of it. And the truth is that, while Buber was conveying his extreme sensitivity to these illuminations which involve the particular in its starkness

[1] *Morals and Revelation*, chap. 9.

and finality, he was also at one and the same time feeling after certain other matters of equal, and perhaps greater importance. Nor was it clear at all to Buber himself, alas, just how these different insights shaded into one another, and how they stand apart. This is why we have to work so hard to be sure what he wants to say.

A further thought which is obviously very much in Buber's mind in this context, though much overlaid by others, is that anything we may encounter, animate and inanimate alike, lead out eventually to God or the infinite. God is involved in the being of anything, and there are moments of illumination when this is seen sharply in our contemplation of particular things. This has been impressively put by Professor E. L. Mascall when he refers to 'the common experience of people making their first retreat, that after the first day or so natural objects seem to acquire a peculiar character of transparency and vitality, so that they appear as only very thinly veiling the creative activity of God'.[1] In this way there may be a meeting with things which is also a meeting with God; and it is evident that Buber has this very much in mind. He writes:

'Every particular *Thou* is a glimpse through to the eternal *Thou*; by means of every particular *Thou* the primary word addresses the eternal *Thou*. Through this mediation of the *Thou* of all beings fulfilment, and non-fulfilment, of relations comes to them: the inborn *Thou* is realized in each relation and consummated in none. It is consummated only in the direct relation with the *Thou* that by its nature cannot become *It*'.[2]

It may be that Buber does not understand 'the glimpse through to the eternal *Thou*' in quite the same way as Mascall and others when they find natural objects thinly veiling the activity of God. But if so, then I think that is due largely to his own failure or reluctance to sort out his various insights effectively. One of the ways in which his work rings the bell with many people is, I much suspect, just this involvement of the eternal in every particular and the moments of illumination when this becomes plain.

This sort of illumination has much in common with the way particular things may become articulate in art and kindred ways.

[1] *He Who Is*, p. 80.
[2] *I and Thou*, p. 75.

But the two sorts of insights must not be confused or conflated. The artist is not bound to be, even implicitly, a religious visionary. He may just hit on the means to make what is normally present to us have its proper impact, and he need not in any way be a minor artist if that is all he does. On the other hand the artistic insight may readily become a religious one, and as there are further ways in which, in divine disclosure, the eternal involves itself in particular things and events, the blending of art and religion may be exceptionally close and fruitful, as may well be seen in the history of both. It is not surprising, therefore, that what Buber has to say has been found impressive by different people in very different ways.

The religious aspect of the *I-Thou* relation is not, in my understanding, the whole of it for Buber. But it is for him essential, and for that reason it tends to eclipse what may be said about other features of it on their own account. On its religious side, it is understandable that the *I-Thou* relation should be apt to be taken entirely in the sense of taking one's stand in the relation. For where God, as eternal or transcendent being, is concerned, there is nothing specific that we learn about Him in the immediate sense of His presence in all things.[1] We simply know that He has to be as the ultimate mysterious ground of the being of all else— He is just 'He who Is'. To that extent we just stand in relation to Him and He to us. This is not a relation to nothing, or some bare relation without terms, whatever that could be. God is real, supremely so, and we are real. But in the immediate awareness we have of God, as involved in the being of everything else, we do not learn anything expressly about the essence of God, we do not understand what it is to be God, as we have at least some partial understanding of any finite entity we postulate to explain natural phenomena in the ordinary way. God is not known as an object among objects, or some term in the finite relations of things. He remains to that extent an unfathomable mystery. This point has been very much stressed of late, and I shall not dwell upon it. But it can be understood how, in the light of this reflection, it becomes plausible to say that, in our initial awareness of God which is regulative for all further awareness of Him, we do not experience Him in the ordinary way but stand in relation to Him.

I am not maintaining that this is the best way, or even a satisfactory way, of putting the matter. For the insight we have into

[1] See my 'God and Mystery' in *Prospect for Metaphysics*, ed. I. T. Ramsey.

there having to be God is itself an experience, and it is an experience in which we apprehend what is of the utmost consequence in all other experience. It is not without content, but has the richest content of all. At the same time what we apprehend is grasped, not in the delineation of its properties, but in the inevitability of its being and the perfection therein involved. It is to that extent some sort of standing in a relation.

If, however, Buber had not allowed this idea to be so dominant over his other ideas and draw the latter into itself, he might well have been put in the way of presenting his religious thought in a way that would have allowed a much more fruitful development. For the sense that he has of the impact which objects may make upon us, and the way they could thus become alive and articulate, could have opened up a way of thinking of encounter and meeting which did not have to be conceived so finely and cautiously as to empty it of all but the standing in relation. It would not be devoid of content, though its content would not be the world as we normally experience it; it would not be sharply opposed, in all respects, to experience as such.

This would have two results. It would have taken the sting out of much of the usual criticisms of the theology of encounter. For the latter need not then have taken the course it has so often taken, namely that of by-passing all problems of our particular knowledge of God, on the score that, in true religion, it is not 'knowledge about' God that we have but encounter. It has often been urged, by myself among many others, that there can be no mere encounter. This seems certainly true in our ordinary dealings with each other. How can I encounter anyone unless I know something about him? In like manner religious life, at least all but the most incipient, has some filling or content obtained from some experience of God or divine disclosure. Religion is not just the sense of the being of God. It contains more precise beliefs about what God is like, how He deals with us and how we experience Him, what He requires of us and so forth. Some account must be given of this and the way it is warranted. We cannot just cry 'Encounter', and dodge the issue. Many have been tempted to do so, and they have taken their cue from Buber. But if they had learnt the lesson of other insights that Buber has, they might have been much less disposed to do so.

In the second place, there would have been not only an appreciation of the limitation of the idea of meeting as such or of bare encounter, but also a way would have been opened up of indicating how, in peculiar relationships like those of religion, this takes place. For the way things become alive and articulate to us in their impact upon us, as the artist in particular mediates it, provides a peculiarly fruitful approach to problems of the way God, who cannot be known as He is in Himself, may be found by us through some impact He indirectly makes upon us through the events of our lives and history. There is in Buber much which, if only it were enabled to stand out more sharply on its own account, is most suggestive for the student of the philosophical problem of revelation.

There is also the bearing of Buber's teaching on the place which is given to the idea of respect for persons in a social or ethical context. This is an important principle, although it is hard to see the precise implication of it for practice. The distinction that is sometimes drawn between treating people as persons and treating them as things or as a means is certainly not absolute. We never strictly treat a person as 'a thing', if this means wholly disregarding the fact that he is a person. Into our respect for persons there surely enters the thought of what they are like. There is also something more of which I shall give an indication in a moment. But this something more is not to be detached from what Buber has in mind when he talks of the way we experience persons; and if he had paid more heed to the content of our normal exchanges and the way we evaluate them, he could have made his more original and germinative thought about the subject a good deal more fruitful in its application to practice.

This brings us back to what seems to me central in Buber's position. I believe that what has impressed him most, although he does not sort it out and present it as explicitly as he might, is the fact that we just cannot characterize or identify the self by some distinctive feature in the respect in which it is uniquely known and identified for itself. There is nothing to be said about the self at this level, we do not learn about it, and for that reason we see why it is not quite appropriate to say that we experience it. We can, as is quite obvious, have experience of one another in another way. We can learn what other persons feel and think, what has been their history and so forth. But the basic sense in which it is the history of this particular person, the way his experiences belong to him, this, in the last analysis, we cannot know. Each must know it for himself in his own case. He knows himself as a distinct and ultimate being in a way that is not dependent on what he happens to think and feel, and so on, and what has occurred to him. We never expressly share the consciousness each one has of himself in this way, we only ascribe it, without further justification, on the assumption that what we do ascribe, on the basis of our observations and so forth, in the way of experience must carry with it, in the case of another person, the same recognition of an irreducible distinctness as we find in our own case.

There is, thus, a sense in which other persons are essentially mysterious to us. This is not the mystery of transcendent being, as in the case of God, although we do come closer here to the irreducible mystery of transcendence than anywhere else in our limited existence. It is not that we have no notion at all what it must be to be the other person. We presume that he has a mind, or thoughts and feelings, not unlike our own. For him to be thinking about philosophy is substantially the same as for me to do so, he suffers and he enjoys things as I do. But what it is for all this to happen to *him*, that I cannot explicitly know at all. I can only presume that he knows it as I know who I am. The other is in some sense essentially mysterious.

It is hardly necessary to add that the present sense in which each is some kind of world of his own has nothing directly to do with the fact that there is a great deal which we are not, in fact, able to learn about one another. There are depths in our hearts and thoughts which others may find it particularly difficult to probe, and there are many things we deliberately keep away from others. There are many disguises we wear, and it needs the trained observer or the novelist to get behind them. There is much which, in some measure at least, we hide from ourselves. But this is contingent, there is no reason in principle why all may not be laid bare, at the present level, to ourselves or to others, however unlikely in fact. This is altogether different from the inherent or irreducible mystery of the other, in the sense that only the other person properly knows what it is for him to be himself.

There are, however, moments when we become peculiarly conscious of the fact that the other person is distinctively other and strange in the sense indicated. These are moments of exceptional intimacy, sometimes sweet and sometimes disturbing and alarming. We are truly closer to the other just because he also stands in our presence as a stranger. We must not presume too much, although now we are truly face to face, we are in the presence of a being who is as irreducibly and finally himself, one might almost say a world of his own, as we are. This adds great depth and enrichment to our mutual awareness, whether our relation be friendly or hostile, and it has the utmost significance for major problems of human existence, as I hope to show.

In the meantime it must suffice here to show how plausible it is to speak of the moments of encounter, in the sense indicated, as a case of taking one's stand in relation, not having experience of or learning about another. It is a confrontation, although this does not mean that we abstract from experience or what is 'learnt about'. The distinctive thing is the sense of the other as other, although in further ways the encounter draws its significance from the specific content of our experience.

A weakness in Buber's own position is that he tends to think of the moment of standing in relation in too great a detachment from the varied content of all the experience we have of one another. It is not that he denies such experience; he acknowledges, on the contrary, that we have it and need it to continue the round of our lives. But he is apt also to treat it as altogether inferior, almost an encumbrance, and not very different in worth or importance from the knowledge of natural objects we require in order to manipulate them. *I-It* is thus on an altogether different plane, even in the case of persons, from the *I-Thou*, and the ideal must be always to pass beyond the world of *I-It*, although for regrettable practical reasons we cannot disregard it, to the more rarefied and truly significant world of *I-Thou*.

This is, indeed, a very grave mistake. It takes away all that gives point and direction to our aspirations and our dealings with each other. It renders negligible the judgment, the discernment, the sympathy, the forbearance, which we should cultivate in seeking to know one another and supply one another's needs, the need for fellowship above all. The art of mutual understanding is a supreme one in the right conduct of human life, but we are not likely to succeed in it if we withdraw from the world in which we feel and think this or that to a world which is altogether above such disparities and above the battle they present.

Indeed, if this withdrawal is too complete, it may even defeat the aim of recognizing the other in his ultimate distinctness as other. It may lead to a conflation in which no one properly takes his stand in relation to the other, a merging such as we find in some forms of mysticism. This is not because the distinctness is made what it is by the particular events of our lives and experience. The corrective is not found by just stressing those, and if we thought this we should miss the point of what is most suggestive and profound in Buber's own insight. It is simply that the very insight into the finality of our distinctness, as each one apprehends it in his own case, is put in jeopardy if it is viewed in the sort of void which is created by thinking of persons entirely in terms of the confrontation of one by the other in the finality of his otherness. This is the obverse of the error which we find, as I hope to show in due course, in idealist philosophy.

This error is bound up with another. We have already seen that Buber's conception of the *I-Thou* relation is much affected by his sense of the eternal *Thou* and the way this is involved in any other relation to a *Thou*. That affords one reason for the proneness of Buber to think of us, in what is distinctive and of worth in our lives, as merely standing in a relation. For in one sense, as we saw, this is very nearly how we must conceive of ourselves in relation to transcendent being, although this, as was also stressed, is far from being the whole story. But, in like manner, the pre-occupation with persons in the sense in which they stand starkly opposed as other, to the neglect of the peculiarities of their natures and history, has repercussions on the way Buber thinks of God and our relation to Him. For the way he conceives of the *I-Thou* relation at the finite level, and the rarefied notion of it solely in terms of standing in relation, tends to determine for him also the character of the relation we have with the eternal Thou. This becomes also tenuous in all respects and the way is prepared thus again for the sort of mysticism in which all distinctness is lost.

There are, undoubtedly, strains of this kind of mysticism in Buber, and it is by no means easy to determine how far he has travelled in that direction. But to the extent that he does so we have one of those curious paradoxes we find in the history of thought by which a slight distortion of some position brings about an affirmation of almost the opposite of it—as when extreme individualism in political thought culminates in the doctrine of the general will. For what is of the utmost importance in Buber's thought is just the recognition of the irreducible way in which I confront a *Thou*. Of this he writes with great sensitivity and it is for this that we are indebted to him. But, if I am right, the clue to what is central and most impressive in Buber's teaching, and the way to avoid the pitfalls along the course he is taking, is to have due appreciation of the elusiveness of the self in its ultimacy and distinctness whereby it is more than its experiences or its aptitudes and character, but more in a way which cannot in turn be described or characterized any more than it could be thought to subsist in isolation from its experiences and the propensities which condition them. This is the self which each one knows himself to be and which he ascribes to another, as known to him, in the moments of confrontation which give the greatest depth and significance to our commerce together in this world—and beyond it.

CHAPTER XIV

IDEALISM

Idealism was the dominant philosophy in the latter half of the nineteenth century, not only in English speaking countries but almost everywhere where the subject was studied. It was brought into English, and thereby American, philosophy largely through the influence of T. H. Green, sometimes described as the father of English idealism, but the most notable figure in the movement, as few will doubt today, is that of F. H. Bradley. Behind all these thinkers lies the massive work of Hegel, now happily coming to its own again; and Hegel's work, like that of many outstanding European thinkers, was given its shape most decisively by the need to cope with a problem bequeathed by Kant to his successors.

According to Kant, we can only have knowledge of objects which are conditioned or affected in certain ways by the fact that we know or experience them. This does not, for Kant, make the knowledge viciously subjective. He starts from the fact that we know or experience a world of objects which are not of our own creation. His main question is—How is such experience possible? He specifies the conditions which make it possible for us to have the knowledge we do have. But these conditions do carry with them some limitation, sometimes put in the form that the world of our knowledge or experience is relative, not indeed to each of us as individuals, but to our 'faculty of cognition'. The objects involved are objects of our type of experience, subject to conditions which, it is at least sometimes suggested, are imposed by our minds. Even if not so imposed, they carry with them a certain restriction. They give us a world of things as they are *for us*, and not 'in themselves'.

Contrasted with this world of phenomena is the noumenal world, or the world of things in themselves. We can have no knowledge of these, for they do not conform to the ways in which knowledge is possible for us. But we are led to think of them, the door is opened as it were, by the limitations of the sort of knowledge or experience we do have. In addition, Kant maintains, we can have some sort of assurance about the existence and nature of the kind of reality which lies altogether beyond the world we can properly be said to know. To this Kant gives the name 'faith', but it is not faith in the way we normally think of it in religion. There are certain postulates or requirements of a moral order of things, described also as 'the postulates of practical reason'. In this way there is established the existence of God, freedom and the immortality of the soul.

The soul had already come into the picture in another way. For a basic condition of our having the sort of knowledge we do have, had been, for Kant, that everything in our experience should be organized or co-ordinated, it must be given its place and not be random, it must admit of being identified and characterized. But this is only possible if there is some focus or centre from which the unification takes place, and thus, just as there must be certain objective conditions or modes of unification of things which we can be said to know, the conditions which Kant himself claims to delineate, so there must also be a subject by which the order and continuity of our experience is sustained from one moment to the next—'an abiding self' as it has been put. We do not properly know this self, it is itself the condition of knowledge; and there is nothing that can be said about it beyond the fact that it is required in this way to make possible a knowledge of a world of objects. We do have a phenomenal self, consisting of the way our impressions and desires occur to us, but the pure non-empirical self must be thought of quite differently as the subject in all experience; it is not accessible to us as an object of experience, it is that through which all experience is co-ordinated, an 'imaginary focus' as it is even put on occasion; never can the subject itself be part of the world of phenomena.

But this presents many problems, especially where the sharp bifurcation of the self into an empirical and a noumenal self is concerned. These are most acute in ethics. On the one hand we have the empirical self—determined in the same general way as events in the external world, the mode of it being in fact hedonistic, on Kant's view, for all our desires; and, on the other, we have a pure self which is free in a way that seems to remove it altogether from the course of events in the world. Indeed, the pure self does not seem to be in time at all, and some of Kant's followers have not hesitated to speak of a 'timeless self'. Are we then to consider ourselves morally accountable solely in respect of some once for all choice which determines the set of our conduct for the rest of our lives, or is there some other way in which the self as noumenon makes itself effective in the course of our conduct? These are notorious difficulties in Kantian ethics, though this is not the place to consider them closely.

But these difficulties are only peculiarly sharp examples of the straits in which we seem to be generally landed by the supposition that the objects of which we can be said to have knowledge in the proper sense, or the objects of our experience, are altogether different from the sort of realities, the 'things in themselves', of which we have some other assurance through the postulates of practical reason. We seem to have two quite separate worlds, the world of things in themselves and the world of appearances or phenomena, and there seems to be no commerce between them, they are not even real in the same sense; indeed, in spite of the prestige which the term 'things in themselves' appears to confer, it is not very clear that we are entitled to take these to be realities at all, although Kant in some respects takes them to be of the utmost importance. There is a grave ambiguity about them, as there is also in a different way about the world of mere phenomena.

The dilemma in which Kant has placed himself here is more understandable in the case of our knowledge of God than of other things in themselves. For, if God is a transcendent being, we certainly do not know Him in His essence as many of us claim that we do know other things. He remains, in a very radical sense, a mystery. But even so we have the intuition of His being as a supreme and perfect reality; and, in most religions at least, we have the additional claim that much is known beyond this about God through the impact He makes on certain finite things or some other mode of divine disclosure. None of this is easy unless the media by which God is known admit of being known by us in themselves in some dependable way.

It was the problems bequeathed in these ways by Kant to his successors that determined the main course of speculative thought in subsequent times. Profound dissatisfaction was felt with the sharp bifurcation of reality in the Kantian system. Some closer commerce between the world as it shapes itself for us and the world as it truly is and in its fulness came to be sought; and the obvious way to accomplish this was to find some clue within the limited world of our experience to whatever reality is thought to extend beyond that. The 'world as will' was one such suggestion, but by far the most influential and widely-developed solution was that of reason or rational necessity as the ultimate determinant of all there is.

The chief architect of this form of metaphysics was Hegel and it was in his work that the main lines of the course of later idealism were laid. The universe came to be regarded as one comprehensive system in which there was no room for ultimate division. The whole is what it is in virtue of the parts and the parts in virtue of the whole, the dependence of whole and part is complete; some Hegelians went further and held that reason itself requires that everything should be as it is in this way. The knowledge we have is thus always partial and inadequate, it always involves some distortion, as we never see anything as it truly is in the system as a whole. But the more we extend our knowledge and make it coherent the closer we draw to the ideal of knowledge, namely a complete self-explanatory system. There are, as many idealists would put it, degrees of truth and also degrees of reality. In finite experience we never get beyond that. But our inadequate finite understanding is not, on the other hand, wholly removed from the one genuine reality. There is only the one universe, although there are partial and inadequate apprehensions of it. The whole is present, at least in principle, in our limited understanding; and we embrace the one true reality with ever increasing adequacy the more we widen and develop the knowledge we already have.

There are, however, obvious difficulties in this view of the universe and of our knowledge of it. One of these presents itself when we think of what is sometimes described as the 'given' element in experience. There seems to be an element of brute fact in all that we encounter in the world around us. This may be hard to isolate or get at in its neatness, and this is why some idealists would follow the fashion of T. H. Green when he spoke of reality as 'an all-inclusive system of relations'. But it is difficult to see how there could be nothing but relations. There must be room for something which is related as well, however difficult to give an account of it; and to that extent there must be something in experience of which an exhaustive rational account is not possible, something which is just what it is and is just there.

A further difficulty is the fact of evil, in its moral and non-moral forms. The idealist scheme of things, in the form I have just been noting, requires that there should be no ultimate evil. Things only appear evil to our limited comprehension. If we understood better we would see that everything has its place in a system which is perfect throughout. There is no inherent evil but only the good that is displaced, some misalliance of inherently worthwhile things; and this itself can only have place in the limited partial understanding we have. Things appear evil to us, but there is no room for evil in the universe as it truly is and as it would appear to a perfect understanding. This is, however, a difficult view to maintain. For is there not some kind of blot in the system of things due to the mere fact that some things appear at least to be evil? From where does the very notion of evil come? And how plausible is it to think of acute and protracted physical or mental suffering as only seemingly bad, or as some form of goodness in the wrong place? Is it not plain bad? And what of error? Is not this, by contrast with mere limitations of knowledge, positive in a way that hardly fits into a wholly rational scheme of things?

Idealists sought in various ways to cope with these problems. They pointed out, for example, that good may often come out of bad and, in this way, prepared for the view that, if we understood all, we would see that all evil, as it seems to us, contributed in some way to an eventual good which compensated for it. Pain, it was observed, led to an enrichment of experience or an ennobling of character. But how far can we go in this way? Not many would agree today that we can offer an exhaustive rational account of all non-moral evil in these terms; there is much which they do not seem to cover, although some of the explanations contain important elements of truth. In addition there is moral evil, which presents the idealist with a peculiarly intractable problem.

This is because of the exceptionally positive character of moral evil. It seems quite plainly inherent in some of our attitudes or procedures and irreducible; and this in turn is closely dependent on the element of deliberation which it involves. It is not something which befalls us, we incur it directly by what we intend, it is a form of rebelliousness and involves a power, if I may so put it, of standing out against the universe and resisting its demands. How is this possible, how can we be the independent agents which moral good and evil require, if we are ourselves some modes or limitations of the one system or reality of which the universe consists? How can there be inherent or deliberate evil in our lives if those are some part of the life or the being of God?

We come here to the point where the central problem of idealist metaphysics is most acute. This is the problem of the status of finite individuals. We tend to think of ourselves as distinct or separate beings; and that is what the idea of creation normally implies. But this is put in jeopardy at once if we are to suppose that there is only one reality of which everything else is some phase or limitation. Admittedly, we do have our part to play, we make a genuine contribution to the life of the whole. But this is in turn organic to what the system as a whole is like. Nor is the place we have in this system precisely what it seems to us in our finite existence to be. The way we understand ourselves is not the way we properly are, the status of appearance does not give the true or ultimate reality of anything. Nor has anything the sort of distinctness which, to the superficial view, it may seem to have.

The position is not radically altered if, as in the case of Bradley, we pass beyond strictly rational idealism and substitute for it the idea of a supra-rational absolute. For although this opens the way for the solution of some of the problems which idealism presents, it still leaves us, for Bradley at least, with an absolute of which every finite reality is some phase or limitation.

This problem became the crux for a great deal of philosophical debate at the turn of the century. Some thinkers, like Bernard Bosanquet, were not very much daunted by the implications of the position they held. Others, like G. F. Stout, Pringle-Pattison and A. E. Taylor were deeply concerned about them and went to considerable pains to try to accommodate their general acceptance of the prevailing idealism to what we usually believe and what seemed to be required by morals and religion. I shall not follow the course of the controversy in further detail in its general form, highly instructive though it is. Nor shall I here consider the ramifications of it as they affected the thought of Eastern countries whose culture had much in common with nineteenth century idealism. But I am anxious, now that I have sketched the general position, to bring out the bearing of what has been said in preceding chapters about the elusive nature of the self on some of the main arguments in the discussion as it centred on the question of personal identity.

To do this I shall refer especially to a celebrated discussion of the subject at a conference held in London in 1918. This took the form of a symposium on the subject, 'Do Finite Individuals Possess a Substantive or an Adjectival Mode of Being?', the papers being published in a volume of the *Proceedings of the Aristotelian Society* under the title, *Life and Finite Individuality*.

The discussion, in the symposium I have mentioned, is opened by Bosanquet. He begins by drawing a fairly sharp distinction between 'spirits' and other things or 'reals'. The problem of the finite individual seems to him very much more acute in the case of the former than of the latter—indeed he is convinced that there is no very serious problem until we consider spirits or persons. In respect to all other entities the affirmation of thinghood or identity seems to him plainly provisional and relative. It depends on our purpose in dividing things up in the world around us. As he puts it himself

'There is no ultimate reason for taking one complex, at least below conscious individuals, as a single thing more than another. They include one another in innumerable subordinations, from the Sahara, for example, or any patch of it, down to any grain of sand in it. A thing, therefore, as an existence, can have no claim to be an ultimate subject. It is, as such, a provisional subject, and has, of course, a being and reality, and is necessary to the universe. But it is selected for convenience of special knowledge or practice, and justifies its selection in infinitely varied degrees.'[1]

It is a little strange that the line should be drawn here at the level of 'spirits' understood as 'conscious individuals' in a sense that excludes, as it seems to do, other animate and sentient existence, including 'all minds of brutes'.[2] When we think of brutes as beings apart we do so on further grounds than those which lead us to single out inanimate objects. Their identity has at least some affinity with that which we ascribe to ourselves on the basis of inner states or experiences. We do not, initially at least, think of it solely in terms of convenient demarcations. That would be odd even if, in the last resort, we found that there was nothing else to be said. The proper place to draw a line seems to me to be at the point of sentient existence.

I shall not pursue this further now but simply note that, for Bosanquet, there can be no question of drawing, even initially, 'an absolute boundary line round any reals but spirits'.[3] There is for him no problem except in the case of 'spiritual finite beings'. Nor shall I go further here into the difficulties of the view that the

[1] *Op. cit.*, p. 79.
[2] *Op. cit.*, p. 78.
[3] *Op. cit.*, p. 83.

divisions we make generally among natural objects can be under-stood entirely in terms of our purposes and convenience. There seem to be inherently natural groupings. This may not involve a wholly unobservable material substance, and what it finally does involve is a very hard problem. But I have no need for my purpose to consider it. Let us confine ourselves to what Bosanquet says about spirits. Initially, even on his view, these seem to have some sort of finality; and this is where the problem is a live one for him.

It is so, however, not because of any immediate sense, real or illusory, that we have of our distinctness or finality as beings on our own account, but because of 'an indefeasible unity'[1] which is characteristic of human experience. 'We are confident of our individual unity,'[2] 'it is our nature to be a single self. We claim it as a right, and accept it as a duty',[3] but the essential reason for this is that 'to be a thinking being is to demand a unity, and every act of such a being is an attempt to realize it'.[4] It is as the reflection of this unity, and of the demand to realize it more completely, that 'the popular attitude in considering finite individuals, whether things or persons, is frankly pluralist'.[5] In the case of external things we make the mistake of looking for unity in 'a linear or successional continuity' rather than in the essential inter-related-ness of things. But the principle of individuality is ultimately a matter of unity, and this is what is focused with peculiar sharpness in conscious experience. That is why, as 'spirits' we have an exceptionally clear consciousness of 'distinct individuality'.

When the matter is thought of in this way, it is not hard to see why one's nature 'as a single self', our 'distinct individuality' should also be thought to be 'a question of degree'.[6] It is as much a demand as an actual attainment. It is never completely realized. 'Our unity is a puzzle and an unrealized aspiration.'[7] The self 'is a substance and an ultimate subject, but not in its own right. Its existence, as an existence, bears the umistakeable stamp of the fragmentary and the provisional'.[8] There is thus nothing final in our distinctness, even as spirits or human beings. Indeed, the unity which confers such distinctness upon us in a pre-eminent way as spirits proclaims, in that very context, more markedly than elsewhere its own involvement in a completer realization of itself.

[1, 4, 8] *Op. cit.*, p. 93.
[2, 3, 7] *Op. cit.*, p. 92.
[5] *Op. cit.*, p. 89.
[6] *Op. cit.*, p. 91.

On the one hand, our existence, as finite beings, is provisional. 'Can there be anyone who does not feel it so in every act and every thought? But through all this, and operative in it, there shines the intellectual unity. It is not my monad nor my star. It is the life which lives in me, but it is more of that life than I succeed in living.'[1]

It is in terms of this principle that Bosanquet gives an account of the freedom which we exercise as moral and religious creatures and which presents one way in which the distinctness and autonomy of spirits is very sharply displayed. To be accountable, it would seem, we require to be beings whose actions can be regarded as pre-eminently their own. But on this agelong problem Bosanquet is content to follow the line usually taken by idealist writers from T. H. Green to the present day, namely that of thinking of freedom in terms of a self-determination which is a matter of degree and never fully realized short of the absolute itself. Our conduct is free in the measure of the richness and co-ordination of its content. The forces which affect us do not determine us solely from outside or mechanically but as taken up into the organic unity of our own experience. I am thus free in the unity and structure of the ends at which I aim.

As Bosanquet puts it, a man is thus free 'in so far as he wills the universal object'.[2] 'It is only what is free from self-contradiction that can be willed without obstruction . . . I am only free in such objects of volition as confront with adequate solutions the situations which I apprehend.'[3]

We do not, however, at any time fully achieve the adequacy posited here—short of willing 'the whole'. The more we do achieve it the more we are at one with the whole, and this leads Bosanquet to 'the familiar paradox', as he calls it, that 'it is only in a will above my own that I can find my own will and my freedom and independence'.[4] 'The moral universe in me expresses itself thus. There is always an incoming wave of identical object-consciousness.'[5] To the extent that this occurs our wills, in becoming identical with the whole, become also identical with one another. There is in this, as in respect to other modes of experience, a 'confluence of selves'. One's will becomes part of 'the communal will'. This communal will, 'though revealed in a number of

[1] *Op. cit.*, p. 93.
[2] *Op. cit.*, p. 94.
[3], [4], [5] *Op. cit.*, p. 95.

individuals, is a single thing as much as external nature, which is revealed in the same way. Participation in its structure makes every particular unit an individual, that is, a particular in which the universal or the identity assumes a special modification. His will is made out of the common substance and, even when he rejects and reverses the form in which it is seen elsewhere, his volition is still dependent on it'.[1]

Much has been written in criticism of the notion of freedom as self-determination whereby the finite individual is also determined by the universal or absolute will which is operative within him. Does it not imply, as Bosanquet himself puts it, that it is 'in error and in sin' that 'I come nearest to being a substantive in my own right'?[2] Is that true to the way we think of moral achievement and our distinctiveness at the crucial point of moral effort? I do not think so, but I shall not press these points of criticism now. My concern is more to show by what sort of considerations Bosanquet arrived at these well-known conclusions of idealist metaphysics.

The point to note especially is the preoccupation with the content of experience and its unification, whether in thinking or in action. Bosanquet is quite explicit in his rejection of the idea of the ego as some entity with a describable character or nature of its own. That would only push our problems back a stage, for all the main questions would have to be asked again about this separate entity. How does it come to be known and how is it found? And in this respect Bosanquet seems altogether right, the mistake of thinking of the self as some reality with a discernible nature of its own has already been sufficiently stressed in earlier chapters. But Bosanquet also concludes that the only alternative to thinking of the self in this way is to think of it wholly in terms of the content of experience and its particular structure. Once this move is made, the important thing about us, as persons, seems to be the unification and extension of experience by which it becomes identical with the experience of others, and it is on this particular point that Bosanquet himself, understandably and quite properly once the initial move is made, lays the main emphasis at the most crucial points. As he writes:

'It is this property of being a centre, in which the universal spirit applies itself to the concrete situation, which gives the spiritual individual just that note of independence which is claimed

[1] *Op. cit.*, p. 95.
[2] *Op. cit.*, p. 93.

for him'.[1] If we fully 'possessed our self we should be the absolute, for certainly we should then include or be blended with innumerable other selves'.[2] 'If the self is to be free and self-modelling, the ego must be a mere spirit of unity working in and throughout experiences. Otherwise, it must bring with it some character or nature which would be an antecedent condition biassing and restricting the development of the soul or self.'[3] So much is this the case that we even find Bosanquet himself insisting that it is 'a grave injustice that a man should be severely punished for an offence of very old date'.[4] For in the reshaping that has taken place over the years the self has become wellnigh another person. On Bosanquet's premises this seems a very natural view to hold.

For this reason also Bosanquet seems to score heavily, in point of rigidity and consistency of argument, over his immediate opponent in the symposium, namely Pringle-Pattison. Bosanquet himself contends that the difference between him and Pringle-Pattison is mainly a matter 'of proportion and degree'. They share the same initial assumptions and they should arrive at the same conclusions. But Pringle-Pattison echoes more the 'frankly pluralist' attitude of common sense, and he shows a considerable suspicion of any move towards the absorption of the finite individual in the absolute or the blending of persons. He is convinced that the main interests of morals and religion are seriously jeopardized by such a move. 'On Professor Bosanquet's theory, error and sin are totally inexplicable'.[5] So is worship. For how can we 'bow to a higher will' unless there is 'some otherness in the relation between us'?[6] And how can we regard evil, as Bosanquet must, 'as simply good in the wrong place?'[7]

Pringle-Pattison rings the changes on these and kindred themes at some length and with much vigour. He clearly feels that something of the utmost importance is altogether imperilled by Bosanquet's views, and he does not spare his opponent in making this plain. The accents of moral fervour are unmistakable in his paper. And in this, I think, he is justified. It is, in my opinion, a departure from the plain facts of experience, and a repudiation of all the main concerns of morals and religion, to speak of ourselves as merely modes of unification within the one ultimate reality in

[1,2] *Op. cit.*, p. 96.
[3] *Op. cit.*, p. 97.
[4] *Op. cit.*, p. 100.
[5,6] *Op. cit.*, p. 115.
[7] *Op. cit.*, p. 117.

which we have our true existence; and it seems peculiarly inconsistent with the Christian religion to identify ourselves in this fashion with the being of God rather than understand ourselves as separate created finite beings, distinct from God and from one another.

To that extent, and above all in respect to what our main concerns in morals and religion require, I thus find myself entirely on the side of Pringle-Pattison. And yet it seems to me that the interests which Pringle-Pattison is anxious to safeguard cannot be properly defended without acknowledgement of a feature of personal existence which is as little evident in Pringle-Pattison's contentions as in those of Bosanquet. On the assumptions which they both initially share, Bosanquet seems to have the best of the argument and he has less need of fervent protest, much though I also feel that there is something radically wrong with his position and that we must somehow be rescued from the shipwreck which seems inevitable on the course which he steers with firmness and resolve.

Admittedly, Pringle-Pattison does put his finger on some of the weaknesses in Bosanquet's position. He insists that we should not 'restrict our attention to knowledge content', for, if we do so, 'there is no ground discernible for the distinction and multiplication of personalities. These are at best only different points of view—peepholes so to speak—from which an identical content is contemplated.'[1] He also complains that 'in speaking of finite selves he (Bosanquet) seems never to look at them from the inside'.[2] 'The logical analysis of knowledge is substituted for an account of living experience.'[3] 'The idea of blending or absorption depends entirely on material analogies which can have no application in the case of selves.'[4] But what then are we to substitute for the abstract and rarefied view of the self which we find in Bosanquet's work? How shall we think of the living experience which is to take the place of a logical analysis of knowledge?

The main point which Pringle-Pattison himself makes, in supplementation of his general condemnation of the reduction of persons to 'peepholes from which an identical content is contemplated', is that we can not reduce reality at any point to mere

[1] *Op. cit.*, p. 116.
[2] *Op. cit.*, p. 113.
[3] *Op. cit.*, p. 115.
[4] *Op. cit.*, p. 121.

'connections of content' within the one Reality or 'connections of qualities'[1] of the one ultimate subject. That procedure 'ignores entirely the concrete texture of existence as distinguished from the abstractions of the intellect. For the existence of a world at all just means individuation. Every existent is a "this", a "one", a being in the strict sense unique'.[2] Every part of a whole 'exhibits the same characteristic of concrete thisness'.[3] But it is by no means clear what is at issue here that Bosanquet could not accept. For the 'reference to reality' comes very close to providing the element of thisness, itself very much stressed by Bradley in his *Logic*, which Pringle-Pattison requires. If Pringle-Pattison admits, as he does, 'that the bounds of what we treat as an individual depend largely on our immediate interest or practical purpose', have we reserved for finite existence any sort of thisness which guarantees the kind of distinctness we wish to ascribe to persons? It may be wrong to think too exclusively in terms of connections of content or qualities where concrete things are concerned. We must ascribe genuine reality to things, but in what does this consist beyond their having the qualities they do have in unique relation to others? Short of restoring the idea of a wholly unobservable substance, in what does the thinghood of material things consist that is not reasonably catered for by Bosanquet? And even if there is something essential which the latter overlooks, does this require us to bestow some kind of finality on the divisions we make among objects? Does not that remain largely a matter of our own interest or purpose, even if inadequately or misleadingly presented in the metaphysics of absolute idealism?

In that case we have not advanced very far towards that distinctness of persons which common sense and Pringle-Pattison's instinctive response assure us that we must somehow preserve. Pringle-Pattison himself senses this, and tacitly conceding the point of Bosanquet that the crux of the problem is found in other existence than the material one, he prepares to take a firmer stand in the case where 'living and sentient beings' are concerned. It is here, he admits, 'that we seem first to meet the real individual'.[4] And in this, although the matter need not be put in those terms, he seems to me certainly on the right tack, he has made the right move.

But having made it he seems to fall very far short of the true implications of it. For what he is also concerned to emphasize

[1], [2], [3] *Op. cit.*, p. 106.
[4] *Op. cit.*, p. 107.

most is 'the centrality or focalized unity' which he considers to be 'the essential characteristic of a self'.[1] Bosanquet is taken to task, both in respect to his theory of the absolute and in his account of finite beings, for not having proper regard to the sort of unity which selfhood involves. It is a unique 'focalization' of unity which is irreducible and has thus its indispensable place in the universe as a whole. It does not lose its significance from the point of view of the whole, it is in this sense distinct and ultimate, it is irreplaceable, but as a focus of unity. The demarcations remain, as it were, even when the whole picture is before us. On Bosanquet's view, it is at least alleged by his critic, they just disappear in the unity of the system as a whole. But what is preserved is still some unique centre of unification within the whole.

How far this is fair to Bosanquet may not be easy to determine, and it would certainly take us far afield to consider the question closely. Bosanquet certainly does not want to regard the finite self as 'a mere appearance'. The absolute would not be what it is without it. It is only partly unreal, and while this is indeed a difficult doctrine it does not involve the total repudiation of finite existence. The absolute is not the sort of whole in which all differences disappear, they are just transmuted. But in writing of all finite reality as merely 'adjectival' of the whole Bosanquet was probably underestimating or distorting the function which he himself wanted to reserve for finite existence as having, in its proper place, a contribution to the life of the whole. Pringle-Pattison is providing a corrective, but is it not the sort which justifies Bosanquet's own insistence that the difference between them is a matter of degree? It does not seem to be nearly as deep as Pringle-Pattison's fervour seems to imply. It is a disagreement within certain general assumptions which do not confer on the finite existent any reality other than as an element within the one whole of being.

It is because his concern is pre-eminently with unity or focalization that Pringle-Pattison considers the idea of individuality to be only properly exemplified when we pass to living or sentient beings. The uniqueness of the mere occupation of different parts of space is 'the lowest or most imperfect form in which individuation manifests itself'.[2] It is only in ' "living or sentient beings" that we seem first to meet the real individual, for in these the unity and

[1] p. 109 (the author is here quoting from his own *The Idea of God*)
[2] *Op. cit.*, p. 107.

centrality are in no wise imposed upon the facts by our way of regarding them. They are objective in the sense that they express the essential mode of the creature's existence.'[1] It is for this reason that 'the higher we go, the more clearly does individuation impress itself upon us'.[2]

This gives individuation, for Pringle-Pattison, an increasingly important place in the scheme of things. It is indeed 'the only conceivable goal of the divine endeavour'.[3] But it is so essentially because it is a distinctive focus of unity within the whole. Even in that respect it has no reality apart from the whole. Finite selves are still 'subordinate to the systematic whole in which they are included as parts'.[4] How far this does justice to the individuation of external things is a question which a critic might well want to raise in a general discussion. The point I want to stress is that the difference between Pringle-Pattison and Bosanquet, so far as the distinctness of sentient and conscious beings are concerned, is far less substantial than might be gathered from the role the former ascribes to himself as the champion of the distinctness of persons and of the place of this in moral and religious concerns, against a thinker who is taken to put the whole principle in complete jeopardy. Is there all that difference, so far as the present issue is concerned, between being, in Pringle-Pattison's terms, 'a unique focalization of the universe'[5] and being, as Bosanquet conceives it, 'a centre, in which the universal spirit applies itself to the concrete situation'? Have we advanced much, in Pringle-Pattison's view of the matter, from the 'spirit of unity' or 'the self which has existence as a function which is a system of functions'? Have we still not too rarefied a view of the individual person, and is the independence required in morality and religion, so keenly championed by Pringle-Pattison, guaranteed at all by 'a unique focalization of the universe'? The latter may not be quite consistent with the idea of the 'confluence of selves', but does it not come perilously near it in the respects that matter?

It is not, however, hard to understand how this situation comes about. Pringle-Pattison and Bosanquet alike are acutely conscious of the danger of setting up the self as an entity with 'a prior content', in Bosanquet's phrase, or, in Pringle-Pattison's words, 'the old

[1, 2] *Op. cit.*, p. 107.
[3] *Op. cit.*, p. 108.
[4] *Op. cit.*, p. 104.
[5] *Op. cit.*, p. 109.

K

doctrine of the soul-substance as a kind of metaphysical atom'. The self, as has been stressed, has no characterizable nature as a thing apart or an entity which could subsist apart from experience. It is natural, in the light of this, to take it as the only alternative that the self is nothing but some kind of centre or focus for the unification of experience. Pringle-Pattison senses quite rightly that our autonomy and independence as finite persons is essential for our main concerns and firmly reflected in the way we normally think and talk. His philosophical good sense, if I may so put it, is sound, but he is hindered in his attempt to justify what this requires, not only by his general adherence to an absolutist metaphysics, but also by his understandable failure to confer on the self any reality as a being apart which would not at once set it up as a substance with a nature of its own. He is caught on the horns of a grave dilemma, to bestow on the self the sort of reality it plainly does not have or to reduce it to a centre or focus of unity for experience. It is this which makes him ineffective as the champion of a worthy cause.

This situation might have been avoided if Pringle-Pattison had followed out more effectively his own insistence that we should look at finite selves 'from the inside'. For it is then that we properly see how the self is not merely a focus to which our various experiences are referred, but a reality on its own account, however much also involved in having its experiences, a reality which is known to itself to be uniquely itself in a way which cannot be reduced at all to the specification of distinctive characteristics. This is what I have described as the peculiar elusiveness of the self, and it is in virtue of this elusiveness that we find Bosanquet and Pringle-Pattison engaged in a somewhat unreal battle, like two champions who never come quite to grips with one another, over a quarry which has escaped from the nets of both of them alike. In the moral life, as I hope to stress again in due course, the self which is more than its formed character has a function which does much more justice to the requirements of moral accountability than the self whose freedom can only consist in the sort of self-determination of which idealist philosophers speak. That it has importance for religion in further vital ways will also, I hope, be plain in due course.

The third contributor to the symposium is G. F. Stout. He also maintains that Bosanquet has failed to do justice to the distinctness of persons, and he takes up a general position not very different from that of Pringle-Pattison. There are, however, some additional features of their common line of criticism which call for comment, although briefly in view of what has already been said.

Stout directs attention very expressly to the more technical features of Bosanquet's arguments and in particular to the notion that finite things must be thought of as adjectival of the one Reality or the universe as a whole. Stout maintains that this idea is only plausible if we assume that the relation of whole and part is the same as the relation of adjectives to their subjects. If that assumption were sound 'the adjectival complex which is the whole contains the adjectival complex which is the part. The tail is then an adjective of the dog in essentially the same sense as sweetness is an adjective of sugar'.[1] But Stout maintains against this that 'where from the adjective of the part we pass to a corresponding adjective of the whole, this always presupposes the relation of whole and part as ultimately distinct from that of subject and adjective'.[2]

It is thus maintained that the part of a whole must always have some reality or nature of its own. 'The relatedness of a thing is "nothing" apart from its nature. Admitting, at least for the sake of argument, that the nature of a thing can be nothing apart from relatedness, I deny the totally different proposition that the nature of a thing is *nothing but* its relatedness. If this were so there would be nothing to be related.'[3] It appears, therefore, that finite things, although for Stout as for Pringle-Pattison they are parts of one whole of being, have a genuine reality on their own account and can themselves be quite properly distinct subjects or predicates.

This leads Stout to reject the idea of a 'communal will' as a 'single thing' or a 'single mind' with 'its members as partial phases or modes of it'.[4] He admits that 'the life of a community is a single thing with a unity and identity of its own'. Yet, he insists, 'this unity and identity is essentially distinct from that of a single mind'.[5] 'There is nothing in the social system which thinks, feels, or wills, except its individual members taken severally.'[6] The 'higher' system does not diminish the 'distinct individuality' of its members.

[1] *Op. cit.*, p. 129.
[2] *Op. cit.*, p. 131.
[3] *Op. cit.*, p. 133.
[4] *Op. cit.*, p. 139.
[5], [6] *Op. cit.*, p. 140.

'The whole being of a member of society cannot consist in the knowledge which others have of him and the interest which others take in him.'[1]

All the same this does not prevent Stout from entertaining the possibility of 'a confluence' of minds. 'It would be rash to take for granted that the self-development of the individual excludes confluence with other individuals.'[2] This may even involve 'a transitory' loss of identity although normally 'the "I" before coalescence may be recognizable as the same with the "I" after coalescence'.[3] It is thus not surprising that, in his subsequent work, *God and Nature*, Stout defends the idea of a 'Universal Mind' by which 'the temporal order, being real, is known and willed as what it really is'.[4] This does indeed confer some distinctness on the temporal order. 'Eternal being,' we are told, is 'not the absolute whole of being.'[5] But what sort of distinctness do we have as finite minds if 'the time-order as a whole' is 'willed by the Universal Mind',[6] or if, in apprehending the part as essentially incomplete, we have to apprehend it 'as continued beyond itself within a more comprehensive being'?[7]

It is, however, to this idea of the essential incompleteness of finite things that Stout attaches most weight. It plays an indispensable part in the arguments by which it is sought to establish the existence of a Universal Mind; and although we are not ourselves part of the Universal Mind, the fundamental thing about us is that we find the completion of our own being in 'the unity of the whole', 'the unity of the universe'. 'Just as the primary demand for causal connection is founded on the essential incompleteness of temporal occurrences, which require to be supplemented by their causal conditions and consequences, so there is a primary demand for psychical existence beyond the self, founded on the essential incompleteness of the finite individual.'[8]

These arguments turn much on the unity involved in our knowledge of the world, but they also fail to take particular heed of the special nature and unity of the self as it is inwardly known to itself. Impressive efforts are made to stretch the idea of unity, as it is

[1] *Op. cit.*, p. 141.
[2, 3] *Op. cit.*, p. 148.
[4] *God and Nature*, p. 228.
[5, 6] *Op. cit.*, p. 228.
[7] *Op. cit.*, p. 288.
[8] *Op. cit.*, p. 248.

found in the world in general, to allow for all that has to be preserved in the way of the distinctness and worth of persons, but
there is no serious reckoning with the way a person finds himself
to be peculiar and irreducible as a distinct being in his own experience of himself. Short of this, it becomes very hard for us to deny
some continuity of our being with that of the world around us
which is not consistent with what we find to be true about ourselves and, in particular, about the requirements of morals and
religion. Variations within the general themes of idealist philosophy, or refinements on the sort of arguments I have outlined,
will not, therefore, suffice. It is not some specific point here and
there that needs to be corrected, we need to change altogether the
conspectus within which the problem is viewed by idealists. We
need to look beyond the sort of unity we find in experience and the
world around us to peculiarities of sentient and personal existence
which they exhibit in what everyone in his own case finds them
to be.

For this reason, my excursus into the the debates of traditional
metaphysics, in the form they took at the start of this century, has
not taken the form of a general survey. That would, indeed, require
considerable space. My concern has been solely to give some indication of the way the vital considerations were overlooked by
failure to grasp the true import of Pringle-Pattison's own insistence that we should look at experience and personal existence as
they appear to us 'from the inside'. In the failure to do this adequately idealists have much in common with the philosophers who
are more in the fashion today, in English-speaking countries; and
it is not surprising that, in the arguments of many of our contemporaries and those of idealists of an age that seems philosophically very remote, there should be so many meetings of extremes.
I should like to note one peculiarly significant example of this
before I close my discussion of the present topic.

It is that the way is eased for Stout, in maintaining that our
finite existence is continued beyond itself in a more comprehensive
being, by his disinclination to allow that we have distinct cognitive
processes. Stout does not deny that there is mental activity, but he
conceives it in a way that makes much easier the transition from
the experience of one person to that of another, and an eventual
coalescence. For the essential inwardness of the distinct cognitive
process is obscured by thinking of it mainly in conative terms. As
he puts it himself, 'it includes all questioning, inquiry, seeking,

searching, watching, waiting, taking notice, *being on the alert*,[1] grappling with a problem, following the thread of an argument, concentration on a topic, etc'.[2] This does not go quite as far as Ryle, although Stout does firmly deny that there is anything 'which can be strictly and properly called an act of knowing'.[3] In the case of Stout, and other idealists, the immediate consciousness of ourselves and our mental processes tends to be overlooked in favour of other processes and concomitants of our experiences in a way that has much in common with the more expressly behaviourist views of our day. The latter are sometimes directly anticipated in some features of idealist thought, as may well be seen in the passage I have just quoted.

---

[1] Italics mine.
[2] *God and Nature*, p. 274.
[3] *Op. cit.*, p. 274.

CHAPTER XV

MYSTICISM AND MONISM

There are many uses of the word 'monism'. We have met one of these earlier, in discussing the problem of mind and body. In that context it stood for the view that no sharp distinction may be drawn between mind and body. A man is not a composite being but one entity which is both mental and physical. Opposed to this is the dualist view of mind and body which I have been seeking to defend. But these terms may also be used of general views that may be held about the nature of the universe as a whole and of our place in it. On a monist view, in this metaphysical context, there is only one ultimate being, the universe as a whole, and everything which can be thought to exist must be somehow included within it. By contrast we have various forms of pluralism, according to which there are many beings in the universe, the word 'dualism' being used most commonly here when contrasting our own distinct existence with that of some supreme or eternal Reality on which we take ourselves to be dependent.

There are many forms of monism. Note has already been taken of one of them, namely idealism. According to idealism, even in its more extreme and rigorous forms, an important place is retained for finite things. They have an indispensable part to play in the system of reality as a whole. They are not quite unreal or illusory, it is simply that their nature and status is not what it seems to be, the extent of the transformation involved, by their having their proper place in the system, varying a great deal from one type of idealism to another. There is no question of annulling or completely denying the reality of finite things.

There are, however, more extreme forms of monism. These tend to question or repudiate the world of change and multiplicity altogether. There is only the One, an undifferentiated whole in which there are no distinguishable parts. All else is illusion and unreality, a kind of dream world perhaps from which we may escape by a happy identification of ourselves with the one whole of being, an immersion of ourselves and our private identity in the one Reality. This escape may be achieved in various ways, among them high and selfless moral attitudes and certain forms of meditation, including in some cases physical disciplines and postures.

These sorts of monism are found, in their neatest and most uncompromising forms, in oriental literatures and religions, notably Hinduism and Buddhism. They are not easy to describe, the language being often symbolic and obscure and the senses in which the present world is abjured or thought to be illusory being by no means as precise or explicit in all cases as one would like. Some of those who have professed a monistic attitude and firmly denied the reality of our present existence have also been apt to display a marked concern about their own lot in the world and their standing with men. But no movement, in philosophy or religion, should be judged by its least consistent adherents. The notion that the world is a place of total illusion has been seriously maintained over a long period and endorsed by men who have undoubtedly proved themselves in other ways to be persons of great probity and wisdom. Their view is not one we can just thrust aside as of no consequence or interest. They must have had some reason for holding it.

It must not be supposed, however, that extreme monism is the only form of Hinduism or Buddhism. That is far from being the case. Nor are all the utterances which appear at first to be rigorously monistic always to be taken at their face value. They are qualified or corrected by what is said in other contexts. There are, it should also be noted, instances of extreme monism in Western thought and religion, although the West, in conformity with the teaching of its main religions, is normally dualist in its view of man and God and little inclined to monism. Our concern at the moment is with the forms of monism, widespread and sustained as they seem to have been, in which individual existence and multiplicity are firmly and seriously questioned.

Such opinions appear to be wholly at odds with the obvious facts of our own experience. Nothing seems plainer than that there are a multiplicity of things in the world around us and that these, and our experience of them, are constantly changing. To deny the reality of change, variety and multiplicity seems to be the most bizarre of all religious or metaphysical procedures, and it is understandable that it should try the patience of tough empirically minded philosophers and earn their contempt. Here it would seem, more than anywhere, is the proliferation of nonsense which one would expect the clear-headed down-to-earth philosophy of our day to expose and arrest for good. It is from this source that the most gloomy examples of allegedly metaphysical nonsense are often culled. There are in addition, it is urged, the gravest consequences of holding the 'illusionist' view, as it is sometimes called, of our present existence. For, if we take it that our existence in this world is entirely illusory, it is not likely that we shall mind much what our lives in the world are like. Perhaps few have the logical ruthlessness to match their acceptance of an extreme form of monism with total indifference to their own lot or that of others, and it is often a feature of monistic religions to require selflessness and compassion as part of the discipline by which escape from the present world of unreality is made possible. But it can hardly be doubted that the more extreme forms of monistic religions and cultures have been apt to induce or encourage attitudes of in-difference or apathy in moral and social matters.

This is why some prominent Hindu thinkers, in recent times especially, have been very sharp in their own denunciation of the excessively other-worldly elements in their own religion. An excellent example is that of Sri Aurobindo. He does not doubt that progress, in ethical and social matters, has been much re-tarded in India by an attitude of resignation and apathy induced in large measure by religion, most of all as involving the view that our present existence is an unreal or illusory one—a dream-world of some kind. There is little incentive to cope with poverty and ignorance and the general wretchedness of an improvident mode of existence, to say nothing of ills that lie deep in a stagnant social system and sharp caste distinctions, if thought is centred entirely on the hope of the total dissolution of our individual temporal existence or the exhibition of the unreality of our present life as it is made evident to us that there is only one undifferentiated being in which all multiplicity and particularity is lost. It is not surprising, therefore, that Aurobindo, like other Indian thinkers of late, makes the most dramatic and eloquent pleas[1] for the abandon-ment of the forms of Hinduism or Buddhism which involve what he himself calls the 'theory of universal illusionism'. This does not mean the total surrender of monism, but it does require the surrender of the view that has no room at all for change and multiplicity within the one whole of being.

It seems, therefore, that it is not just common sense that is

[1] See the quotations from Aurobindo's writings on pages 180–182 of *World Religions* by R. L. Slater and H. D. Lewis.

outraged by the form of monism which denies all differentiation. Questions of social justice and moral accountability are also much involved. A world-denying monism seems to be on all counts a serious offender. It has nonetheless been upheld and defended by thinkers of undoubted intellectual power and insight, including some outstanding writers of the present day. How does this come about? What can lend support to a view that seems so patently at odds with the facts? Idealism did not question outright the reality of all the varied facts of our experience. It denied that they were self-subsistent or independent, it refused, in some forms at least, to accord them a substantival existence of their own, it claimed that their nature and status could not be rightly understood apart from the whole to which they belong. But this is one thing. It is quite another to deny any place at all to plurality and change. We must surely take some account of the course of events in the world and in our own lives as we find them. Even as dreams or illusions these events must have a place of some kind in whatever we finally deem to be real. To deny any place to change and multiplicity, including the course of one's own life, seems absurd. It is belied by the most obvious facts of which a philosopher must take account. We could not be at all without some multiplicity. There would be just a void.

How then does it happen that such a position is held and seriously defended? Among the main arguments used in support of the view that the universe is one of undifferentiated unity are those that have come down to us from Parmenides. These have rarely been absent from any serious discussion of the subject in the Western World, and they have their close analogues in Eastern philosophy. They can be stated very simply. Parmenides began with an analysis of what thought or predication involves. Whenever we think, we are maintaining that something is the case. Even to doubt or question, we must sort things out in a preliminary way to start, and this means that some things are taken, at least provisionally, to be of a certain sort. But to affirm anything in this way is also to deny, to deny all that is not consistent with what we affirm. Thus if I say that this book is blue I *ipso facto* imply that it cannot be black or white—in the same respect. It may be blue in front and back behind, but it cannot be both in respect of the same part of the same surface. Likewise, if I affirm that the book is on the table, I imply that it is not on the shelves, on the floor, in some other room and so forth. There is an endless variety of things that I deny in making any affirmation. But to deny, as Parmenides understood it, is to say that something 'is not', it involves the idea of 'non-being'; and non-being was taken by Parmenides in this context to mean something which altogether is not the case, the wholly unreal. But no one can entertain the thought of something which has no reality of any kind. We cannot even deny where absolute non-being is concerned. But if negation is not possible, neither is affirmation. For these seem to involve one another. There appears thus to be something radically wrong with thought as such, and with its presuppositions. The presuppositions are that we must operate within some system in which entities are distinguished from one another and also found to stand in certain relations. There is a plurality. By contrast we must now conclude that the sort of requirements which thought sets out before us, the principles of rational necessity as they may be put, give us an impossible impression of the world, they seem to defy their own purpose and thus themselves to lead us to the idea that the universe has a different and more ultimate sort of unity, that it is One, not in the sense of a number of terms related to one another, but in the sense of a unity in which none of the diversifications required by thought have a place. Thought is transcended in the true reality and unity of the universe, and it is to this conclusion that thought itself propels us when its presuppositions are properly investigated.

The picturesque way in which Parmenides is led by these ideas (and by the streak of materialism in his thought) to conceive of being, namely like the mass of a rounded sphere equally real in every direction, does not much concern us. But the arguments do; and it is plain that there is something radically wrong with them. Plato was not slow to point this out. He observed that the idea of non-being, as involved in our thought about negation and error, is not the idea of something which is wholly unreal but of something which is just other than something else; and so we come back again to the notion of the unity of terms within a system. That is what thought itself requires of reality. Plato, in consequence of what he took over and developed from the thought of Heraclitus and Protagoras, did not think the conditions of systematic unity, as involving the complete interdependence of whole and part required by intelligibility, could ever be properly found in the external world or the events of our lives. These had, therefore, an uncertain place in the world of becoming. True reality is of the

forms and it is of these, in the unity inherent in each of them and
more completely in their interdependence, that genuine knowledge
is possible. Even here, however, there is imperfection, the system
does not wholly explain itself, and we are thus led to the idea of the
Form of the Good as the ultimate condition of all being and
intelligibility. It is itself beyond being and knowledge. We thus
arrive again at the idea of some ultimate unity, itself required by
the modes of unification we ourselves grasp in our understanding
of reality, which is beyond the multiplicity even of the forms,
much more the flow of events in the world of becoming. Ultimate
reality is thus again a unity that goes beyond all diversification and
understanding, although some persons may have a glimpse or
noesis of it after suitable training. This takes us part of the way
back to Parmenides. But not the whole way. There is a radical
difference.

The One, or as Plato named it the Good, is no longer the whole
of being. It is the source of all being and of intelligibility, but it is
not exhaustive. There is in addition the world of forms, and Plato
himself at times protests against the lifelessness of this world of
formal systems, as if he felt that something of the doubtful world
of becoming had to have its place there as well. This provided the
model for one way of thinking of the reality which is supreme and
ultimate in the universe, namely as one which is complete and
perfect in a way that is beyond our understanding—indeed beyond
all understanding—but which is properly *beyond*. The rest of the
universe is conditioned by it, and what this involves is itself
beyond our proper understanding. Everything exhibits the dependence in question, but nothing affords a proper clue to its nature.
The One which is supreme or infinite is involved in all things,
but it is itself, in itself and in its relation to the world, essentially
mysterious. It is, in more recent language, transcendent, but in a
way which itself requires that all other reality be distinct from it,
however dependent. There are many ways in which the significance
of the transcendent source of our being for us is understood, and
we come here to various problems of divine disclosure and
revelation. They do not concern us at the moment. The point is
that the arguments which start with Parmenides and proceed via
Plato and others as a demand for some ultimate and perfect unity,
beyond the incompleteness of unity in multiplicity as we find it in
our normal understanding of the world and ourselves, can be taken
to require a truly supreme and transcendent reality without the

implication that all other reality is absorbed into it, and thus without the repudiation of the obvious multiplicity and change of our finite existence.

Further philosophical thought, together with various cultures and religions, have sometimes followed this model of the ultimate and transcendent unity of the universe; others revert to the position initially typified by Parmenides, the universe, as our thought of the present world of our own experience requires, being all-inclusive and complete in a way which precludes all diversification and particular existence, the latter being some kind of colossal illusion which we must dispel as soon as we can.

In Western thought, when there is recognition, in religion or in philosophical and kindred thought, of a transcendent reality, this usually follows the model set out by Plato, although without being always consciously indebted to Plato. This is in close accordance with the teaching of the main Western religions, Judaism, Christianity and Islam. In these religions the idea of creation is basic. The world is not a part of God, or an emanation of His being, it is a created world brought into being by the fiat of God. The insights which the Hebrews showed into the implications of this idea, and their grasp of its importance, despite the unavoidable crudity of their cosmology, is remarkable and it has remained a formative and indispensable feature of the main forms of religion in the West to the present day. No sound understanding of Christian doctrine is possible without it. On the other hand there have been, in the West as well as in the East, instances of the form of monism typified by Parmenides and often following closely his way of thinking.

This has been mainly due to the influence of mystical experience and of philosophical thought about it. The distinctive feature of mysticism is the claim to have union with God. But this is a claim, in essentials, which most religions make. What is truly distinctive of mysticism is the further claim that the union with God is direct or immediate. This may, however, be understood in various ways. It could be thought to refer merely to the insight or intuition we have into there having to be a transcendent ground of all finite existence. Rightly understood this is at the opposite extreme to the claim to be strictly at one with God, for it sets the creature in a position where that is not possible. The claim of the mystic could also be understood in the sense of some further unmediated knowledge of God. This is also, in my view, not possible. But it is a very different claim to make from the claim that one is strictly identified with God. To know God is one thing, to become part of Him another. This is also true if the relation to God is thought of, as in the case of Martin Buber, in some other form than that of knowing Him. Buber himself is much averse to thinking of the *I–Thou* relation as any kind of identification, it is encounter with the strictly other. The immediacy in question may again be thought of symbolically. Familiar hindrances are removed, there is an exceptionally intimate relationship, but without any question of literal identification or of knowing the other strictly as he is for himself. The claim may, however, be made that, in mystical experience, we are literally at one with God; and this is how many mystics have understood the matter themselves.

There is more than one way in which this may come about. Professor W. T. Stace, in his important work *Mysticism and Philosopy*, draws attention to two sorts of mysticism, the extrovert and the introvert. The former takes its start from the facts of the world around us, and from oneself mainly as a fact on the same level with others. It finds that all things run into one another in a unity in which all separate existence and variety is lost. There is nothing but the One, but the One is seen 'in or through the multiplicity of objects'.[1] This is a curiously paradoxical position, and I shall note in a moment more closely how Stace himself understands that. For the present it is enough to note that, although the unity is itself unqualified, that in a sense there is nothing but the One, we nonetheless come to it or it is 'seen through a multiplicity',[2] our physical senses are at work and material things, although each is the other and the all, are perceived as such.

There is no doubt that some mystics do think of their experience in this way, and Stace is convinced that they are fully entitled to do so. It seems to me, however, that what, in fact, occurs, in the sort of mystical experience to which Stace is alluding here, and of which he provides full and interesting examples, may not be what Stace himself (and many of the mystics he quotes) takes it to be. We have to recall the way the transcendent was found to be peculiarly involved in the facts of our present existence. It is, in a sense, known in and through them, they 'thinly veil' it, as Mascall puts it. In addition there are ways in which some configurations of

---

[1] *Mysticism and Philosophy*, p. 79.
[2] *Op. cit.*, p. 62.

finite things may become distinctively revelatory of the transcendent which cannot be known in itself, the divine becomes articulate in them. It is not surprising then that persons who acquire a profound and disturbing sense of the transcendent, displacing many of their normal concerns and valuations and investing the world around them with something of its own elusive and incomprehensible nature, should come to describe their experience as if nothing remained of it besides the transcendent taking it over. The Beyond would be all in all in the present.

It does not follow that the mystic himself is always misled in such cases. He may be under no misapprehension himself, although his language would suggest that to others. After all, this is a context where suitable terms are not readily available and where hyperbole, symbolism, and paradox are not easily avoided. Things must be put 'slantwise', as the famous term has it. Others, and they could well be the majority, may be meaning just what they say, as Stace maintains that they do. In that case their position is very odd indeed. For they also make explicit reference to particular items of experience, the 'blades of grass, wood, and stone', in the famous instance from Eckhart quoted by Stace. This indeed is what is distinctive of the extrovert type of mysticism. It is set going by facts of experience, and these seem required also to sustain it. One might account for this in a boldly paradoxical way, as is done by Stace, by asserting that the mystic wishes to deny the plurality outright at the same time as he is forced to acknowledge it, and one might seek to justify this attitude. I do not think, however, that we ought to be driven to so desperate a course when there is available an explanation more consistent with the way we otherwise think of the transcendent and with the evidence available, as adduced by Stace himself, about the extrovert type of mysticism.

We are, moreover, told of 'borderline cases' of extrovert mysticism. What characterizes these is the firmness with which it is maintained that items of present experience continue to be recognized as such. They may be 'in the margin of attention', as in the description given of Arthur Koestler's experience,[1] or they may be very firmly noted, it being simply a case of 'all the usual things' being seen 'in a miraculous new light',[2] as in the case of Margaret Montague. Indeed, Stace himself tells us how 'the

[1] *Op. cit.*, p. 122.
[2] *Op. cit.*, p. 83.

extrovert mystic, using his physical senses, perceives the multiplicity of external material objects—the sea, the sky, the houses, the trees—mystically transfigured so that the One, or the Unity, *shines through them*'.[1]

Being 'mystically transfigured' is one thing, it falls very far short of a denial of any distinct reality; the trees, the houses and so forth are known for what they are in themselves. 'Shining through' is a peculiarly significant phrase in this context, bringing us close to Mascall's account of objects 'thinly veiling' the Reality beyond them. In allusions of this kind we seem to be much more in the world of a transcendent reality which is closely involved in particular things, and in some fashion investing or permeating them with its own reality, than in the world of a total repudiation of all particularity. The particular seems, in fact, to have an indispensable role to play.

There may be other regards in which the experiences in question now may be thought to be borderline or incomplete cases of mysticism. But might they not, at the same time, be taken to indicate the questionable character of the account eventually given of the full or properly typical sort of mysticism when this takes the form of denying that the plurality has a place as such in the experience at all?

It is quite the opposite course, however, that is taken by Stace himself. The examples in question are 'borderline' just because the particular items of present experience are not thrust aside or doubted; and, in complete consistency with this procedure, Stace goes on further to qualify all forms of merely extrovert mysticism as incomplete approximations to mysticism in its proper form. It is 'a distinct type' but 'on a lower level', and this is precisely because the multiplicity has not been 'wholly obliterated', it has been 'only half absorbed in the unity'.[2] 'The multiple items are still there' and 'so also must be at least the spatial relations between the items and possibly in some cases the time relations too'.[3] They are 'all one' but they are stubbornly 'there', and the boldest of paradoxes must be invoked on their account.

We have paradox too, and in its way yet more outrageous, in the full and ultimate form of mysticism, namely the introvert type. For here a much bolder line is taken about the multiplicity. Before we note that, let it be observed, in recapitulation of what I have

---

[1] *Op. cit.*, p. 61, italics mine.
[2], [3] *Op. cit.*, p. 132.

maintained about the inferior type of mysticism noted by Stace, namely the extrovert type, that there is nothing in the account which is given of it which could not be properly accommodated within an explanation of the experience in terms of an apprehension of a transcendent which is other than ourselves and our environment, although involved in them in a peculiarly intimate way and disclosed in them. Indeed there is much in what is said about extrovert mysticism to reinforce and illumine that account of the transcendent and the mode of its apprehension.

It is thus only when seen in the light of the second type of mysticism, and as having its character finally settled through what is alleged in that way to be generally true of all mysticism, that the lower type of mysticism can be seriously considered to involve the repudiation of all plurality. The issue, therefore, turns on what can be said about the second and more ultimate type of mysticism in which the inferior extrovert type finds its completion. This is introvert mysticism.

It is this kind of mysticism, in the account which Stace gives of it, that is of special interest to us in this book. We take our start here from within, with the self. But the self concerned here is not the empirical self, it is the pure self; and what is distinctive of the pure self, as Stace understands it, is that it has no empirical content, indeed it has no proper characteristics or content at all. As such there appears to be nothing about it to set it in opposition to the equally undifferentiated unity of the whole. Our experience points to a reality beyond the incomplete and fragmented items of the normal content of experience, and this cannot itself have the limits and determinations of ordinary objects. It is also without characterization, and, therefore, as we centre attention on the pure self or withdraw from the world of the multiple content of experience, the blending of the self with the equally undefined reality of the ultimate principle of being becomes easier and indeed unavoidable. There seems to be nothing to distinguish the one from the other.

This is a curious argument, and it still leaves us with the thought that the 'multiple content' must have a place somewhere, however we avert our attention from it. Stace has his own strange way of coping with this. But in the meantime we must note first how insistent he is, for the purpose of his main thesis, on the empty, characterless nature of the self as it is primarily involved in mystical experience. The introvertive mystic excludes from his consciousness all 'particular mental contents' and so attains a state of 'pure consciousness' which 'has no content except itself'.[1] This is a 'complete vacuum', a 'void' or 'nothingness'. But for that reason it must be also 'the One' and 'the Infinite'.[2] 'That there are in it no particular existences is the same as saying that there are no distinctions in it, or that it is an undifferentiated unity. Since there is no multiplicity in it, it is the One. And that there are no distinctions in it or outside it means that there are no boundary lines in it between anything and anything. It is, therefore, the boundless or the infinite'.[3]

Many examples of mysticism seeming to take this form are given. We are told of a passage in *The Upanishads* which speaks of 'a unitary consciousness' in which 'multiplicity is completely obliterated'. 'It is One without a second. It is the Self.'[4] This gives us, it is said, an 'identity of my pure ego with the pure ego of the Universe'.[5] In a quotation from Ruysbroeck we read how 'the God-seeing man' can enter 'into the inmost part of his spirit'. 'It (his spirit) is undifferentiated and without distinction, and, therefore, it feels nothing but the unity.'[6] It is in the same sense, we are told, that other mystics speak of ' "darkness", "emptiness", "nothingness", "silence", "nakedness", "nudity" etc'.[7] It is all a case of 'emptying the mind of all empirical content' to find oneself at one with 'the barren Godhead'. God, as Eckhart says, 'leads the human spirit into the desert, into his own unity, which is pure One'.[8] In St John of the Cross the soul learns to bring to a 'halt the operation of the faculties in particular acts' and 'becomes more and more collected in one undivided and pure act'.[9] A Mahayana Sutra tells us that 'Mind-Essence' 'does not belong to any kind of describable nature' and for this reason is 'free from all manner of individuation'.[10] In these and kindred examples we are shown how 'The boundaries of the "I", the walls which separate it from the infinite, are broken through and disappear'.[11]

In his own account of these passages, Stace takes it for granted

[1, 2, 3] *Op. cit.*, p. 86.
[4] *Op. cit.*, p. 88.
[5] *Op. cit.*, p. 90.
[6] *Op. cit.*, p. 94.
[7] *Op. cit.*, p. 100.
[8] *Op. cit.*, p. 99.
[9] *Op. cit.*, p. 103.
[10] *Op. cit.*, p. 108.
[11] *Op. cit.*, p. 119.

that the unitary consciousness must be understood in each case along the lines of a Kantian 'unity of apperception'. This is, in his view,[1] the proper reply to make to Hume, when he complained that he could not catch himself without a perception and so forth. But, even on this basis, it would seem that some account has to be given of distinct centres of unification, as even idealist philosophers, to whom Stace is approximating here more closely than elsewhere, were anxious to admit. This makes it hard for the walls to disappear entirely. On the other hand, Stace does seem properly justified in his insistence that the self is not some entity like others with an ascertainable nature. It is not, as he puts the point, 'another thing or substance, distinct from its contents'. This must, however, be understood cautiously. The self is not an entity with specifiable characteristics. But it is not, as I have stressed, a mere principle of unification. There could be no such unity without a subject properly distinct from the world it apprehends; and I have also urged that the self is known as a being in its own right by each individual in his own case. It is known to be what it is in just that way, not by further description. But it was also urged that the self, so understood, could not be thought to subsist independently of some experience and is to that extent involved in having its experience. This makes it impossible for us to neglect the content of experience or induce it to disappear from the picture; and even on Stace's view, indeed one might almost say more obviously so, the contents have to be reckoned with, the self being nothing without the contents of its experience. The multiplicity seems stubbornly present in this way again and it is hard to see how it could be conjured away.

It is odd, therefore, that Stace should suggest, on occasion at least, that the true nature of the self would be best disclosed to us in some state, like that of dreamless sleep, when there appears to be no content of consciousness at all. It is very hard to see what such a self could be when it is also insisted, quite rightly, that it has no distinct nature or character of its own. When the self withdraws into this inner state of itself, divorced from all involvement with an apprehended content, just what is there for it to recognize or know of itself at all? In particular, if the self is understood as a principle of unification, just how can it be accorded any status when there is nothing to unify? Would it not just cease to be with the disappearance of all unified content?

[1] *Op. cit.*, p. 87.

This is not, however, the point I most wish to stress. My special concern at this point is with the way the self is affirmed not to have a describable nature. For while this might appear, in one sense, to facilitate the view that, so far as the nature of the self as such is concerned, the 'walls' or boundaries between selves, and thus between finite selves and the Infinite, can be made to dissolve away fairly easily, there being nothing distinctive, no precise characteristic, to resist such dissolution, yet, in fact, the opposite is the case when it is rightly understood why the self must be thought of as an entity which can not be properly characterized. For we have seen that the reason for this is, not that the self is some mere principle of unification, but rather that it is peculiarly known to be what it is, and very distinctively a being in its own right, by each individual in his own case. There is a finality and ultimacy about this sort of distinctness which is not present in the same way when entities are distinguished from each other solely through some characterization. We can more readily see how the boundaries could become fluid in the latter case than when the distinctiveness and particularity is of the very essence of what we purport to discriminate. It is in knowing oneself to be oneself that one really knows that one exists. This is a very ultimate sort of particularity and it is, accordingly, peculiarly irreducible.

The point to which Stace himself attaches most importance, in his account of the elimination of the individual in mystical experience, seems, therefore, to cut in precisely the opposite direction to the one he intends. On the other hand it does also help us to understand how the mystics themselves should, in so many cases, suppose that all distinction between themselves and the infinite has been eliminated, that they are strictly at one, or identified with, God or some supreme and limitless reality. For the more their eyes are averted from the flow of events around them, as they withdraw into inner citadels of experience, the less is there in the way of content to bar the way to such union, particularly where the self in its true distinctiveness, as it is for itself, is concerned. At the same time, the Infinite itself, in its properly transcendent character, is without determination, not because it is nothing or just a void, but because it is transcendent in its richness or completeness and so beyond the sort of determination which we find at finite levels of noting things and relating them to one another as terms in a system. How such a transcendent is possible eludes our understanding, though what we manage to understand points to it or to its inevitability. But if the transcendent is also elusive and without characteristics in any way we can grasp, albeit this is altogether different from the elusiveness of the finite self which we do properly know, even though only in recognizing it to be what it is, we can understand how the mystics, withdrawn into themselves in some of their profounder experiences, and at the same time acutely conscious of a supreme transcendent Reality encompassing all there is but elusive and not identifiable in any normal way, should come to suppose that the partition between themselves and the Infinite had been rent and that they were literally one with God. In the way partitions normally present themselves, there might not seem to be any left, and in the rapture and intensity of his consciousness of God, caught up in this to the exclusion of all other thought, the mystic, in these conditions, could genuinely feel, as no doubt many of them did, that their own being, at the very core of it, had been wholly taken up into the being of God.

In this they would be quite mistaken, there could hardly be a greater mistake. But it is a mistake which we can easily understand; and we can also see how the very features of personal existence to which Stace draws attention, in his own account of the dissolution of individual existence in mystical experience, could, on the one hand, be understood in a way which strongly favoured his conclusion although, on the other hand, when their true purport is properly understood, they support exactly the opposite view.

There are further reasons, more familiar ones in the normal conduct of this controversy, why the mystics should, on occasion at least, give an account of their experience which appears sharply at odds with what, if my main submissions earlier are right, must, in fact, be the case. Stace himself is fully aware of these, and he is also fully conscious of the difficulty presented for his view by the fact that, even on his own showing, *some* account must be given of the varied contents of experience and the seemingly obvious multiplicity of the facts of the world around us. We are not all mystics, and even the greatest mystics do not stay permanently in the fulness of their mystical experience. Life must be lived in the world as we find it, and, whatever impression the mystics may have in moments of mystical illumination, the multiple facts of the world and our own varied experiences are bound to obtrude themselves at some stage. A truer sense of the distinctness of one's own individual existence may also assert itself, and although Stace

himself would not, in view of his own account of the self, be much
perturbed by this, it accentuates the problem of particularity for
others. No philosopher can, therefore, refuse to take account of it.
Nor is Stace unaware of this. How, then, does he deal with it and
with the explanation of mystical claims which are offered by those
who do not always take such claims at their face value?

He does so by retreating to a very curious position, and a seemingly desperate one. He holds, on the one hand that the mystic is
entitled to speak of the dissolution of the individual and of a
'distinctionless experience';[1] there is no place for 'the many', but
only 'the One'. On the other hand he does not subscribe to a
position of unqualified monism, there must after all be some room
for 'the many', there is no case for a 'simple assertion of identity
between God and the world'.[2] To take up the latter position is
'silly', and Stuart Hampshire is taken to task for ascribing it
to Spinoza.[3] On the view that 'God alone is real, and God is an
undifferentiated unity wherein there is no multiplicity of finite
objects', Stace comments, 'Has anybody ever seriously maintained
such a view?'. It is hard to avoid the impression in many places
that Professor Stace does so, and that he ascribes it to those he
much admires. But if this is not after all his position, but one which
earns his contempt, what does he hold? What he holds apparently
is that we must affirm the reality of 'the many' and at the same
time deny it, and do both things in a quite unambiguous, unqualified way. We must not be afraid of contradiction. We must
rather say boldly:

'1. The world is identical with God.

'2. The world is distinct from, that is to say, not identical with,
God.'[4]

It is this basic, and most extraordinary paradox that Stace wishes
to sustain in its most unqualified form.

In this vein he praises Hegel for his recognition of the principle
of 'the identity of opposites'. But Hegel is also taken severely to
task for trying to modify the outright character of it and continue
to rationalize it as a logical principle on the basis of 'a new super-
logic'. He thus makes 'a terrible mess of it'. For it is 'a definitely
antilogical idea. It is the expression of a nonrational element in the

[1] *Op. cit.*, p. 107.
[2] *Op. cit.*, p. 211.
[3] *Op. cit.*, p. 237.
[4] *Op. cit.*, p. 212.

human mind'.[1] By failing to recognize this Hegel lapsed into 'a
species of chicanery', 'palpable fallacies' and 'simply punning on
words' which brought his cause into very ill repute.

The Vedanta, we are told, have much the advantage over Hegel
here, for they are much bolder and more uncompromising in
asserting 'both the identity of Brahman and the World, and their
difference'.[2] Indian folklore is also alleged to take the same course.
'The secret of Maya', he quotes from Zimmer, 'is the identity of
opposites.'

It is admitted, however, that the position, on the face of it, is
different in the case of most Western mystics. For St John of the
Cross ('no first-class intellect' we are told) the union with God is
not thought of in the form of a literal identity, but only as a
conformity and resemblance of wills. According to Henry Suso,[3]
'the spirit . . . does not become God by nature. . . . It is still a
something which has been created out of nothing and continues
to be this everlastingly'. Meister Eckhart is more ambiguous.
He declares: 'God and I: We are one' and 'Between the Son and
the soul there is no distinction'; but in his defence against charges
of heresy he wavers and says that if his statements 'should be
taken to mean that I am God, this is false'. He is only 'a member'
of God, a position which Stace understandably finds difficult.[4]
The Sufi mystic Al Ghazzali speaks of identity only in the sense
of being 'engrossed in your beloved', separate existence being only
forgotten. Those who go beyond this are 'foolish babblers',[5]
indeed to speak of being amalgamated with God is sin.

It might be thought possible to cope with this, from Stace's
point of view, on the basis of a radical difference in types of
mystical experience. It would, indeed, have been odd if the differences coincided as sharply as the case requires with the difference
of East and West. But this is not in any case the course which
Stace is anxious to take. He maintains, on the whole it seems to me
with justice, that the differences could not be as radical as that
between dualism and monism when the 'inner nucleus' of the
experience seems to be described in such similar terms in all
cases. It is much more likely that substantially similar experiences
were subjected to different interpretations in various cases.

[1, 2] *Op. cit.*, p. 213.
[3] *Op. cit.*, p. 223.
[4] *Op. cit.*, p. 225.
[5] *Op. cit.*, p. 228.

This raises the general question of interpretation. I agree that interpretation is in order and that it may over-ride in some respects the express avowals of the subject of experience himself. This is parallel to other cases, for example perception. We do not take firm and sincere avowals to be decisive here. The issue may not be clearly seen by those with no flair for philosophy or acquaintance with it. A Berkeleyan view will often seem absurd to the layman because he does not really see what is involved. The evidence, perspectival distortions for example, must be sifted to see what is the most plausible account to give of it on careful reflection. We must not disregard the evidence, we must start with it, but bearing in mind that things may not be, in fact, what they firmly seem to be at first glance. They may wear a different look when proper analysis is made of them. This applies to religious experience as much as any.

It must be stressed also that the interpretation must take proper cognizance of what the facts are truly like, and these include insights of various sorts according as the evidence points to them. An experience, before it is interpreted, need not be a mere subjective state. But we have to consider what is probable and plausible in the evidence as adduced, whether it refers to insights or anything else. I am far, therefore, from thinking that the last word must lie with those who have claims to the most first-hand evidence in religious matters, and I believe that this is of first importance in the study of religions today; it should curb the excessive confidence and pretensions sometimes displayed by those most concerned in the first-hand investigation of relevant material, literary, sociological or whatever else it may be. To quote the sources is not always decisive.

In the sifting of evidence, and of claims based upon it, an important place must be accorded to what we generally consider to be likely or possible. If someone (or even a very large number of people) claimed to have seen a square circle, however sincere I took him to be, I should reject his claim outright. I would do so in a very different way from that in which I would reject the claim of someone who said he had seen a flying saucer. The evidence for flying saucers is thin and there is a great deal that tells against. But it is just conceivable that there should be such things, those who say they have seen them may be right or nearly right. There just could not, however, be objects which are round and square in exactly the same respect. If someone says that he has seen them,

I may admit that he has seen something odd, but not what he himself strictly says he saw.

It is here that I am at odds with Professor Stace. His view is that the explicit evidence of mystical experience, or of first-hand reports of it, points invariably towards the identity of opposites in the sense he has in mind in this context, namely as involving an identification of the many with the One, in the strictest sense, while at the same time repudiating it. Western mystics, he holds, gave a different account when it came to interpreting their experience, the interpretation in this case being closely interwoven with the first-hand report. But he cannot sustain this position solely by noting seemingly monistic elements in the utterances of such mystics, for the whole question is how such utterances are to be understood. There is no good reason for taking them literally if we find in the same context equally firm affirmations not consistent with that, unless, that is, we call the latter in question in some further way, either by showing it to be inherently unsound or in some way unreliable. In the first of these respects Stace attempts nothing, his case resting mainly on simply producing the first-hand utterances; and all that he adds to this is the insinuation that Western mystics were unduly subject to ecclesiastical influence and allowed this to colour their impression of an experience which was not in itself a dualistic one. Their statements show 'a strong tendency to drift towards the monistic position' and 'they are only prevented from adopting it by the menaces and pressure of the theologians and ecclesiastical authorities'.[1] Being 'pious men, obedient to the constituted authorities', they took 'a step backwards into dualism'.[2] Unfortunately, although this accusation is made in many places there is little documentation or other evidence adduced to support it.

It is true that what the Western mystics said, in respect of its dualism, was in accord with ecclesiastical teaching. But that should not in itself make it suspect. The teaching may be sound and the experience, in essentials and in direct impressions of it, may not owe much to the teaching except as a causal factor not relevant here. If it does, then this must be expressly shown. In any case, Western mystics, like others, could be mistaken in their own impression of what their experience involved, and ecclesiastical authorities could be justified, in aim if not in method, in seeking to correct it.

[1] *Op. cit.*, p. 232.
[2] *Op. cit.*, p. 234.

By contrast there seems to be a case for maintaining that Oriental mystics, to the extent that they follow the line ascribed to them by Stace, are misrepresenting the experience which, in fact, they have, whatever the reason may be for their doing so. For, on the one hand, there are the undoubted facts of the world around us (an obvious multiplicity in some sense), and, on the other, the necessity there seems to be upon us to think of all finite things as having some supreme transcendent source which cannot be known in the way finite things are known and must be thought to be radically other than them. A sound view of the transcendent as well as of finite beings (and the two things go largely together) seems to preclude from the start any possibility of our being strictly identical with God. The claim that we are so is bound to be mistaken, whatever the mystic may feel or experience. At the same time, the very same insight into the way we should think of supreme or transcendent being makes it easier for us to understand how some persons should come to think and speak of their being in some state of a literal union with God. Some indication of this has already been given, and there are yet further ways in which we may account for the confused state of mind of some mystics, even when their vision is in some respects extremely clear, and of their being deluded about their own experience or speaking about it in ways which are misleading to others.

A mystical experience is, for obvious reasons, hard to describe, and a mystic will be jealous of the peculiar distinctive character of it. This will make him reluctant to modify the terms in which he describes it. But when we consider the matter 'in a cool hour' and bring to bear on it what we must otherwise think of the transcendent and what we find other religious experiences to be like, then it seems impossible to concede to any mystics the sort of claims which Stace considers that many of them make. This will not affect what we think in other ways of the merits and importance of mystical experience. It is simply that, in the question of interpretation, I take the opposite view to that of Stace. If there is the difference he alleges between Eastern and Western mystics, and I am far from being convinced that Eastern mysticism is as uniform in nature or style of utterance as he supposes, then it seems plain to me that Western Mystics have a sounder view of what the experience in all its forms is bound to be in essentials.

Let me add now that Stace himself makes no attempt to diminish the outright character of his basic paradox or, as it had better be described, contradiction. He has no recourse to obscure metaphors or evasion. He sees quite clearly what he wishes to maintain, he holds firmly to it and leaves us in no doubt about it. This is most commendable, above all in a subject that lends itself to obscurity and evasion; but it also helps us to see more clearly where we are expected to go. Stace rejects, for example, the notion of a merely 'rhetorical paradox' designed to make us 'stop and think'.[1] The idea of a 'pure unity' is not a mere 'literary flourish'. He likewise discards the idea of misdescription, stressing the range and high quality of the testimony for his own view, coming as it does from 'all over the world' and 'the main higher cultures';[2] and on this the point made already about interpretation must suffice as a comment. The 'double location' theory is also rejected. This is the theory that the paradox may be got rid of if the opposing terms of it are taken to apply to different objects or different aspects of the same object. That, he says, will not apply to the contradiction that the world is both identical with and distinct from God. For the same reason we must not fall back on the 'theory of ambiguity'. There is no ambiguity or 'double meaning' in the statement: 'I cease to be this individual, and yet I remain this individual'. The contradiction, here as elsewhere, must be taken in its strictest undiminished form. It is an essentially contradictory view that has to be defended. But is not this a fatal avowal for any philosopher?

Stace himself tries to cope with this in various ways. He maintains, for example, that a contradiction, while it is certainly not true, is not, as we normally assume, devoid of meaning. If we fail to resolve a paradox and find ourselves affirming outright that A is B and A is not B in precisely the same sense and same respect, then we would normally be taken not to be saying or thinking anything at all. There is no thought which could take this form, it is just words. But Stace rejects this. He argues that a theory is refuted if it is shown to be contradictory, but to refute is to show something to be false, and nothing can be false if it is without meaning. On this I will only comment that the word 'refute' may be ambiguous here; if it presupposes that the initial contention is genuine or meaningful, then it may not always be the proper term to use; but we could then say instead that a theory had been exploded. The justification for using the term 'refute' is, partly at

[1] *Op. cit.*, p. 254.
[2] *Op. cit.*, p. 259.

least, that it is not initially evident always that a nonsensical or contradictory claim is so at the start.

We have also the following argument: 'If "A is B" is a meaningful statement, and if "A is not B" is also meaningful, it is impossible that the connective "and" placed between them should render the conjunction of the two meaningful statements meaningless.'[1] It is strange that a gifted professional philosopher should write in this way. The obvious comment is that the meaning of the statement must be found in it as a whole, it is not the parts separately that are being asserted; and in what it purports to be as a whole statement the statement is devoid of meaning, it does not present any thought we can entertain or consider.

It might be expected that Professor Stace would have some recourse here to the idea of alternative logics, of which much has been made today. He does not do so. He declares firmly that 'there is only one kind of logic, namely the logic discussed by logicians';[2] there is not, we are assured any analogy between mysticism and non-Euclidean geometry. Nor will it do to think of the laws of logic as 'only linguistic or semantic rules'.[3] They 'do tell us something about the world of our everyday experience'.[4] On the other hand we must also reject 'the popular dogma' 'that no experience could ever contravene the laws of logic'.[5] 'For logic applies only to *some* actual or possible worlds, not to all possible worlds as is usually supposed'.[6] There is a 'sphere of logic' and also of 'nonlogic', and 'the position of mysticism in violating these laws (of logic) is not another kind of logic, but is simply non-logical'.[7] In mysticism we have to do with the sphere of nonlogic.

The sphere of logic is that of 'the many'. It must thus 'apply to any world in which there exists multiplicity'.[8] Its laws are just the 'necessary rules for thinking of or dealing with a *multiplicity* of separate items'.[9] In that sphere we cannot escape it or reduce the rigidity of its rules. But we do not need it when we are not dealing with a multiplicity, 'The many is the sphere of logic, the One not so',[10] and it is with 'the One' that we have to do in mystical experience and in attempts to understand it. 'For this reason, there is no clash between mysticism and logic. The logic and the illogic

---

[1] *Op. cit.*, p. 267.
[2, 7] *Op. cit.*, p. 268.
[3, 9] *Op. cit.*, p. 270.
[4, 6, 8] *Op. cit.*, p. 273.
[5] *Op. cit.*, p. 272.
[10] *Op. cit.*, p. 271.

occupy different territories of experience'.[1] We need not be per-turbed by paradox and contradiction when we deal with a territory of experience which does not belong to logic.

This is a very bold line to take, but it is not without some plausibility. For, as we have seen, the facts of the world as we find them, and as we understand them, point to some Reality beyond them which is altogether different and incapable, from the very demand which posits it, of fragmentation; it is complete in a way of which we can form no positive conception, because all our thought has to do with the relating of terms in a system. God, as it is sometimes put, is not an object among objects, He is transcendent and what this means in itself we can never know; nor can we know properly what is the relation of God to the world which we describe in the only terms available as our own dependence and so forth. There is an irreducible mystery of God and a mystery of creation. Of this nothing further of a positive kind may be said, no account of it may be given in rational terms beyond the intimation of it in finite natures; and to this extent we are in a sphere of nonlogic. But we have also to be very wary here; for we are given no licence to make positive affirmations which contravene the laws of logic or reason. It is simply that, at this point in religious thinking, we are not entitled to make any positive affirmations at all. This does not preclude us from making affirmations about God through items of experience by which knowledge of God is mediated to us, in the way noted already, without reducing the mystery of His essence. The part which reason plays in this process, helping us to note and sift the appropriate items and set out their significance, must be in conformity with the normal requirements of consistency in all exercise of reason. This is sometimes overlooked in theological controversy, some theologians assuming that because they are dealing with a transcendent Reality they can disregard ordinary standards of consistency, on occasion making even a merit of unreason and irresponsible paradox at the expense, among other things, of fundamental ethical principles. Stace does not lapse in this way. But he falls into the same basic misconception at a more radical or initial level.

This is because, in spite of all that he himself says about non-logic and so forth, he does, in fact, try to understand more than is possible about the transcendent and its essential relation to the world. At a point where the proper course is cautious agnosticism

[1] *Op. cit.*, p. 271.

he tries to reach out into further intellectual mastery. As he himself puts it, we must 'scale down' the mystical consciousness 'to the logical plane of the intellect', and when we do this we find 'that there is no distinction in the One, that there is no distinction of object and object and that there is no distinction of subject and object'. But these curious conclusions, and the paradoxes of affirming the many and denying them at the same time are just the perplexing consequences that are inevitable if we persist in trying to make sense, in ordinary rational terms, of the demand which leads us to the transcendent and of the facts of experience. A sound understanding of the nature of transcendence should warn us not to attempt this, but just to recognize the transcendent as a Reality other than the world of finite experience as such and essentially incomprehensible in itself and in its essential relation to us and to the world. We would not then try to say that it is One in an indifferentiated sense and also many. We would just recognize the mystery of the transcendent in its absolute irreducible nature and the inevitability of it as evidenced in all finite natures. By taking a more presumptuous course, by seeking to scale down to the level of the intellect a reality which is essentially beyond the grasp of intellect, Stace is led to his denial of the facts and distinctness of finite realities for which he must somehow, by paradox and contradiction, find some room in his system.

If the paradox could be allowed, the way would be open for Stace to deal with a number of objections to his position of which he himself is very conscious. For example, it might be urged that a God to whom we can pray must be a personal God. Stace's reply is that, in his theory, God is both personal and impersonal, and we make the usual sort of prayer to him as a personal being. This is obviously proper if the basic contradiction can be maintained, if we can insist that God is personal at the same time as we are affirming, not that he is suprapersonal, but that he is, as undifferentiated unity, not personal at all, if, in other words we can have it both ways.

Likewise with the problem of evil. Stace first observes here that evil is in any case a serious problem for any view that does not reduce God to the level of a being who is essentially finite like ourselves, the celebrated doctrine of a 'finite God'. He is right, in my view, in rejecting the idea of a finite God; it is not compatible with either the attitude of worship and religious experience or with the way we are induced to think that there must be a God.

But if we do not take refuge in the idea of a finite God the problem of evil in some of its forms is very acute. We may see how, in principle, some kinds of evil can be reconciled with the infinite goodness and wisdom of God, but it is hard to extend this to all the evil we find in the world, for example to protracted and seemingly pointless suffering. Normally, I think, the religious person lives with the tensions of this problem in the strength of the faith which is independently founded and which does not require him to be able to fathom all the mystery of God. But for Stace the position is simpler. In the world of 'distinctions' the problem persists and there is no 'intellectual solution', but in the Godhead all distinctions disappear and we have no longer any evil. But this in turn depends on being able to maintain the paradox that there are the many although there is also only the one, and this gives us only another subtle form of the basic misguided attempt to scale down the transcendence of God to the logical plane of the intellect. It seems wiser to acknowledge the point at which comprehension is not possible and rest secure in what we are, in fact, able to understand through our initial awareness of the essential goodness of God as supreme and perfect reality and the further disclosure of His concern in ways in which He has revealed himself immediately in finite experience.[1]

---

[1] See my *The Philosophy of Religion* chap. XXI.

CHAPTER XVI

THE ELUSIVE SELF IN
MORALS AND RELIGION

In this book I have sought to defend two closely related themes. I have maintained that mental processes are of a quite different nature from physical ones or any observable external reality. They are private and only known directly in the process of having them. But we know one another's minds in a mediated way, usually by observing one another's bodies. I have also held that experiences belong to an entity distinct from one's body and also from any particular feature in the course of our experiences. No account can be given of the sort of belonging in question, but everyone knows his experiences as belonging to him in this unique way in having any experience. Nor is it possible to ascribe particular characteristics or determinations to the self that has the experiences. This does not mean that a self is not determinate or that it is somehow unbounded or one with the infinite, as Stace supposed. On the contrary, it is very distinctively individual, the most inescapably individual thing we know. It is limited to knowing itself in the special way in question, *and no other*; and it knows itself as essentially individual. The self is also limited by the way it is involved in its experiences, its particular aptitudes and dispositions. It could not be without these in some form. But my identity, in the most basic sense, is not dependent on having any particular kind of experience or disposition. Nor can the self to which these belong be further described. There are no criteria by which it is identified. Everyone, man or brute, knows in this basic sense who he is, whether he takes particular cognizance of the fact or not. We know ourselves in this way in being ourselves. There is a finality and directness in this knowledge which precludes any further analysis. But we ascribe selves in this way to others when we have reason to ascribe any experience or mental process to them, and we learn to characterize one another in more precise ways on the basis of the course of experience and mental activity we ascribe to various persons—and any dispositional tendencies which these disclose. We can also identify ourselves in the same way, building around the continuity of our own existence, as established in our memories, all that we learn in other ways about ourselves. I can identify myself in this way as the person who was born at a certain time, has lived in various places, has a particular profession, has certain likes and dislikes, and so on. But I also know all this about myself as a distinct being, indivisible and incapable of being any other. My history might have been different, and I may suffer from a split personality or similar derangement, but I know also that all this happened to the irreducibly distinct person I find myself to be.

It is for these reasons that I have used the phrase 'elusive self'. The self is not elusive in the sense that we do not know what it is—we know quite well—but only in the sense that we can say nothing further about it and do not posit it in the same way as other specifiable entities. It eludes our grasp if we try to capture it in a particular way but not otherwise.

I shall say nothing more in this book in further defence or amplification of this position. But I wish, before I close, to give some indication of the implications of the views I have advanced for other major problems in philosophy and religious thought. In a sequel to the present work I shall take up further the theme of the elusive self and its implications for ethics and religion. I must, therefore, be content for the present with the briefest outline of the course to be followed later. The main items are these:

(1) *Freedom and responsibility.* It is widely agreed that the main concerns of ethics and religion require us to continue to think of ourselves as morally responsible creatures. The form this notion takes varies a great deal in different types of ethics and religion, but there are few in which it does not appear in some form. The idea of responsibility seems to presuppose freedom of some kind. I cannot be held to account for something which I do not choose to do. But what sort of choice is this? It does not seem to be enough to have the power merely of carrying our purposes into effect. We must actually choose what we do. But, in that case, what about the influence of character and circumstances? Is it enough to say that an action is free as the expression of a distinctive character? Character is not moulded mechanically, it develops. But the development nonetheless appears to be in some way inevitable, and if so the question still remains—can we help what we do? To meet this situation some have recourse to the idea of a choice that is not determined at all, except in the sense that the limits and

L

occasions for it are set by our character at the time and the situation, including, of course, the moral obligations which arise in various situations. This seems to me to be in accordance with moral experience and the requirements of moral principle.[1] But there is one very serious objection, namely that a choice which is not the expression of our own character at the time is not in any proper sense our own choice. It seems to be a blind happening. To meet this objection it is, however, urged that the self is more than its formed character, or set of dispositions, at any time. It is such a self which can act contrary to one's main inclination or take a course not in the line of least resistance. But how can there be such a self or a choice which is not itself in turn determined by more superior elements in our natures? It is here that we turn to the notion of the self being a genuine entity, known by each one to be such in his own case, but at the same time having no specific nature or attributes. It is the unique thing which a self is. If we take our model from other sorts of entities, then the question becomes very insistent—must not the self which is more than character still have some nature which determines how its choice is made, and if so does it not in effect fall back into some aspect of one's character, a superior one perhaps but still so much absorbed into our nature, as formed at some time, as to defeat the purpose of postulating a self which is effectively and finally more than character? Such a problem does not arise, however, if we understand aright how the self, as subject and agent, is known to itself in being itself as a unique entity whose distinctiveness is not found in particular attributes but in the recognition by each one of the distinct person he finds himself to be.

At this point then, the idea of the elusive self, as outlined already, can have the utmost relevance to a problem of major importance for moral philosophy in an aspect of it that impinges very closely on religious thought.

(2) *Persons and their relations.* A great deal in our personal relationships, and in those features of these which present us with some of our more complicated ethical problems, can only be fully understood in the light of the way each person is, in a sense, a world of his own, however full also his fellowship with other persons may be. One of the reasons for the imbalance in our ethical judgments is that our perspective is restricted and distorted by the effect on

[1] See my *Morals and Revelation* chapters 5,6,7 and my *Freedom and History.*

our judgments of the inescapable inwardness which is a feature of our finite natures. This adds a new and subtle dimension to any self-concern we may have in other ways. It hinders the more completely objective view we should take of our problems. We judge things too much in their immediate impact on ourselves or see them too exclusively in the light they have as they appear within the orbit of our personal concerns. We can correct this limitation more easily when we understand the source of it.

A profounder feature of the same basic complication is the rebelliousness we are prone to exhibit against the inwardness of our ultimate being and experience and the consequent mediated character of our knowledge of one another. There is nothing properly that should disturb us here. We do have the most rich and intimate associations with one another. But when we do not understand our situation aright, and when various frustrations make us impatient and anxious, we are apt to seek that sort of immediate contact with other persons which by our nature is precluded for us. We want to know other beings as we know ourselves, or as God knows us, we wish to storm and penetrate the inner citadels of the being of other persons, to throw down all barriers and all possibility of misunderstanding. This we do not, in fact, ever accomplish. We do not begin to get any nearer to it in paranormal experience, such as telepathy. For whatever happens here, it is not a case of knowing the person 'from within' as he knows himself. That is not just difficult, it is inherently impossible. But it can *seem* possible in those situations where the usual disguises are penetrated or whisked away, when reserve gives way to abandon in moments of great emotional excitement or concentration or fear or anguish. Thus it comes about, as is well attested in sociological study and in current art and fiction, that people seek, in extremes of passion or the torment of one another's souls, a way of forcing themselves beyond a barrier which we should, on the contrary, just learn to accept and thus discover better how to cope with it and the complications it presents. Many perversions and distortions of aim, sadism and deviations of sexual interest owe a great deal to this side of our situation, however much other more obvious factors come into them as well. Much that is otherwise quite bewildering in our reactions and concerns can be understood better in the light of the desperate, though misguided, attempt to break through inevitable barriers and invade one another's privacy and sanctity in ways which are, in fact neither possible nor proper. How much of human tragedy may be traced to this source is a question too vast to be examined closely now. I can only hint at the possibilities of new understanding it offers and the scope we have here for a closer *rapprochement* of religious and literary studies. The proper answer to the problems of loneliness and the inevitable barriers lies in a better grasp of our religious situation. Viewing our lot in the right relation of ourselves to God, we become better placed to accept the limitations of our finite lot and to see its own otherwise illimitable possibilities and exciting variations better. This is one of the main ways in which religion helps us to cope with our situation and its problems, including especially those problems which have been thrown into prominence and accentuated by the various acute crises and complexities of our own age. The bearing of religious study here, not only on morals, but on sociology and general culture is very extensive. It should be one of the main points of concentration in such studies today.

(3) *Immortality.* Belief in some kind of after-life is a central theme of most religions. It takes many forms. One of these is the idea of a limited re-birth culminating in our entrance into some state of nirvana, it being not always clear what becomes of continued identity in the latter case. There are also many, as we have seen, who think of our ultimate destiny in terms of absorption into some universal mind or supreme soul. In the Christian religion, at least in its orthodox forms, immortality is thought of as involving essentially some continuation of our present existence. Some even think of a literal resuscitation of our corpses. It is hard for us today to take that view seriously, even allowing that 'with God all things are possible'. But it is, on the other hand, hard to avoid the expectation that, if we believe in life eternal at all, it will involve, among other things, some continuation of our own personalities. This may involve having a body in some way like our present bodies, the sort of body one has in a dream perhaps. That would make the metamorphosis less drastic and help us to maintain the sense of a continued identity. But it would not be indispensable for one's ultimate identification of oneself. For what matters essentially here, if the thesis of this book is sound, is that each one should have the unique awareness of himself that he has in being himself. This would be ensured even in the absence of any remembrance of a previous existence. On the other hand it seems

to me that survival would lose most of its significance without some remembrance of our earlier state, and some contribution which one existence makes to the other; and that would have great importance for any religious reasons we might have for the belief in survival. There remains also the question of how we could be identified for one another in a future existence. That would be simplified if we had bodies in some ways resembling our present ones, but I do not think that it would be ruled out even in a totally disembodied state. If telepathy and kindred phenomena are genuine they tell us something about communications that dispense with at least the usual physical media, although they happen between persons who are identified in the first place in ways which involve their bodies. Certain patterns within one's own experience, and peculiar insistent variations upon these, might provide the principle on which discrimination between some merely unexpected turn of our own thoughts and communications from without might be made. At the same time a believer in survival does not have to have any precise notion of the form this could take, although speculation about it should be a part of religious thought. One might have religious reasons for believing in after-life and leave it quite open 'what we shall be'. There must be much in the universe which is entirely beyond our present experience and understanding. On the other hand, we need a concept of the self which makes it conceivable that identity is maintained in a continued existence; and this is where the view of the self which I have outlined seems to me to have special importance. I can do no more than hint at its relevance now, but it should be evident that many difficulties can be simplified if we can think of the self as an entity which is more than a pattern of physical or mental events and which is identified uniquely to itself in the way suggested.

These problems can, of course, be by-passed if we can speak of resurrection and life eternal in a way that involves no implication of our continued existence in any form. But although many seem to think in these terms today I fail altogether to understand their position. It seems to be just a juggling with words.

(4) *The Distinctness of Persons.* We have already considered earlier certain forms of monistic metaphysics in which the distinctness of persons is not ultimate. On some of these views a finite being is a mode or limitation of the absolute; for others, 'the sphere of the

many' is an illusion, there being only 'the One'. This accords well with some religious views and we have also seen how it was defended by W. T. Stace as the only sound account to be given of mystical experience. The idea of the 'elusive self', as I have presented it, has bearing on this controversy in many ways, and I urged that a sound understanding of the way the self is, in a basic respect, without determination establishes also its irreducible finality in a way that cuts in precisely the opposite way to that supposed by Stace. More than anything else it precludes a merging of selves. I can never have the sort of knowledge of other persons which I have of myself, however well I may know other persons in other ways.

In addition there is the following consideration. We must suppose that God knows us as we know ourselves and not as we know one another. We can have no conception how this is possible. But in the case of an infinite Being we must suppose things possible in some fashion which altogether transcends our sort of understanding. It follows that we must consider God to be involved in a peculiarly intimate way in the lives of all persons, to be, so to speak, truly within them. This does not mean that God is strictly identified with His creation, or that the creature becomes God; there is no diminution of our own being, and we retain a will of our own. But there is also a sense in which God is all in all and by which the cultivation of His presence is a surrender to a reality that is peculiarly all-encompassing and close. It is this that is often misrepresented to give the impression that one's own being is totally lost in the being of God, and that this is the ultimate goal. Here again a sound understanding can save us from grievous error.

(5) *Sin and Salvation.* There are grave misrepresentations of important truths in many doctrines of sin and salvation. These come about, in Christian contexts especially, in juristic versions of such doctrines which start from too literal an interpretation of legal metaphors taken out of their context in the full experience they reflect. This brings religion into ill repute among enlightened people. To redeem this situation we need a fresh examination of the ideas of sin and salvation and of metaphors like 'the penalty of sin', being 'bought', being 'redeemed', being 'washed in the blood of the Lamb' and so forth. This is a very comprehensive task and it presents us with one of the major concerns of the philosophy of religion today; it needs much literary insight as well as theological

scholarship for its proper discharge. Here I confine myself to one point.

One of the main results of deliberate wrong-doing is to drive men back on that inward aspect of their existence which is an unavoidable feature of their finite natures. Instead of coping with this feature of existence, cultivating along with it a due and humble sense of fellowship with men and God, we become confined, in serious concern, in an inner life of our own. Contact with others, while being outwardly maintained in seemingly normal ways, becomes weak and unreal; men suffer from an 'inner emptiness' and debility of spirit of which much has been written, directly or by implication, in recent literature. It is in the lostness, the death of the spirit, the helplessness and sense of impending doom and soul-destroying guilt induced in these ways that we find the true penalty of sin. This is no theological anachronism or psychological fantasy. Psychology as such only touches the edges of it. It is a sombre reality of present experience which can only be properly understood in terms of man's relation to God and the alienation wrought by sin, not only in the immediate impact upon the individual but in the cumulative effect of this as it permeates our total situation. It is in that context that redeeming activity has its place, and while I would be going far beyond the limits of my present aim if I sought to indicate how this helps us to see the true import of Christian notions of divine grace and redeeming activity in 'the work of Christ', I venture to suggest that the imaginative rediscovery of the relevance of these ideas today will owe a great deal to the understanding available to us, in consequence of recent controversy, of the true import of the preoccupation, in general literature as in philosophy, with inwardness and privacy. It is in this context above all that it is important to grasp what is truly involved in the inwardness and elusiveness of the self; and it is for this reason that I find it so regrettable that, while some discerning thinkers direct our attention effectively towards these features of our situation, they do so with little close consideration of its nature and implications, while others turn away with scorn from notions so alien to the tough-minded empiricism which has dominated so much of the most rigorous and powerful philosophical thinking in English-speaking countries.

(6) *Theism.* The idea of the kind of redeeming activity to which I have just drawn attention has a close bearing also on the general

question of theism, especially in its Christian forms. But that is in turn bound up with the reasons we may have for believing that a truly transcendent reality can also disclose itself in human experience and history in a way sufficiently distinctive to be regarded as a personal dealing with us and the perfection of a fellowship with God. This raises issues that fall well outside the scope of this book. I have given some indication of the way I view them in earlier writings, and especially in my *Our Experience of God*. In the sequel to the present volume I hope to show how much light is thrown on the distinctive processes of divine disclosure, and the way these may be best apprehended in sophisticated thought of today, by a sound understanding of finite personality. That will relate, on the one hand, to the problems involved in any claims to have apprehension of transcendent activity. On the other hand, it will help to deepen the sense of this activity as a dealing with us directed especially to the sanctity and inviolable character of our own personality—and, thereby, itself a pre-eminently personal activity. These are, however, very large themes, and I can only give the most general indication of them, in this wholly provisional way, as some intimation of the field of investigation which opens out before us if the main themes of the present study can be sustained. How much I myself can cover that field remains to be seen.

ADDENDUM

PRIVATE AND PUBLIC SPACE[1]

I

The distinction between public and private Space is one which in some sense or other many philosophers feel impelled to draw. And the reason is not hard to seek. They have in mind such things as optical illusions, hallucinations, mental images, objects seen in mirrors or pictures and the contents of dreams. None of these are thought to be in Space in the ordinary way or, as we sometimes put it, 'they are not in real Space'. Some have wished to say that they are not real at all. But, however that may be, it seems certainly possible to say some things of a spatial nature about all such objects. We can describe their shapes and say that one is to the right or to the left of the other; and I hope to stress that we can say even more specific things than this. But since there appear to be very strong reasons for denying that these objects are in the Space of which we normally think when referring to material things, there appears to be no alternative but to relegate them all to a peculiar private Space. This step is often taken as a matter of course and with very few qualms, as if, at this stage at least, no particular problem presents itself.

Such assurance seems to me very misplaced. And the first point I wish to make to bring out the oddity of the distinction that is commonly drawn between public and private Space is that it is not merely two Spaces that are involved but a public Space and a vast number of private Spaces; each private Space belongs to someone, and the presumption then is that there are as many such Spaces as there are experients, human and non-human, capable of apprehending spatial distinctions. Any arguments which would seem to establish one such Space commits us to the view also that they are legion.

Now I certainly do not think that this can be true as normally understood and in the sense which the reader is likely to have in mind at this point. I hold that the distinction of public and private Space, as normally conceived, is quite untenable, and much that I shall say will be intended to show this. But it will

[1] Originally read as a paper to the Aristotelian Society and published in the *Proceedings of the Aristotelian Society* 1952–53.

also be well to warn the reader thus early that I shall myself eventually confront him with something rather like the accepted view—so far as *multitudinous* Spaces are concerned.

To embark on this course, let us first take up matters like optical illusions. The celebrated 'bent stick in water' would serve the purpose well, but to make quite clear the point I wish to make I should prefer to think of a stick that is wholly immersed but which is bent or distorted, as seems to the onlooker, by waves or some other cause, much as faults in the glass of a window cause fantastic distortions of things. Now there seem to be very good reasons for saying that the 'distorted stick' is not in Space in the way both the straight stick and the water are. For the place where the bent stick appears to be, or at least part of it, is already occupied by something else, water for example. Nor could we locate this stick by the tests we would employ to supplement vision in the case of the 'real' straight stick. We cannot sink our hands in the water and feel round it, it would not be there to touch, but only the water and the 'real' stick. Nonetheless, we can say a great deal about this 'unreal' or illusory object. We can give its colour and its shape, and roughly, at the very least, its size. We can say that its point is towards the shore, that its handle is much shorter than the rest of it; and, if pressed to say where it is, we could point it out and add 'There it is, over there, just under the pier'. We could give the most precise directions for locating it, and we could shoot an arrow through it. I see no reason why we should not also measure it, contortions and all. For, although we could not apply a tape to it, we could measure it as we would other objects from a distance, or as we would a real bent stick on the ground which we were forbidden to touch, or as we would measure a shadow from afar—and a shadow is itself a not unlikely candidate for our private Space. Not even the most sceptical could deny the sense of saying that the bent stick is much shorter than the pier, although a trick of the light or other optical condition could make it much longer. We seem, therefore, to be able to say a great deal of a spatial character about the stick which, it is alleged, is not in 'ordinary Space' at all.

This goes also for reflections. The columns that hold up the pier are mirrored *underneath*. We can point to where they are, a real fish can swim through them, we can make paintings of them and take photographs of them from our position on the pier, and this would obviously not be possible unless we knew in what direction to point the camera. In fact, we can learn and say anything about these reflections, in principle, which we could learn, by looking, about a real inverted pier supporting the present one. Their appearance is substantially the same as that of real things. And it is for this reason that we can say so much of a spatial character about them.

But now note that the great bulk of what we do say in this way about the reflections or the distorted stick is said in relation to positions and objects in real Space; and even if there are some things that can be said about the pier on which I walk that cannot be ascertained or properly said about its double underneath, the main point stands, namely, that we can at least say a great deal about the illusory appearances which is dependent entirely on relations between them and real things in Space. The reflections are there below the pier on which I stand, they are not in the sky above my head. The distorted stick points to the real shore. Admittedly not all the spatial qualities of the appearances involve this. If there is a white patch on one of the supports of the pier I shall be able to say of the reflection that a part of it is white surrounded by black. Even here there is, of course, a causal relation. The white patch in the water is surrounded by black because it is reflecting the real support up above it. But that is a point that need not concern us now. It is much more important to insist that even if some of the spatial qualities of the appearances in the water do not involve any direct reference beyond themselves, a great many others do. And it seems to me that if we can affirm any spatial relations between the illusory appearances and the real objects in Space, then it must be because they are both in the same Space. To say 'there are the reflections below us', even if we say no more than this and leave it open whether they really go down into the water or are on the surface or any other alternative if one is conceivable (and I should maintain that none is), or to declare 'there is the distorted stick' and shoot an arrow through it—all this is possible only if these appearances occupy the same Space as other things from which their position is located. Short of that, we should need some kind of intra-spatial relations cutting across public and private Spaces of which it is hard to form any clear conception. And this seems, moreover, so plain to me that I find it astonishing that anyone should have persisted for any length of time in the notion of public and private Spaces as homes respectively for real and illusory things; and yet that is what many philosophers seem to have thought in recent years.

Is there any special reason why they should have done so? I think there is, but before we can come to it we must continue with some further examination of candidates for private Space.

Take, now, the case of hallucination. Macbeth sees the dagger. No one else sees it, and no one would be aware of it or be able to say anything about it except on the basis of Macbeth's own reporting. Here, then, is something which is in some sense very private. It is not open to public inspection in the same way as the pier mirrored in the sea, which all can observe. Nonetheless, the dagger would not be a dagger unless it had distinct spatial qualities. It has shape and parts. The blade may be twice as long as the handle; and there is no reason to suppose, although this does not matter much, that its outline is blurred in any way. These are internal relations, not quite in the technical philosophical sense, but in the sense that they concern nothing directly besides the hallucinatory object itself. Even so, I do not think we could really apprehend them except on the basis of their belonging to the same Space as everything else. But we need not ponder this. For it is evident in any case that a great many further things may be said about the dagger which do unmistakably relate it to other objects. Macbeth sees the dagger 'before me, the handle toward my hand'—not to the right or to the left. It is not in the far corner of the room but here before him. If it were on the table he could locate it as precisely as any other knife. He could not, presumably, take hold of it, although there is no reason why strong hallucinations should not take that form; they certainly extend to hearing. Nor could he kill someone with it or cut his meat. Or, at any rate, if we start postulating those possibilities we shall have to go into some very nice questions about when is a dagger a dagger, and what is a miracle and so on. All this we can by-pass. For the stark fact on which it is necessary to insist is that Macbeth knows very well where the dagger is, and if only it behaved like an ordinary dagger he would know exactly how to set about getting hold of it. So far as that is concerned there is no difference between it and a real one.

Likewise, when the ghost of Banquo comes in at the feast. No one else sees him, but what Macbeth sees is a figure which he knows at once to be familiar. Presumably it makes its first appearance at the door, although apparitions are credited with a disconcerting habit of just 'being there' suddenly out of nowhere. As the part is usually acted in the play at any rate, the ghost *moves across* the room, and Macbeth at least has no doubts about the route it takes. It also sits in the place that Macbeth usually occupied. Macbeth could describe all this, and for him the ghost fills the space that Macbeth himself filled when he took his place at table. If the ghost obliged by putting his hand on the table, there is no reason why Macbeth could not, if his nerves were steadier, call for a quill and draw the outline of it for all to see. But this also means that, however private to Macbeth the vision may be, it stands in some clearly definable relation to the public objects which are there all the time. It enters *by* the door and sits *at* the table. And how could this possibly be if it were not in the same Space as the door and the table? If it sits on the stool at the place Macbeth normally fills, then that is the place in which it is, a place in that particular hall and no other. Macbeth knows quite well in what hall he is—he is not dreaming—and so do the others. If a fuller account of where 'Banquo' sat is required he could give it in relation to the North Pole or the North Star or anywhere else in Space, if sufficiently instructed. The place where the ghost sits is a real place where real people sit, and it is described and identified as such—there can be only the one. But in that case the ghost is also in the same Space as the other occupants of the room. He is not in any private Space, and I do not think we can possibly go back on this even though we may be much tempted to do so when we consider, as we are now bound to do, the question —what of the stool that the other guests see or of some reveller who might have shifted into the place where Macbeth should be and where Macbeth sees the apparition, or the air which fills the place if no one 'really' sits there? Can two or more things be in the same space?

Before turning to this question, however, a word must be added here about other candidates for private space—in some respects stronger ones. These are mental images of various kinds and the objects we see in a dream. Some philosophers would say that these are in no sense in Space, and there is much to be said for that view. For, while it is easy to say where the ghost or the 'dagger' are, one is rather nonplussed if pressed to say where was the tree I saw in a dream or the mental image I have now of the College. Even so, there are spatial things we do say about these and I should maintain that we can discover spatial relations between them and the physical objects which are the normal occupants of Space. I should say, for example, that the image I have of the College is before me, while I picture the pier somewhere behind me.[1] I can visualize a friend coming into the room. It seems to follow that if the pictures I conjure up in this way are in Space at all, they must be in the same space as the other entities to which they stand in some spatial relation. Dreams constitute a harder problem, but here, again, I should hold that the difference between the entities I see in a dream and physical things is not that the former are not in Space at all, but that they are much wilder and looser inhabitants of Space than the latter. In essentials the difference is thus one of correlation,[2] the objects I see in a dream not observing the same rules as material things; the difficulty we would encounter in locating an object seen in a dream is thus a practical one, not one of principle. This, however, is not a matter I wish to debate in detail now. All I wish to insist upon is that, if there is a case for regarding mental images and what we see in dreams as entities in some kind of Space, then such privacy as we do accord to these affords no warrant for relegating them to some Space other than that in which material things are located. I thus reject the view that there is a case to be made for the distinction between public and private Space in any sense which would involve a sharp division within experience of entities we relegate to private Space and entities in public Space. Those who agree with the main

[1] Mainly because that is where I take them to be.

[2] We can clearly relate things to one another spatially within a dream. Thus I may see someone come, in my dream, through the gate at the foot of my garden and walk up the path raising his arm in greeting and touching the branch of a tree above his head. There is no difference here from anything we might say in waking life. We would describe the shapes and movements of things in the same way, we could see the distant hills as well as the garden. The difficulty is placing all this in relation to the physical space of waking experience. Nothing we see in a dream seems to have that location. But suppose we found that some dreams had close consistency in themselves and also a correlation with events in waking life. Suppose I dreamt an entire incident, a visit from someone or a football match, and suppose I found afterwards that this tallied closely with all that, in fact, occurred. If this happened to me often I might conclude that this was more than a chance occurrence, although not capable of being explained in terms of the causal relations normally involved in perception. I might then also get into the way of saying that I had seen the football match, much as we already say that we saw the car that was following us when we looked in the mirror or saw someone on television. There are indeed causal relations in these latter cases which are not found in the dream. But might we not get into the way, nonetheless, of placing things we saw in the dreams, in the peculiar conditions envisaged, in terms of their location as normally established. Just as I say that I saw a car behind me swerve, so I might say (and if my credibility in clairvoyance were firmly established give evidence to settle an important issue) that I had seen one horse take the lead at the tape or a shot being fired, at a certain place. Would this be altogether different from the way things are normally given their location?

point I have been making hitherto, namely, that optical illusions or hallucinations are in the same Space as material things will, I submit, find it hard to reserve a special kind of Space solely for mental images or dreams. Is there, then, any other sort of case to be made for the notion of private Space which will not involve the bifurcation of experience usually implied by that notion? I believe that there is, and it is to that matter that I wish to turn now.

II

I hope that what I have said hitherto will not convey the impression that it is a simple business to give an account of the difference between mental images or dreams and real or material things solely in terms of the completer correlations we find in the one case but not in the other. Phenomenalism notoriously bristles with difficulties. I shall not try to consider these now. I wish, instead, to proceed to another matter to which students of perception have not in my opinion sufficiently attended. This concerns the correlations of sensible impressions and images to which I have referred as providing a basis for distinguishing between real things and appearances. These correlations include correlations with the experiences of other persons than the subject himself, and this raises a peculiar difficulty about Space, the implications of which it is my main concern to exhibit in this paper.

This difficulty begins to appear if we go back now to the problem which I mentioned rather lightly earlier, but which is really the whole crux of the matter. In dealing with Macbeth's hallucinations, I deferred the question of the location of some real person (or the air) which fills the place where the ghost is also supposed to be, and is seen to be by Macbeth. Now, so far as Macbeth himself is concerned, there is no overwhelming problem here. For we can think of any rival for the space in which the ghost appears in terms of what Macbeth would see under normal conditions. He does not see that now; he only sees 'Banquo'. *But other people see it.* And thus, if we are to say that literally one and the same space is occupied both by 'Banquo' and by Lennox, let us say, we seem to defy all consistency.

To this the reply may be made that, although the ghost appears in a definite part of Space and seems to fill it, a ghost does not really fill space. It was in the same way that G. E. Moore spoke of after-images being merely 'presented' in Space. I very much doubt, however, whether this distinction is as simple and as absolute as is frequently assumed. We certainly cannot say that the ghost and the 'dagger' are wholly unreal; nor will it do to seek the shelter of the comfortably ambiguous phrase that Macbeth is simply thinking that he sees a dagger or a ghost. Macbeth's error is not a purely intellectual one. It is not as though he had misread instructions or miscalculated; nor is it even a case of misconceiving a real object that is presented to his senses, as when a rope is taken to be a snake. The dagger and the ghost are distinct entities of some kind, and they are not merely in Macbeth's mind in the metaphorical sense in which a thought is in his mind, but quite simply and literally in an easily ascertainable part of Space—as we have already seen. The most that we can say, in support of the view that they do not *fill* Space is that they may not present themselves to all our senses and that they are not correlated with other sense impressions in the same way as real things. The ghost may not be tangible as well as visible, and, while having a frontal surface, it may have no obverse side; it may present no lateral view. One might also add that it has no inside, but I think it is very hard to say what exactly we mean by the inside of a material thing; and I should myself wish to supply the answer in terms of what one would experience if one performed certain operations on what one does perceive now, such as cutting it with a knife. But even if we admit that the ghost has no inside in this, or any other, sense, and that it is intangible and so forth, it does have some kind of monopoly of a certain surface. It may well be the case that if Macbeth reaches forth his hands he will have sensations other than those of clasping a body or a dagger; he may touch nothing at all or the table. But this does not eliminate what he *sees*, the coloured surface does not become transparent by not offering resistance to his hands. Admittedly, Macbeth's outstretched hands may pass through the body of the ghost, but if they were seen by him to be doing so he would not see the body of 'Banquo' in the area through which his hands passed while that happened. Where he sees a ghost he can see nothing else. Is not that, moreover, ultimately due to the fact that *if a surface is coloured in one way, whether in a dream or hallucination or in normal sense experience, it cannot at the same time be coloured in any other way or made transparent?* Does not this follow from the nature of colour? And does it not follow from this again that we cannot say of one and the same surface that it is red, let us say, for me, green or transparent for you?

The reply may be made to this that, in point of fact, we do see colours of one sort precisely where other people see colours of a different sort. The reflections I see below the pier may be green, but other people looking at the same place from another position or 'point of view' may only see the blue surface of the water. The first part of this paper has, moreover, been mainly devoted to showing that such things as the green reflections and the blue sea are in the same Space. It seems, therefore, a plain fact of experience that, in different conditions and from different 'points of view', various persons see different colours in the same place just as they may see through a coloured surface which obscures the further vision of other persons. If my friend wears red spectacles he will see a red surface where I see a green one.

It seems, therefore, quite beyond dispute that, just as we may say that some entities are only partially in Space or in Space only from a certain point of view, for example, when they are presented to some senses but not to others, so also these entities may be presented even to the *same* sense from one point of view but not from others. And if we can accept the further conclusion that it is only proper to speak of entities 'occupying' Space when they present themselves, not from some special 'point of view', but under more systematic conditions which only obtain for one entity in respect of the same part of Space, then our problem vanishes. We do not have different entities competing for the same position in Space.

Nevertheless, this does not seem to be satisfactory. For while I see no particular difficulty about the way we may have some sense experience, for example, a visual one, without the other sense experiences we normally expect to accompany it, for example certain tactual ones, there appears to me to be something radically wrong with the assumption on which so much of our thought about these problems proceeds, namely, that a coloured surface, to keep to the example of vision, can present itself to one person in a place where different-coloured surfaces appear to others at the same time. A coloured surface is no less real because it appears in hallucination or dreams or perspectival distortion. But once we admit its reality does it not also follow from the very nature of colour that nothing but that coloured surface can be seen where it is? I know of no further proof of this, but it seems to me to be a conclusion to which we are bound to come if we reflect on the nature of colour. The reason why it has not always been evident is that attention has been diverted from it to the equally obvious fact that various observers seem to see different colours in the same place when they look under different conditions. As the latter fact is the most important for ordinary experience and thought, it has tended to monopolize attention. But it seems to me that both facts are equally certain and that some quite radical modification of our ordinary thought about such questions is needed to solve our dilemma.

A short way out of this dilemma may be sought by simply insisting that even the same individual may, in fact, see two different things in the same place, for example when he looks at the shining surface of the table and sees both the table and the reflections of other objects in it; this may also be said to be the case when two trains are level at a station and the occupants of a carriage in the one train see both the occupants of a similar carriage opposite them in the other and reflections of themselves. But I am quite sure that this does not strictly happen. There may be close intermingling of what we see of the other train and of the reflections, and there may be swift interchanges as our interest shifts. This may create the illusion for the unwary of having two distinct views at the same time of the same surface or place. But it is quite certain that this does not happen, and we settle the question, I submit, not by experiments of any kind, such as trying to see what sort of impressions we do have in such cases, but by knowing without further ado that it cannot happen. This holds also for Macbeth and his ghost. Nothing can compete with the ghost so long as he is there—*for Macbeth*. His place is secure enough, and it is wholly and solely his so far as vision is concerned. *But the other revellers have a different impression altogether*. They see a stool or they see Lennox, and they see him sitting up at the same real table in relation to which the ghost is located also. They see him where the ghost is.

It is this, I am sure, more than anything else, that accounts for the persistence of the belief in public and private Spaces, as commonly held by philosophers and not infrequently by laymen, and for the failure to face up to the obvious difficulties. It is felt that there must be some simple solution to the sort of dilemmas I have propounded, much as we know that Achilles overtakes the tortoise, and I suspect we are helped in all this by the ease with which we form mental pictures of Space itself in terms of some spatial figure—a sphere for example, which, would allow of some intersection with other spheres and similar correspondences. There is an extremely interesting field for the psychologist to investigate here, and it might throw light on many problems. But whether it would or not, the temptation to identify the one Space, extending (in this regard in an all-inclusive way) to infinity in all directions, with some part of itself, is an insidious one. It can breed endless confusions and bogus questions. Are we also misled by the confusion between Space and particular 'spaces'? That would certainly be *naïve*, and I doubt whether it would apply here. But *naïve* errors have certainly been a source of trouble for philosophers *of all schools*.

The main point, however, is that the notion of public and private Spaces, in the form in which recourse is so commonly had to it in this connection, namely, that which supposes that there is some one real public Space filled by real things together with more or less complete duplicates which exist along with it in some fashion and for some length of time to house other entities, is, quite apart from other difficulties, totally inadequate to meet the present problem. There would not be a problem, at least not the one I have raised, if the ghost and Lennox appeared in quite different Spaces. For in that case a place could easily be reserved in their respective spheres for both, whatever other problems might remain. But what puzzles us now is that we seem bound to locate both entities in the same part of the one Space.

But if the usual recourse to public and private Space is denied us, what alternative have we? The alternative I would like to suggest, but very tentatively in as short a paper as this, will seem to many a strange one. It is that Space, as I find it in my own experience, is not public at all but private to me, a particular individual. I know what it is but no one else. There is at least some kind of precedent for this. For do we not often remind ourselves that what I mean by 'yellow' may never be the same exactly as what others mean? It does not for colour-blind persons, and for all we know the occasions on which I speak of red may be occasions on which other people, if they could literally have my experience now, would say 'yellow'. There is not, to my mind, any way of refuting this, unless we assume that differences which cannot be verified cannot exist, and that seems to me a most unwarranted assumption. All this concerns the content rather than the form of experience, I admit, but if private access is inevitable to the extent suggested, need we boggle at extending it, and may we not find that the whole problem, the subject of so much recent controversy, arises because we refuse to be thorough enough and take up impossible half-way positions open to equally deadly attack from either side?

Let us, however, keep to our immediate problem. If what I have just suggested about Space is sound, we have no longer any need to worry about a location for ghosts, hallucinatory daggers, illusions, mental images, or objects seen in a mirror, in consequence of some way in which they are ousted by some other entities from the position originally accorded to them in Space as we really find it. For this does not strictly happen. Consider the case of the mirror. My contention is that, so far as the immediate experience is concerned, there is no essential difference between seeing things in a mirror and seeing 'real' things in the ordinary way. And I think this goes for pictures also, the difference between pictures and mirrors, for this purpose, being largely incidental and consisting mainly, it seems to me, in the fact that the shapes and general appearance of things in the picture are so much at variance with their surroundings that they impose upon us less easily and do not, therefore, create the expectation of their behaving as things of the same sort are generally found to behave. Would a really good picture of what I expect to see in a mirror on the wall opposite be distinguishable in any but casual ways from the latter? I think not, and in any case the main point is that the view I have of things in the mirror is just like any other view of similar things in all but irrelevant detail. Suppose, for example, that a mirror was set up to cover the whole face of the wall opposite me now. I would see the present room reflected in it; and, if not very familiar with my present surroundings, I might well have the impression—have we not all had it?—that the room in the mirror was a real extension of this one. And if someone removed the mirror and cunningly substituted for it, while I dozed, the sort of room I now only see in the mirror I would not know the difference if I had stayed in my seat. In short, the difference between the things I see only in the mirror and my view of the real room is that if I try to approach the former I find myself disconcertingly arrested by banging my head against a glass surface, and so forth; and if I go outside and look into the room opposite through a window I should not, in the one case, see what I see now, but I should in the other—and should be able to handle things and sit in a chair. All this, and more of the same kind, is meant by correlation, but it is not meant that the space behind the mirror is literally filled by tables and chairs of one sort at the time when I see tables and chairs of another sort there. It *is* meant further, however, that other people may be having experiences *of some kind* which are *in some way* correlated with the experience I have myself. Precisely what are the modes in which other people have these experiences I cannot tell; nor can I possibly know what for other people is the equivalent of Space for me. But I know that it cannot be the same. For the very infinity of Space as I find it precludes that. I could—in principle—go to any part of it and see there—in a mirror, perhaps —different kinds of things from those which other people see in what we normally describe as the same place. The Space of other people is not another planet but another 'dimension' or 'attribute' of existence (in Spinozistic language) which is nonetheless correlated with ours.

To develop this suggestion further and meet objections many matters would need to be considered. I should have to maintain, for example, that Kant was nearer the truth than his critics in maintaining that Space was 'an infinite given whole'. The question of communication would also have to be examined, for while it follows from the view I have outlined that each person is confined to a private world of his own, it is also a fact which none of us wishes to deny that in some way we have intimate contacts with other persons. These, in my view, are made possible by inferences from features of experience that are themselves private to each individual, the peculiarly radical nature of this privacy, as I conceive it, being logically or emotionally no more disconcerting, I should maintain, than any inferential view of our knowledge of other minds. For ordinary purposes we have to allow the world to impose upon us and behave as if it were public in a fashion which does not turn out to be correct when considered at the philosophical level. These matters, and especially the question of the precise sense in which it can be said that there is a public as well as a private 'world' (and the important question what is meant by 'world' in this connection) can hardly be discussed to any purpose now. Nor can any of the general metaphysical implications of the view I have outlined be indicated. But to obviate misunderstanding, I should like to stress one matter in coming to a close.

The view I have suggested must be sharply distinguished from a theory such as that of Bertrand Russell in *Our Knowledge of the External World*. For, although Russell also speaks of Spaces and worlds that are private to each individual, he does so in a less radical sense than the one I have suggested. On Russell's view the same individual could occupy different spaces at various times, and these different spaces would themselves be related to one another in a way not substantially different from the relations of particular entities within each of them individually. The use of the word Space, in Russell's notion of a 'private space', is in fact rather arbitrary. It presupposes Space in the more usual meaning of the word. The distinctions which Russell draws, and I believe they are substantially sound as well as ingenious, have also to do mainly with differences between illusions and real things, whether this be in the experience of one individual or many. But I have maintained that it is just because we have to think of 'real' things and illusions as being in the same Space that we have also to suppose that the Space of one person is distinct from the Space of another. The private-world theory which I am suggesting cuts across the far less radical distinction into public and private worlds suggested by Russell. It has also much closer affinity with Leibniz.

In the very brief sketch of a theory which, if it is sound, will have ramifications in many fields of philosophy besides Perception, I have confined myself almost wholly to the problems of visual experience. This is partly because vision and touch seem more fundamental than other modes of sense experience for our understanding of Space. But I also wished to avoid unnecessary complications in a short paper. The substance of my argument is not imperilled, so far as I can see, by any implications it may have for a theory of Perception in all its aspects. I believe, on the contrary, that the view I have outlined will make many features of sensible experience less bewildering than they are for us commonly today. If true, it will also rule out any theory of material things as existing quite independently of sensible impressions, and, in particular, the suggestion, made lately by Dr Ewing, that secondary qualities such as colours may be ascribed to such 'independent' objects. There may be no reason for holding that colours are necessarily mind-dependent. But indirect considerations of the kind I have adduced in this paper seem to me fatal to Dr Ewing's suggestion and to most other forms of realism, and I am surprised that they have not figured more prominently in the 'realist' controversy. These are, however, matters of which I can only make passing mention here. I have trailed my coat enough for one paper and have myself occupied quite enough space in the *Proceedings* for one contributor.

INDEX OF PROPER NAMES

INDEX OF SUBJECTS

GEORGE ALLEN & UNWIN LTD

Head Office
40 Museum Street, London W.C.1
Telephone: 01-405 8577

Sales, Distribution and Accounts Departments
Park Lane, Hemel Hempstead, Herts.
Telephone: 0442 3244

Athens: 34 Panepistimiou Street
Auckland: P.O. Box 36013, Northcote Central N.4
Barbados: P.O. Box 222, Bridgetown
Beirut: Deeb Building, Jeanne d'Arc Street
Bombay: 103/5 Fort Street, Bombay 1
Buenos Aires: Escritorio 454-459, Florida 165
Calcutta: 285J Bepin Behari Ganguli Street, Calcutta 12
Cape Town: 68 Shortmarket Street
Hong Kong: 105 Wing On Mansion, 26 Hancow Road, Kowloon
Ibadan: P.O. Box 62
Karachi: Karachi Chambers, McLeod Road
Madras: 2/18 Mount Road, Madras
Mexico: Villalongin, 32 Mexico 5, D.F.
Nairobi: P.O. Box 30583
Philippines: P.O. Box 157, Quezon City D-502
Rio de Janeiro: Caixa Postal 2537-Zc-00
Singapore: 36c Prinsep Street, Singapore 7
Sydney N.S.W.: Bradbury House, 55 York Street
Tokyo: C.P.O. Box 1728, Tokyo 100-91
Toronto: 81 Curlew Drive, Don Mills

Further Titles in the Muirhead Library of Philosophy Series

Perception and Our Knowledge of the External World
DON LOCKE

The philosophical problems of perception have traditionally played a central role in Empiricist and Analytic philosophy, and in undergraduate courses in the subject. The author argues that it is necessary to distinguish two problems, the problem of the nature and status of what we perceive, and the problem of the nature and status of our knowledge of the external world.

Philosophy and Religion
AXEL HÄGERSTRÖM

' . . . an interesting and much needed book, which any who take part in contemporary radical thinking should reckon with, if only to discover a fresh way of tackling the problems of the modern intellect.' *British Weekly*
'This is a volume which must be taken into account in any historical review of twentieth-century thought.'
London Quarterly and Holborn Review

Philosophy of Space and Time
MICHAEL WHITEMAN

A mathematician who is also a mystic is exceptionally well qualified to survey the mysterious subject of space and time. Dr Whiteman, Associate Professor of Applied Mathematics at Cape Town University and author of *The Mystical Life*, brings the mathematician's detachment and the mystic's insight to this book and presents the most thorough treatment of space and time yet seen. For the expert he provides an indispensable textbook likely to stand unchallenged for many years; for the intelligent layman, an opening into an absorbing field of knowledge, in a world where religious beliefs about the nature of the universe have lost their authority, but interest in the infinite is at its greatest.

Philosophical Papers
G. E. MOORE

' . . . those who are prepared for serious reading will find much stimulus here, and will be in touch with one of the most penetrating minds of this century.' *British Weekly*

The Analysis of Mind

BERTRAND RUSSELL

'Brilliant . . . one of the most interesting and important books that Mr Russell has yet given us.' *Nation*

'Here are the old clarity and the old charm; the restrained, illuminating with . . . a most brilliant essay in psychology.' *New Statesman*

'Most interesting . . . a most valuable contribution to its subject.' *Manchester Guardian*

'This interesting and fascinating book . . . is a perfect model of what such books should be . . . the style is so clear and technicalities so carefully explained that the reading of the book is an intellectual pleasure rather than a mental effort.' *Church Times*

G. E. Moore, Essays in Retrospect

Edited by ALICE AMBROSE and MORRIS LAZEROWITZ

The contribution made by G. E. Moore (1873–1958) to the philosophy of the twentieth century has yet to be fully assessed. This collection of essays illustrates the extent to which Moore's work has impressed and influenced the arguments of many other important contemporary philosophers. These essays present in detail his general, metaphysical and ethical philosophical attitudes and afford both an exhaustive critique and appraisal of them. The papers were written in or after 1958 by philosophers whom Moore respected— A. J. Ayer, Gilbert Ryle, A. C. Ewing, C. D. Broad and so on—and *in toto* they undertake a scholarly examination of his analytical method and the direction he gave to philosophical investigation.

In addition to specific essays on Moore's views concerning utilitarianism, the naturalistic fallacy, free will, propositions and time, linguistics, etc, the book includes more general and biographical ones. In particular, areas of Moore's philosophy hitherto neglected are discussed: many of his ideas were, for instance, contained in the form of unpublished lecture notes. The appreciation felt by Alice Ambrose and Morris Lazerowitz, editors of *Essays in Retrospect*, for G. E. Moore assures the future progress of philosophical enquiry into his works.

Our Experience of God

H. D. LEWIS

'An important contribution towards a philosophical study of the nature of religious belief. . . . He has much to say on these topics which is both reverent and sensible.'　　　　*Church Times*
'This is an eminently sound and sensible study. To write dispassionately and yet with insight and conviction upon religious topics is at best a difficult task but one which in the present instance is admirably successful.'　　　　*Philosophical Studies*

Freedom and History

H. D. LEWIS

Professor Lewis here discusses the nature of history, of objectivity in history, of religion and history, and of responsibility in law and morality. The work of well-known recent writers like Reinhold Niebuhr, Barbara Wootton, Ian Ramsey, Leonard Hodgson, is subjected to close examination, and by contrast with the views he opposes, the author presents his own ideas about the relation of theology to historical fact. The book throughout expresses a deep concern about freedom and the way it is imperilled by misunderstandings and abuses.
'Sensitive and intelligent this delightfully reasoned book by a scholar of deep Christian devotion is most welco me.'

Cork Examiner

LONDON: GEORGE ALLEN AND UNWIN LTD